A Framework for Marketing Management

A FRAMEWORK FOR MARKETING MANAGEMENT

Sixth Edition

Philip Kotler

Northwestern University

Kevin Lane Keller

Dartmouth College

PEARSON

Boston   Columbus   Indianapolis   New York   San Francisco   Amsterdam   Cape
Town   Dubai   London   Madrid   Milan   Munich   Paris   Montréal   Toronto
Delhi   Mexico City   São Paulo   Sydney   Hong Kong   Seoul   Singapore   Taipei   Tokyo

Vice President, Business Publishing: Donna Battista
Editor-in-Chief: Stephanie Wall
Acquisitions Editor: Mark Gaffney
Development Editor: Elisa Adams
Program Manager Team Lead: Ashley Santora
Program Manager: Jennifer Collins
Editorial Assistant: Daniel Petrino
Vice President, Product Marketing: Maggie Moylan
Director of Marketing, Digital Services and Products: Jeanette Koskinas
Executive Product Marketing Manager: Anne Fahlgren
Field Marketing Manager: Lenny Ann Raper
Senior Strategic Marketing Manager: Erin Gardner
Project Manager Team Lead: Judy Leale
Project Manager: Becca Groves
Operations Specialist: Carol Melville
Creative Director: Blair Brown

Senior Art Director: Janet Slowik
Interior and Cover Designer: Integra Software Services Pvt Ltd.
Vice President, Director of Digital Strategy & Assessment: Paul Gentile
Manager of Learning Applications: Paul Deluca
Digital Editor: Brian Surette
Digital Studio Manager: Diane Lombardo
Digital Studio Project Manager: Robin Lazrus
Digital Studio Project Manager: Alana Coles
Digital Studio Project Manager: Monique Lawrence
Digital Studio Project Manager: Regina DaSilva
Full-Service Project Management and Composition: Integra Software Services Pvt Ltd.
Printer/Binder: Courier/Westford
Cover Printer: Moore Langen
Text Font: 10/12, Minion Pro Regular

Library of Congress Cataloging-in-Publication Data

Kotler, Philip.
  A framework for marketing management/Philip Kotler, Kevin Lane Keller.—6e [edition].
    pages cm
  Includes index.
  ISBN 978-0-13-387131-9—ISBN 0-13-387131-2
  1. Marketing—Management.   I. Keller, Kevin Lane, 1956–   II. Title.
  HF5415.13.K636 2016
  658.8—dc23

                                                                2014044334

10 9 8 7 6 5 4 3 2 1

ISBN 10:   0-13-387131-2
ISBN 13: 978-0-13-387131-9

Brief Contents

Contents

Preface

The sixth edition of *A Framework for Marketing Management* is a concise paperback adapted from Philip Kotler and Kevin Lane Keller's fifteenth edition of *Marketing Management*. Its streamlined approach will appeal to those who want an authoritative account of current marketing management practices and theory plus a text that is short enough to allow the incorporation of outside cases, simulations, and projects. Like previous editions, the sixth edition of *A Framework for Marketing Management* is dedicated to helping companies, groups, and individuals adapt their marketing strategies and management to the marketplace of the twenty-first century.

What's New In The Edition

- A new chapter (Chapter 16, Managing Digital Communications: Online, Social Media, and Mobile) highlights expanded coverage of the latest digital trends and their marketing implications.
- New combined coverage of consumer and business markets in a single chapter (Chapter 5, Analyzing Consumer and Business Markets) explores the similarities and differences in marketing to individual consumers, businesses, government agencies, and institutions.
- The positioning chapter (Chapter 7) now follows the segmentation and targeting chapter (Chapter 6) to align with the conventional STP sequencing of topics.
- The marketing strategy and planning chapter (Chapter 2) now includes all material on marketing implementation, metrics, and control, emphasizing the importance of advance planning for measuring and managing marketing performance.
- New opening vignettes for each chapter show marketing management in action at real-world companies and provide effective discussion starters for chapter concepts. Companies featured include LinkedIn, PepsiCo, USAA, Gatorade, Pandora, Cisco, and Patagonia.
- New "Marketing Insights" boxes discuss a wide range of cutting-edge topics and marketing situations, including Marketing 3.0, marketing double jeopardy, showrooming, playing tricks to build a brand, and other subjects.
- New coverage throughout the text of contemporary marketing developments and issues, including omnichannel marketing, mobile apps, geofencing and mobile commerce, privacy concerns, shopper marketing, and the sharing economy.

Features of The Edition

Major Themes

This new edition explores how the powerful forces of globalization, technology, and social responsibility—individually and in combination—can affect the success of modern marketing programs. Incorporating the latest concepts with recent examples and current academic research, this edition examines the complexities and possibilities of holistic marketing today, encompassing relationship marketing, integrated marketing, internal marketing, and performance marketing.

Instructor Resources

At the Instructor Resource Center, www.pearsonhighered.com/irc, instructors can easily register to gain access to a variety of instructor resources available with this text in downloadable format. If assistance is needed, our dedicated technical support team is ready to help with the media supplements that accompany this text. Visit http://247.pearsoned.com for answers to frequently asked questions and toll-free user support phone numbers.

The following supplements are available with this text:

- Instructor's Resource Manual
- Test Bank
- TestGen® Computerized Test Bank
- PowerPoint Presentation

Acknowledgments

This edition of *A Framework for Marketing Management* bears the imprint of many people who have contributed to the previous edition of this text and to the fifteenth edition of *Marketing Management.* We reserve special thanks to Marian Burk Wood for her extensive development and editorial work on this edition. Many thanks also to the professional editorial and production teams at Pearson. We gratefully acknowledge the many reviewers who helped shape this book over the years.

John H. Antil, University of Delaware
Bill Archer, Northern Arizona University
Timothy W. Aurand, Northern Illinois University
Ruth Clottey, Barry University
Jeff Conant, Texas A&M University
Mike Dailey, University of Texas, Arlington
Brian Engelland, Mississippi State University
Brian Gibbs, Vanderbilt University
Thomas Gruca, University of Iowa
Mark Houston, University of Missouri, Columbia
Nicole Howatt, University of Central Florida
Gopal Iyer, Florida Atlantic University
Jack Kasulis, University of Oklahoma
Susan Keaveney, University of Colorado, Denver
Bob Kent, University of Delaware
Robert Kuchta, Lehigh University
Jack K. H. Lee, City University of New York Baruch College
Ning Li, University of Delaware
Steven Lysonski, Marquette University
Naomi Mandel, Arizona State University
Ajay K. Manrai, University of Delaware
Denny McCorkle, Southwest Missouri State University
James McCullough, Washington State University

Ron Michaels, University of Central Florida

George R. Milne, University of Massachusetts, Amherst

Marian Chapman Moore, Duke University

Steve Nowlis, Arizona State University

Louis Nzegwu, University of Wisconsin, Platteville

K. Padmanabhan, University of Michigan, Dearborn

Mary Anne Raymond, Clemson University

William Robinson, Purdue University

Carol A. Scott, University of California at Los Angeles

Stanley F. Slater, Colorado State University

Robert Spekman, University of Virginia

Edwin Stafford, Utah State University

Vernon Stauble, California State Polytechnic

Mike Swenson, Brigham Young University

Kimberly A. Taylor, Florida International University

Bronis J. Verhage, Georgia State University

Philip Kotler

S. C. Johnson & Son Distinguished Professor of International Marketing

Kellogg School of Management

Northwestern University

Evanston, Illinois

Kevin Lane Keller

E.B. Osborn Professor of Marketing

Tuck School of Business

Dartmouth College

Hanover, New Hampshire

A Framework
for Marketing
Management

Chapter 1

Defining Marketing for the New Realities

In this chapter, we will address the following questions:

1. Why is marketing important? (Page 2)
2. What is the scope of marketing? (Page 2)
3. What are some core marketing concepts? (Page 5)
4. What forces are defining the new marketing realities? (Page 7)
5. What tasks are necessary for successful marketing management? (Page 10)

Marketing Management at Unilever

Under the leadership of ex-P&G marketing executive Paul Polman and marketing whiz Keith Weed, Unilever is steering in an aggressive new direction. Its "Crafting Brands for Life" model establishes social, economic, and product missions for each brand, including Dove, Ben & Jerry's, and Knorr. One part of the mission, for instance, is sustainability—specifically, to halve its ecological footprint while doubling revenues. To improve marketing communications, it aims to strike a balance between "magic" and "logic," doubling marketing training expenditures and emphasizing ad research. Unilever has set its sights on developing and emerging markets, hoping to draw 70 percent to 75 percent of revenues from these markets by 2020. The company has also adopted "reverse innovation" by applying marketing innovations from developing markets to recession-hit developed markets. In Spain, it now sells Surf detergent in five-wash packs. In Greece, it offers mayonnaise in small packages.[1]

Good marketing is no accident. It is both an art and a science, and it results from careful planning and execution using state-of-the-art tools and techniques. In this book, we describe how skillful marketers are updating classic practices and inventing new ones to find creative, practical solutions to new marketing realities. In the first chapter, we lay our foundation by reviewing important marketing concepts, tools, frameworks, and issues.

The Value of Marketing

Finance, operations, accounting, and other business functions won't really matter without sufficient demand for products and services so the firm can make a profit. In other words, there must be a top line for there to be a bottom line. Thus, financial success often depends on marketing ability. Marketing's value extends to society as a whole. It has helped introduce new or enhanced products that ease or enrich people's lives. Successful marketing builds demand for products and services, which, in turn, creates jobs. By contributing to the bottom line, successful marketing also allows firms to more fully engage in socially responsible activities.[2]

Many firms, even service and nonprofit, now have a chief marketing officer (CMO) to put marketing on a more equal footing with other C-level executives such as the chief financial officer (CFO) or chief information officer (CIO).[3] In an Internet-fueled environment where consumers, competition, technology, and economic forces change rapidly and consequences quickly multiply, marketers in every organization must choose features, prices, and markets and decide how much to spend on advertising, sales, and online and mobile marketing—while under intense pressure to make every marketing dollar count.

At greatest risk are those that fail to carefully monitor their customers and competitors, continuously improve their value offerings and marketing strategies, or satisfy their employees, stockholders, suppliers, and channel partners in the process. Thus, skillful marketing is a never-ending pursuit. Despite these challenges, some businesses are adapting and thriving in these changing times.

The Scope of Marketing

To be a marketer, you need to understand what marketing is, how it works, who does it, and what is marketed.

What Is Marketing?

Marketing is about identifying and meeting human and social needs. One of the shortest good definitions of marketing is "meeting needs profitably." When Google recognized that people needed to more effectively and efficiently access information on the Internet, it created a powerful search engine that organized and prioritized queries. When IKEA noticed that people wanted good furnishings at substantially lower prices, it created knockdown furniture. These two firms demonstrated marketing savvy and turned a private or social need into a profitable business opportunity.

The American Marketing Association offers the following formal definition: *Marketing is the activity, set of institutions, and processes for creating, communicating, delivering, and exchanging offerings that have value for customers, clients, partners, and society at large.*[4] We see **marketing management** as *the art and science of choosing target markets and getting, keeping, and growing customers through creating, delivering, and communicating superior customer value.* Cocreation of value among consumers and with businesses and the importance of value creation and sharing have become important themes in the development of modern marketing thought.[5]

Note that selling is *not* the most important part of marketing. Peter Drucker, famed management theorist, says that "the aim of marketing is to know and understand the customer so well that the product or service fits him and sells itself. Ideally, marketing should result in a customer who is ready to buy. All that should be needed then is to make the product or service available."[6] When Apple launched its iPad tablet computer and when Toyota introduced its Prius hybrid automobile, these manufacturers were swamped with orders because they designed the right product, based on careful marketing homework.

What Is Marketed?

Marketers market 10 main types of entities: goods, services, events, experiences, persons, places, properties, organizations, information, and ideas.

Goods   Physical goods constitute the bulk of most countries' production and marketing efforts. Each year, U.S. companies market billions of fresh, canned, bagged, and frozen food products and other tangible items.

Services   As economies advance, a growing proportion of their activities focuses on the production of services. The U.S. economy today produces a services-to-goods mix of roughly two-thirds to one-third.[7] Services include the work of airlines, hotels, car rental firms, barbers and beauticians, maintenance and repair people, and accountants, bankers, lawyers, engineers, doctors, software programmers, and management consultants. Many market offerings mix goods and services, such as a fast-food meal.

Events   Marketers promote time-based events, such as major trade shows, artistic performances, and company anniversaries. Global sporting events such as the Olympics and the World Cup are promoted aggressively to companies and fans.

Experiences   By orchestrating several services and goods, a firm can create, stage, and market experiences. Walt Disney World's Magic Kingdom lets customers visit a fairy kingdom, a pirate ship, or a haunted house. Customized experiences include a week at a baseball camp with retired baseball greats, as one example.[8]

Persons   Artists, musicians, CEOs, physicians, high-profile financiers, and other professionals often get help from marketers.[9] Management consultant Tom Peters, himself a master at self-branding, has advised each person to become a "brand."

Places   Cities, states, regions, and whole nations compete to attract tourists, residents, factories, and company headquarters.[10] Place marketers include economic development specialists, real estate agents, commercial banks, local business associations, and advertising and public relations agencies.

Properties   Properties are intangible rights of ownership to either real property (real estate) or financial property (stocks and bonds). They can be bought and sold and therefore require marketing through the efforts of real estate agents, investment companies, and banks.

Organizations   Museums, performing arts organizations, corporations, and nonprofits all use marketing to boost their public images and compete for audiences and funds. Some universities have created chief marketing officer (CMO) positions to better manage their school identity and image, via everything from admission brochures and Twitter feeds to brand strategy.[11]

Information Information is essentially what books, schools, and universities produce, market, and distribute at a price to parents, students, and communities.

Ideas Every market offering includes a basic idea. Charles Revson of Revlon once observed: "In the factory we make cosmetics; in the drugstore we sell hope." Products and services are platforms for delivering some idea or benefit. Social marketers promote such ideas as "Friends Don't Let Friends Drive Drunk" and "A Mind Is a Terrible Thing to Waste."

Who Markets?

A **marketer** is someone who seeks a response—attention, a purchase, a vote, a donation—from another party, called the **prospect**. If two parties are seeking to sell something to each other, we call them both marketers.

Increasingly, marketing is *not* done only by the marketing department. Marketers now must properly manage all possible *touch points* (where a customer directly or indirectly interacts with the company), including store layouts, package designs, product functions, employee training, and shipping and logistics. To create a strong marketing organization, marketers must think like executives in other departments, and executives in other departments must think more like marketers. Interdepartmental teamwork that includes marketers is needed to manage key processes like production innovation, new-business development, customer acquisition and retention, and order fulfillment.

What Is a Market?

Traditionally, a "market" was a physical place where buyers and sellers gathered to buy and sell goods. Economists describe a *market* as a collection of buyers and sellers who transact over a particular product or product class (such as the housing market or the grain market). Marketers use the term **market** to describe customer groups. They talk about need markets (the diet-seeking market), product markets (the shoe market), demographic markets (the "millennium" youth market), geographic markets (the Chinese market), or voter markets, labor markets, and donor markets. Four key customer markets are consumer, business, global, and nonprofit.

Figure 1.1 shows how sellers and buyers are connected by four flows. Sellers send goods and services and communications such as ads and direct mail to the market; in return they receive money and information such as customer attitudes and sales data. The inner loop shows an exchange of money for goods and services; the outer loop shows an exchange of information.

FIGURE 1.1 A Simple Marketing System

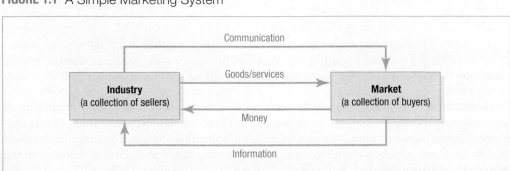

Core Marketing Concepts

To understand the marketing function, we need to understand the following core set of concepts.

Needs, Wants, and Demands

Needs are the basic human requirements such as for air, food, water, clothing, and shelter. Humans also have strong needs for recreation, education, and entertainment. These needs become *wants* when directed to specific objects that might satisfy the need. A U.S. consumer needs food but may want a Chicago-style "deep-dish" pizza and a craft beer. A person in Afghanistan needs food but may want rice, lamb, and carrots. Our wants are shaped by our society. *Demands* are wants for specific products backed by an ability to pay. Many people want a Mercedes; only a few can buy one. Companies must measure not only how many people want their product, but also how many are willing and able to buy it.

These distinctions shed light on the criticism that "marketers get people to buy things they don't want." Marketers do not create needs: Needs pre-exist marketers. Marketers might promote the idea that a Mercedes satisfies a person's need for social status. They do not, however, create the need for social status.

Some customers have needs of which they are not fully conscious or that they cannot articulate. What does the customer mean in asking for a "powerful" lawn mower or a "peaceful" hotel? We can distinguish five types of needs:

1. Stated needs (The customer wants an inexpensive car.)
2. Real needs (The customer wants a car whose operating cost, not initial price, is low.)
3. Unstated needs (The customer expects good service from the dealer.)
4. Delight needs (The customer would like the dealer to include an onboard GPS system.)
5. Secret needs (The customer wants friends to see him or her as a savvy consumer.)

Responding only to the stated need may shortchange the customer.[12] Consumers did not know much about tablet computers when they were first introduced, but Apple worked hard to shape consumer perceptions of them. To gain an edge, companies must help customers learn what they want.

Target Markets, Positioning, and Segmentation

Not everyone likes the same cereal, restaurant, university, or movie. Marketers therefore identify distinct segments of buyers by identifying demographic, psychographic, and behavioral differences between them. They then decide which segment(s) present the greatest opportunities. For each of these *target markets,* the firm develops a *market offering* that it *positions* in target buyers' minds as delivering some key benefit(s). Porsche targets buyers who seek pleasure and excitement in driving and want to make a statement about their wheels.

Offerings and Brands

Companies address customer needs by putting forth a **value proposition**, a set of benefits that satisfy those needs. The intangible value proposition is made physical by an *offering,* which can be a combination of products, services, information, and experiences. A *brand* is an offering from a known source. A brand name such as Apple carries many different kinds of associations in people's minds that make up its image: creative, innovative, easy-to-use, fun, cool, iPhone, and iPad to name just a few. All companies strive to build a brand image with strong, favorable, and unique brand associations.

Marketing Channels

To reach a target market, the marketer uses three kinds of marketing channels. *Communication channels* deliver and receive messages from target buyers and include newspapers, magazines, radio, television, mail, telephone, smart phone, billboards, posters, and the Internet. Firms also communicate through the look of their retail stores and Web sites and other media, adding dialogue channels such as e-mail, blogs, text messages, and URLs to familiar monologue channels such as ads.

Distribution channels help display, sell, or deliver the physical product or service(s) to the buyer or user. These channels may be direct via the Internet, mail, or mobile phone or telephone or indirect with distributors, wholesalers, retailers, and agents as intermediaries. To carry out transactions with potential buyers, the marketer also uses *service channels* that include warehouses, transportation companies, banks, and insurance companies. Marketers clearly face a design challenge in choosing the best mix of communication, distribution, and service channels.

Paid, Owned, and Earned Media

We can group communication options for interacting with customers into three categories.[13] *Paid media* include TV, magazine and display ads, paid search, and sponsorships, all of which allow marketers to show their ad or brand for a fee. *Owned media* are communication channels marketers actually own, like a company or brand brochure, Web site, blog, Facebook page, or Twitter account. *Earned media* are streams in which consumers, the press, or other outsiders voluntarily communicate something about the brand via word of mouth, buzz, or viral marketing methods. The emergence of earned media has allowed some companies, such as Chipotle, to reduce paid media expenditures.[14]

Impressions and Engagement

Marketers now think of three "screens" or means to reach consumers: TV, Internet, and mobile. *Impressions,* which occur when consumers view a communication, are a useful metric for tracking the scope or breadth of a communication's reach that can also be compared across all communication types. The downside is that impressions don't provide any insight into the results of viewing the communication. *Engagement* is the extent of a customer's attention and active involvement with a communication, which is more likely to create value for the firm. Some online measures of engagements are Facebook "likes," Twitter tweets, comments on a blog or Web site, and sharing of video or other content.

Value and Satisfaction

The buyer chooses the offerings he or she perceives to deliver the most *value,* the sum of the tangible and intangible benefits and costs. Value, a central marketing concept, is primarily a combination of quality, service, and price, called the *customer value triad*. Value perceptions increase with quality and service but decrease with price.

Satisfaction reflects a person's judgment of a product's perceived performance in relationship to expectations. If performance falls short of expectations, the customer is disappointed. If it matches expectations, the customer is satisfied. If it exceeds them, the customer is delighted.

Supply Chain

The supply chain is a longer channel stretching from raw materials to components to finished products carried to final buyers. The supply chain for coffee may start with farmers who plant, tend, and pick the coffee beans and sell their harvest. After farmers sell their harvest to wholesalers or perhaps a Fair Trade cooperative, the beans are prepared and then transported to the developed world for sale through wholesale or retail channels. Each company in the chain captures only a certain percentage of the total value generated by the supply chain's value delivery system. When a company acquires competitors or expands upstream or downstream, its aim is to capture a higher percentage of supply chain value.

Competition

Competition includes all the actual and potential rival offerings and substitutes a buyer might consider. An automobile manufacturer can buy steel from U.S. Steel, from a firm in Japan or Korea, or from a mini-mill. Alternatively, it can buy aluminum parts from Alcoa to reduce the car's weight or engineered plastics instead of steel. Clearly, U.S. Steel is more likely to be hurt by substitute products than by other integrated steel companies and would be defining its competition too narrowly if it didn't recognize this.

Marketing Environment

The marketing environment consists of the task environment and the broad environment. The *task environment* includes the actors engaged in producing, distributing, and promoting the offering. These are the company, suppliers, distributors, dealers, and target customers. In the supplier group are material suppliers and service suppliers, such as marketing research agencies, advertising agencies, banking and insurance companies, transportation companies, and telecommunications companies. Distributors and dealers include agents, brokers, manufacturer representatives, and others who facilitate finding and selling to customers.

The *broad environment* consists of six components: demographic environment, economic environment, social-cultural environment, natural environment, technological environment, and political-legal environment. Marketers must pay close attention to the trends and developments in these and adjust their marketing strategies as needed.

The New Marketing Realities

The marketplace is dramatically different from even 10 years ago, with new marketing behaviors, opportunities, and challenges emerging. In this book we focus on three transformative forces: technology, globalization, and social responsibility.

Technology

The pace of change and the scale of technological achievement can be staggering. With the rapid rise of e-commerce, the mobile Internet, and Web penetration in emerging markets, the Boston Consulting Group believes brand marketers must enhance their "digital balance sheets."[15] Massive amounts of information and data about almost everything are now available to consumers and marketers. In fact, the technology research firm Gartner predicts that by 2017, chief marketing officers will spend more time on information technology than chief information officers.

The old credo "information is power" is giving way to the new idea that "sharing information is power."[16] Even traditional marketing activities are profoundly affected by technology. As just one example, drug maker Roche decided to issue iPads to its entire sales team to improve sales force effectiveness. Now sales personnel can do real-time data entry, improving the quality of the data entered while freeing up time for other tasks.[17]

Globalization

The world has become a smaller place. New transportation, shipping, and communication technologies have made it easier for us to know the rest of the world, to travel, to buy and sell anywhere. By 2025, annual consumption in emerging markets will total $30 trillion and contribute more than 70 percent of global GDP growth.[18] A staggering 56 percent of global financial services consumption is forecast to come from emerging markets by 2050, up from 18 percent in 2010.

Globalization has made countries increasingly multicultural. U.S. minorities have much economic clout, and their buying power is growing faster than that of the general population. As a result, one survey found that 87 percent of companies planned to increase or maintain multicultural media budgets.[19] Companies can now take marketing ideas and lessons from one country and apply them to another. After years of little success with premium ultrasound scanners in the Chinese market, GE successfully developed a portable, ultra-low-cost version that addressed the country's unique market needs. Later, it began to successfully sell the product throughout the developed world for use in ambulances and operating rooms where existing units were too big.[20]

Social Responsibility

Poverty, pollution, water shortages, climate change, wars, and wealth concentration demand our attention. The private sector is taking some responsibility for improving living conditions, and firms all over the world have elevated the role of corporate social responsibility. Because marketing's effects extend to society as a whole, marketers must consider the ethical, environmental, legal, and social context of their activities.[21] "Marketing Insight: Getting to Marketing 3.0" describes how companies need to change to do that.

A Dramatically Changed Marketplace

These three forces—technology, globalization, and social responsibility—have dramatically changed the marketplace and provided both consumers *and* companies with new capabilities, as shown in Table 1.1.

One of the reasons consumers have more choices is that channels of distribution have changed. Store-based retailers face competition from catalog houses; direct-mail firms; newspaper, magazine, and TV direct-to-customer ads; home shopping TV; and e-commerce. In

---

TABLE 1.1 New Capabilities in the Changed Marketplace

New Consumer Capabilities:

- Can use the Internet as a powerful information and purchasing aid
- Can search, communicate, and purchase on the move
- Can tap into social media to share opinions and express loyalty
- Can actively interact with companies
- Can reject marketing they find inappropriate

New Company Capabilities:

- Can use the Internet as a powerful information and sales channel, including for individually differentiated goods
- Can collect fuller and richer information about markets, customers, prospects, and competitors
- Can reach customers quickly and efficiently via social media and mobile marketing, sending targeted ads, coupons, and information
- Can improve purchasing, recruiting, training, and internal and external communications
- Can improve cost efficiency

Getting to Marketing 3.0

Philip Kotler, Hermawan Kartajaya, and Iwan Setiawan believe today's customers want marketers to treat them as whole human beings and acknowledge that their needs extend beyond pure consumerism. Successful marketing is thus distinguished by its human or emotional element. A third wave of thinking, values-driven and heralded as "Marketing 3.0," has moved us beyond the product-centric and consumer-centric models of the past, these authors say. Its three central trends are increased consumer participation and collaborative marketing, globalization, and the rise of a creative society.

- We live with sustained technological development—low-cost Internet, cheap computers and mobile phones, open source services and systems. Expressive and collaborative social media, such as Facebook and Wikipedia, have changed the way marketers operate and interact with consumers.
- Culturally relevant brands can have far-reaching effects. A cultural brand might position itself as a national or local alternative to a global brand with poor environmental standards, for instance.
- Creative people are increasingly the backbone of developed economies. Marketing can now help companies tap into creativity and spirituality by instilling marketing values in corporate culture, vision, and mission.

These authors believe the future of marketing will be consumer-to-consumer. They say the recent economic downturn has not fostered trust in the marketplace and customers are increasingly turning to one another for credible advice and information when selecting products.

Sources: Philip Kotler, Hermawan Kartajaya, and Iwan Setiawan, *Marketing 3.0: From Products to Customers to the Human Spirit* (Hoboken, NJ: Wiley, 2010); Michael Krauss, "Evolution of an Academic: Kotler on Marketing 3.0," *Marketing News*, January 30, 2011; Vivek Kaul, "Beyond Advertising: Philip Kotler Remains One of the Most Influential Marketing Thinkers," *The Economic Times*, February 29, 2012. For related ideas, see also Jim Stengel, *Grow: How Ideals Power Growth and Profit at the World's Greatest Companies* (New York: Crown, 2011).

response, entrepreneurial retailers are building entertainment into their stores with coffee bars, demonstrations, and performances, marketing an "experience" rather than a product assortment. Early dot-coms such as Amazon.com successfully created *disintermediation* in the delivery of products and services by intervening in the traditional flow of goods. Now traditional companies are engaging in *reintermediation* and becoming "brick-and-click" retailers, adding online services to their offerings.

While globalization has created intense competition among domestic and foreign brands, the rise of private labels (marketed by powerful retailers) and mega-brands (and brands extended into related product categories) plus a trend toward deregulation and privatization have also increased competition. Many countries have deregulated industries to create greater competition and growth opportunities. In the United States, laws restricting financial services, telecommunications, and electric utilities have all been loosened in the spirit of greater competition. Meanwhile, many countries have converted public companies to private ownership and management to increase efficiency, which also adds to the competitive pressure.

Marketers are increasingly asked to justify their investments in financial and profitability terms as well as in terms of building the brand and growing the customer base. Organizations recognize that much of their market value comes from intangible assets, particularly brands, customer base, employees, distributor and supplier relations, and intellectual capital. They are thus applying more metrics—brand equity, customer lifetime value, return on marketing investment—to understand and measure their marketing and business performance and a broader variety of financial measures to assess the direct and indirect value their marketing efforts create.

Company Orientation Toward the Marketplace

Given these new marketing realities, what philosophy should guide a company's marketing efforts? Let's first review the evolution of marketing philosophies.

The Production Concept

The **production concept** is one of the oldest concepts in business. It holds that consumers prefer products that are widely available and inexpensive. Managers of production-oriented businesses concentrate on achieving high production efficiency, low costs, and mass distribution. This orientation has made sense in developing countries such as China, where the largest PC manufacturer, Lenovo, has taken advantage of the country's huge, inexpensive labor pool to dominate the market. Marketers also use the production concept when they want to expand the market.

The Product Concept

The **product concept** proposes that consumers favor products offering the most quality, performance, or innovative features. However, managers are sometimes caught in a love affair with their products. They might commit the "better-mousetrap" fallacy, believing a better product will by itself lead people to beat a path to their door. As many start-ups have learned the hard way, a new or improved product will not necessarily be successful unless it's priced, distributed, advertised, and sold properly.

The Selling Concept

The **selling concept** holds that consumers and businesses, if left alone, won't buy enough of the organization's products. It is practiced most aggressively with unsought goods—goods buyers don't normally think of buying, such as insurance and cemetery plots—and when firms with overcapacity aim to sell what they make rather than make what the market wants. Marketing based on hard selling is risky. It assumes customers coaxed into buying a product not only won't return or bad-mouth it or complain to consumer organizations but might even buy it again.

The Marketing Concept

The **marketing concept** emerged in the mid-1950s as a customer-centered, sense-and-respond philosophy. The job is to find not the right customers for your products, but the right products for your customers. The marketing concept holds that the key to achieving organizational goals is being more effective than competitors in creating, delivering, and communicating superior customer value to your target markets. Harvard's Theodore Levitt drew a perceptive contrast between the selling and marketing concepts:[22]

> Selling focuses on the needs of the seller; marketing on the needs of the buyer. Selling is preoccupied with the seller's need to convert his product into cash; marketing with the idea of satisfying the needs of the customer by means of the product and the whole cluster of things associated with creating, delivering, and finally consuming it.

The Holistic Marketing Concept

The **holistic marketing concept** is based on the development, design, and implementation of marketing programs, processes, and activities that recognize their breadth and interdependencies. Holistic marketing acknowledges that everything matters in marketing—and that a broad, integrated perspective is often necessary. Holistic marketing thus recognizes and reconciles the scope and complexities of marketing activities. Figure 1.2 provides a schematic overview of four broad components characterizing holistic marketing: relationship marketing, integrated marketing, internal marketing, and performance marketing. We'll examine these major themes throughout this book.

Relationship Marketing **Relationship marketing** aims to build mutually satisfying long-term relationships with key constituents in order to earn and retain their business.[23] Four key constituents for relationship marketing are customers, employees, marketing partners (channels, suppliers, distributors, dealers, agencies), and members of the financial community (shareholders, investors, analysts). Marketers must create prosperity among all these constituents and balance the returns to all key stakeholders.

The ultimate outcome of relationship marketing is a unique company asset called a **marketing network**, consisting of the company and its supporting stakeholders—customers, employees, suppliers, distributors, retailers, and others—with whom it has built mutually profitable business relationships. The operating principle is simple: build an effective network of relationships with key stakeholders, and profits will follow.[24] Thus, more companies are choosing to own brands rather than physical assets, and they are subcontracting activities to firms that can do them better and more cheaply while retaining core activities at home.

Companies are also shaping separate offers, services, and messages to *individual customers*, based on information about their past transactions, demographics, psychographics, and media

FIGURE 1.2 Holistic Marketing Dimensions

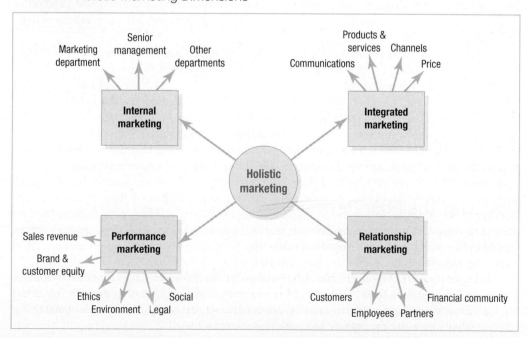

and distribution preferences. By focusing on their most profitable customers, products, and channels, these firms hope to achieve profitable growth, capturing a larger share of each customer's expenditures by building high customer loyalty. They estimate individual customer lifetime value and design their market offerings and prices to make a profit over the customer's lifetime. Marketing must skillfully conduct not only customer relationship management but partner relationship management as well. Companies are deepening their partnering arrangements with suppliers and distributors, seeing them as partners in delivering value to final customers so everybody benefits.

Integrated Marketing   Integrated marketing occurs when the marketer devises activities and programs to create, communicate, and deliver value for consumer such that "the whole is greater than the sum of its parts." Two key themes are that (1) many different marketing activities can create, communicate, and deliver value; and (2) marketers should design and implement each marketing activity with all other activities in mind. When a hospital buys an MRI machine from General Electric, for instance, it expects good installation, maintenance, and training services to go with the purchase. All company communications also must be integrated so they reinforce and complement each other. A marketer might selectively employ television, radio, and print advertising, public relations and events, and PR and Web site communications so each contributes on its own and improves the effectiveness of the others while delivering a consistent brand message at every contact.

Internal Marketing   **Internal marketing**, an element of holistic marketing, is the task of hiring, training, and motivating able employees who want to serve customers well. Smart marketers recognize that marketing activities within the firm can be as important as, or even more important than, those directed outside the company.

Performance Marketing   **Performance marketing** requires understanding the financial and nonfinancial returns to business and society from marketing activities and programs. As noted previously, top marketers are increasingly going beyond sales revenue to interpret what is happening to market share, customer loss rate, customer satisfaction, product quality, and other measures. They are also considering the legal, ethical, social, and environmental effects of marketing activities and programs.

When they founded Ben & Jerry's, Ben Cohen and Jerry Greenfield embraced the performance marketing concept by dividing the traditional financial bottom line into a "double bottom line" that also measured the environmental impact of their products and processes. That later expanded into a "triple bottom line" to represent the positive and negative social impacts of the firm's entire range of business activities. Some firms have failed to live up to their legal and ethical responsibilities, and consumers are demanding more responsible behavior. One research study reported that at least one-third of consumers around the world believed that banks, insurance providers, and packaged-food companies should be subject to stricter regulation.[25]

Updating The Four Ps

Many years ago, McCarthy classified various marketing activities into *marketing-mix* tools of four broad kinds, which he called *the four Ps* of marketing: product, price, place, and promotion.[26] The marketing variables under each P are shown in Figure 1.3.

Given the breadth, complexity, and richness of marketing, however—as exemplified by holistic marketing—clearly these four Ps are not the whole story anymore. Updating them to reflect the holistic marketing concept results in a more representative set that encompasses modern marketing realities: people, processes, programs, and performance, as in Table 1.2.

FIGURE 1.3 The Four P Components of the Marketing Mix

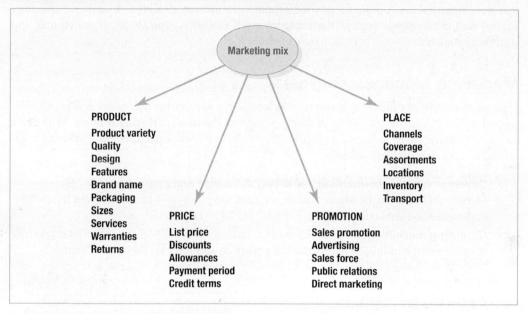

PRODUCT
Product variety
Quality
Design
Features
Brand name
Packaging
Sizes
Services
Warranties
Returns

PRICE
List price
Discounts
Allowances
Payment period
Credit terms

PLACE
Channels
Coverage
Assortments
Locations
Inventory
Transport

PROMOTION
Sales promotion
Advertising
Sales force
Public relations
Direct marketing

TABLE 1.2	The Evolution of Marketing Management
Marketing Mix Four Ps	**Modern Marketing Management Four Ps**
Product	People
Place	Processes
Promotion	Programs
Price	Performance

People reflects, in part, internal marketing and the fact that employees are critical to marketing success. Marketing will only be as good as the people inside the organization. It also reflects the fact that marketers must view consumers as people to understand their lives more broadly and not just as shoppers who consume products and services.

Processes are all the creativity, discipline, and structure brought to marketing management. Marketers must ensure that state-of-the-art marketing ideas and concepts play an appropriate role in all they do, including creating mutually beneficial long-term relationships and imaginatively generating insights and breakthrough products, services, and marketing activities.

Programs are all the firm's consumer-directed activities, encompassing the old four Ps as well as a range of other marketing activities that might not fit as neatly into the old view of marketing. Regardless of whether they are online or offline, traditional or nontraditional, these activities must be integrated such that their whole is greater than the sum of their parts and they accomplish multiple objectives for the firm.

Performance reflects, as in holistic marketing, the range of possible outcome measures that have financial and nonfinancial implications (profitability as well as brand and customer equity) and implications beyond the company itself (social responsibility, legal, ethical, and community related).

Marketing Management Tasks

Figure 1.4 summarizes the three major market forces, two key market outcomes, and four fundamental pillars of holistic marketing that help to capture the new marketing realities. With these concepts in place, we can identify a specific set of tasks that make up successful marketing management and marketing leadership.

- **Developing and implementing marketing strategies and plans.** The first task is to identify and plan for the organization's potential long-run opportunities, given its market experience and core competencies. See Chapter 2 for more detail.
- **Capturing marketing insights.** Each organization should closely monitor its marketing environment, continually assess market potential, and forecast demand. Chapter 3 looks at marketing information and research, market demand, and the marketing environment.
- **Connecting with customers.** Management must decide how to best create value for the firm's chosen target markets and how to develop strong, profitable, long-term relationships with customers, as discussed in Chapters 4 and 5.
- **Building strong brands.** The organization must divide the market into major market segments, evaluate each one, and target those it can best serve, as explained in Chapter 6.

FIGURE 1.4 The New Marketing Realities

Next, it needs to craft a brand positioning and plan to compete effectively, as shown in Chapter 7. Also, it should understand how customers perceive its brands and plan for growth, topics covered in Chapter 8.

- **Creating value.** At the heart of the marketing program is the product—the firm's tangible offering to the market—which includes the product quality, design, features, and packaging, all explored in Chapter 9. Chapter 10 looks at how firms can design and market services, and Chapter 11 examines critical marketing decisions related to pricing.

- **Delivering value.** Based on its products and services, how can the firm deliver value to its target market? Chapter 12 discusses channel activities needed to make the product accessible and available to customers. Chapter 13 explores the marketing decisions made by retailers, wholesalers, and physical-distribution firms.

- **Communicating value.** Each marketer needs to communicate to the target market the value embodied by its offerings. This requires an integrated marketing program that maximizes the individual and collective contribution of all communication activities, as shown in Chapter 14. Chapter 15 examines mass communications such as advertising, sales promotion, events, and public relations, while Chapter 16 discusses online, social media, and mobile options for reaching consumers. Chapter 17 looks at personal communications such as direct and database marketing as well as personal selling.

- **Managing the marketing organization for long term success.** The marketing strategy should take into account changing global opportunities and challenges as well as social responsibility and ethics. Management must also establish an appropriate marketing organization. See Chapter 18 for more detail.

Executive Summary

Marketing is the activity, set of institutions, and processes for creating, communicating, delivering, and exchanging offerings that have value for customers, clients, partners, and society at large. Marketing management is the art and science of choosing target markets and getting, keeping, and growing customers through creating, delivering, and communicating superior customer value. Marketers can market goods, services, events, experiences, persons, places, properties, organizations, information, and ideas in four different marketplaces: consumer, business, global, and nonprofit.

Today's marketplace is fundamentally different than in the past, resulting in many new consumer and company capabilities. Technology, globalization, and social responsibility are creating new opportunities and challenges and significantly changing the management of marketing. Organizations can conduct business under the production concept, the product concept, the selling concept, the marketing concept, or the holistic marketing concept. The holistic marketing concept (including relationship marketing, integrated marketing, internal marketing, and performance marketing) is based on the development, design, and implementation of marketing programs, processes, and activities that recognize their breadth and interdependencies. Successful marketing management includes developing and implementing marketing strategies and plans, capturing marketing insights, connecting with customers, building strong brands, creating, delivering, and communicating value, and managing the marketing organization within the global economy.

Notes

1. "'Captain Planet,' The HBR Interview: Unilever CEO Paul Polman," *Harvard Business Review*, June 2012; "Unilever Reframes Marketing," February 8, 2012, www.warc.com; "Unilever Gets Back to Basics," www.warc.com, September 11, 2012; "Unilever Confident on China," www.warc.com, September 17, 2012; Geoffrey Precourt, "Engaging with Media and Markets: Unilever's Prowl for Experiential Improvement," *WARC Events Report: 4A's Transformation*, March 2011; "Unilever Targets Russia," www.warc.com, October 4, 2012; "Unilever Adopts 'Reverse Engineering,'" www.warc.com, October 1, 2012; "Unilever Seeks New Way Forward," www.warc.com, October 23, 2012; "Unilever Prioritises Emerging Markets," www.warc.com, October 31, 2012; Peter Evans, "Unilever Flags Further Emerging-Market Slowdown," *Wall Street Journal*, July 24, 2014.

2. Philip Kotler, "Marketing: The Underappreciated Workhorse," *Market Leader* Quarter 2 (2009), pp. 8–10.

3. Peter C. Verhoef and Peter S. H. Leeflang, "Understanding the Marketing Department's Influence within the Firm," *Journal of Marketing* 73 (March 2009), pp. 14–37; Pravin Nath and Vijay Mahajan, "Marketing in the C-Suite: A Study of Chief Marketing Officer Power in Firms' Top Management Teams," *Journal of Marketing* 75 (January 2012), pp. 60–77; Christian Schulze, Bernd Skiera, and Thorsten Weisel, "Linking Customer and Financial Metrics to Shareholder Value: The Leverage Effect in Customer-Based Valuation," *Journal of Marketing* 76 (March 2012), pp. 17–32.

4. American Marketing Association, "Definition of Marketing," www.marketingpower.com/AboutAMA/Pages/DefinitionofMarketing.aspx; Lisa Keefe, "Marketing Defined," *Marketing News*, January 15, 2008, pp. 28–29.

5. Robert F. Lusch and Frederick E. Webster Jr., "A Stakeholder-Unifying, Cocreation Philosophy for Marketing," *Journal of Macromarketing* 31, no. 2 (2011), pp. 129–34. See also Robert F. Lusch and Frederick E. Webster Jr., "Elevating Marketing: Marketing Is Dead! Long Live Marketing!," *Journal of Academy of Marketing Science* 41 (January 2013), pp. 389–99.

6. Peter Drucker, *Management: Tasks, Responsibilities, Practices* (New York: Harper and Row, 1973), pp. 64–65.

7. Lisa Mataloni and Andrew Hodge, "Gross Domestic Product: First Quarter 2012 (Second Estimate)," *Bureau of Economic Analysis*, May 31, 2012.

8. B. Joseph Pine II and James Gilmore, *The Experience Economy* (Boston: Harvard Business School Press, 1999); Bernd Schmitt, *Experience Marketing* (New York: Free Press, 1999); Philip Kotler, "Dream Vacations: The Booming Market for Designed Experiences," *The Futurist*, October 1984, pp. 7–13.

9. Irving J. Rein, Philip Kotler, Michael Hamlin, and Martin Stoller, *High Visibility*, 3rd ed. (New York: McGraw-Hill, 2006).

10. Philip Kotler, Christer Asplund, Irving Rein, and Donald H. Haider, *Marketing Places in Europe: Attracting Investments, Industries, Residents, and Visitors to European Cities, Communities, Regions, and Nations* (London: Financial Times Prentice Hall, 1999); Philip Kotler, Irving J. Rein, and Donald Haider, *Marketing Places: Attracting Investment, Industry, and Tourism to Cities, States, and Nations* (New York: Free Press, 1993).

11. Emily Glazer and Melissa Korn, "Marketing Pros: Big Brands on Campus," *Wall Street Journal*, August 5, 2012.

12. Nikolaus Franke, Peter Keinz, and Christoph J. Steger, "Testing the Value of Customization: When Do Customers Really Prefer Products Tailored to Their Preferences?" *Journal of Marketing* 73 (September 2009), pp. 103–21.

13. Sean Corcoran, "Defining Earned, Owned and Paid Media," *Forrester Blogs*, December 16, 2009. For an empirical examination, see Andrew T. Stephen and Jeff Galak, "The Effects of Traditional and Social Earned Media on Sales: A Study of a Microlending Marketplace," *Journal of Marketing Research* 49 (October 2012), pp. 624–39.

14. Jim Edwards, "How Chipotle's Business Model Depends on NEVER Running TV Ads," *Business Insider*, March 16, 2012; Dan Klamm, "How Chipotle Uses Social Media to Cultivate a Better World," *Spredfast*, March 21, 2012; Danielle Sacks, "For Exploding All the Rules; Chipotle: The World's 50 Most Innovative Companies in 2012," *Fast Company*, October 2012.

15. "Digital Focus Vital for Brands," www.warc.com, January 30, 2012.

16. David Kirkpatrick, "Social Power and the Coming Corporate Revolution," *Forbes*, September 26, 2011.

17. Peter Mansell, "Pharma Sales and the Digital Rep," *Eye for Pharma*, May 28, 2012.

18. Yuval Atsmon, Peter Child, Richard Dobbs, and Laxman Narasimhan, "Winning the $30 Trillion Decathalon: Going for Gold in Emerging Marketing Markets," *McKinsey Quarterly*, August 2012.

19. "Multicultural Shoppers Attract U.S. Brands," www.warc.com, October 8, 2012.

20. Vijay Govindarajan and Chris Trimble, *Reverse Innovation: Create Far from Home, Win Everywhere* (Boston: Harvard Business School Publishing, 2012).

21. Rajendra Sisodia, David Wolfe, and Jagdish Sheth, *Firms of Endearment: How World-Class Companies Profit from Passion* (Upper Saddle River, NJ: Wharton School Publishing, 2007).

22. Theodore Levitt, "Marketing Myopia," *Harvard Business Review,* July–August 1960, p. 50.

23. Evert Gummesson, *Total Relationship Marketing* (Boston: Butterworth-Heinemann, 1999); Regis McKenna, *Relationship Marketing* (Reading, MA: Addison-Wesley, 1991); Martin Christopher, Adrian Payne, and David Ballantyne, *Relationship Marketing* (Oxford, UK: Butterworth-Heinemann, 1991).

24. James C. Anderson, Hakan Hakansson, and Jan Johanson, "Dyadic Business Relationships within a Business Network Context," *Journal of Marketing* (October 15, 1994), pp. 1–15.

25. "Many Shoppers Support Regulation," www.warc.com, July 10, 2012.

26. E. Jerome McCarthy and William D. Perreault, *Basic Marketing: A Global-Managerial Approach,* 14th ed. (Homewood, IL: McGraw-Hill/Irwin, 2002).

Chapter 2

Developing and Implementing Marketing Strategies and Plans

In this chapter, we will address the following questions:

1. How does marketing affect customer value? (Page 19)
2. How is strategic planning carried out at different organizational levels? (Page 21)
3. What does a marketing plan include? (Page 26)
4. How can companies monitor and improve marketing activities and performance? (Page 28)

Marketing Management at Hewlett-Packard

A true technology pioneer, Hewlett-Packard (HP) has encountered much difficulty in recent years, culminating in a massive quarterly charge of more than $9.5 billion in 2012. Of that total, $8 billion was a write-down in the value of its IT services unit as the result of a disastrous acquisition of EDS. Revenue for the unit dropped when customers stopped signing large, long-term outsourcing contracts that were at the core of the unit's business model. In a maturing market with few good new products, PC sales slowed so much that HP announced it was exiting the business. Printer and ink sales dropped as consumers began to print less. CEO Meg Whitman vowed to increase the company's emphasis on design, reorganizing the PC group to come up with a cleaner, minimalist sensibility. Admitting that the company did not yet have a strategy for mobile phones, Whitman acknowledged there was much work to be done.[1] Therefore, HP is revising its corporate strategy to reflect all these significant changes in the marketing environment.

Developing the right marketing strategy requires a blend of discipline and flexibility. Firms must stick to a strategy but also constantly improve it. In today's fast-changing marketing world, identifying the best long-term strategies is crucial—but challenging—as HP has been finding out. This chapter examines some of the strategic marketing implications in creating customer value, planning for marketing, and assessing marketing performance.

Marketing and Customer Value

The task of any business is to deliver customer value at a profit. A company can win only by fine-tuning the value delivery process and choosing, providing, and communicating superior value to increasingly well-informed buyers.

The Value Delivery Process

The traditional—but dated—view of marketing is that the firm makes something and then sells it, with marketing taking place during the selling process. Companies that take this view succeed only in economies marked by goods shortages where consumers are not fussy about quality, features, or style—for example, basic staple goods in developing markets.

In economies with many different types of people, each with individual wants, perceptions, preferences, and buying criteria, the smart competitor must design and deliver offerings for well-defined target markets. This realization inspired a new view of business processes that places marketing at the *beginning* of planning. Instead of emphasizing making and selling, companies now see themselves as part of a value delivery process.

The value creation and delivery sequence consists of three phases.[2] In the first phase, *choosing the value*, marketers segment the market, select the appropriate target, and develop the offering's value positioning. The formula "segmentation, targeting, positioning (STP)" is the essence of strategic marketing. The second phase is *providing the value* through identifying specific product features, prices, and distribution. The third phase is *communicating the value* by utilizing the Internet, advertising, sales force, and other communication tools to announce and promote the product. The value delivery process begins before there is a product and continues through development and after launch.

The Value Chain

Harvard's Michael Porter has proposed the **value chain** as a tool for identifying ways to create more customer value.[3] According to this model, every firm is a synthesis of activities performed to design, produce, market, deliver, and support its product. Nine strategically relevant activities—five primary and four support activities—create value and cost in a specific business.

The *primary activities* are (1) inbound logistics, or bringing materials into the business; (2) operations, or converting materials into final products; (3) outbound logistics, or shipping out final products; (4) marketing, which includes sales; and (5) service. Specialized departments handle the *support activities*—(1) procurement, (2) technology development, (3) human resource management, and (4) firm infrastructure (including general management, planning, finance, accounting, legal, and government affairs).

The firm's task is to examine its costs and performance in each value-creating activity, *benchmarking* against competitors, and look for ways to improve. Even the best companies can benchmark, against other industries if necessary, to improve their performance. The firm's success depends not only on how well each department performs its work but also on how well the company coordinates departmental activities to conduct *core business processes*.[4] These processes include:

- *The market-sensing process*—gathering and acting upon information about the market
- *The new-offering realization process*—researching, developing, and launching new high-quality offerings quickly and within budget

- *The customer acquisition process*—defining target markets and prospecting for new customers
- *The customer relationship management process*—building deeper understanding of, relationships with, and offerings for individual customers
- *The fulfillment management process*—receiving and approving orders, shipping goods on time, and collecting payment

Strong companies are reengineering their work flows and building cross-functional teams to be responsible for each process.[5] Ford established a cross-functional team to help reduce water usage per vehicle by 30 percent.[6] A firm also needs to look for competitive advantages beyond its own operations in the value chains of suppliers, distributors, and customers. Many companies have partnered with specific suppliers and distributors to create a superior **value delivery network**, also called a **supply chain**.

Core Competencies

Companies today outsource less-critical resources if they can obtain better quality or lower cost. The key is to own and nurture the resources and competencies that make up the essence of the business. A **core competency** has three characteristics: (1) it is a source of competitive advantage and makes a significant contribution to perceived customer benefits; (2) it has applications in a wide variety of markets; and (3) it is difficult for competitors to imitate. Competitive advantage also accompanies *distinctive capabilities* or excellence in broader business processes. Wharton's George Day sees market-driven organizations as excelling in three distinctive capabilities: market sensing, customer linking, and channel bonding.[7]

In terms of market sensing, Day believes tremendous opportunities and threats often begin as "weak signals" from the "periphery" of a business.[8] He suggests systematically developing peripheral vision by asking three questions related to learning from the past, evaluating the present, and envisioning the future. Over time, businesses may need to realign themselves to maximize core competencies, by (re)defining the business concept or "big idea," (re)shaping the business scope, and (re)positioning the company's brand identity.

The Central Role of Strategic Planning

Marketers must prioritize strategic planning in three key areas: (1) managing their businesses as an investment portfolio, (2) assessing the market's growth rate and the company's position in that market, and (3) establishing a strategy. Most large companies consist of four organizational levels: corporate, division, business unit, and product. Corporate headquarters designs a corporate strategic plan to guide the whole enterprise; it makes decisions on the amount of resources to allocate to each division as well as on which businesses to start or eliminate. Each division establishes a plan covering the allocation of funds to each business unit within the division. Each business unit develops a strategic plan to carry that business unit into a profitable future. Finally, each product level (product line, brand) develops a marketing plan for achieving its objectives.

The *marketing plan* is the central instrument for directing and coordinating the marketing effort, operating at both the strategic and tactical levels. The **strategic marketing plan** lays out the target markets and the firm's value proposition, based on an analysis of the best market opportunities. The **tactical marketing plan** specifies the marketing tactics, including product features, promotion, merchandising, pricing, sales channels, and service. The complete strategic planning, implementation, and control cycle is shown in Figure 2.1.

FIGURE 2.1 Strategic Planning, Implementation, and Control

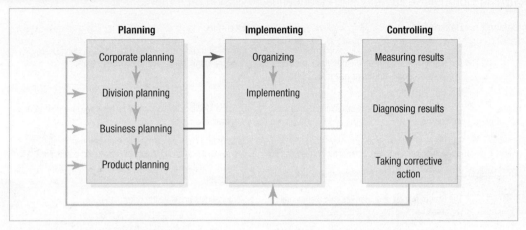

Corporate and Division Strategic Planning

All corporate headquarters undertake four planning activities: (1) defining the corporate mission, (2) establishing strategic business units, (3) assigning resources to each unit, and (4) assessing growth opportunities. These activities are discussed next.

Defining the Corporate Mission

An organization exists to accomplish something: to make cars, lend money, provide a night's lodging. Over time, the mission may change to respond to new opportunities or market conditions. Amazon.com changed its mission from being the world's largest online bookstore to aspiring to be the world's largest online store. To define its mission, a company should address Peter Drucker's classic questions:[9] What is our business? Who is the customer? What is of value to the customer? What will our business be? What should our business be? These simple-sounding questions are among the most difficult a company will ever face. Successful companies continuously ask and answer them.

A clear, thoughtful **mission statement**, developed collaboratively with and shared with managers, employees, and often customers, provides a shared sense of purpose, direction, and opportunity. Good mission statements focus on a limited number of goals, stress the firm's major policies and values, and define the major competitive spheres within which the firm will operate. They also take a long-term view and are short, memorable, and meaningful. Table 2.1 shows key competitive dimensions for mission statements along with examples.

Establishing Strategic Business Units

Large companies normally manage quite different businesses, each requiring its own strategy. A **strategic business unit (SBU)** has three characteristics: (1) it is a single business, or a collection of related businesses, that can be planned separately from the rest of the company; (2) it has its own set of competitors; and (3) it has a manager responsible for strategic planning and profit performance who controls most of the factors affecting profit. The purpose of identifying the company's strategic business units is to develop separate strategies and assign appropriate funding. Senior management knows its portfolio of businesses usually includes a number of "yesterday's has-beens" as well as "tomorrow's winners."

TABLE 2.1	Defining Competitive Territory and Boundaries in Mission Statements	
Competitive Dimension	Description	Example
Industry	Some companies operate only in one industry; some only in a set of related industries; some only in industrial goods, consumer goods, or services; and some in any industry.	Caterpillar focuses on the industrial market; John Deere operates in the industrial and consumer markets.
Products and applications	The range of products and applications that a firm will supply.	St. Jude Medical develops medical technology and services for physicians.
Competence	The range of technological and other core competencies that a firm will master and leverage.	Japan's NEC has core competencies in computing, communications, and components to support production of laptop computers, television receivers, and handheld telephones.
Market segment	The type of market or customers that a company will serve.	Gerber serves primarily the baby market.
Vertical sphere	The number of channel levels, from raw material to final product and distribution, in which a company will participate.	At one extreme are companies with a large vertical scope. At the other extreme are "hollow corporations," which outsource the production of nearly all goods and services.
Geographical sphere	The range of regions, countries, or country groups in which a company will operate.	Some firms operate in a specific city or state. Others are multinationals like Royal Dutch/Shell, which operates in more than 100 countries.

Assigning Resources to Each SBU[10]

Once SBUs have been defined, management must decide how to allocate corporate resources to each unit. Newer methods of portfolio planning rely on shareholder value analysis and on whether the market value of a company is greater with an SBU or without it. These value calculations assess the potential of a business based on growth opportunities from global expansion, repositioning or retargeting, and strategic outsourcing.

Assessing Growth Opportunities

Assessing growth opportunities includes planning new businesses, downsizing, and terminating older businesses. If there is a gap between future desired sales and projected sales, corporate management will need to develop or acquire new businesses to fill it. One option is to identify opportunities for growth within current businesses (intensive opportunities). A second option is to build or acquire businesses related to current businesses (integrative opportunities). A third option is to add attractive unrelated businesses (diversification opportunities).

- **Intensive growth.** Marketers can use a "product-market expansion grid" to consider the firm's strategic growth opportunities in terms of current and new products and markets. The company first considers whether it could gain more market share with its current products in current markets, using a *market-penetration strategy*. Next it considers whether it can find or develop new markets for its current products in a *market-development strategy*. Then it considers whether it can develop new products for its current markets with a *product-development strategy*. Later the firm will also review opportunities to develop new products for new markets in a *diversification strategy*.

- **Integrative growth.** A business can increase sales and profits through backward integration (acquiring a supplier), forward integration (acquiring a distributor), or horizontal integration (acquiring a competitor). Horizontal mergers and alliances don't always work out, however.
- **Diversification growth.** This makes sense when good opportunities exist outside the present businesses—the industry is highly attractive and the company has the right mix of business strengths to succeed. The firm might seek new products that have technological or marketing synergies with existing product lines, though appealing to a different group of customers. Or it might use a horizontal strategy to search for unrelated new products that appeal to current customers. Finally, the company might seek new businesses with no relationship to its current technology, products, or markets, adopting a conglomerate strategy to diversification.

Also, companies must carefully prune, harvest, or divest tired old businesses to release needed resources for other uses and reduce costs.

Organization and Organizational Culture

Strategic planning happens within the context of the *organization,* the firm's structures, policies, and corporate culture, all of which can become dysfunctional in a rapidly changing business environment. **Corporate culture** has been defined as "the shared experiences, stories, beliefs, and norms that characterize an organization." A customer-centric culture can affect all aspects of an organization. Enterprise Rent-A-Car featured its own employees in a recent "The Enterprise Way" ad campaign. One ad in the campaign, themed "Fix Any Problem," reinforced how any local Enterprise outlet has the authority to take actions to maximize customer satisfaction.[11] Whereas managers can change structures and policies (though with difficulty), the company's culture is very hard to change. Yet adapting the culture is often the key to successfully implementing a new strategy.

Organizations develop strategy by choosing their view of the future. The Royal Dutch/Shell Group has pioneered **scenario analysis**, which develops plausible representations of a firm's possible future using assumptions about forces driving the market and different uncertainties. Managers think through each scenario with the question "What will we do if it happens?," adopt one scenario as the most probable, and watch for signposts that might confirm or disconfirm it.[12]

Business Unit Strategic Planning

The business unit strategic-planning process consists of the steps shown in Figure 2.2. We examine each step in the sections that follow.

The Business Mission

Each business unit needs to define its specific mission within the broader company mission. Thus, a television-studio-lighting-equipment company might define its mission as "To target major television studios and become their vendor of choice for lighting technologies that represent the most advanced and reliable studio lighting arrangements." Notice this mission does not mention winning business from smaller studios, offering the lowest price, or offering non-lighting products.

SWOT Analysis

The overall evaluation of a company's strengths, weaknesses, opportunities, and threats is called *SWOT analysis.* It's a way of monitoring the external and internal marketing environment.

FIGURE 2.2 The Business Unit Strategic-Planning Process

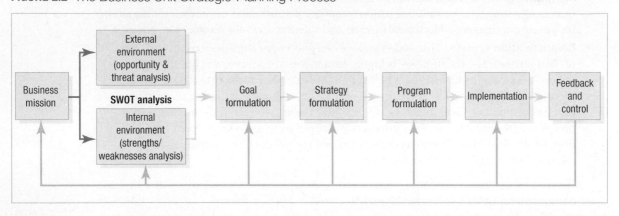

External Environment (Opportunity and Threat) Analysis A business unit must monitor key *macroenvironment forces* and significant *microenvironment factors* that affect its ability to earn profits. It should track trends and important developments and any related opportunities and threats.

Good marketing is the art of finding, developing, and profiting from these opportunities.[13] A **marketing opportunity** is an area of buyer need and interest that a company has a high probability of profitably satisfying. There are three main sources of market opportunities.[14] The first is to offer something that is in short supply. The second is to supply an existing product or service in a new or superior way. How? The *problem detection method* asks consumers for their suggestions, the *ideal method* has them imagine an ideal version of the product or service, and the *consumption chain method* asks them to chart their steps in acquiring, using, and disposing of a product. This last can often lead to a totally new product or service, which is the third main source of market opportunities.

Marketers need to be good at spotting opportunities created from:

- **Converging industry trends.** These may open opportunities to introduce new hybrid products or services, the way cell phone manufacturers have released phones with Global Positioning Systems (GPS) and other features.
- **Making a buying process more convenient or efficient.** Mobil introduced Speed Pass, one of the first widely deployed RFID (radio-frequency identification) payment systems, to allow consumers to quickly and easily pay for gas at the pump.
- **Meeting the need for information and advice.** Angie's List connects individuals with local home improvement and other services that have been reviewed by others.
- **Customizing an offering.** Timberland allows customers to choose colors for different parts of their boots, add initials or numbers, and select different stitching and embroidery.
- **Introducing a new capability.** Consumers can create and edit digital "iMovies" with the iMac and upload them to share with friends around the world.
- **Delivering products or services faster.** FedEx pioneered a way to deliver packages much more quickly than the U.S. Postal Service.
- **Offering a much lower price.** Pharmaceutical firms have created generic versions of brand-name drugs that often sell for less than the branded versions.

To evaluate opportunities, companies can use *market opportunity analysis (MOA)* and ask questions like: (1) Can we articulate the benefits convincingly to the defined target market(s)? (2) Can we locate the target market(s) and reach them with cost-effective media and trade channels? (3) Does our company possess or have access to the critical capabilities and resources we need to deliver the customer benefits? (4) Can we deliver the benefits better than any actual or potential competitors? (5) Will the financial rate of return meet or exceed our required threshold for investment?

An **environmental threat** is a challenge posed by an unfavorable trend or development that, in the absence of defensive marketing action, would lead to lower sales or profit. The company needs contingency plans to deal with major threats that have a high probability of occurrence and can seriously hurt the company. Although minor threats can be ignored, the firm will want to carefully monitor emerging threats in case they grow more serious.

Internal Environment (Strengths and Weaknesses) Analysis   It's one thing to find attractive opportunities and another to be able to take advantage of them. Each business needs to evaluate its internal strengths and weaknesses. Clearly, the business doesn't have to correct *all* its weaknesses, nor should it gloat about all its strengths. The big question is whether it should limit itself to those opportunities for which it possesses the required strengths or consider those that might require it to find or develop new strengths.

Goal Formulation

After SWOT analysis, the next step is *goal formulation,* developing specific goals for the planning period. *Goals* are objectives that are specific with respect to magnitude and time. Most business units pursue a mix of objectives, including profitability, sales growth, market share improvement, risk containment, and innovation. The business unit sets these objectives and then manages by objectives (MBO). For an MBO system to work, the unit's objectives must be (1) arranged hierarchically, from most to least important; (2) quantitative whenever possible; (3) realistic; and (4) consistent. Other important trade-offs include short-term profit versus long-term growth, deep penetration of existing markets versus development of new markets, profit goals versus nonprofit goals, and high growth versus low risk. Each choice calls for a different marketing strategy.[15]

Strategy Formulation

Goals indicate what a business unit wants to achieve; **strategy** is a game plan for getting there. Every business must design a strategy for achieving its goals, consisting of a *marketing strategy* and a compatible *technology strategy* and *sourcing strategy.* Michael Porter has proposed three generic strategies that provide a good starting point for strategic thinking: overall cost leadership, differentiation, and focus.[16]

- **Overall cost leadership.** Firms work to achieve the lowest production and distribution costs so they can underprice competitors and win market share. They need less skill in marketing. The problem is that other firms will usually compete with still-lower costs.
- **Differentiation.** The business concentrates on achieving superior performance in an important customer benefit area valued by a large part of the market.
- **Focus.** The business focuses on one or more narrow market segments, gets to know them intimately, and pursues either cost leadership or differentiation within the target segment.

Competing firms directing the same strategy to the same target market constitute a *strategic group.*[17] The firm that carries out the strategy best will make the most profits. Porter draws a distinction between operational effectiveness and strategy. Competitors can quickly copy the operationally effective company using benchmarking and other tools, thus diminishing the advantage of operational effectiveness. Strategy, on the other hand, is "the creation of a unique and valuable position involving a different set of activities." A company can claim it has a strategy when it "performs different activities from rivals or performs similar activities in different ways."

Even giant companies—AT&T, Philips, and Starbucks—often cannot achieve leadership, either nationally or globally, without forming alliances with domestic or multinational companies that complement or leverage their capabilities and resources. Marketing alliances may involve products or services (licensing or jointly marketing an offering), promotions (one company carrying a promotion for another), logistics (delivering or distributing another firm's product), or pricing (offering mutual price discounts). To keep strategic alliances thriving, firms are developing organizational structures to support them, and many have come to view the ability to form and manage partnerships as core skills called **partner relationship management (PRM)**.

Strategy and Implementation

Strategy addresses the *what* and *why* of marketing programs and activities; implementation addresses the *who, where, when,* and *how.* According to McKinsey & Company, strategy is only one of seven elements—all of which start with the letter *s*—in successful business practice.[18] The first three—strategy, structure, and systems—are considered the "hardware" of success. The next four—style, skills, staff, and shared values—are the "software." When these elements are present, companies are usually more successful at strategy implementation.[19] Implementation depends on management exercising control over marketing programs that support the strategy. A company's strategic fit with the environment will inevitably erode because the market environment changes faster than the company's seven Ss. Thus, a company might remain efficient yet lose effectiveness. Peter Drucker pointed out that it is more important to "do the right thing"—to be effective—than "to do things right"—to be efficient. The most successful companies, however, excel at both.

Organizations, especially large ones, are subject to inertia. It's difficult to change one part without adjusting everything else. Yet organizations can be changed through strong leadership, preferably in advance of a crisis. The key to organizational health is willingness to examine the changing environment and adopt new goals and behaviors. "Marketing Insight: Businesses Charting a New Direction" describes how some companies are adjusting to the new marketing realities.

The Marketing Plan

Working within the strategies and plans set by the levels above them, marketing managers come up with a marketing plan for individual products, lines, brands, channels, or customer groups. A **marketing plan** is a written document that summarizes what the marketer has learned about the marketplace and indicates how the firm plans to reach its marketing objectives.[20] It contains tactical guidelines for the marketing programs and financial allocations over the planning period.[21] The most frequently cited shortcomings of current marketing plans, according to marketing executives, are lack of realism, insufficient competitive analysis, and a short-run focus.

Contents of a Marketing Plan

A marketing plan usually contains the following sections.

- **Executive summary and table of contents.**
- **Situation analysis.** This section presents relevant background data on sales, costs, the market, competitors, and the macroenvironment. How do we define the market, how big

Businesses Charting a New Direction

Continued prosperity or even survival may depend on how quickly and effectively a firm is able to chart a strategy for a new direction. Consider these examples.

- With consumers increasingly using smart phones for directions and maps, Garmin, the biggest maker of GPS devices, found sales declining rapidly. Its solution was to partner with automakers and embed GPS systems in dashboard "command centers." Hedging its bets, Garmin also developed its own smart-phone app.

- When Dow Chemical found its commodity chemical strategy was no longer profitable, it shifted focus to unique, innovative high-margin products like solar shingles to capitalize on four main trends: clean energy,

health and nutrition, consumerism in the emerging world, and infrastructure.

- The runaway success of Amazon's Kindle, Apple's iPad, and other tablet products has turned the book industry upside down. Bookstores, libraries, and publishers are all recognizing that the sale and delivery of a book are now just a download away. Libraries can lend e-readers and e-books, and when the due date arrives, the book just disappears!

Sources: Erik Rhey, "A GPS Maker Shifts Gears," *Fortune*, March 19, 2012; Geoff Colvin, "Dow's New Direction," *Fortune*, March 19, 2012; Ben Bradford, "Libraries Grapple with the Downside of E-books," www.npr.org, May 29, 2012; Sharon Tregaskis, "Buy the Book," *Cornell Alumni Magazine*, November–December 2012; "Great Digital Expectations," *The Economist*, September 10, 2011.

is it, how fast is it growing, and what are the relevant trends and critical issues? Firms use all this information to carry out a SWOT analysis.

- **Marketing strategy.** The marketing manager defines the mission, marketing and financial objectives, and needs the market offering is intended to satisfy as well as its competitive positioning. This requires inputs from areas such as purchasing, manufacturing, sales, finance, and human resources.

- **Marketing tactics.** Here the marketing manager outlines the marketing activities that will be undertaken to execute the marketing strategy, including decisions about the product or service offering, pricing, channels, and communications.

- **Financial projections.** Financial projections include a sales forecast (by month and product category), an expense forecast (broken down into finer categories), and a break-even analysis (how many units the firm must sell to offset its fixed costs and average per-unit variable costs).

- **Implementation controls.** Management outlines the controls for monitoring activities and adjusting implementation. Typically, this section spells out the goals and budget for each month or quarter so management can review results and take corrective action as needed.

From Marketing Plan to Marketing Action

Most companies create yearly marketing plans. They start planning well in advance of the implementation date to allow time for marketing research, analysis, management review, and coordination between departments. As each action program begins, they monitor ongoing results, investigate any deviation from plans, and take corrective steps as needed to keep marketing performance on track. Some firms prepare contingency plans so they can update and adapt the marketing plan at any time.

Marketing Implementation, Control, and Performance

Marketing implementation is the process that turns marketing plans into action assignments and ensures they accomplish the plan's stated objectives.[22] A brilliant strategic marketing plan counts for little if not implemented properly. Therefore, the marketing plan typically outlines budgets, schedules, and marketing metrics for monitoring and evaluating results over time. With budgets, marketers can compare planned and actual expenditures for a given period. Schedules show when tasks were supposed to be completed and when they actually were. Marketing metrics track actual outcomes of marketing programs to see whether the company is moving forward toward its objectives. These and other tools enable management to measure marketing performance and control the implementation of marketing programs.

Although marketing expenses are easily quantified in the short run, the resulting outputs such as broader brand awareness, enhanced brand image, greater customer loyalty, and improved new product prospects may take months or years to manifest themselves. Two complementary approaches to measuring marketing productivity are: (1) *marketing metrics* to assess marketing effects and (2) *marketing-mix modeling* to estimate causal relationships and measure how marketing activity affects outcomes. *Marketing dashboards* are a structured way to disseminate the insights gleaned from these two approaches.

Marketing Metrics

Marketing metrics is the set of measures that help marketers quantify, compare, and interpret their performance.[23] Marketers today have better marketing metrics for measuring the performance of marketing plans (see Table 2.2 for some examples).[24] Firms can choose metrics based on the particular issues or problems they face. London Business School's Tim Ambler believes firms can split evaluation of marketing performance into two parts: (1) short-term results and (2) changes in brand equity.[25] Short-term results often reflect profit-and-loss concerns as shown by sales turnover, shareholder value, or some combination of the two. Brand-equity measures could include customer awareness, attitudes, and behaviors; market share; relative price premium; number of complaints; distribution and availability; total number of customers; perceived quality; and loyalty and retention.[26]

Marketing-Mix Modeling

Marketing accountability means that marketers must more precisely estimate the effects of different marketing investments. *Marketing-mix models* analyze data from a variety of sources, such as retailer scanner data, company shipment data, pricing, media, and promotion spending data, to understand the effects of specific marketing activities.[27] To deepen understanding, marketers can conduct multivariate analyses, such as regression analysis, to sort through how each marketing element influences marketing outcomes such as brand sales or market share. Especially popular with packaged-goods marketers such as Procter & Gamble and Colgate, the findings from marketing-mix modeling help allocate or reallocate expenditures. Analyses explore which part of ad budgets are wasted, what optimal spending levels are, and what minimum investment levels should be.

Although marketing-mix modeling helps to isolate effects, it is less effective at assessing how different marketing elements work in combination. Wharton's Dave Reibstein also notes three

TABLE 2.2	Marketing Metrics

Sales Metrics

- Sales growth
- Market share
- Sales from new products

Customer Readiness to Buy Metrics

- Awareness
- Preference
- Purchase intention
- Trial rate
- Repurchase rate

Customer Metrics

- Customer complaints
- Customer satisfaction
- Ratio of promoters to detractors
- Customer acquisition costs
- New-customer gains
- Customer losses
- Customer churn
- Retention rate
- Customer lifetime value
- Customer equity
- Customer profitability
- Return on customer

Distribution Metrics

- Number of outlets
- Share in shops handling
- Weighted distribution
- Distribution gains
- Average stock volume (value)
- Stock cover in days
- Out of stock frequency
- Share of shelf
- Average sales per point of sale

Communication Metrics

- Spontaneous (unaided) brand awareness
- Top of mind brand awareness
- Prompted (aided) brand awareness
- Spontaneous (unaided) advertising awareness
- Prompted (aided) advertising awareness
- Effective reach
- Effective frequency
- Gross rating points (GRP)
- Response rate

other shortcomings:[28] (1) it focuses on incremental growth instead of baseline sales or long-term effects; (2) it has limited integration of metrics related to customer satisfaction, awareness, and brand equity; and (3) it generally fails to incorporate metrics related to competitors, the trade, or the sales force.

Marketing Dashboards

Management can assemble a summary set of relevant internal and external measures in a marketing dashboard for synthesis and interpretation. Marketing dashboards are like the instrument panel in a car or plane, visually displaying real-time indicators to ensure proper functioning. Formally, **marketing dashboards** are "a concise set of interconnected performance drivers to be viewed in common throughout the organization."[29]

As input to the marketing dashboard, companies should include two key market-based scorecards that reflect performance and provide possible early warning signals. A *customer-performance scorecard* records how well the company is doing year after year on such customer-based measures as the percentage of customers who say they would repurchase the product. A *stakeholder-performance scorecard* tracks the satisfaction of various constituencies who have a critical interest in and impact on the company's performance: employees, suppliers, banks, distributors, retailers, and stockholders. Again, management should take action when one or more groups register increased or above-norm levels of dissatisfaction.[30] A company might aim to delight its customers, perform well for its employees, and deliver a threshold level of satisfaction to its suppliers. It must not violate any stakeholder group's sense of fairness about the treatment it is receiving relative to the others.

Marketing Control

Marketing control is the process by which firms assess the effects of their marketing activities and make necessary changes and adjustments. Table 2.3 lists four types of marketing control: annual-plan control, profitability control, efficiency control, and strategic control.

Annual-plan control ensures the company achieves the sales, profits, and other goals established in its annual plan. To do this, management sets monthly or quarterly goals, monitors marketing performance in the marketplace, determines the causes of serious performance deviations, and takes corrective action to close gaps between goals and performance (see Figure 2.3). Profitability control is used to determine whether to expand, reduce, or eliminate any products or marketing activities.

Efficiency control helps the company look at better ways to manage marketing spending and investments. Some companies have established a marketing controller position to improve marketing efficiency. Marketing controllers examine adherence to profit plans, help brand managers prepare budgets, measure the efficiency of promotions, analyze media production costs, evaluate customer and geographic profitability, and educate marketing staff on the financial implications of marketing decisions.

With strategic control, the firm should periodically reassess its strategic approach to the marketplace, using a **marketing audit**, a comprehensive, systematic, independent, and periodic examination of a company's or business unit's marketing environment, objectives, strategies, and activities, to identify problem areas and opportunities and recommend a plan for improving marketing performance. A good marketing audit covers the macroenvironment, task environment,

TABLE 2.3	Types of Marketing Control		
Type of Control	Prime Responsibility	Purpose of Control	Approaches
I. Annual-plan control	Top management Middle management	To examine whether the planned results are being achieved	• Sales analysis • Market share analysis • Sales-to-expense ratios • Financial analysis • Market-based scorecard analysis
II. Profitability control	Marketing controller	To examine where the company is making and losing money	Profitability by: • product • territory • customer • segment • trade channel • order size
III. Efficiency control	Line and staff management Marketing controller	To evaluate and improve the spending efficiency and impact of marketing expenditures	Efficiency of: • sales force • advertising • sales promotion • distribution
IV. Strategic control	Top management Marketing auditor	To examine whether the company is pursuing its best opportunities with respect to markets, products, and channels	• Marketing effectiveness rating instrument • Marketing audit • Marketing excellence review • Company ethical and social responsibility review

FIGURE 2.3 The Control Process

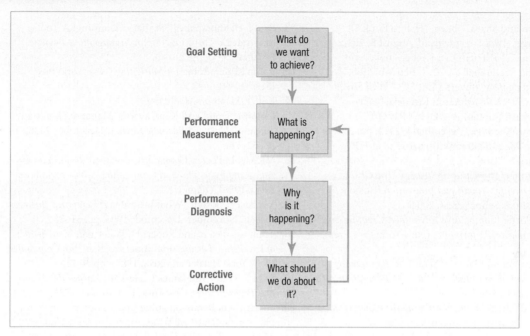

marketing strategy, marketing organization, marketing systems, marketing productivity, and marketing functions. Regular marketing audits can benefit companies in good health as well as those in trouble.

Executive Summary

The value chain is a tool for identifying key activities that create customer value and costs in a specific business. The value delivery process includes choosing (or identifying), providing (or delivering), and communicating superior value. Market-oriented strategic planning is the managerial process of developing and maintaining a viable fit between the organization's objectives, skills, and resources and its changing market opportunities.

Strategic planning occurs at multiple levels: corporate, division, business unit, and product. Corporate strategy includes defining the mission, establishing strategic business units (SBUs), assigning resources, and assessing growth opportunities. This is the framework within which divisions and SBUs prepare their strategic plans. The marketing plan summarizes what the firm knows about the marketplace and how it will reach its marketing objectives, operating at both the strategic and tactical levels. Marketing implementation turns marketing plans into action assignments to achieve the plan's objectives. Firms use marketing metrics, marketing-mix modeling, and marketing dashboards to monitor and assess marketing productivity. By applying marketing control, management can assess the effects of marketing activities and make improvements.

Notes

1. Ben Worthen and Shara Tibken, "H-P to Book $8 Billion Charge," *Wall Street Journal*, August 8, 2012; Ben Worthen, "H-P Tries On a Sleeker Look," *Wall Street Journal*, September 17, 2012; Ben Worthen, "H-P, Dell Struggle as Buyers Shun PCs," *Wall Street Journal*, August 22, 2012; Aaron Ricadela, "Why Hewlett-Packard Impulse Buy Didn't Pay Off," *Bloomberg Businessweek*, December 3, 2012, pp. 35–36; Jack Hough, "Meg Whitman's Turnaround at HP," *Barron's*, April 5, 2014.

2. Nirmalya Kumar, *Marketing as Strategy: The CEO's Agenda for Driving Growth and Innovation* (Boston: Harvard Business School Press, 2004).

3. Michael E. Porter, *Competitive Advantage: Creating and Sustaining Superior Performance* (New York: Free Press, 1985).

4. Michael Hammer and James Champy, *Reengineering the Corporation: A Manifesto for Business Revolution* (New York: Harper Business, 1993).

5. Hammer and Champy, *Reengineering the Corporation*; Jon R. Katzenbach and Douglas K. Smith, *The Wisdom of Teams* (Boston: Harvard Business School Press, 1993); Matias G. Enz and Douglas M. Lambert, "Using Cross-Functional, Cross-Firm Teams to Co-Create Value: The Role of Financial Measures," *Industrial Marketing Management*, 41 (April 2012), pp. 495–507.

6. "Ford Targets 30% Water Reduction per Vehicle," *Manufacturing Close-Up*, January 10, 2012.

7. George S. Day, "Closing the Marketing Capabilities Gap," *Journal of Marketing* 75 (July 2011), pp. 183–95.

8. George S. Day and Paul J. H. Schoemaker, *Peripheral Vision: Detecting the Weak Signals That Will Make or Break Your Company* (Cambridge, MA: Harvard Business School Press, 2006); Paul J. H. Schoemaker and George S. Day, "How to Make Sense of Weak Signals," *MIT Sloan Management Review* (Spring 2009), pp. 81–89.

9. Peter Drucker, *Management: Tasks, Responsibilities and Practices* (New York: Harper and Row, 1973), chapter 7.

10. This section is based on Robert M. Grant, *Contemporary Strategy Analysis*, 8th ed. (New York: John Wiley & Sons, 2013), chapter 5.

11. Beth Snyder Bulik, "Customer Service Playing Bigger Role as Marketing Tool," *Advertising Age*, November 7, 2011.

12. Paul J. H. Shoemaker, "Scenario Planning: A Tool for Strategic Thinking," *Sloan Management Review* (Winter 1995), pp. 25–40.

13. Philip Kotler, *Kotler on Marketing* (New York: Free Press, 1999).

14. Kotler, *Kotler on Marketing*.

15. Dominic Dodd and Ken Favaro, "Managing the Right Tension," *Harvard Business Review*, December 2006, pp. 62–74.

16. Michael E. Porter, *Competitive Strategy: Techniques for Analyzing Industries and Competitors* (New York: Free Press, 1980), chapter 2.

17. Michael E. Porter, "What Is Strategy?" *Harvard Business Review*, November–December 1996, pp. 61–78.

18. Thomas J. Peters and Robert H. Waterman Jr., *In Search of Excellence: Lessons from America's Best-Run Companies* (New York: Harper and Row, 1982), pp. 9–12.

19. John P. Kotter and James L. Heskett, *Corporate Culture and Performance* (New York: Free Press, 1992).

20. An excellent hands-on guide to developing a marketing plan can be found with Alexander Chernev, *The Marketing Plan Handbook* (Chicago, IL: Cerebellum Press, 2011), on which some of the discussion in this section is built. See also Marian Burk Wood, *The Marketing Plan Handbook*, 5th ed. (Upper Saddle River, NJ: Pearson, 2014); Tim Calkins, *Breakthrough Marketing Plans* (New York: Palgrave MacMillan, 2008).

21. Donald R. Lehmann and Russell S. Winer, *Product Management*, 3rd ed. (Boston: McGraw-Hill/Irwin, 2001).

22. For more on developing and implementing marketing plans, see H. W. Goetsch, *Developing, Implementing, and Managing an Effective Marketing Plan* (Chicago: NTC Business Books, 1993). See also Thomas V. Bonoma, *The Marketing Edge: Making Strategies Work* (New York: Free Press, 1985). Much of this section is based on Bonoma's work.

23. Elisabeth Sullivan, "Measure Up," *Marketing News*, May 30, 2009, pp. 8–11.

24. For other examples, see Paul W. Farris, Neil T. Bendle, Phillip E. Pfeifer, and David J. Reibstein, *Marketing Metrics: 50+ Metrics Every Executive Should Master* (Upper Saddle River, NJ: Wharton School Publishing, 2006).

25. Tim Ambler, *Marketing and the Bottom Line: The New Methods of Corporate Wealth*, 2nd ed. (London: Pearson Education, 2003).

26. Kusum L. Ailawadi, Donald R. Lehmann, and Scott A. Neslin, "Revenue Premium as an Outcome Measure of Brand Equity," *Journal of Marketing* 67 (October 2003), pp. 1–17.

27. Gerard J. Tellis, "Modeling Marketing Mix," Rajiv Grover and Marco Vriens, eds., *Handbook of Marketing Research* (Thousand Oaks, CA: Sage Publications, 2006).

28. David J. Reibstein, "Connect the Dots," *CMO Magazine*, May 2005.

29. For insightful discussion of the design and implementation of marketing dashboards, see Koen Pauwels, *It's Not the Size of the Data, It's How You Use It: Smarter Marketing with Analytics and Dashboards* (New York: AMACOM: 2014) and consult the resources at www.marketdashboards.com.

30. Robert S. Kaplan and David P. Norton, *The Balanced Scorecard* (Boston: Harvard Business School Press, 1996).

Chapter 3

Capturing Marketing Insights and Forecasting Demand

In this chapter, we will address the following questions:

1. What are the components of a modern marketing information system? (Page 35)
2. How can companies collect marketing intelligence? (Page 36)
3. What constitutes good marketing research? (Page 37)
4. How can companies accurately measure and forecast market demand? (Page 42)
5. What are some influential developments in the macroenvironment? (Page 45)

Marketing Management at Campbell Soup Company

The Campbell Soup Company's iconic red-and-white soup can represents one of the most famous U.S. brands. Recently, though, overall consumption of canned soup has declined 13 percent, and the firm's market share has dropped from 67 percent to 53 percent. To help stop the sales slide, Campbell's set out to better understand the habits and tastes of 18- to 34-year-olds. Executives visited "hipster market hubs" to observe Millennials during "live-alongs," where they shopped and ate at home with young consumers, and "eat-alongs," where they dined with them in restaurants. The key insight: Millennials love spices and eat more exotic food than their parents—they just can't cook it at home! The solution: a new line of Campbell's Go! Soup—ready-to-eat, boldly-flavored meals sold in pouches (and at a price more than three times the basic red-and-white line). Since the target market is tech-savvy, the product line was promoted entirely online on music and humor sites, gaming platforms, and social media.[1]

Virtually every industry has been touched by dramatic shifts in the economic, sociocultural, natural, technological, demographic, and political-legal environments. In this chapter, we consider how Campbell's and other firms can collect and store information, conduct marketing research, develop good forecasts to support marketing management, and analyze trends in the macroenvironment.

The Marketing Information System and Marketing Intelligence

The major responsibility for identifying significant marketplace changes falls to the company's marketers. Marketers have two advantages for the task: disciplined methods for collecting information and time spent interacting with customers and observing competitors and other outside groups. Some firms have marketing information systems that provide rich detail about buyer wants, preferences, and behavior.

Every firm must organize and distribute a continuous flow of information to its marketing managers. A **marketing information system (MIS)** consists of people, equipment, and procedures to gather, sort, analyze, evaluate, and distribute needed, timely, and accurate information to marketing decision makers. It relies on internal company records, marketing intelligence activities, and marketing research.

Internal Records and Database Systems

To spot important opportunities and potential problems, marketing managers rely on internal reports of orders, sales, prices, costs, inventory levels, receivables, and payables.

The Order-to-Payment Cycle   The heart of the internal records system is the order-to-payment cycle. Sales representatives, dealers, and customers send orders to the firm. The sales department prepares invoices, transmits copies to various departments, and back-orders out-of-stock items. Shipped items generate shipping and billing documents. Because customers favor firms that can promise timely delivery, companies need to perform these steps quickly and accurately.

Sales Information Systems   Marketing managers need timely and accurate reports on current sales. Walmart operates a sales and inventory data warehouse that captures data on every item for every customer, every store, every day and refreshes it every hour. Marketers must carefully interpret sales data, however, to avoid drawing wrong conclusions.

Databases, Data Warehousing, and Data Mining   A **customer database** is an organized collection of comprehensive information about individual customers or prospects that is current, accessible, and actionable for lead generation, lead qualification, sales, or customer relationship management. **Database marketing** is the process of building, maintaining, and using customer databases and other databases (products, suppliers, resellers) to contact, transact with, and build relationships with customers. Information captured by the company is organized into a **data warehouse** where marketers can capture, query, and analyze data to draw inferences about individual customers' needs and responses. Marketing analysts use **data mining** to extract from the mass of data useful insights about customer behavior, trends, and segments.

The explosion of data brought by the maturation of the Internet and mobile technology gives companies unprecedented opportunities to engage customers. It also threatens to overwhelm decision makers. "Marketing Insight: Digging into Big Data" describes opportunities and challenges in managing massive data sets.[2] On the other hand, some customers may not want a relationship with the company and may resent having personal data collected and stored. The use of *behavioral targeting* to track customers' online behavior for marketing purposes allows advertisers to better target online ads—but some consumers object to the practice. Chapter 17 discusses database marketing in the context of direct marketing.

Digging into Big Data

In one year, people store enough data to fill 60,000 Libraries of Congress. YouTube receives 24 hours of video *every minute*. Manufacturers are putting sensors and chips into appliances and products, generating even more data. However, more data are not better unless they can be properly processed, analyzed, and interpreted. And therein lies the opportunity and challenge of Big Data, data sets that cannot be effectively managed with traditional tools.

One industry expert, James Kobielus, sees Big Data as distinctive because of: *Volume* (from hundreds of terabytes to petabytes and beyond); *Velocity* (up to and including real-time delivery); *Variety* (encompassing structured, unstructured, and semi-structured formats such as messages, images, and GPS signals); and *Volatility* (with hundreds of new data sources in apps, Web services, and social networks).

Some companies are harnessing Big Data. UK supermarket giant Tesco uses the 1.5 billion pieces of data it collects every month to set prices and promotions; U.S. kitchenware retailer Williams-Sonoma uses its customer data to customize versions of its catalog. Amazon reports generating 30 percent of its sales through its recommendation engine ("You may also like"). On the production side, GE set up a team of developers in Silicon Valley to improve the efficiency of the jet engines, generators, locomotives, and CT scanners it sells. Even a 1 percent improvement in the operation of commercial aircraft would save $2 billion for GE's airline customers.

Sources: Schumpeter, "Building with Big Data," *The Economist*, May 28, 2011; Jessica Twentyman, "Big Data Is the 'Next Frontier,'" *Financial Times*, November 14, 2011; Jacques Bughin, John Livingston, and Sam Marwaha, "Seizing the Potential of Big Data," *McKinsey Quarterly* 4 (October 2011); "Mining the Big Data Goldmine," Special Advertising Section, *Fortune*, 2012; "Financial Brands Tap Big Data," www.warc.com, September 13, 2012; Thomas H. Davenport, Paul Barth, and Randy Bean, "How 'Big Data' Is Different," *MIT Sloan Management Review* 54 (Fall 2012), pp. 43–46; Andrew McAfee and Erik Brynjolfsson, "Big Data: The Management Revolution," *Harvard Business Review*, October 2012, pp. 60–68; Ashlee Vance, "GE Tries to Make Its Machines Cool and Connected," *Bloomberg Businessweek*, December 10, 2012, pp. 44–46.

Marketing Intelligence

A **marketing intelligence system** is a set of procedures and sources that managers use to obtain everyday information about developments in the marketing environment. The internal records system supplies *results* data, but the marketing intelligence system supplies *happenings* data. Marketing managers collect marketing intelligence by reading books, newspapers, and trade publications; talking to customers, suppliers, distributors, and other company managers; and monitoring online social media. Table 3.1 shows eight ways to improve the quality and quantity of marketing intelligence.

Companies that make good use of "cookies," records of Web site usage stored on personal browsers, are smart users of targeted marketing. Many consumers are happy to cooperate: Not only do they *not* delete cookies, but they also expect customized marketing appeals and deals once they accept them.

The Marketing Research System

Marketing managers often commission formal marketing studies of specific problems and opportunities, like a market survey, a product-preference test, a sales forecast by region, or an advertising evaluation. It's the job of the marketing researcher to produce insight to help

TABLE 3.1	Improving Marketing Intelligence
Action	**Example**
Train and motivate the sales force to spot and report new developments.	Have sales representatives observe how customers use products in innovative ways, which can lead to new product ideas.
Motivate distributors, retailers, and other intermediaries to pass along important intelligence.	Intermediaries are closer to the customer and can offer helpful insights, such as observing that certain consumers switch to different products during specific seasons.
Hire external experts to collect intelligence.	Use mystery shoppers to uncover problems with quality, services, and facilities.
Network internally and externally.	Buy competitors' products, attend open houses and trade shows, read competitors' published reports, and collect competitors' ads.
Set up a customer advisory panel.	Invite the company's largest, most outspoken, most sophisticated, or most representative customers to provide feedback.
Take advantage of government data.	Check U.S. Census Bureau data to learn about population swings, demographic groups, regional migrations, and changing family structure.
Buy information from outside research firms and vendors.	Obtain data from well-known suppliers such as Nielsen and NPD.
Collect marketing intelligence on the Internet.	Check online forums, distributor feedback sites, customer complaint sites, blogs, and social media for comments and opinions about competing goods and services.

the marketing manager's decision making. *Marketing insights* provide diagnostic information about how and why we observe certain effects in the marketplace and what that means to marketers.[3]

Gaining marketing insights is crucial for marketing success. To improve the marketing of its $3 billion Pantene hair care brand, Procter & Gamble researched women's feelings about hair, using surveys with mood scales from psychology, high-resolution EEG research to measure brain waves, and other methods. As a result, the company reformulated Pantene products, redesigned packages, pared the line down, and fine-tuned the ad campaign.[4]

Defining Marketing Research

The American Marketing Association defines **marketing research** as "the function that links the consumer, customer, and public to the marketer through information—information used to identify and define marketing opportunities and problems; generate, refine, and evaluate marketing actions; monitor marketing performance; and improve understanding of marketing as a process. Marketing research specifies the information required to address these issues, designs the method for collecting information, manages and implements the data collection process, analyzes the results, and communicates the findings and their implications."[5]

Most companies use multiple resources to study their industries, competitors, audiences, and channel strategies. They normally budget marketing research at 1 percent to 2 percent of company sales and spend much of that on outside firms. Marketing research firms fall into three categories. Syndicated-service research firms such as Nielsen gather consumer and trade information, which they sell for a fee. Custom marketing research firms design studies, implement them, and report the findings. Specialty-line marketing research firms provide specific services such as field interviewing.

The Marketing Research Process

To take advantage of all the resources and practices available, good marketers adopt a formal marketing research process that follows the six steps shown in Figure 3.1. We illustrate these steps in the following situation. Assume that American Airlines is reviewing new ideas for serving first-class passengers on very long flights, mainly businesspeople whose high-priced tickets pay most of the freight. Among these ideas are: (1) ultra high-speed Wi-Fi service, (2) 124 channels of high-definition satellite cable TV, and (3) a 250-CD audio system that lets each passenger create a customized in-flight playlist. The marketing research manager will investigate how first-class passengers would rate these services, specifically ultra high-speed Wi-Fi, and how much extra they would be willing to pay.

Step 1: Define the Problem, Decision Alternatives, and Research Objectives

Marketing managers must not define the problem too broadly or too narrowly for the marketing researcher. In this case, the researcher and the marketing manager are defining the problem as follows: "Will offering ultra high-speed Wi-Fi service create enough incremental preference and

FIGURE 3.1 The Marketing Research Process

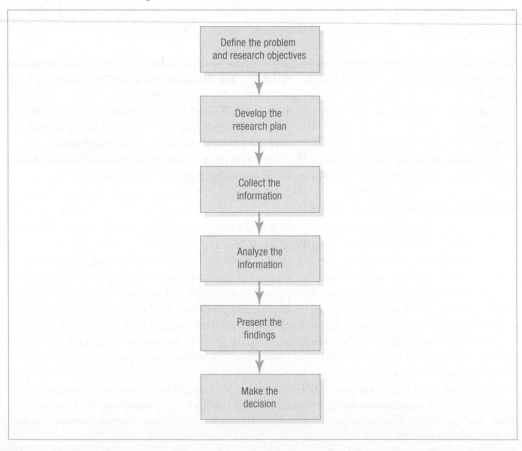

profit to justify its cost against other service enhancements American might make?" They specify five research objectives: (1) What types of first-class passengers would respond most to ultra high-speed Wi-Fi service? (2) How many are likely to use it at different price levels? (3) How many might choose American because of this new service? (4) How much long-term goodwill will this service add to American's image? (5) How important is ultra high-speed Wi-Fi service to first-class passengers relative to other services, such as a power plug?

Not all research can be this specific. Some is *exploratory*—its goal is to identify the problem and to suggest possible solutions. Some is *descriptive*—it seeks to quantify demand, such as how many first-class passengers would purchase ultra high-speed Wi-Fi service at $25. Some research is *causal*—its purpose is to test a cause-and-effect relationship.

Step 2: Develop the Research Plan

To design a research plan, marketing managers need to make decisions about the data sources, research approaches, research instruments, sampling plan, and contact methods.

Data Sources   The researcher can gather secondary data, primary data, or both. *Secondary data* are data that were collected for another purpose and already exist somewhere. *Primary data* are data freshly gathered for a specific purpose or project. Researchers usually start by examining secondary data. If the needed data don't exist or are dated, inaccurate, incomplete, or unreliable, the researcher will need to collect primary data.

Research Approaches   Marketers collect primary data in five main ways: through observation, focus groups, surveys, behavioral data, and experiments.

- **Observational research.** Researchers can gather fresh data by observing unobtrusively as customers shop or consume products or by holding informal interview sessions at a café or bar.[6] **Ethnographic research** uses concepts and tools from anthropology and other social science disciplines to provide deep cultural understanding of how people live and work.[7] The American Airlines researchers might meander around first-class lounges to hear how travelers talk about different carriers or sit next to passengers on planes.

- **Focus group research.** A **focus group** is a gathering of 6 to 10 people selected for demographic, psychographic, or other considerations and convened to discuss various topics at length, with a professional moderator, for a small payment. In the American Airlines research, the moderator might start with a broad question, such as "How do you feel about first-class air travel?" Questions then move to how people view different airlines, existing services, proposed services, and, specifically, ultra high-speed Wi-Fi service.

- **Survey research.** Companies undertake surveys to assess people's knowledge, beliefs, preferences, and satisfaction and to measure these magnitudes in the general population. Cash register receipts from Walmart, Petco, and Staples include an invitation to fill out a survey with a chance to win a prize.[8] American Airlines might prepare its own survey questions, or it might add questions to an omnibus survey that carries the questions of several companies at a much lower cost. It can also pose questions to an ongoing consumer panel, have researchers survey people in a shopping mall, or add a survey request at the end of customer service calls.

- **Behavioral data.** Customers leave traces of their purchasing behavior in store scanning data, catalog purchases, and customer databases. Actual purchases reflect consumers' preferences and often are more reliable than statements they offer to market researchers. American Airlines can analyze ticket purchase records and online behavior.

- **Experimental research.** The most scientifically valid research is **experimental research,** designed to capture cause-and-effect relationships by eliminating competing explanations of the findings. American Airlines might introduce ultra high-speed Wi-Fi service on one of its international flights, charging $25 one week and $15 the next week. If the plane carried approximately the same number of first-class passengers each week and the particular weeks made no difference, the airline could relate any significant difference in the number of passengers using the service to the price charged.

Research Instruments   Marketing researchers use three main research instruments in collecting primary data: questionnaires, qualitative measures, and technological devices. A *questionnaire* consists of a set of questions presented to respondents. Because of its flexibility, it is by far the most common instrument used to collect primary data. The form, wording, and sequence of the questions can all influence the responses, so testing and de-bugging are necessary. *Closed-end questions* specify all the possible answers, and the responses are easier to interpret and tabulate. *Open-end questions* allow respondents to answer in their own words. They are especially useful in exploratory research, where the researcher is looking for insight into how people think.

Some marketers prefer qualitative methods for gauging consumer opinion because they feel consumers' actions don't always match their answers to survey questions. *Qualitative research techniques* are relatively indirect and unstructured measurement approaches, limited only by the marketing researcher's creativity, that permit a range of responses. They can be an especially useful first step in exploring consumers' perceptions because respondents may be less guarded and reveal more about themselves in the process.

Technological devices are also used for marketing research. Galvanometers can measure the interest or emotions aroused by exposure to a specific ad or picture. The tachistoscope flashes an ad to a subject with an exposure interval that may range from a fraction of a second to several seconds. After each exposure, respondents describe everything they recall. Researchers have also benefited from advances in visual technology techniques studying a consumer's eyes and face.[9] Technology now lets marketers use skin sensors, brain wave scanners, and full-body scanners to get consumer responses.[10] For example, biometric-tracking wrist sensors can measure electrodermal activity, or skin conductance, to note changes in sweat levels, body temperature, and so on.[11]

Sampling Plan   After choosing the research approach and instruments, the marketing researcher must design a sampling plan. This calls for three decisions:

1. *Sampling unit: Whom should we survey?* In the American Airlines survey, should the sampling unit consist of first-class business travelers, first-class vacation travelers, or both? Should it include travelers under age 18? With the sampling unit chosen, marketers must next develop a sampling frame so everyone in the target population has an equal or known chance of being sampled.

2. *Sample size: How many people should we survey?* Large samples give more reliable results, but it's not necessary to sample the entire target population to achieve reliable results. Samples of less than 1 percent of a population can often provide good reliability with a credible sampling procedure.

3. *Sampling procedure: How should we choose the respondents?* Probability sampling allows marketers to calculate confidence limits for sampling error and makes the sample more representative.

Contact Methods   Now the marketing researcher must decide how to contact the subjects: by mail, by telephone, in person, or online. The advantages and disadvantages of each method are shown in Table 3.2.

TABLE 3.2	Marketing Research Contact Methods	
Contact Method	Advantages	Disadvantages
By mail	Good for reaching people who would not give personal interviews or whose responses might be biased or distorted by the interviewer.	Response rate is usually low or slow.
By telephone	Good for gathering information quickly and clarifying questions if respondents do not understand. Response rate is typically higher than for mailed questionnaires.	Interviews must be brief, not too personal. Telephone contact getting more difficult because of consumers' growing antipathy toward telemarketers.
In person	Most versatile because researcher can ask more questions and record additional observations about respondents, such as dress and body language.	Most expensive method, subject to interviewer bias, and requires more planning and supervision.
Online	Inexpensive, fast, versatile. Responses tend to be honest and thoughtful. Firms can post questionnaires online, host a consumer panel or virtual focus group, sponsor a chat room or blog, analyze clickstream data, use text messaging.	Samples can be skewed and small. Online research can suffer from technological problems and inconsistencies. Online panels can suffer from excessive turnover.

Step 3: Collect the Data

The data collection phase of marketing research is generally the most expensive and error-prone. Some respondents will be away from home, offline, or otherwise inaccessible; they must be contacted again or replaced. Others will refuse to cooperate or will give biased or dishonest answers.

Step 4: Analyze the Information

The next step in the process is to extract findings by tabulating the data and developing summary measures. The researchers now compute averages and measures of dispersion for the major variables and apply some advanced statistical techniques and decision models to try to discover additional findings. They may test different hypotheses and theories, applying sensitivity analysis to test assumptions and the strength of the conclusions.

Step 5: Present the Findings

Now the researcher presents the findings. Researchers are increasingly asked to play a proactive, consulting role in translating data and information into insights and recommendations. They're also considering ways to make the findings understandable and compelling. In the American Airlines situation, management learns that about 5 of 10 first-class passengers would use Wi-Fi service during a flight if priced at $25; at $15, about 6 would. Thus, a fee of $15 would produce less revenue ($90 = 6 × $15) than $25 ($125 = 5 × $25). Assuming the same flight takes place 365 days a year, American could collect $45,625 (= $125 × 365) annually. Given an investment of $90,000 per plane, it would take two years for each to break even. Offering ultra high-speed Wi-Fi service would also strengthen American Airlines' image as an innovative carrier and earn it some new passengers and customer goodwill.

Step 6: Make the Decision

The American Airlines managers who commissioned the research need to weigh the evidence. If they have little confidence in the findings, they may decide against introducing the new Wi-Fi service. If they are predisposed to launching it, the findings support their inclination. They may even decide to study the issue further. The decision is theirs, but the research has provided them with insight into the problem.

Forecasting and Demand Measurement

Conducting marketing research and collecting marketing intelligence can help to identify marketing opportunities. The company must then measure and forecast the size, growth, and profit potential of each new opportunity. Sales forecasts prepared by marketing are used by finance to raise cash for investment and operations; by manufacturing to establish capacity and output; by purchasing to acquire the right amount of supplies; and by human resources to hire the needed workers. If the forecast is off the mark, the company will face excess or inadequate inventory. Because it's based on estimates of demand, managers need to define what they mean by market demand.

The Measures of Market Demand

There are many productive ways to break down the market:

- The **potential market** is the set of consumers with a sufficient level of interest in a market offer. However, their interest is not enough to define a market unless they also have sufficient income and access to the product.
- The **available market** is the set of consumers who have interest, income, *and* access to a particular offer. Eligible adults constitute the *qualified available market*—the set of consumers who have interest, income, access, and qualifications for the market offer.
- The **target market** is the part of the qualified available market the company decides to pursue.
- The **penetrated market** is the set of consumers who are buying the company's product.

These definitions are a useful tool for market planning. If the company isn't satisfied with current sales, it can try to attract a larger percentage of buyers from its target market. It can lower the qualifications for potential buyers. It can expand its available market by opening distribution elsewhere or lowering its price, or it can reposition itself in the minds of its customers.

The Market Demand Function

Market demand for a product is the total volume that would be bought by a defined customer group in a defined geographical area in a defined time period in a defined marketing environment under a defined marketing program. Market demand is not a fixed number, but rather a function of the stated conditions. For this reason, we call it the *market demand function*. Its dependence on underlying conditions is illustrated in Figure 3.2(a). The horizontal axis shows different possible levels of industry marketing expenditure in a given time period. The vertical axis shows the resulting demand level. The curve represents the estimated market demand associated with varying levels of marketing expenditure.

Some base sales—called the *market minimum* and labeled Q_1 in the figure—would take place without any demand-stimulating expenditures. Higher marketing expenditures would yield higher levels of demand, first at an increasing rate, then at a decreasing rate. Marketing expenditures beyond a certain level would not stimulate much further demand, suggesting an upper limit called the *market potential* and labeled Q_2 in the figure.

Markets and Market Potential   Two extreme types of markets are the expansible and the nonexpansible. The size of an *expansible market* is greatly affected by the level of industry marketing expenditures. As shown in Figure 3.2(a), the distance between Q_1 and Q_2 is relatively large. The size of a *nonexpansible market* is not much affected by the level of marketing expenditures,

FIGURE 3.2 Market Demand Functions

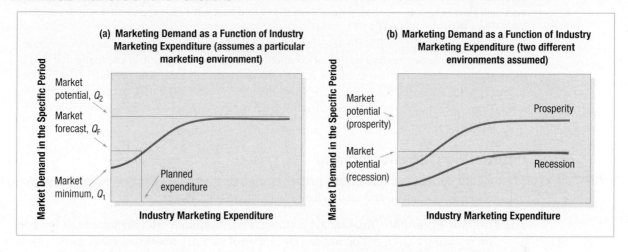

(a) Marketing Demand as a Function of Industry Marketing Expenditure (assumes a particular marketing environment)

Market Demand in the Specific Period

Market potential, Q_2

Market forecast, Q_F

Market minimum, Q_1

Planned expenditure

Industry Marketing Expenditure

(b) Marketing Demand as a Function of Industry Marketing Expenditure (two different environments assumed)

Market Demand in the Specific Period

Market potential (prosperity)

Market potential (recession)

Prosperity

Recession

Industry Marketing Expenditure

so the distance between Q_1 and Q_2 is relatively small. Organizations selling in a nonexpansible market must accept the market's size—the level of *primary demand* for the product class—and direct their efforts toward winning a larger **market share** for their product, that is, a higher level of *selective demand* for their product.

Remember that the market demand function is not a picture of market demand over time. Rather, it shows alternate current forecasts of market demand associated with possible levels of industry marketing effort. Only one level of industry marketing expenditure will actually occur. The market demand corresponding to this level is called the **market forecast.** This forecast shows the expected demand, not the maximum demand.

Market potential is the limit approached by market demand as industry marketing expenditures approach infinity for a given marketing environment. The phrase "for a given market environment" is crucial. Consider the market potential for automobiles. It's higher during prosperity than during a recession, as illustrated in Figure 3.2(b). Companies cannot do anything about the position of the market demand function, which is determined by the marketing environment. However, they influence their particular location on the function when they decide how much to spend on marketing.

Company Demand and Sales Forecast **Company demand** is the company's estimated share of market demand at alternative levels of company marketing effort in a given time period. It depends on how the company's products, services, prices, and communications are perceived relative to the competitors'. Other things equal, the company's market share depends on the relative scale and effectiveness of its market expenditures. Marketing model builders have developed sales response functions to measure how a company's sales are affected by its marketing expenditure level, marketing mix, and marketing effectiveness.[12]

Once marketers have estimated company demand, they choose a level of marketing effort. The **company sales forecast** is the expected level of company sales based on a chosen marketing plan and an assumed marketing environment. We represent the company sales forecast graphically with sales on the vertical axis and marketing effort on the horizontal axis, as in Figure 3.2.

A **sales quota** is the sales goal set for a product line, company division, or sales representative. It is primarily a managerial device for defining and stimulating sales effort, often set slightly higher than estimated sales to stretch the sales force's effort. A *sales budget* is a conservative estimate of the expected volume of sales, primarily for making current purchasing, production, and cash flow decisions. It's based on the need to avoid excessive risk and is generally set slightly lower than the sales forecast.

Company sales potential is the sales limit approached by company demand as company marketing effort increases relative to that of competitors. The absolute limit of company demand is the market potential. The two would be equal if the company captured 100 percent of the market. In most cases, company sales potential is less than the market potential, even when company marketing expenditures increase considerably. Each competitor has loyal buyers unresponsive to other companies' efforts to woo them.

Estimating Current Demand

In estimating current market demand, marketing executives want to estimate total market potential, area market potential, and total industry sales and market shares.

Total Market Potential   *Total market potential* is the maximum sales available to all firms in an industry during a given period under a given level of industry marketing effort and environmental conditions. A common way to estimate total market potential is to multiply the potential number of buyers by the average quantity each purchases and then by the price. If 100 million people buy books each year and the average book buyer buys three books a year at an average price of $20 each, then the total market potential for books is $6 billion (100 million × 3 × $20). The most difficult component to estimate is the number of buyers. Marketers often start with the total population, eliminate groups that obviously would not buy the product, and conduct research to eliminate groups without interest or income to buy.

Area Market Potential   Because companies must allocate their marketing budget optimally among their best territories, they need to estimate the market potential of different cities, states, and nations. Two major methods are the market-buildup method, used primarily by business marketers, and the multiple-factor index method, used primarily by consumer marketers. The *market-buildup method* calls for identifying all the potential buyers in each market and estimating their potential purchases. It produces accurate results if we have a list of all potential buyers and a good estimate of what each will buy. Unfortunately, this information is not always easy to gather.

An efficient method of estimating area market potentials makes use of the *North American Industry Classification System (NAICS)*, developed by the U.S. Bureau of the Census with the Canadian and Mexican governments.[13] The NAICS classifies all manufacturing into 20 major industry sectors and further breaks each sector into a six-digit, hierarchical structure. To use the NAICS, a lathe manufacturer would first determine the six-digit NAICS codes that represent products whose manufacturers are likely to require lathe machines. Then the lathe manufacturer would determine an appropriate base for estimating the number of lathes each industry will use, such as customer industry sales. Once the company estimates the rate of lathe ownership relative to the customer industry's sales, it can compute the market potential.

Consumer companies also need to estimate area market potentials, but because their customers are too numerous to list, they commonly use a straightforward index. A drug manufacturer might assume the market potential for drugs is directly related to population size. If the state of Virginia has 2.55 percent of the U.S. population, Virginia might be a market for 2.55 percent of total drugs sold. Yet a single factor is rarely a complete indicator of sales opportunity. Thus, it makes sense to develop a multiple-factor index and assign each factor a specific weight. Suppose Virginia has 2.00 percent of U.S. disposable personal income, 1.96 percent of U.S. retail sales, and 2.28 percent of U.S. population, and the respective weights for these factors are 0.5, 0.3, and 0.2. The buying-power index for Virginia is then 2.04 [0.5(2.00) + 0.3(1.96) + 0.2(2.28)].

Industry Sales and Market Shares   Besides estimating total potential and area potential, a company needs to know the actual industry sales taking place in its market. This means identifying competitors and estimating their sales. The industry trade association will often collect and publish total industry sales, although it usually does not list individual company sales. With this information, each company can evaluate its own performance against the industry's. If a company's sales are increasing by 5 percent a year and industry sales are increasing by 10 percent, the company is losing its relative standing in the industry. Another way to estimate sales is to buy reports from a marketing research firm that audits total sales and brand sales.

Estimating Future Demand

Forecasting is the art of anticipating what buyers are likely to do under a given set of conditions. The few products or services that lend themselves to easy forecasting generally enjoy an absolute level or a fairly constant trend and competition that is either nonexistent (public utilities) or stable (pure oligopolies). In most markets, good forecasting is a key factor in success.

Companies commonly prepare a macroeconomic forecast, followed by an industry forecast and then a company sales forecast. The macroeconomic forecast projects inflation, unemployment, interest rates, consumer spending, business investment, government expenditures, and other variables. The end result is a forecast of gross domestic product (GDP), which the firm uses, along with other environmental indicators, to forecast industry sales. The company derives its sales forecast by assuming it will win a certain market share. Five methods for sales forecasting are shown in Table 3.3.

Analyzing the Macroenvironment

By learning to spot and analyze trends in the macroenvironment, marketers can identify new market opportunities. A **trend** is a direction or sequence of events with momentum and durability, revealing the shape of the future. A **fad** is a craze that is unpredictable, of brief duration, and

TABLE 3.3	Sales Forecast Methods	
Forecast Method	Description	Use
Survey of buyers' intentions	Survey customers about purchase probability, present and future finances, and expectations about the economy.	To estimate demand for industrial products, consumer durables, purchases requiring advance planning, and new products.
Composite of sales force opinions	Ask sales representatives to estimate their future sales.	To understand developing trends and gather detailed estimates by product, territory, customer, and sales rep.
Expert opinion	Obtain forecasts from experts, including dealers, distributors, suppliers, consultants, and trade associations, or buy from economic-forecasting firms.	To gather estimates from knowledgeable specialists who may offer insights.
Past-sales analysis	Use time-series analysis, exponential smoothing, statistical demand analysis, or econometric analysis to assess past sales as the basis of sales forecasts.	To project future demand based on analyses of past demand.
Market-test method	Conduct a direct-market test to understand customer response and estimate future sales.	To forecast sales of new products or sales of an established product in a new channel or area.

without long-term significance. A company can cash in on a fad, but getting it right requires luck and good timing. Marketing research and demand analyses are, as discussed earlier, necessary to determine the profit potential of new market opportunities based on macroenvironmental trends.

Identifying the Major Forces

Firms must monitor six major forces in the broad environment: demographic, economic, sociocultural, natural, technological, and political-legal (see Table 3.4). We'll describe them separately, but remember their interactions will lead to new opportunities and threats. For example, explosive population growth (demographic) leads to more resource depletion and pollution (natural), which leads consumers to call for more laws (political-legal), which stimulate new technological solutions and products (technological) that, if they are affordable (economic), may actually change attitudes and behavior (sociocultural).

The Demographic Environment

The main demographic factor marketers monitor is *population,* including the size and growth rate of population in cities, regions, and nations; age distribution and ethnic mix; educational levels; and household patterns.

Worldwide Population Growth   The global population currently tops 7 billion people and is forecasted to rise to 8.82 billion by 2040 and exceed 9 billion by 2045.[14] Developing regions house 84 percent of the world's population and are growing at 1 percent to 2 percent per year;

TABLE 3.4	Major Forces in the Macroenvironment
Force	Key Elements to Monitor
Demographic environment	• Worldwide population growth • Population age mix • Diversity within markets • Educational groups • Household patterns
Economic environment	• Consumer psychology • Income distribution • Income, savings, debt, and credit
Sociocultural environment	• World views • Core cultural values • Subcultures
Natural environment	• Shortage of raw materials • Increased cost of energy • Increased pollution levels • Changing role of governments • Corporate environmentalism
Technological environment	• Accelerating pace of change • Unlimited opportunities for innovation • Varying research and development budgets • Regulation of technological change
Political-legal environment	• Increase in business legislation • Growth of special-interest groups

developed countries' populations are growing at only 0.3 percent.[15] In developing countries, modern medicine is lowering the death rate, but birthrates remain fairly stable. A growing population does not mean growing markets unless there is sufficient purchasing power. Education can raise the standard of living but is difficult to accomplish in most developing countries. Nonetheless, companies that carefully analyze these markets can find opportunities and sometimes lessons they can apply at home.

Population Age Mix   There is a global trend toward an aging population. In 1950, there were only 131 million people 65 and older; in 1995, their number had almost tripled to 371 million. By 2050, 1 of 10 people worldwide will be 65 or older.[16] Marketers generally divide the population into six age groups: preschool children, school-age children, teens, young adults age 20 to 40, middle-aged adults 40 to 65, and older adults 65 and older. Some marketers focus on *cohorts*, groups of individuals born during the same time period who travel through life together. The defining moments they experience as they come of age and become adults (roughly ages 17 through 24) can stay with them for a lifetime and influence their values, preferences, and buying behaviors.

Diversity within Markets   Ethnic and racial diversity varies across countries, which affects needs, wants, and buying patterns. At one extreme is Japan, where almost everyone is native Japanese; at the other extreme is the United States, 12 percent of whose people were born in another country. In the United States, more than half the growth between 2000 and 2010 came from the increase in the Hispanic population, which grew by 43 percent, from 35.3 million to 50.5 million, representing a major shift in the nation's ethnic center of gravity. Geographically, the 2010 Census revealed that Hispanics were moving to states like North Carolina where they had not been concentrated before and that they increasingly live in suburbs.[17] Such demographic trends affect the market for all kinds of products, including food, clothing, music, and cars. Yet marketers must not overgeneralize—within each group are consumers quite different from each other.[18] Diversity also goes beyond ethnic and racial markets. More than 51 million U.S. consumers have disabilities, and they constitute a market for home delivery companies such as Internet grocer Peapod.

Educational Groups   The population in any society falls into five educational groups: illiterates, high school dropouts, high school diplomas, college degrees, and professional degrees. More than two-thirds of the world's 793 million illiterate adults are found in only eight countries (Bangladesh, China, Egypt, Ethiopia, India, Indonesia, Nigeria, and Pakistan); of all illiterate adults in the world, two-thirds are women.[19] The United States has one of the world's highest percentages of college-educated citizens.[20] This educational level drives strong demand for high-quality books, magazines, and travel and creates a supply of skills.

Household Patterns   The traditional U.S. household included a husband, wife, and children under 18 (sometimes with grandparents). By 2010, only 20 percent of U.S. households met this definition, down from about 25 percent a decade before and 43 percent in 1950. Married couples have dropped below half of all U.S. households for the first time (48 percent), far below the 78 percent of 1950. The median age at first marriage has never been higher: 26.5 for U.S. brides and 28.7 for U.S. grooms.[21] Nontraditional households are growing more rapidly than traditional households as more people divorce, separate, choose not to marry, or marry later. Other types of households are single live-alones (27 percent), single-parent families (8 percent), childless married couples and empty nesters (32 percent), living with nonrelatives only (5 percent), and other family structures (8 percent). Each type of household has distinctive needs and buying habits that marketers need to study and understand.

The Economic Environment

Purchasing power depends on consumers' income, savings, debt, and credit availability as well as the price level. As the recent economic downturn vividly demonstrated, fluctuating purchasing power strongly affects business. Marketers must understand consumer psychology and levels and distribution of income, savings, debt, and credit.

Consumer Psychology   The recession that began in 2008 initiated new consumer spending patterns. Were these temporary adjustments or permanent changes?[22] Identifying the more likely long-term scenario—especially for the coveted 18- to 34-year-old group—would help managers decide how to invest their marketing money. Executives at Sainsbury, the third-largest UK supermarket chain, concluded that the recession had created a more risk-averse British consumer who now saves more, pays off debts instead of borrowing, and shops in more cost-conscious ways. Even wealthy UK consumers traded down to lower-cost items. As one executive said, "There's nobody who can afford not to try to save."[23]

Income Distribution   There are four types of industrial structures: *subsistence economies* like Papua New Guinea, with few opportunities for marketers; *raw-material-exporting economies* like Saudi Arabia (oil), with good markets for equipment, tools, supplies, and luxury goods for the rich; *industrializing economies* like India, where a new rich class and a growing middle class demand new types of goods; and *industrial economies* like Western Europe, with rich markets for all sorts of goods. Marketers often distinguish countries using five income-distribution patterns: (1) very low incomes; (2) mostly low incomes; (3) very low, very high incomes; (4) low, medium, high incomes; and (5) mostly medium incomes.

Income, Savings, Debt, and Credit   U.S. consumers have a high debt-to-income ratio, which slows expenditures on housing and large-ticket items. When credit became scarcer in the recession, especially for lower-income borrowers, consumer borrowing dropped for the first time in two decades. An economic issue of increasing importance is the migration of manufacturers and service jobs offshore, which affects incomes in the United States and the countries where jobs are relocated.

The Sociocultural Environment

From our sociocultural environment we absorb, almost unconsciously, a world view that defines our relationships to ourselves, others, organizations, society, nature, and the universe.

- **Views of ourselves.** Some "pleasure seekers" chase fun, change, and escape; others seek "self-realization." Some are adopting more conservative behaviors and ambitions.
- **Views of others.** People are concerned about the homeless, crime and victims, and other social problems. At the same time, they seek out those like themselves, suggesting a growing market for social-support products and services such as health clubs, cruises, and religious activity as well as "social surrogates" like television, video games, and social networking sites.
- **Views of organizations.** After a wave of layoffs and corporate scandals, organizational loyalty has declined. Companies need new ways to win back consumer and employee confidence. They need to be good corporate citizens and ensure their consumer messages are honest.
- **Views of society.** Some people defend society (preservers), some run it (makers), some take what they can from it (takers), some want to change it (changers), some are looking for something deeper (seekers), and still others want to leave it (escapers).[24] Consumption

patterns often reflect these social attitudes. Makers are high achievers who eat, dress, and live well. Changers usually live more frugally, drive smaller cars, and wear simpler clothes. Escapers and seekers are a major market for movies, music, surfing, and camping.

- **Views of nature.** Business has responded to increased awareness of nature's fragility and finiteness by making more green products, seeking new energy sources, and reducing their environmental footprint.
- **Views of the universe.** Most U.S. citizens are monotheistic, although religious conviction and practice have waned through the years or been redirected into an interest in evangelical movements or Eastern religions, mysticism, the occult, and the human potential movement.

Other cultural characteristics of interest to marketers are core cultural values and subcultures.

Core Cultural Values   Most people in the United States still believe in working, getting married, giving to charity, and being honest. *Core beliefs* and values are passed from parents to children and reinforced by social institutions—schools, churches, businesses, and governments. *Secondary beliefs* and values are more open to change. Believing in the institution of marriage is a core belief; believing people should marry early is a secondary belief.

Marketers have some chance of changing secondary values but little chance of changing core values. The nonprofit organization Mothers Against Drunk Drivers (MADD) does not try to stop the sale of alcohol but promotes lower legal blood-alcohol levels for driving. Although core values are fairly persistent, cultural swings do take place. In the 1960s, hippies, the Beatles, and other cultural phenomena had a major impact on hairstyles, clothing, sexual norms, and life goals. Today's young people are influenced by new heroes and activities: music entertainer and mogul Jay-Z, singer Lady Gaga, and snowboarder and skateboarder Shaun White.

Subcultures   Each society contains **subcultures,** groups with shared values, beliefs, preferences, and behaviors emerging from their special life experiences or circumstances. Marketers have always loved teenagers because they are trendsetters in fashion, music, entertainment, ideas, and attitudes. Attract someone as a teen, and you will likely keep the person as a customer later in life.

The Natural Environment

In Western Europe, "green" parties have pressed for public action to reduce industrial pollution. In the United States, experts have documented ecological deterioration, and watchdog groups such as the Sierra Club commit to political and social action. Steel companies and public utilities have invested billions of dollars in pollution-control equipment and environmentally friendly fuels, making hybrid cars, low-flow toilets and showers, organic foods, and green office buildings everyday realities. Opportunities await those who can reconcile prosperity with environmental protection.

Corporate environmentalism recognizes the need to integrate environmental issues into the firm's strategic plans. Trends for marketers to be aware of include the shortage of raw materials, especially water; the increased cost of energy; increased pollution levels; and the changing role of governments.[25]

- The earth's raw materials consist of the infinite, the finite renewable, and the finite nonrenewable. Firms whose products require *finite nonrenewable resources*—oil, coal, platinum—face substantial cost increases as depletion approaches. Firms that can develop substitute materials have an excellent opportunity.

- One finite nonrenewable resource, oil, has created serious problems for the world economy. As oil prices soar, companies search for practical means to harness solar power and other alternative energies.
- Some industrial activity will inevitably damage the natural environment, creating a large market for pollution-control solutions such as scrubbers, recycling centers, and landfill systems as well as for alternative ways to produce and package goods.
- Many poor nations are doing little about pollution, lacking the funds or the political will. It is in the richer nations' interest to help control pollution, but even richer nations today lack the necessary funds.

The Technological Environment

The essence of market capitalism is a dynamism that tolerates the creative destructiveness of technology as the price of progress. Marketers should monitor the following technology trends: the accelerating pace of change, unlimited opportunities for innovation, varying R&D budgets, and increased regulation of technological change.

- **Accelerating pace of technological change.** More ideas than ever are in the works, and the time between idea and implementation is shrinking. In the first two-and-a-half years of the iPad's existence, Apple sold a staggering 97 million units worldwide.[26] In many markets, the next technological breakthrough seems right around the corner.
- **Unlimited opportunities for innovation.** Some of the most exciting innovations today are taking place in biotechnology, microelectronics, telecommunications, robotics, and designer materials.
- **Varying R&D budgets.** The United States is the world leader in research and development, spending $436 billion in 2012. A growing portion of U.S. R&D, however, goes to the development side, not research, raising concerns about whether the nation can maintain its lead in basic science. Too many companies seem to be putting their money into copying competitors' products with minor improvements. China, Israel, and Finland all are beginning to spend a larger percentage of their GDP on R&D than the United States.[27]
- **Increased regulation of technological change.** Government has expanded its agencies' powers to investigate and ban potentially unsafe products. Safety and health regulations have increased for food, automobiles, clothing, electrical appliances, and construction.

The Political-Legal Environment

The political and legal environment consists of laws, government agencies, and pressure groups that influence organizations and individuals. Sometimes the political-legal environment can create new business opportunities. Mandatory recycling laws boosted the recycling industry and launched dozens of new companies making products from recycled materials. On the other hand, overseas governments can impose laws or take actions that create uncertainty and even confusion for companies. Two key trends are the increase in business legislation and the growth of special-interest groups.

Increased Business Legislation   Business legislation is intended to protect companies from unfair competition, protect consumers from unfair business practices, protect society from unbridled business behavior, and charge businesses with the social costs of their products or production processes. Each new law may also have the unintended effect of sapping initiative and slowing growth. The United States has many consumer protection laws covering competition, product safety and liability, fair trade and credit practices, and packaging and labeling. The European Commission has established new laws covering competitive behavior, privacy, product standards, product liability, and commercial transactions for member nations.

Growth of Special-Interest Groups   Political action committees (PACs) lobby government officials and pressure business executives to respect the rights of consumers, women, senior citizens, minorities, and gays and lesbians. The *consumerist movement* organized citizens and government to strengthen the rights and powers of buyers in relationship to sellers. Consumerists have won many rights, including to know the real cost of a loan and the nutritional quality and freshness of food. Privacy issues and identity theft, which are key public policy issues, will remain hot buttons as long as consumers are willing to swap personal information for customized products—from marketers they trust.[28] Many companies have established public affairs departments to formulate policies and deal with important issues.

Executive Summary

Marketing managers need a marketing information system (MIS) to assess information needs, develop the needed information, and distribute it in a timely manner. An MIS relies on: (1) an internal records system, including information about the order-to-payment cycle and sales information systems; (2) a marketing intelligence system to obtain information about the marketing environment; and (3) a marketing research system. The marketing research process consists of six steps: define the problem and objectives, develop the plan, collect the data, analyze the data, present the findings, and make the decision. Companies use forecasting and demand measurement to evaluate the size, growth, and profit potential of each new opportunity.

Marketers must monitor six major environmental forces: demographic, economic, sociocultural, natural, technological, and political-legal. In the demographic environment, they should examine worldwide population growth, mixes of age, ethnic composition, and educational levels; and household patterns. In the economic arena, they should focus on consumer psychology, income distribution, and levels of savings, debt, and credit. In the sociocultural arena, marketers must understand people's views of themselves, others, organizations, society, nature, and the universe, as well as the role of core cultural values and subcultures. In the natural environment, marketers should be aware of increased concern about the natural environment and sustainability. In the technological arena, marketers should examine the accelerating pace of change, opportunities for innovation, varying R&D budgets, and increased regulation. In the political-legal environment, marketers must work within the many laws regulating business practices and with various special-interest groups.

Notes

1. David Welch, "Campbell Looks Way Beyond the Tomato," *Bloomberg BusinessWeek*, August 13, 2012; Candice Choi, "Campbell Soup Tries to Reinvent Itself," *Huffington Post*, September 7, 2012; Karl Greenberg, "Campbell's Go Soups Add Zing for Millennial Palates," *Marketing Daily*, November 13, 2012; Craig Torres and Anthony Field, "Campbell's Quest for Productivity," *Bloomberg BusinessWeek*, November 29, 2012; Jenna Goudreau, "Kicking the Can," *Forbes*, December 24, 2012, pp. 46–51; Dale Buss, "Campbell's Soup Can't Seem to Find Slurp-Happy Consumers," *BrandChannel.com*, May 21, 2014.

2. For thought-provoking academic perspectives on the challenges of Big Data, see George S. Day, "Closing the Marketing Capabilities Gap," *Journal of Marketing* 75 (July 2011), pp. 183–95.

3. See Robert Schieffer, *Ten Key Customer Insights: Unlocking the Mind of the Market* (Mason, OH: Thomson, 2005) for an in-depth discussion of how to generate customer insights to drive business results.

4. Ellen Byron, "Wash Away Bad Hair Days," *Wall Street Journal*, June 30, 2010.

5. www.marketingpower.com/AboutAMA, accessed February 16, 2014.

6. Fiona Blades, "Real-time Experience Tracking Gets Closer to the Truth," *International Journal of Market Research* 54, no. 2 (2012), pp. 283–85; Emma K. Macdonald, Hugh N. Wilson, and Umut Konuş, "Better Consumer Insight—in Real Time," *Harvard Business Review*, September 2012, pp. 102–108; Lynda Andrews, Rebekah Russell Bennett, and Judy Drennan, "Capturing Affective Experiences Using the SMS Experience Sampling (SMS-ES) Method," *International Journal of Market Research* 53, no. 4 (2011), pp. 479–506.

7. For a detailed review of some relevant academic work, see Eric J. Arnould and Amber Epp, "Deep Engagement with Consumer Experience," Rajiv Grover and Marco Vriens, eds., *Handbook of Marketing Research* (Thousand Oaks, CA: Sage Publications, 2006). For a range of academic discussion, see the following special issue: "Can Ethnography Uncover Richer Consumer Insights?" *Journal of Advertising Research* 46 (September 2006). For some practical tips, see Richard Durante and Michael Feehan, "Leverage Ethnography to Improve Strategic Decision Making," *Marketing Research* (Winter 2005).

8. William Grimes, "When Businesses Can't Stop Asking, 'How Am I Doing,'" *New York Times*, March 16, 2012.

9. Evan Ramstead, "Big Brother, Now at the Mall," *Wall Street Journal*, October 8, 2012; Natasha Singer, "Face Recognition Makes the Leap from Sci-Fi," *The New York Times*, November 13, 2011; Emily Glazer, "The Eyes Have It: Marketers Now Track Shoppers' Retinas," *Wall Street Journal*, July 12, 2012; Lessley Anderson, "A Night on the Town with SceneTap," *The Verve*, May 29, 2012; Kashmir Hill, "SceneTap Wants to One Day Tell You the Weights, Heights, Races and Income Levels of the Crowd at Every Bar," www.forbes.com, September 25, 2012.

10. Laurie Burkitt, "Battle for the Brain," *Forbes*, November 16, 2009, pp. 76–77.

11. Emily Steel, "Does Shopping Stress You Out Too Much?," *Wall Street Journal*, November 23, 2011. For an academic application of some techniques, see Thales Teixeira, Michel Wedel, and Rik Pieters, "Emotion-Induced Engagement in Internet Video Advertisements," *Journal of Marketing Research* 49 (April 2012), pp. 144–59.

12. For further discussion, see Gary L. Lilien, Philip Kotler, and K. Sridhar Moorthy, *Marketing Models* (Upper Saddle River, NJ: Prentice Hall, 1992); Gary L. Lilien, "Bridging the Academic-Practitioner Divide in Marketing Decision Models," *Journal of Marketing* 75 (July 2011), pp. 196–210.

13. www.naics.com, accessed February 7, 2010; www.census.gov/epcd/naics02, December 9, 2010.

14. World POPClock Projection, U.S. Census Bureau, www.census.gov, 2011; Statistical Abstract of the United States 2011, U.S. Census Bureau.

15. "World Development Indicators Database," *World Bank*, http://siteresources.worldbank.org/DATASTATISTICS / Resources/POP.pdf, September 15, 2009; "World Population Growth," www.worldbank.org/depweb /english/beyond/beyondco/beg_03.pdf.

16. "Facts and Statistics," U.S. Census Bureau, November 30, 2011.

17. Christine Birker, "The Census and the New American Consumer, *Marketing News*, May 15, 2011.

18. Mark R. Forehand and Rohit Deshpandé, "What We See Makes Us Who We Are," *Journal of Marketing Research* 38 (August 2001), pp. 336–48.

19. *The Central Intelligence Agency's World Factbook*, www.cia.gov/library/publications/the-world-factbook, June 25, 2012.

20. www.census.gov/newsroom/releases/archives /facts_for_features_special_editions/cb11-ff15.html; Richard Pérez-Peña, "U.S. Bachelor Degree Rate Passes Milestone," www.nytimes.com, February 23, 2012.

21. Sabrina Tavernise, "Married Couples Are No Longer a Majority, Census Finds," *The New York Times*, May 26,

2011; D'Vera Cohn, Jeffrey Passel, Wendy Wang and Gretchen Livingston, "Barely Half of U.S. Adults Are Married—A Record Low," www.pewsocialtrends.org, December 14, 2011.

22. For a data-rich examination of the post-recession consumer, see John Gerzema and Michael D'Antonio, *Spend Shrift: How the Post-Crisis Values Revolution Is Changing the Way We Buy, Sell and Live* (San Francisco: Jossey-Bass, 2011).

23. Michael Barnett, "They're Shopping, but Not as We Know It," *Marketing Week,* June 14, 2012.

24. "Clearing House Suit Chronology," *Associated Press,* January 26, 2001; Paul Wenske, "You Too Could Lose $19,000!" *Kansas City Star,* October 31, 1999.

25. Philip Kotler, "Reinventing Marketing to Manage the Environmental Imperative," *Journal of Marketing* 75 (July 2011), pp. 132–35; Subhabrata Bobby Banerjee, Easwar S. Iyer, and Rajiv K Kashyap, "Corporate Environmentalism: Antecedents and Influence of Industry Type," *Journal of Marketing* 67 (April 2003), pp. 106–22.

26. Apple quarterly press releases, culminating in "Apple Reports Fourth Quarter Results," www.apple.com, October 25, 2012.

27. Allison Lim, "The U.S Is Still No. 1 in R&D Spending, but…," www.nbcnews.com, August 17, 2012; Martin Grueber and Tim Studt, *R&D,* December 16, 2011.

28. Paul Ohm, "Don't Build a Database of Ruin," *HBR Blog Network,* August 23, 2012.

Chapter 4

Creating Long-Term Loyalty Relationships

In this chapter, we will address the following questions:

1. How can companies deliver customer value, satisfaction, and loyalty? (Page 55)
2. What is the lifetime value of customers, and how can marketers maximize it? (Page 59)
3. How can companies attract and retain the right customers and cultivate strong customer relationships and communities? (Page 60)

Marketing Management at Pandora

Technological advances have changed the way consumers purchase, listen to, and share music, and music-streaming services are in a virtual arms race for their loyalty. Internet radio company Pandora has staked a claim to be the market leader with its automated music discovery and recommendation service, which has helped attract more than 200 million registered users. Based on a listener's musical selection, Pandora recommends other musical selections. Listener feedback to those recommendations and more than 400 different musical attributes judged by professional music lovers are combined and analyzed to suggest future songs. Pandora launched its smart-phone app in 2008, making its service available "anywhere, anytime." Now Pandora faces steep competition from Spotify and other rivals, each of which has unique features that may drive customer preference and loyalty.[1]

Successful marketers carefully cultivate customer satisfaction and loyalty. In this chapter, we spell out the different ways they can go about winning customers, encouraging loyalty, and beating competitors.

Building Customer Value, Satisfaction, and Loyalty

With the rise of digital technologies, increasingly informed consumers expect companies to do more than connect with them, more than satisfy them, and even more than delight them. They expect companies to *listen* and *respond* to them. Even the best-run companies have to be careful not to take customers for granted. Consumers are better educated and better informed than ever, and they have the tools to verify companies' claims and seek out superior value alternatives.

Customer-Perceived Value

Customer-perceived value (CPV) is the difference between the prospective customer's evaluation of all the benefits and costs of an offering and the perceived alternatives (see Figure 4.1). **Total customer benefit** is the perceived monetary value of the bundle of economic, functional, and psychological benefits customers expect from a given market offering because of the product, service, people, and image. **Total customer cost** is the perceived bundle of costs customers expect to incur in evaluating, obtaining, using, and disposing of the given market offering, including monetary, time, energy, and psychological costs.

Suppose the buyer for a construction company wants to buy a tractor for residential construction from either Caterpillar or Komatsu. After evaluating the two tractors on the basis of reliability, durability, performance, and resale value, the buyer decides Caterpillar has greater

FIGURE 4.1 Determinants of Customer-Perceived Value

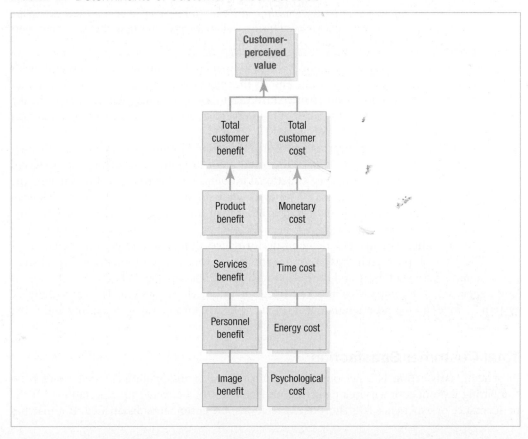

product benefits. He also decides Caterpillar provides better service and has more knowledgeable and responsive staff. Finally, he places higher value on Caterpillar's corporate image and reputation. He adds up all the benefits from product, services, people, and image, and perceives Caterpillar as delivering greater customer benefits.

The buyer also examines his total cost of transacting with Caterpillar versus Komatsu, including time, energy, and psychological costs expended in product acquisition, usage, maintenance, ownership, and disposal. Then he considers whether Caterpillar's total customer cost is too high compared to total customer benefits. If it is, he might choose Komatsu. The buyer will choose whichever source delivers the highest perceived value.

In this situation, Caterpillar can improve its offer in three ways. First, it can increase total customer benefit by improving economic, functional, and psychological benefits of its product, services, people, and/or image. Second, it can reduce the buyer's time, energy, and psychological investment. Third, it can reduce its product's monetary cost to the buyer.

Some marketers might argue that this process is too rational. Suppose the customer chooses the Komatsu tractor. How can we explain this choice? Here are three possibilities.

1. *The buyer might be under orders to buy at the lowest price.* Caterpillar's task is then to convince the buyer's manager that buying on price alone will result in lower long-term profits and customer value for the buyer's company.

2. *The buyer will retire before the company realizes the Komatsu tractor is more expensive to operate.* Caterpillar's task is to convince other people in the customer company that Caterpillar delivers greater customer value.

3. *The buyer enjoys a long-term friendship with the Komatsu salesperson.* Here, Caterpillar must show the buyer that the Komatsu tractor will draw complaints from the tractor operators when they discover its high fuel cost and need for frequent repairs.

Customer-perceived value is a useful framework that applies to many situations and yields rich insights. It suggests that the seller must assess the total customer benefit and total customer cost associated with each competitor's offer in order to know how its own offer rates in the buyer's mind. It also implies that the seller at a disadvantage has two alternatives: increase total customer benefit or decrease total customer cost.

Consumers have varying degrees of loyalty to specific brands, stores, and companies. **Loyalty** has been defined as "a deeply held commitment to rebuy or repatronize a preferred product or service in the future despite situational influences and marketing efforts having the potential to cause switching behavior."[2] The *value proposition* consists of the whole cluster of benefits the company promises to deliver; it is more than the core positioning of the offering. For example, Volvo's core positioning has been "safety," but the buyer is promised more than just a safe car; other benefits include good performance, design, and safety for the environment. The value proposition is thus a promise about the experience customers can expect from the company's market offering and their relationship with the supplier. Whether the promise is kept depends on the company's ability to manage its value delivery system. The **value delivery system** includes all the experiences the customer will have on the way to obtaining and using the offering.[3]

Total Customer Satisfaction

In general, **satisfaction** is a person's feelings of pleasure or disappointment that result from comparing a product or service's perceived performance (or outcome) to expectations.[4] If the performance or experience falls short of expectations, the customer is dissatisfied. If it matches expectations, the customer is satisfied. If it exceeds expectations, the customer is highly satisfied or delighted.[5] Customer assessments of product or service performance depend on many factors, including the type of loyalty relationship the customer has with the brand.[6]

Although the customer-centered firm seeks to create high customer satisfaction, that is not its ultimate goal. Increasing customer satisfaction by lowering price or increasing services may result in lower profits. The company might be able to increase its profitability by means other than increased satisfaction (for example, by improving manufacturing processes). The company also has many stakeholders, including employees, dealers, suppliers, and stockholders. Spending more to increase customer satisfaction might divert funds from increasing the satisfaction of other "partners." Ultimately, the company must try to deliver a high level of customer satisfaction subject to also delivering acceptable levels to other stakeholders, given its total resources.

Monitoring Satisfaction

Many companies are systematically measuring how well they treat customers, identifying the factors shaping satisfaction, and changing operations and marketing as a result.[7] A highly satisfied customer generally stays loyal longer, buys more as the company introduces new and upgraded products, talks favorably to others about the company and its products, pays less attention to competing brands and is less sensitive to price, offers product or service ideas to the company, and costs less to serve than new customers because transactions can become routine.[8]

The link between customer satisfaction and customer loyalty is not proportional, however. Suppose customer satisfaction is rated on a scale from 1 to 5. At a very low level of satisfaction (level 1), customers are likely to abandon the company and even bad-mouth it. At levels 2 to 4, customers are fairly satisfied but still find it easy to switch to better offers. At level 5, the customer is very likely to repurchase and even spread good word of mouth about the company. High satisfaction or delight creates an emotional bond with the brand or company, not just a rational preference.

Yet customers define good performance differently. Good delivery could mean early delivery, on-time delivery, or order completeness, and two customers can report being "highly satisfied" for different reasons. One may be easily satisfied most of the time, and the other might be hard to please but was pleased on this occasion. It is also important to know how satisfied customers are with competitors in order to assess "share of wallet" or how much of the customer's spending the company's brand enjoys: The more highly the consumer ranks the company's brand in terms of satisfaction and loyalty, the more the customer is likely to spend on the brand.[9]

Companies use a variety of methods to measure customer satisfaction. "Marketing Insight: Net Promoter and Customer Satisfaction" describes why some companies believe one well-designed question is all that is necessary to assess customer satisfaction.[10]

Some companies think they're getting a sense of customer satisfaction by tallying complaints, but studies show that while customers are dissatisfied with their purchases about 25 percent of the time, only about 5 percent complain. The other 95 percent either feel complaining is not worth the effort or don't know how or to whom to complain. They just stop buying.[11]

Of the customers who complain, 54 percent to 70 percent will do business with the organization again if their complaint is resolved. The figure goes up to a staggering 95 percent if the customer feels the complaint was resolved *quickly*. Customers whose complaints are satisfactorily resolved tell an average of five people about the good treatment they received.[12] The average dissatisfied customer, however, gripes to 11 people.

marketing insight

Net Promoter and Customer Satisfaction

Bain's Frederick Reichheld suggests only one question matters in measuring customer satisfaction: "How likely is it that you would recommend this product or service to a friend or colleague?" Reichheld was inspired in part by the experiences of Enterprise Rent-A-Car. When the company cut its customer satisfaction survey to two questions—one about the quality of the rental experience and the other about the likelihood customers would rent from the company again—it found those who gave the highest ratings to their rental experience were three times as likely to rent again than those who gave the second-highest rating.

In a typical Net Promoter survey, customers are given a 1-to-10 scale on which to rate their likelihood of recommending the company. Marketers then subtract *Detractors* (those who gave a 0 to 6) from *Promoters* (those who gave a 9 or 10) to arrive at the Net Promoter Score (NPS). Customers who rate the brand with a 7 or 8 are deemed *Passively Satisfied* and are not included.

Many client firms praise the simplicity of Net Promoter and the strong relationship to financial performance. However, a common criticism is that many different patterns of responses may lead to the same NPS. Another criticism is that it is not a useful predictor of future sales or growth because it ignores important cost and revenue considerations. Finally, some critics question its actual research support.

Sources: Fred Reichheld, *Ultimate Question: For Driving Good Profits and True Growth* (Cambridge, MA: Harvard Business School Press, 2006); Fred Reichheld, "The One Number You Need to Grow," *Harvard Business Review*, December 2003; Neil A. Morgan and Lopo Leotte Rego, "The Value of Different Customer Satisfaction and Loyalty Metrics in Predicting Business Performance," *Marketing Science* 25 (September–October 2006), pp. 426–39; Timothy L. Keiningham, Lerzan Aksoy, Bruce Cooil, and Tor W. Andreassen, "Linking Customer Loyalty to Growth," *MIT Sloan Management Review* (Summer 2008), pp. 51–57; Suhail Khan, "How Philips Uses Net Promoter Scores to Understand Customers," *HBR Blog Network*, May 10, 2011; Robert East, Jenni Romaniuk, and Wendy Lomax, "The NPS and ACSI: A Critique and an Alternative Metric," *International Journal of Market Research* 53, no. 3 (2011), pp. 327–45; Randy Hanson, "Life after NPS," *Marketing Research* (Summer 2011), pp. 8–11; Jenny van Doorn, Peter S. H. Leeflang, and Marleen Tijs, "Satisfaction as a Predictor of Future Performance: A Replication," *International Journal of Research in Marketing* 30 (September 2013), pp. 314–18; www.satmetrix.com.

The following practices can help to recover customer goodwill after a negative experience.[13]

1. Set up a seven-day, 24-hour toll-free hotline (by phone, fax, or e-mail) to receive and act on complaints—make it easy for the customer to complain.

2. Contact the complaining customer as quickly as possible. The slower the response, the more dissatisfaction may grow and lead to negative word of mouth.

3. Accept responsibility for the customer's disappointment; don't blame the customer.

4. Use friendly, empathic customer service people.

5. Resolve the complaint swiftly and to the customer's satisfaction. Some complaining customers are looking for a sign that the company cares, not for compensation.

Product and Service Quality

Satisfaction will also depend on product and service quality. What exactly is quality? Various experts have defined it as "fitness for use," "conformance to requirements," and "freedom from variation." We will use the American Society for Quality's definition: **Quality** is the totality of features and characteristics of a product or service that bear on its ability to satisfy stated or implied needs.[14] The seller has delivered quality whenever its product or service meets or exceeds the customers' expectations. It's important to distinguish between *conformance* quality and *performance* quality (or grade). A Lexus provides higher performance quality than a Hyundai: The Lexus rides more smoothly, accelerates faster, and runs problem-free longer. Yet both a Lexus and a Hyundai deliver the same conformance quality if all the units deliver their promised quality.

Studies have shown a high correlation between relative product quality and company profitability.[15] Marketing plays an especially important role in helping companies deliver high-quality goods to target customers by (1) correctly identifying customers' needs and requirements; (2) communicating customer expectations properly to product designers; (3) making sure that customers' orders are filled correctly and on time; (4) checking that customers have received proper instructions, training, and technical assistance for product usage; (5) staying in touch after the sale to ensure customers are and remain satisfied; and (6) gathering customer ideas for improvements and conveying them to the appropriate departments. When marketers do all this, they make substantial contributions to total quality management and customer satisfaction as well as to customer and company profitability

Maximizing Customer Lifetime Value

Ultimately, marketing is the art of attracting and keeping profitable customers. Yet every company loses money on some of its customers. The well-known 80–20 rule states that 80 percent or more of the company's profits come from the top 20 percent of its customers. Some cases may be more extreme—the most profitable 20 percent of customers (on a per capita basis) may contribute as much as 150 percent to 300 percent of profitability. The least profitable 10 percent to 20 percent, on the other hand, can actually reduce profits between 50 percent and 200 percent per account, with the middle 60 percent to 70 percent breaking even.[16] The implication is that a company could improve its profits by "firing" its worst customers.

It's not always the company's largest customers who yield the most profit. The smallest customers pay full price and receive minimal service, but the costs of transacting with them can reduce their profitability. Midsize customers who receive good service and pay nearly full price are often the most profitable.

Customer Profitability

A **profitable customer** is a person, household, or company that over time yields a revenue stream exceeding by an acceptable amount the company's cost stream for attracting, selling, and serving that customer. Note the emphasis is on the *lifetime* stream of revenue and cost, not the profit from a particular transaction.[17] Marketers can assess customer profitability individually, by market segment, or by channel. Many companies measure customer satisfaction, but few measure individual customer profitability.[18]

A useful type of profitability analysis is shown in Figure 4.2.[19] Customers are arrayed along the columns and products along the rows. Each cell contains a symbol representing the profitability, positive or negative, of selling that product to that customer. Customer 1 is very profitable; he buys two profit-making products. Customer 2 yields mixed profitability; she buys one profitable product and one unprofitable product. Customer 3 is a losing customer because he buys one profitable product and two unprofitable products. What can the company do about customers 2 and 3? (1) It can raise the price of its less profitable products or eliminate them, or (2) it can try to sell customers 2 and 3 its profit-making products. In fact, the company should encourage them to switch to competitors.

Customer profitability analysis is best conducted with the tools of an accounting technique called *activity-based costing (ABC)*. The company estimates all revenue coming from

FIGURE 4.2 Customer-Product Profitability Analysis

Products		Customers: C_1	C_2	C_3	
	P_1	+	+	+	Highly profitable product
	P_2	+			Profitable product
	P_3		–	–	Unprofitable product
	P_4			–	Highly unprofitable product
		High-profit customer	Mixed-bag customer	Losing customer	

the customer, less all costs (including the direct and indirect costs of serving each customer). Companies that fail to measure their costs correctly are also not measuring their profit correctly and are likely to misallocate their marketing effort.

Measuring Customer Lifetime Value

The case for maximizing long-term customer profitability is captured in the concept of customer lifetime value.[20] **Customer lifetime value (CLV)** describes the net present value of the stream of future profits expected over the customer's lifetime purchases. The company must subtract from its expected revenues the expected costs of attracting, selling, and servicing the account of that customer, applying the appropriate discount rate (say, between 10 percent and 20 percent, depending on cost of capital and risk attitudes). Lifetime value calculations for a product or service can add up to tens of thousands of dollars or even run to six figures.[21]

CLV calculations provide a formal quantitative framework for planning customer investment and help marketers adopt a long-term perspective. Many methods exist to measure CLV.[22] Columbia's Don Lehmann and Harvard's Sunil Gupta illustrate their approach by calculating the CLV of 100 customers over a 10-year period (see Table 4.1). In this example, the firm acquires 100 customers with an acquisition cost per customer of $40. Therefore, in year 0, it spends $4,000. Some of these customers defect each year. The present value of the profits from this cohort of customers over 10 years is $13,286.52. The net CLV (after deducting acquisition costs) is $9,286.52, or $92.87 per customer.[23]

Cultivating Customer Relationships

Companies are using information about customers to enact precision marketing designed to build strong and profitable long-term relationships.[24] **Customer relationship management (CRM)** is the process of carefully managing detailed information about individual customers and all customer "touch points" to maximize loyalty.[25] CRM is important because a major driver of company profitability is the aggregate value of the company's customer base. A *touch point* is

TABLE 4.1	A Hypothetical Example to Illustrate CLV Calculations										
	Year 0	Year 1	Year 2	Year 3	Year 4	Year 5	Year 6	Year 7	Year 8	Year 9	Year 10
Number of Customers	100	90	80	72	60	48	34	23	12	6	2
Revenue per Customer		100	110	120	125	130	135	140	142	143	145
Variable Cost per Customer		70	72	75	76	78	79	80	81	82	83
Margin per Customer		30	38	45	49	52	56	60	61	61	62
Acquisition Cost per Customer	40										
Total Cost or Profit	−4,000	2,700	3,040	3,240	2,940	2,496	1,904	1,380	732	366	124
Present Value	−4,000	2,454.55	2,512.40	2,434.26	2,008.06	1,549.82	1,074.76	708.16	341.48	155.22	47.81

Source: Sunil Gupta and Donald R. Lehmann, "Models of Customer Value," Berend Wierenga, ed., *Handbook of Decision Models* (Springer Science Business Media, 2007).

any occasion when a customer encounters the brand and product—from actual experience to personal or mass communications to casual observation. For a hotel, the touch points include reservations, check-in and checkout, frequent-stay programs, room service, business services, exercise facilities, and restaurants.

CRM enables companies to provide excellent real-time customer service through the effective use of individual account information. Based on what they know about each valued customer, they can customize market offerings, services, programs, messages, and media. *Personalizing marketing* is about making sure the brand and its marketing are as personally relevant as possible to as many customers as possible—a challenge, given that no two customers are identical.

To adapt to customers' increased desire for personalization, marketers have embraced concepts such as *permission marketing*, the practice of marketing to consumers only after gaining their expressed permission. According to Seth Godin, a pioneer in the technique, marketers develop stronger consumer relationships by sending messages only when consumers express a willingness to become more engaged with the brand.[26] "Participatory marketing" may be a more appropriate concept than permission marketing because marketers and consumers need to work together to find out how the firm can best satisfy consumers.

Although much has been made of the newly empowered consumer—in charge, setting the direction of the brand, and playing a much bigger role in how it is marketed—it's still true that only *some consumers* want to get involved with *some of the brands* they use and, even then, only *some of the time*. Consumers have lives, jobs, families, hobbies, goals, and commitments, and many things matter more to them than the brands they purchase and consume. Understanding how to best market a brand given such diversity in customer interests is crucially important.[27]

Attracting and Retaining Customers

Companies seeking to expand profits and sales must invest time and resources searching for new customers. To generate leads, they advertise in media that will reach new prospects, send direct mail and e-mails to possible new prospects, send their salespeople to participate in trade shows where they might find new leads, purchase names from list brokers, and so on.

Different acquisition methods yield customers with varying CLVs. One study showed that customers acquired through the offer of a 35 percent discount had about one-half the long-term value of customers acquired without any discount.[28] Many of these customers were more interested in the offer than in the product itself. Similarly, many local businesses have launched "daily deal" campaigns from Groupon and LivingSocial to attract new customers. Unfortunately, these campaigns have sometimes turned out to be unprofitable in the long run because coupon users were not easily converted into loyal customers.[29]

It is not enough to attract new customers; the company must also keep them and increase their business.[30] Too many companies suffer from high **customer churn** or defection. To reduce the defection rate, the company must first define and measure its retention rate, distinguish the causes of customer attrition and identify those that can be managed better, and compare the lost customer's CLV to the costs of reducing the defection rate. As long as the cost to discourage defection is lower than the lost profit, spend the money to try to retain the customer.

Figure 4.3 shows the main steps in attracting and retaining customers in terms of a funnel. The **marketing funnel** identifies the percentage of the potential target market at each stage in the decision process, from merely aware to highly loyal. Some marketers extend the funnel to include loyal customers who are brand advocates or even partners with the firm. By calculating *conversion rates*—the percentage of customers at one stage who move to the next—the funnel allows marketers to identify any bottleneck stage or barrier to building a loyal customer franchise. The funnel also emphasizes how important it is not just to attract new customers but to retain and cultivate existing ones.

Customer profitability analysis and the marketing funnel help marketers decide how to manage groups of customers that vary in loyalty, profitability, risk, and other factors.[31] Winning companies know how to reduce the rate of customer defection; increase the longevity of the customer relationship; enhance the growth of each customer through "share of wallet," cross-selling, and up-selling; make low-profit customers more profitable or terminate them; and treat high-profit customers in a special way.

FIGURE 4.3 The Marketing Funnel

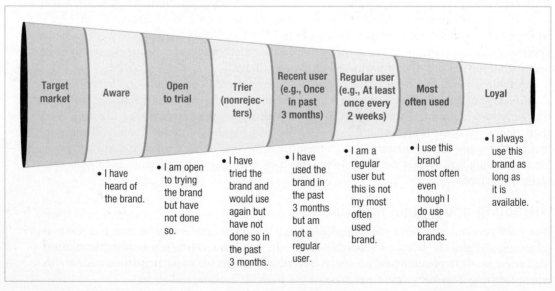

Building Loyalty

Companies should strive to build loyalty for strong, enduring connections with customers. One set of researchers sees retention-building activities as adding financial benefits, social benefits, or structural ties.[32] Next we describe four marketing activities that improve loyalty and retention.

Interact Closely with Customers   Listening to customers is crucial to customer relationship management. Some companies have created an ongoing mechanism that keeps their marketers permanently plugged in to frontline customer feedback. Build-A-Bear Workshop uses a "Cub Advisory Board" as a feedback and decision-input body. The board is made up of 5- to 16-year-olds who review new-product ideas.[33] It is also important to be a customer advocate and, as much as possible, take the customers' side and understand their point of view.[34]

Develop Loyalty Programs   **Frequency programs (FPs)** are designed to reward customers who buy frequently and in substantial amounts. They can help build long-term loyalty with high CLV customers, creating cross-selling opportunities in the process. Pioneered by the airlines, hotels, and credit card companies, FPs now exist in many other industries. Typically, the first company to introduce an FP in an industry gains the most benefit, especially if competitors are slow to respond. After competitors react, FPs can become a financial burden to all the offering companies, but some companies are more efficient and creative in managing them. FPs can also produce a psychological boost and a feeling of being special and elite that customers value.[35]

Club membership programs attract and keep those customers responsible for the largest portion of business. Clubs can be open to everyone who purchases a product or service or limited to an affinity group or those willing to pay a small fee. Although open clubs are good for building a database or snagging customers from competitors, limited membership is a more powerful long-term loyalty builder. Fees and membership conditions prevent those with only a fleeting interest in a company's products from joining.

Create Institutional Ties   The company may supply business customers with special equipment or services that help them manage orders, payroll, and inventory. Customers are less inclined to switch to another supplier when it means high capital costs, high search costs, or the loss of loyal-customer discounts. A good example is Milliken & Company, which provides proprietary software, marketing research, sales training, and sales leads to loyal customers.

Create Value With Brand Communities   Thanks in part to the Internet, companies are collaborating with consumers to create value through communities built around brands. A **brand community** is a specialized community of consumers and employees whose identification and activities focus around the brand.[36] A strong brand community results in a more loyal, committed customer base and can be a constant source of inspiration and feedback for product improvements or innovations.

Three characteristics identify brand communities:[37] (1) a sense of connection to the brand, company, product, or community members; (2) shared rituals, stories, and traditions that help convey meaning; and (3) shared responsibility or duty to the community and individual members. Brand communities come in many different forms.[38] Some arise organically from brand users, such as the Atlanta MGB riders club, while others are company-sponsored and facilitated, such as the Harley Owners Group (H.O.G.). Online, marketers can tap into social media such as Facebook, Twitter, and blogs or create their own online community. Members can recommend products, share reviews, create lists of recommendations and favorites, or socialize together online.

Win-Backs

Regardless of how hard companies may try, some customers inevitably become inactive or drop out. The challenge is to reactivate them through win-back strategies.[39] It's often easier to reattract ex-customers (because the company knows their names and histories) than to find new ones. Exit interviews and lost-customer surveys can uncover sources of dissatisfaction and help win back only those with strong profit potential.[40]

When will consumers choose to engage with a brand? Follow-up analysis of the IBM 2010 CEO Study revealed the following about customer pragmatism: "… most do not engage with companies via social media simply to feel connected … To successfully exploit the potential of social media, companies need to design experiences that deliver tangible value in return for customers' time, attention, endorsement and data." That "tangible value" includes discounts, coupons, and information to facilitate purchase. The IBM analysts also note that many businesses overlook social media's most potent capabilities for capturing customer insights, monitoring the brand, conducting research, and soliciting new-product ideas.[41]

Executive Summary

Customers will buy from the firm that they perceive to offer the highest customer-delivered value, defined as the difference between total customer benefits and total customer cost. A buyer's satisfaction is a function of the product's perceived performance and the buyer's expectations. Recognizing that high satisfaction leads to high customer loyalty, companies must ensure that they meet and exceed customer expectations. Quality is the totality of features and characteristics of a product or service that bear on its ability to satisfy stated or implied needs. Marketers play a key role in achieving high levels of total quality so that firms remain solvent and profitable.

Marketing managers must calculate the customer lifetime values of their customer base to understand the profit implications. They must also determine ways to increase the value of the customer base. A strong brand community can lead to a more loyal, committed customer base and provide inspiration and feedback for product improvements or innovations. Companies are becoming skilled in customer relationship management (CRM). The purpose is to attract the right customers, meet the individual needs of valued customers, improve loyalty and retention of valued customers, and implement win-back strategies to reattract valued ex-customers.

Notes

1. Seth Fiegerman, "Pandora Now Has 200 Million Registered Users," www.mashable.com, April 9, 2013; Drake Baer, "What You Can Learn from Pandora's Near-Death Experience," *Fast Company*, April 4, 2013; Tyler Gray, "Pandora Pulls Back the Curtain on Its Magic Music Machine," *Fast Company*, January 21, 2011; Rob Medich, "Pandora Goes Local," *Adweek*, February 14, 2011; Charlie White, "Music Services Compared," www.mashable.com, February 13, 2013; Benny Evangelista, "Pandora Advertisers Hope to Turn Tunes into Dollars," *San Francisco Chronicle*, May 11, 2014, www.sfgate.com.

2. Gary Hamel, "Strategy as Revolution," *Harvard Business Review,* July–August 1996, pp. 69–82.

3. Vikas Mittal, Eugene W. Anderson, Akin Sayrak, and Pandu Tadilamalla, "Dual Emphasis and the Long-Term Financial Impact of Customer Satisfaction," *Marketing Science* 24 (Fall 2005), pp. 544–55.

4. Michael Tsiros, Vikas Mittal, and William T. Ross Jr., "The Role of Attributions in Customer Satisfaction: A Reexamination," *Journal of Consumer Research* 31 (September 2004), pp. 476–83. For a succinct review, see Richard L. Oliver, "Customer Satisfaction Research," Rajiv Grover and Marco Vriens, eds., *Handbook of Marketing Research* (Thousand Oaks, CA: Sage Publications, 2006), pp. 569–87; for in-depth discussion, see Richard L. Oliver, *Satisfaction: A Behavioral Perspective on the Consumer* (Armonk, NY: M. E. Sharpe, 2010).

5. For some provocative analysis and discussion, see Praveen K. Kopalle and Donald R. Lehmann, "Setting Quality Expectations when Entering a Market: What Should the Promise Be?," *Marketing Science* 25 (January–February 2006), pp. 8–24; Susan Fournier and David Glenmick, "Rediscovering Satisfaction," *Journal of Marketing* 63 (October 1999), pp. 5–23.

6. Jennifer Aaker, Susan Fournier, and S. Adam Brasel, "When Good Brands Do Bad," *Journal of Consumer Research* 31 (June 2004), pp. 1–16; Pankaj Aggrawal, "The Effects of Brand Relationship Norms on Consumer Attitudes and Behavior," *Journal of Consumer Research* 31 (June 2004), pp. 87–101; Florian Stahl, Mark Heitmann, Donald R. Lehmann, and Scott A. Neslin, "The Impact of Brand Equity on Customer Acquisition, Retention, and Profit Margin," *Journal of Marketing* 76 (July 2012), pp. 44–63.

7. Neil A. Morgan, Eugene W. Anderson, and Vikas Mittal, "Understanding Firms' Customer Satisfaction Information Usage," *Journal of Marketing* 69 (July 2005), pp. 131–51.

8. See, for example, Christian Homburg, Nicole Koschate, and Wayne D. Hoyer, "Do Satisfied Customers Really Pay More? A Study of the Relationship between Customer Satisfaction and Willingness to Pay," *Journal of Marketing* 69 (April 2005), pp. 84–96.

9. Timothy L. Keiningham, Lerzan Aksoy, Alexander Buoye, and Bruce Cooil, "Customer Loyalty Isn't Enough. Grow Your Share of Wallet," *Harvard Business Review*, October 2011, pp. 29–31.

10. For a comparison of different methods to measure customer satisfaction, see Neil A. Morgan and Lopo Leotto Rego, "The Value of Different Customer Satisfaction and Loyalty Metrics in Predicting Business Performance," *Marketing Science* 25 (September–October 2006), pp. 426–39.

11. Piyush Sharma, Roger Marshall, Peter Alan Reday, and WoonBong Na, "Complainers vs. Non-Complainers: A Multi-National Investigation of Individual and Situational Influences on Customer Complaint Behaviour," *Journal of Marketing Management* 26 (February 2010), pp. 163–80.

12. Stephen S. Tax and Stephen W. Brown, "Recovering and Learning from Service Failure," *Sloan Management Review* 40 (Fall 1998), pp. 75–88.

13. Philip Kotler, *Kotler on Marketing* (New York: Free Press, 1999), pp. 21–22; Jochen Wirtz, "How to Deal with Customer Shakedowns," *Harvard Business Review*, April 2011, p. 24.

14. "Basic Concepts," *ASQ*, www.asq.org/glossary/q .html, January 16, 2014. For a thorough conceptual discussion, see Peter N. Golder, Debanjan Mitra, and Christine Moorman, "What Is Quality? An Integrative Framework of Processes and States," *Journal of Marketing* 76 (July 2012), pp. 1–23.

15. See Robert D. Buzzell and Bradley T. Gale, "Quality Is King," *The PIMS Principles: Linking Strategy to Performance* (New York: Free Press, 1987), pp. 103–34. (PIMS stands for Profit Impact of Market Strategy.)

16. Lerzan Aksoy, Timothy L. Keiningham, and Terry G. Vavra, "Nearly Everything You Know about Loyalty Is Wrong," *Marketing News,* October 1, 2005, pp. 20–21; Timothy L. Keiningham, Terry G. Vavra, Lerzan Aksoy, and Henri Wallard, *Loyalty Myths* (Hoboken, NJ: John Wiley & Sons, 2005).

17. Werner J. Reinartz and V. Kumar, "The Impact of Customer Relationship Characteristics on Profitable Lifetime Duration," *Journal of Marketing* 67 (January 2003), pp. 77–99; Werner J. Reinartz and V. Kumar, "On the Profitability of Long-Life Customers in a Noncontractual Setting: An Empirical Investigation

and Implications for Marketing," *Journal of Marketing* 64 (October 2000), pp. 17–35.

18. Rakesh Niraj, Mahendra Gupta, and Chakravarthi Narasimhan, "Customer Profitability in a Supply Chain," *Journal of Marketing* 65 (July 2001), pp. 1–16.

19. Thomas M. Petro, "Profitability: The Fifth 'P' of Marketing," *Bank Marketing,* September 1990, pp. 48–52; "Who Are Your Best Customers?," *Bank Marketing,* October 1990, pp. 48–52.

20. V. Kumar, "Customer Lifetime Value," Rajiv Grover and Marco Vriens, eds., *Handbook of Marketing Research* (Thousand Oaks, CA: Sage Publications, 2006), pp. 602–27; Sunil Gupta, Donald R. Lehmann, and Jennifer Ames Stuart, "Valuing Customers," *Journal of Marketing Research* 61 (February 2004), pp. 7–18; Rajkumar Venkatesan and V. Kumar, "A Customer Lifetime Value Framework for Customer Selection and Resource Allocation Strategy," *Journal of Marketing* 68 (October 2004), pp. 106–25.

21. V. Kumar, "Profitable Relationships," *Marketing Research* 18 (Fall 2006), pp. 41–46.

22. For some recent analysis and discussion, see Michael Haenlein, Andreas M. Kaplan, and Detlef Schoder, "Valuing the Real Option of Abandoning Unprofitable Customers when Calculating Customer Lifetime Value," *Journal of Marketing* 70 (July 2006), pp. 5–20; Teck-Hua Ho, Young-Hoon Park, and Yong-Pin Zhou, "Incorporating Satisfaction into Customer Value Analysis: Optimal Investment in Lifetime Value," *Marketing Science* 25 (May–June 2006), pp. 260–77; and Peter S. Fader, Bruce G. S. Hardie, and Ka Lok Lee, "RFM and CLV: Using Iso-Value Curves for Customer Base Analysis," *Journal of Marketing Research* 62 (November 2005), pp. 415–30; V. Kumar, Rajkumar Venkatesan, Tim Bohling, and Denise Beckmann, "The Power of CLV: Managing Customer Lifetime Value at IBM," *Marketing Science* 27 (2008), pp. 585–99.

23. For more on CLV, see: Sunil Gupta and Donald R. Lehmann, "Models of Customer Value," Berend Wierenga, ed., *Handbook of Marketing Decision Models* (Berlin, Germany: Springer Science and Business Media, 2007); Sunil Gupta and Donald R. Lehmann, "Customers as Assets," *Journal of Interactive Marketing* 17, no. 1 (Winter 2006), pp. 9–24; Sunil Gupta and Donald R. Lehmann, *Managing Customers as Investments* (Upper Saddle River, NJ: Wharton School Publishing, 2005); Peter Fader, Bruce Hardie, and Ka Lee, "RFM and CLV: Using Iso-Value Curves for Customer Base Analysis," *Journal of Marketing Research* 42, no. 4 (November 2005), pp. 415–30; Sunil Gupta, Donald R. Lehmann, and Jennifer Ames Stuart, "Valuing Customers," *Journal of Marketing Research* 41, no. 1 (February 2004), pp. 7–18.

24. For a variety of perspectives on brand relationships, see Deborah J. MacInnis, C. Whan Park, and Joseph R. Preister, eds., *Handbook of Brand Relationships* (Armonk, NY: M. E. Sharpe, 2009).

25. For a study of the processes involved, see Werner Reinartz, Manfred Kraft, and Wayne D. Hoyer, "The Customer Relationship Management Process: Its Measurement and Impact on Performance," *Journal of Marketing Research* 61 (August 2004), pp. 293–305. For a thorough examination of the practical issues, see Peter Fader, *Customer Centricity: Focus on the Right Customers for Strategic Advantage* (Philadelphia, PA: Wharton Digital Press, 2012).

26. Seth Godin, *Permission Marketing: Turning Strangers into Friends, and Friends into Customers* (New York: Simon & Schuster, 1999). See also Susan Fournier, Susan Dobscha, and David Mick, "Preventing the Premature Death of Relationship Marketing," *Harvard Business Review,* January–February 1998, pp. 42–51.

27. Martin Mende, Ruth N. Bolton, and Mary Jo Bitner, "Decoding Customer–Firm Relationships: How Attachment Styles Help Explain Customers' Preferences for Closeness, Repurchase Intentions, and Changes in Relationship Breadth," *Journal of Marketing Research* 50 (February 2013), pp. 125–42.

28. Michael Lewis, "Customer Acquisition Promotions and Customer Asset Value," *Journal of Marketing Research* 63 (May 2006), pp. 195–203; see also Romana Khan, Michael Lewis, and Vishal Singh, "Dynamic Customer Management and the Value of One-to-One Marketing," *Marketing Science* 28 (November–December 2009), pp. 1063–79.

29. V. Kumar and Bharath Rajan, "The Perils of Social Coupon Campaigns," *MIT Sloan Management Review* 53 (Summer 2012), pp. 13–14; Karen E. Klein, "Small Businesses See Red over Daily Deals," *Bloomberg Businessweek*, December 3, 2012, pp. 53–54.

30. Werner Reinartz, Jacquelyn S. Thomas, and V. Kumar, "Balancing Acquisition and Retention Resources to Maximize Customer Profitability," *Journal of Marketing* 69 (January 2005), pp. 63–79.

31. Michael D. Johnson and Fred Selnes, "Diversifying Your Customer Portfolio," *MIT Sloan Management Review* 46 (Spring 2005), pp. 11–14; Crina O. Tarasi, Ruth N. Bolton, Michael D. Hutt, and Beth A. Walker, "Balancing Risk and Return in a Customer Portfolio," *Journal of Marketing* 75 (May 2011), pp. 1–17.

32. Leonard L. Berry and A. Parasuraman, *Marketing Services: Competing through Quality* (New York:

Free Press, 1991), pp. 136–42. For an academic examination in a business-to-business context, see Robert W. Palmatier, Srinath Gopalakrishna, and Mark B. Houston, "Returns on Business-to-Business Relationship Marketing Investments: Strategies for Leveraging Profits," *Marketing Science* 25 (September–October 2006), pp. 477–93. See also Irit Nitzan and Barak Libai, "Social Effects on Customer Retention," *Journal of Marketing* 75 (November 2011), pp. 24–38.

33. Ben McConnell and Jackie Huba, "Learning to Leverage the Lunatic Fringe," *Point,* July–August 2006, pp. 14–15; Michael Krauss, "Work to Convert Customers into Evangelists," *Marketing News,* December 15, 2006, p. 6; "Ask Maxine Clark," *Inc.,* July 1, 2008; "How Maxine Clark Built Build-a-Bear," *Fortune,* March 19, 2012.

34. Utpal M. Dholakia, "How Consumer Self-Determination Influences Relational Marketing Outcomes: Evidence from Longitudinal Field Studies," *Journal of Marketing Research* 43 (February 2006), pp. 109–20.

35. Joseph C. Nunes and Xavier Drèze, "Feeling Superior: The Impact of Loyalty Program Structure on Consumers' Perception of Status," *Journal of Consumer Research* 35 (April 2009), pp. 890–905; Joseph C. Nunes and Xavier Drèze, "Your Loyalty Program Is Betraying You," *Harvard Business Review,* April 2006, pp. 124–31.

36. James H. McAlexander, John W. Schouten, and Harold F. Koenig, "Building Brand Community," *Journal of Marketing* 66 (January 2002), pp. 38–54. For some notable examinations of brand communities, see René Algesheimer, Uptal M. Dholakia, and Andreas Herrmann, "The Social Influence of Brand Community: Evidence from European Car Clubs," *Journal of Marketing* 69 (July 2005), pp. 19–34; Albert M. Muniz Jr. and Hope Jensen Schau, "Religiosity in the Abandoned Apple Newton Brand Community," *Journal of Consumer Research* 31 (2005), pp. 412–32; Robert Kozinets, "Utopian Enterprise: Articulating the Meanings of *Star Trek*'s Culture of Consumption," *Journal of Consumer Research* 28 (June 2001), pp. 67–87; John W. Schouten and James H. McAlexander, "Subcultures of Consumption: An Ethnography of New Bikers," *Journal of Consumer Research* 22 (June 1995), pp. 43–61.

37. Albert M. Muniz Jr. and Thomas C. O'Guinn, "Brand Community," *Journal of Consumer Research* 27 (March 2001), pp. 412–32.

38. Susan Fournier and Lara Lee, "The Seven Deadly Sins of Brand Community 'Management,'" Marketing Science Institute Special Report 08-208, 2008; see also Mark Bubula, "The Myth about Brand Communities," *Admap,* November 2012.

39. Jacquelyn S. Thomas, Robert C. Blattberg, and Edward J. Fox, "Recapturing Lost Customers," *Journal of Marketing Research* 61 (February 2004), pp. 31–45.

40. Werner Reinartz and V. Kumar, "The Impact of Customer Relationship Characteristics on Profitable Lifetime Duration," *Journal of Marketing* 67 (January 2003), pp. 77–99; Werner Reinartz and V. Kumar, "The Mismanagement of Customer Loyalty," *Harvard Business Review,* July 2002, pp. 86–97.

41. Carolyn Heller Baird and Gautam Parasnis, *From Social Media to Social CRM* (Somers, NY: IBM Corporation, 2011).

Chapter 5

Analyzing Consumer and Business Markets

In this chapter, we will address the following questions:

1. How do cultural, social, and personal factors influence consumer buying behavior? (Page 69)
2. What major psychological processes influence consumer buying behavior? (Page 72)
3. How do consumers make purchasing decisions? (Page 75)
4. What is the business market, and how does it differ from the consumer market? (Page 80)
5. Who participates in the business buying process, and how are buying decisions made? (Page 82)
6. How can companies build strong relationships with business customers? (Page 86)

Marketing Management at Cisco

At the height of the dot-com boom, Cisco Systems was briefly the most valuable company in the world, with a valuation of $500 billion. Since those heady days, Cisco has faced a number of challenges to its market leadership—but it has also taken bold steps to reinvent itself, reflecting shifts in the global marketing environment. The company prides itself on staying close to its business customers and sees its core competency as helping them get through big transitions by breaking down their corporate silos. Its CEO cites compact and efficient blade servers as a good example of how Cisco helps companies form a common technological vision, noting that Cisco's is the only computing technology that can handle data, voice, and video. The firm spends $6 billion annually on research and development, and it generates 55 percent of its revenue and 70 percent of its growth from overseas.[1]

Adopting a holistic marketing orientation requires fully understanding customers, whether they're consumers or organizational buyers. Cisco, like other smart marketers, puts a high priority on building strong loyalty relationships with its customers. It is also a buyer of goods and services, not just a seller to other businesses. This chapter looks at the buying dynamics of individual consumers and of businesses, government agencies, and institutions.

What Influences Consumer Behavior?

Consumer behavior is the study of how individuals, groups, and organizations select, buy, use, and dispose of goods, services, ideas, or experiences to satisfy their needs and wants.[2] Marketers must fully understand both the theory and the reality of consumer behavior. A consumer's buying behavior is influenced by cultural, social, and personal factors. Of these, cultural factors exert the broadest and deepest influence.

Cultural Factors

Culture, subculture, and social class are particularly important influences on consumer buying behavior. **Culture** is the fundamental determinant of a person's wants and behavior. Through family and other key institutions, a child growing up in the United States is exposed to values such as achievement and success, activity, efficiency and practicality, progress, material comfort, individualism, freedom, external comfort, humanitarianism, and youthfulness.[3] A child growing up in another country might have a different view of self, relationship to others, and rituals.

Each culture consists of smaller *subcultures* that provide more specific identification and socialization for their members. Subcultures include nationalities, religions, racial groups, and geographic regions. When subcultures grow large and affluent enough, companies often design specialized marketing programs to serve them.

Social classes are relatively homogeneous and enduring divisions in a society, hierarchically ordered and with members who share similar values, interests, and behavior. One classic depiction of social classes in the United States defined seven ascending levels: (1) lower lowers, (2) upper lowers, (3) working class, (4) middle class, (5) upper middles, (6) lower uppers, and (7) upper uppers.[4] Social class members show distinct product and brand preferences in many areas.

Social Factors

In addition to cultural factors, social factors such as reference groups, family, and social roles and statuses affect our buying behavior.

Reference Groups   A person's **reference groups** are all the groups that have a direct (face-to-face) or indirect influence on his or her attitudes or behavior. Groups having a direct influence are called **membership groups.** Some of these are *primary groups* with whom the person interacts fairly continuously and informally, such as family, friends, neighbors, and coworkers. People also belong to *secondary groups*, such as religious, professional, and trade-union groups, which tend to be more formal and require less continuous interaction.

Reference groups influence members by exposing an individual to new behaviors and lifestyles, influencing attitudes and self-concept, and creating pressures for conformity that may affect product and brand choices. People are also influenced by groups to which they do *not* belong. **Aspirational groups** are those a person hopes to join; **dissociative groups** are those whose values or behavior an individual rejects.

Where reference group influence is strong, marketers must determine how to reach and influence the group's **opinion leader,** the person who offers informal advice or information about a specific product or category, such as which of several brands is best or how a particular product may be used.[5] Marketers try to reach these individuals by identifying their demographic and psychographic characteristics, identifying the media they read, and directing messages to them.[6]

Cliques   Communication researchers propose a social-structure view of interpersonal communication.[7] They see society as consisting of *cliques,* small groups whose members interact frequently. Clique members are similar, and their closeness facilitates effective communication but also insulates the clique from new ideas. The challenge is to create more openness so cliques exchange information with others in society. One team of viral marketing experts cautions that although influencers or "alphas" start trends, they are often too introspective and socially alienated to spread them. They advise marketers to cultivate "bees," hyperdevoted customers who are not satisfied just knowing about the next trend but live to spread the word.[8] More firms are in fact finding ways to identify and actively engage passionate brand evangelists and potentially lucrative customers online.[9]

Family   The family is society's most important consumer buying organization, and family members constitute the most influential primary reference group.[10] There are two families in the buyer's life. The **family of orientation** consists of parents and siblings. From parents a person acquires an orientation toward religion, politics, and economics and a sense of personal ambition, self-worth, and love.[11] A more direct influence on everyday buying behavior is the **family of procreation**—namely, the person's spouse and children. For expensive products and services such as cars, vacations, or housing, the vast majority of husbands and wives engage in joint decision making.[12] Men and women may respond differently to marketing messages, however.

Another shift in buying patterns is an increase in the influence wielded by children and teens. Research has shown that more than two-thirds of 13- to 21-year-olds make or influence family purchase decisions on audio/video equipment, software, and vacation destinations.[13] By the time children are about 2 years old, they can often recognize characters, logos, and specific brands. They can distinguish between advertising and programming by about ages 6 or 7. A year or so later, they can understand the concept of persuasive intent on the part of advertisers. By 9 or 10, they can perceive the discrepancies between message and product.[14] Teens and young adults watch what their friends say and do as much as what they see or hear in an ad or are told by a salesperson in a store.

Roles and Status   We each participate in many groups—family, clubs, organizations—and these are often an important source of information and help to define norms for behavior. We can define a person's position in each group in terms of role and status. A **role** consists of the activities a person is expected to perform. Each role in turn connotes a **status.** A senior vice president of marketing may have more status than a sales manager, and a sales manager may have more status than an office clerk. People choose products that reflect and communicate their role and their actual or desired status in society. Marketers must be aware of the status-symbol potential of products and brands.

Personal Factors

Personal characteristics that influence a buyer's decision include age and stage in the life cycle, occupation and economic circumstances, personality and self-concept, and lifestyle and values.

Age and Stage in the Life Cycle   Our taste in food, clothes, furniture, and recreation is often related to our age. Consumption is also shaped by the *family life cycle* and the number, age, and gender of people in the household at any point in time. In addition, *psychological* life-cycle stages may matter. Adults experience certain passages or transformations as they go through life.[15] Their behavior during these intervals, such as when becoming a parent, is not necessarily fixed but changes with the times. Marketers should also consider *critical life events or transitions*—marriage, childbirth, illness, relocation, divorce, first job, career change, retirement, death of a spouse—as giving rise to new needs.

Occupation and Economic Circumstances Occupation influences consumption patterns. Marketers try to identify the occupational groups that have above-average interest in their products and services and even tailor products for certain occupational groups: Software companies, for example, design different products for engineers, lawyers, and physicians. Both product and brand choice are greatly affected by economic circumstances like spendable income (level, stability, and pattern over time), savings and assets (including the percentage that is liquid), debts, borrowing power, and attitudes toward spending and saving.

Personality and Self-Concept By **personality,** we mean a set of distinguishing human psychological traits that lead to relatively consistent and enduring responses to environmental stimuli including buying behavior. We often describe personality in terms of such traits as self-confidence, dominance, autonomy, deference, sociability, defensiveness, and adaptability.[16]

Brands also have personalities, and consumers are likely to choose brands whose personalities match their own. We define **brand personality** as the specific mix of human traits that we can attribute to a particular brand. Stanford's Jennifer Aaker researched brand personalities and identified the following traits: sincerity, excitement, competence, sophistication, and ruggedness.[17] Cross-cultural studies have found that some but not all of these traits apply outside the United States.[18]

Consumers often choose and use brands with a brand personality consistent with their *actual self-concept* (how we view ourselves), though the match may instead be based on the consumer's *ideal self-concept* (how we would like to view ourselves) or even on *others' self-concept* (how we think others see us).[19] These effects may also be more pronounced for publicly consumed products than for privately consumed goods.[20] On the other hand, consumers who are high "self-monitors"—that is, sensitive to the way others see them—are more likely to choose brands whose personalities fit the consumption situation.[21] Finally, multiple aspects of self (serious professional, caring family member, active fun-lover) may often be evoked differently in different situations or around different types of people.

Lifestyle and Values People from the same subculture, social class, and occupation may adopt quite different lifestyles. A **lifestyle** is a person's pattern of living in the world as expressed in activities, interests, and opinions. It portrays the "whole person" interacting with his or her environment. Marketers search for relationships between their products and lifestyle groups. A computer manufacturer might find that most computer buyers are achievement-oriented and then aim the brand more clearly at the achiever lifestyle.

Lifestyles are shaped partly by whether consumers are *money constrained* or *time constrained.* Companies aiming to serve the money-constrained will create lower-cost products and services. By appealing to thrifty consumers, Walmart has become the largest company in the world. In some categories, notably food processing, companies targeting time-constrained consumers need to be aware that these very same people want to believe they're *not* operating within time constraints. Marketers call those who seek both convenience and some involvement in the cooking process the "convenience involvement segment."[22]

Consumer decisions are also influenced by **core values,** the belief systems that underlie attitudes and behaviors. Core values go much deeper than behavior or attitude and at a basic level guide people's choices and desires over the long term. Marketers who target consumers on the basis of their values believe that with appeals to people's inner selves, it is possible to influence their outer selves—their purchase behavior.

Key Psychological Processes

The starting point for understanding consumer behavior is the stimulus-response model shown in Figure 5.1. Marketing and environmental stimuli enter the consumer's consciousness, and a set of psychological processes combine with certain consumer characteristics to result in decision processes and purchase decisions. The marketer's task is to understand what happens in the consumer's consciousness between the arrival of the outside marketing stimuli and the ultimate purchase decisions. Four key psychological processes—motivation, perception, learning, and memory—fundamentally influence consumer responses.

Motivation

We all have many needs at any given time. Some needs are *biogenic*; they arise from physiological states of tension such as hunger, thirst, or discomfort. Other needs are *psychogenic*; they arise from psychological states of tension such as the need for recognition, esteem, or belonging. A need becomes a **motive** when it is aroused to a sufficient level of intensity to drive us to act. Motivation has both direction—we select one goal over another—and intensity—we pursue the goal with more or less vigor.

Well-known theories of human motivation carry different implications for consumer analysis and marketing strategy. Sigmund Freud assumed the psychological forces shaping people's behavior are largely unconscious and that people cannot fully understand their own motivations. Someone who examines specific brands will react not only to the brands' stated capabilities but also to less conscious cues such as shape, size, weight, and brand name. A technique called *laddering* lets us trace a person's motivations from the stated instrumental ones to the more terminal ones. Then the marketer can decide at what level to develop the message and appeal.[23]

Cultural anthropologist Clotaire Rapaille works on breaking the "code" behind product behavior—the unconscious meaning people give to a particular market offering. Rapaille worked with Boeing to identify features in the 787 Dreamliner's interior that would have universal appeal. Based in part on his research, the Dreamliner has a spacious foyer; larger,

FIGURE 5.1 Model of Consumer Behavior

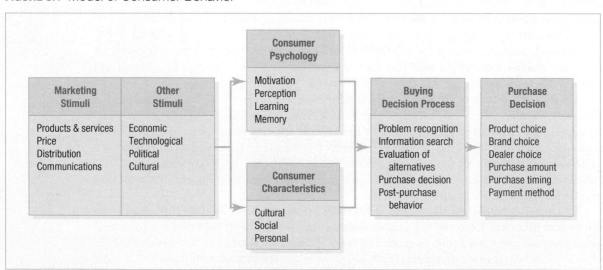

curved luggage bins closer to the ceiling; larger, electronically dimmed windows; and a ceiling discreetly lit by hidden LEDs.[24]

Abraham Maslow sought to explain why people are driven by particular needs at particular times.[25] His answer was that human needs are arranged in a hierarchy from most to least pressing—from physiological needs to safety needs, social needs, esteem needs, and self-actualization needs. People will try to satisfy their most important need first and then move to the next.

Frederick Herzberg developed a two-factor theory that distinguishes *dissatisfiers* (factors that cause dissatisfaction) from *satisfiers* (factors that cause satisfaction).[26] The absence of dissatisfiers is not enough to motivate a purchase; satisfiers must be present. For example, a computer that does not come with a warranty is a dissatisfier. Yet the presence of a product warranty does not act as a satisfier or motivator of a purchase because it is not a source of intrinsic satisfaction. Ease of use is a satisfier. In line with this theory, sellers should do their best to avoid dissatisfiers that might unsell a product and supply the major motivators (satisfiers) of purchase.

Perception

A motivated person is ready to act—*how* is influenced by his or her perception of the situation. In marketing, perceptions are more important than reality because they affect consumers' actual behavior. **Perception** is the process by which we select, organize, and interpret information inputs to create a meaningful picture of the world.[27] Consumers perceive many different kinds of information through sight, sound, smell, taste, and feel.

Sensory marketing has been defined as "marketing that engages the consumers' senses and affects their perception, judgment and behavior." Aradhna Krishna argues that sensory marketing's effects can be manifested in two main ways. One, sensory marketing can be used subconsciously to shape consumer perceptions of more abstract qualities of a product or service (say, different aspects of its brand personality). Two, sensory marketing can also be used to affect the perceptions of specific product or service attributes (such as color, taste, or shape).[28]

People can emerge with different perceptions of the same object because of three perceptual processes: selective attention, selective distortion, and selective retention. Although we're exposed to thousands of marketing stimuli every day, we screen most stimuli out—a process called **selective attention.** Therefore, marketers must work hard to attract consumers' notice. Research shows that people are more likely to notice stimuli that relate to a current need; this is why car shoppers notice car ads but not appliance ads. Also, people are more likely to notice stimuli they anticipate, such as laptops displayed in a computer store. And people are more likely to notice stimuli whose deviations are large in relationship to the normal size of the stimuli. You are more likely to notice an ad offering $100 off than one offering $5 off a product's price.

Even noticed stimuli don't always come across in the way the senders intend. *Selective distortion* is the tendency to interpret information in a way that fits our preconceptions. Consumers will often distort information to be consistent with prior brand and product beliefs and expectations. Selective distortion can work to the advantage of marketers with strong brands when consumers distort neutral or ambiguous brand information to make it more positive. In other words, coffee may seem to taste better and the wait in a bank line may seem shorter, depending on the brand. Moreover, because of *selective retention*, we're likely to remember good points about a product we like and forget good points about competing products. Selective retention again works to the advantage of strong brands. It also explains why marketers need to use repetition—to make sure their message is not overlooked.

Learning

When we act, we learn. **Learning** induces changes in our behavior arising from experience. Most human behavior is learned, though much learning is incidental. Learning theorists believe learning is produced through the interplay of drives, stimuli, cues, responses, and reinforcement. A **drive** is a strong internal stimulus impelling action. **Cues** are minor stimuli that determine when, where, and how a person responds.

Suppose you buy a laptop computer. If your experience is rewarding, your response to the laptop and the brand will be positively reinforced. When you want to buy a printer, you may assume that because the company makes good laptops, it also makes good printers, *generalizing* your response to similar stimuli. A countertendency to generalization is *discrimination*, in which we learn to recognize differences in sets of similar stimuli and adjust our responses accordingly. Learning theory teaches marketers that they can build demand for a product by associating it with strong drives, using motivating cues, and providing positive reinforcement.

Emotions

Consumer response is not all cognitive and rational; much may be emotional and invoke different kinds of feelings. A brand or product may make a consumer feel proud, excited, or confident. An ad may create feelings of amusement, disgust, or wonder. Marketers are increasingly recognizing the power of emotional appeals—especially if rooted in some functional or rational aspects of the brand. An emotion-filled brand story has been shown to trigger's people desire to pass along things they hear about brands, through either word of mouth or online sharing. Firms are therefore giving their communications a stronger human appeal to engage consumers in their brand stories.[29]

Memory

Cognitive psychologists distinguish between short-term memory (STM)—a temporary and limited repository of information—and long-term memory (LTM)—a more permanent, essentially unlimited repository. Most widely accepted views of long-term memory structure assume we form some kind of associative model. For example, the **associative network memory model** views LTM as a set of nodes and links. *Nodes* are stored information connected by *links* that vary in strength. Any type of information can be stored in the memory network, including verbal, visual, abstract, and contextual. A spreading activation process from node to node determines how much we retrieve and what information we can actually recall in any given situation. When a node becomes activated because we're encoding external information (when we read or hear a word or phrase) or retrieving internal information from LTM (when we think about some concept), other nodes are also activated if they're associated strongly enough with that node.

Brand associations consist of all brand-related thoughts, feelings, perceptions, images, experiences, beliefs, attitudes, and so on, that become linked to the brand node. Companies sometimes create mental maps of consumers that depict their knowledge of a particular brand in terms of the key associations likely to be triggered in a marketing setting and their relative strength, favorability, and uniqueness to consumers. Figure 5.2 displays a very simple mental map highlighting some brand beliefs for a hypothetical consumer for State Farm insurance.

Memory encoding describes how and where information gets into memory. The strength of the resulting association depends on how much we process the information at encoding (how much we think about it, for instance) and in what way. The more attention we pay to the meaning of information during encoding, the stronger the resulting associations in memory will be.[30] *Memory retrieval* is the way information gets out of memory. The presence of *other* product

FIGURE 5.2 Hypothetical Mental Map

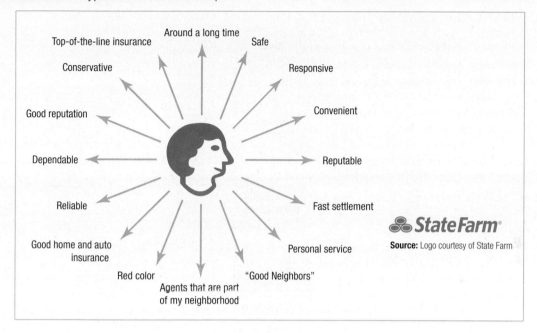

Source: Logo courtesy of State Farm

information in memory can produce interference effects and cause us to either overlook or confuse new data. One marketing challenge in a category crowded with competitors is that consumers may mix up brands. Also, once information becomes stored in memory, its strength of association decays very slowly.

Information may be *available* in memory but not be *accessible* for recall without the proper retrieval cues or reminders. The effectiveness of retrieval cues is one reason marketing *inside* a store is so critical—product packaging and displays remind us of information already conveyed outside the store and become prime determinants of consumer decision making. Accessibility of a brand in memory is important for another reason: People talk about a brand when it is top-of-mind.[31]

The Consumer Buying Decision Process

Smart companies try to fully understand customers' buying decision process—all the experiences in learning, choosing, using, and even disposing of a product. Figure 5.3 shows the five stages of the process: problem recognition, information search, evaluation of alternatives, purchase decision, and postpurchase behavior. Note that consumers don't always pass through all five stages—they may skip or reverse some. The model provides a good frame of reference because it captures the full range of considerations that arise when a consumer faces a highly involving new purchase.

Problem Recognition

The buying process starts when the buyer recognizes a problem or need triggered by internal or external stimuli. With an internal stimulus, one of the person's normal needs—hunger or thirst—rises to a threshold level and becomes a drive. A need can also be aroused by an external stimulus, such as seeing an ad. Marketers want to identify the circumstances that trigger a particular

FIGURE 5.3 Five-Stage Model of the Consumer Buying Process

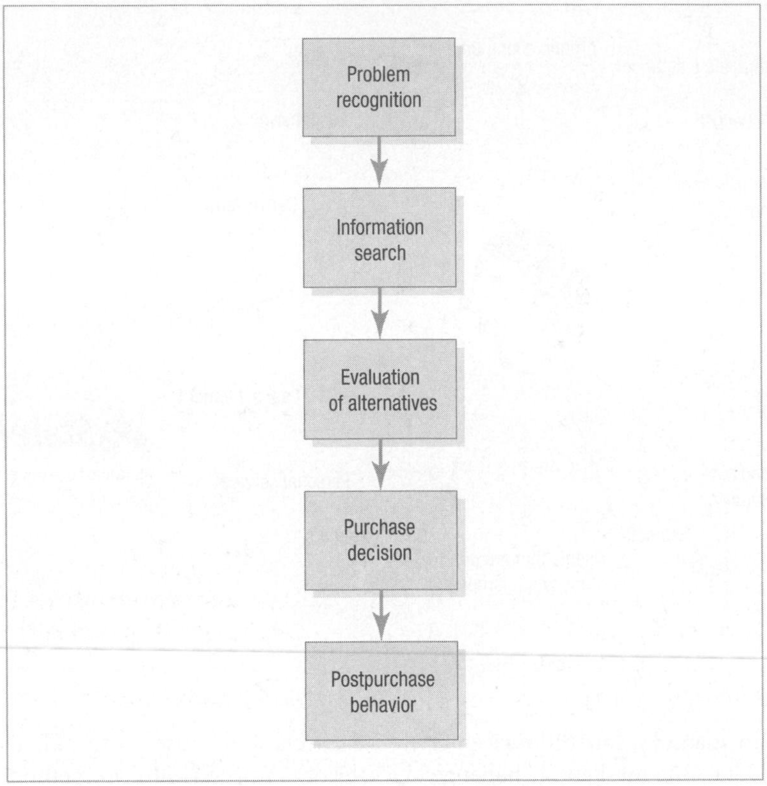

Problem recognition

↓

Information search

↓

Evaluation of alternatives

↓

Purchase decision

↓

Postpurchase behavior

need by gathering information from a number of consumers. They can then develop marketing strategies that spark consumer interest.

Information Search

We can distinguish between two levels of engagement in the information search. The milder search state is called *heightened attention,* in which a person becomes more receptive to information about a product. At the next level, the person may enter an *active information search:* looking for reading material, asking friends, going online, and visiting stores to learn about the product.

Marketers must understand what type of information consumers seek—or are at least receptive to—at different times and places.[32] Information sources for consumers can be categorized as personal (family, friends) commercial (ads, Web sites, salespeople, packaging, displays), public (mass media, social media), and experiential (handling, using the product). Although consumers receive the greatest amount of information about a product from commercial (marketer-dominated) sources, the most effective information often comes from personal or experiential sources or public sources that are independent authorities.[33]

By gathering information, the consumer learns about competing brands and their features. The first box in Figure 5.4 shows the *total set* of brands available. The individual consumer will come to know a subset of these, the *awareness set.* Only some, the *consideration set,* will meet initial buying criteria. As the consumer gathers more information, just the *choice set* will remain strong contenders. The consumer makes a final choice from these.[34] Figure 5.4 shows that a

FIGURE 5.4 Successive Sets Involved in Consumer Decision Making

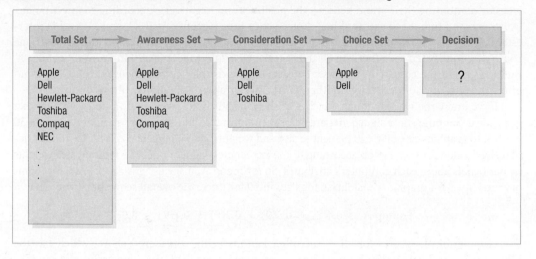

company must get its brand into the prospect's awareness, consideration, and choice sets and identify the other brands in the choice set to plan appropriate competitive appeals. In addition, it should identify the consumer's information sources and evaluate their relative importance so it can prepare effective communications.

Be aware that search behavior can vary online, in part because of the manner in which product information is presented. For example, product alternatives may be presented in order of their predicted attractiveness for the consumer. Consumers may then choose not to search as extensively as they would otherwise.[35]

Evaluation of Alternatives

How does the consumer process competitive brand information and make a final value judgment? There are several processes, and the most current models see the consumer forming judgments largely on a conscious and rational basis.

Some basic concepts will help us understand consumer evaluation processes. First, the consumer is trying to satisfy a need. Second, the consumer is looking for certain benefits. Third, the consumer sees each product as a bundle of attributes with varying abilities to deliver the benefits. The attributes of interest vary by product—for example, the attributes buyers seek in a hotel might be location, atmosphere, and price. Consumers will pay the most attention to attributes that deliver the sought-after benefits. We can often segment the market according to attributes and benefits important to different consumer groups.

Through experience and learning, people acquire beliefs and attitudes, which in turn influence buying behavior. A **belief** is a descriptive thought that a person holds about something. Just as important are **attitudes,** a person's enduring favorable or unfavorable evaluations, emotional feelings, and action tendencies toward some object or idea. People have attitudes toward almost everything: religion, clothes, music, or food. Because attitudes economize on energy and thought, they can be very difficult to change, which is why firms should try to fit their products into existing attitudes rather than try to change attitudes.

The consumer arrives at attitudes toward various brands through an attribute-evaluation procedure, developing a set of beliefs about where each brand stands on each attribute.[36] The

expectancy-value model of attitude formation posits that consumers evaluate products and services by combining their brand beliefs—the positives and negatives—according to importance.

Suppose Linda has narrowed her choice set to four laptops (A, B, C, and D) and is interested in four attributes: memory capacity, graphics capability, size and weight, and price. If one computer dominated the others on all the criteria, we could predict that Linda would choose it. But, as is often the case, her choice set consists of brands that vary in their appeal. One brand offers the best memory capacity, another has the best graphics capability, and so on.

If we knew the weights Linda attaches to the four attributes, we could more reliably predict her choice. Suppose she assigned 40 percent of the importance to the laptop's memory capacity, 30 percent to graphics capability, 20 percent to size and weight, and 10 percent to price. To find Linda's perceived value for each laptop according to the expectancy-value model, we multiply her weights by her beliefs about each computer's attributes. So for brand A, if she assigns a score of 8 for memory capacity, 9 for graphics capability, 6 for size, and 9 for price, the overall score for A would be:

$$\text{Laptop A} = 0.4(8) + 0.3(9) + 0.2(6) + 0.1(9) = 8.0$$

Calculating the scores for all of the other laptops being considered shows which has the highest perceived value. When a marketer knows how buyers form their preferences, it can take steps to influence consumer decisions, such as to redesign the laptop (real repositioning), alter beliefs about the brand (psychological repositioning), alter beliefs about competitors (competitive depositioning), alter the importance weights (persuading buyers to attach more importance to attributes in which the brand excels), call attention to neglected attributes (such as styling), or shift the buyer's ideals (persuading buyers to change their ideal levels for one or more attributes).[37]

Purchase Decision

In the evaluation stage, the consumer forms preferences among the brands in the choice set and may also form an intention to buy the most preferred brand. Even if consumers form brand evaluations, two general factors can intervene between the purchase intention and the purchase decision. The first factor is the *attitudes of others*. The influence of another person's attitude depends on (1) the intensity of the other person's negative attitude toward our preferred alternative and (2) our motivation to comply with the other person's wishes.[38] The more intense the other person's negativism and the closer he or she is to us, the more we will adjust our purchase intention. The converse is also true.

The second factor is *unanticipated situational factors* that may erupt to change the purchase intention. Linda might lose her job, some other purchase might become more urgent, or a store salesperson may turn her off. Preferences and even purchase intentions are not completely reliable predictors of purchase behavior.

A consumer's decision to modify, postpone, or avoid a purchase decision is heavily influenced by one or more types of *perceived risk*.[39] For example, functional risk entails the product not performing to expectations; social risk entails embarrassment in front of others. The degree of perceived risk varies with the amount of money at stake, the amount of attribute uncertainty, and the level of consumer self-confidence. Marketers must understand the factors that provoke a feeling of risk in consumers and provide information and support to reduce it.

Postpurchase Behavior

After the purchase, the consumer might experience dissonance from noticing certain disquieting features or hearing favorable things about other brands and will be alert to information that supports his or her decision. Marketers must therefore monitor postpurchase satisfaction, postpurchase actions, and postpurchase product uses and disposal. A satisfied consumer is more likely to purchase the product again and will also tend to say good things about the brand to others. Dissatisfied consumers may abandon or return the product, take public action (by complaining to the company or complaining to others online), or take private actions (not buying the product or warning friends).[40]

Postpurchase communications to buyers have been shown to result in fewer product returns and order cancellations. Marketers should also monitor how buyers use and dispose of the product. A key driver of sales frequency is product consumption rate—the more quickly buyers consume a product, the sooner they may repurchase it. One strategy to speed replacement is to tie the act of replacing the product to a certain holiday, event, or time of year. Another strategy is to provide consumers with better information about (1) the time they first used the product or need to replace it or (2) its current level of performance. If consumers throw the product away, the marketer needs to know how they dispose of it, especially if—like electronic equipment—it can damage the environment.

Behavioral Decision Theory and Behavioral Economics

Consumers don't always process information or make decisions in a deliberate, rational manner. One of the most active academic research areas in marketing over the past three decades has been *behavioral decision theory* (BDT). Behavioral decision theorists have identified many situations in which consumers make seemingly irrational choices. What such studies reinforce is that consumer behavior is very constructive and the context of decisions really matters. The work of researchers has also challenged predictions from economic theory and assumptions about rationality, leading to the emergence of the field of *behavioral economics*.[41] Here, we review some issues in two key areas: decision heuristics and framing.

Decision Heuristics   Consumers often take "mental shortcuts" called **heuristics** or rules of thumb in the decision process. In everyday decision making, when they forecast the likelihood of future outcomes or events, consumers may use one of these heuristics.

1. The *availability heuristic*—Consumers base their predictions on the quickness and ease with which a particular example of an outcome comes to mind. If an example comes to mind too easily, consumers might overestimate the likelihood of its happening. For example, a recent product failure may lead consumers to inflate the likelihood of a future product failure and make them more inclined to purchase a product warranty.

2. The *representativeness heuristic*—Consumers base their predictions on how representative or similar the outcome is to other examples. One reason package appearances may be so similar for different brands in the same product category is that marketers want their products to be seen as representative of the category as a whole.

3. The *anchoring and adjustment heuristic*—Consumers arrive at an initial judgment and then adjust it—sometimes only reluctantly—based on additional information. For services marketers, a strong first impression is critical to establishing a favorable anchor so subsequent experiences will be interpreted in a more favorable light.

Framing   *Decision framing* is the manner in which choices are presented to and seen by a decision maker. A $200 cell phone may not seem that expensive in the context of a set of $400 phones but may seem very expensive if other phones cost $50. Researchers have found that consumers use a form of framing called *mental accounting* when they handle their money, as a way of coding, categorizing, and evaluating financial outcomes of choices.[42] The principles of mental accounting are derived in part from *prospect theory*, which maintains that consumers frame their decision alternatives in terms of gains and losses according to a value function. Consumers are generally loss-averse. They tend to overweight very low probabilities and underweight very high probabilities.

What is Organizational Buying?

Many marketers sell not to consumers but to organizational buyers. Frederick E. Webster Jr. and Yoram Wind define **organizational buying** as the decision-making process by which formal organizations establish the need for purchased products and services and identify, evaluate, and choose among alternative brands and suppliers.[43] The business market differs from the consumer market in a number of ways.

The Business Market versus the Consumer Market

The **business market** consists of all the organizations that acquire goods and services used in the production of other products or services that are sold, rented, or supplied to others. Some of the major industries making up the business market are aerospace; agriculture, forestry, and fisheries; chemical; computer; construction; defense; energy; mining; manufacturing; construction; transportation; communication; public utilities; banking, finance, and insurance; distribution; and services. Table 5.1 shows 10 unique characteristics of business markets.

TABLE 5.1	Characteristics of Business Markets
Characteristic	**Description**
Fewer, larger buyers	Business marketers normally deal with far fewer, much larger buyers than consumer marketers.
Close supplier-customer relationships	Because of the smaller customer base and the importance and power of larger customers, suppliers are frequently expected to customize offerings to individual customer needs.
Professional purchasing	Trained purchasing agents follow formal purchasing policies, constraints, and requirements. Many of the buying instruments, such as proposals and purchase contracts, are not typically part of consumer buying.
Multiple buying influences	More people influence business buying decisions. Business marketers must send well-trained sales representatives and teams to deal with well-trained buyers and with buying committees.
Multiple sales calls	Because more people are involved, it takes multiple sales calls to win most business orders during a sales cycle often measured in years.
Derived demand	Demand for business goods is ultimately derived from the demand for consumer goods, so business marketers must monitor the buying patterns of end users.
Inelastic demand	Total demand for many business offerings is inelastic—that is, not much affected by price changes, especially in the short run, because producers cannot make quick production changes.
Fluctuating demand	Demand for business offerings tends to be more volatile than demand for consumer offerings. An increase in consumer demand can lead to a much larger increase in demand for plant and equipment necessary to produce the additional output.
Geographically concentrated buyers	More than half of U.S. business buyers are concentrated in seven states: New York, California, Pennsylvania, Illinois, Ohio, New Jersey, and Michigan. The geographical concentration of producers helps to reduce selling costs.
Direct purchasing	Business buyers often buy directly from manufacturers rather than through intermediaries, especially items that are technically complex or expensive.

As an example of the business market, consider the process of producing and selling a simple pair of shoes.[44] Hide dealers must sell hides to tanners, who sell leather to shoe manufacturers, who in turn sell shoes to wholesalers. Wholesalers sell shoes to retailers, who finally sell them to consumers. Each party in the supply chain also buys other goods and services to support its operations.

Institutional and Government Markets

The overall business market includes institutional and government organizations in addition to profit-seeking companies. The *institutional market* consists of schools, hospitals, and other institutions that provide goods and services to people in their care. Many of these organizations have low budgets and captive clienteles. For example, hospitals must decide what quality of food to buy for patients. The objective is not profit because the food is part of the total service package; nor is cost minimization the sole objective because poor food will draw complaints and hurt the hospital's reputation. The hospital must search for vendors whose quality meets or exceeds a certain minimum standard and whose prices are low.

In most countries, government organizations are major buyers of goods and services. The U.S. government now spends more than $500 billion a year—or roughly 14 percent of the federal budget—on private-sector contractors, making it the largest customer in the world.[45] Government buyers typically require suppliers to submit bids and often award the contract to the low bidder, sometimes making allowance for superior quality or a reputation for on-time performance. Governments will also buy on a negotiated-contract basis, primarily in complex projects with major R&D costs and risks and those where there is little competition.

Business Buying Situations

The business buyer faces many decisions in making a purchase. How many depends on the complexity of the problem being solved, newness of the buying requirement, number of people involved, and time required. Three types of buying situations are the straight rebuy, modified rebuy, and new task.[46]

- **Straight rebuy.** In a *straight rebuy*, the purchasing department reorders items like office supplies and bulk chemicals on a routine basis and chooses from suppliers on an approved list. The suppliers make an effort to maintain quality and often propose automatic reordering systems to save time. "Out-suppliers" attempt to offer something new or exploit dissatisfaction with a current supplier. Their goal is to get a small order and then enlarge their purchase share over time.

- **Modified rebuy.** The buyer in a *modified rebuy* wants to change product specifications, prices, delivery requirements, or other terms. This usually requires additional participants on both sides. The in-suppliers become nervous and want to protect the account. The out-suppliers see an opportunity to propose a better offer to gain some business.

- **New task.** A *new-task* purchaser buys a product or service for the first time (an office building, a new security system). The greater the cost or risk, the larger the number of participants, and the greater their information gathering—the longer the time to a decision.[47]

The business buyer makes the fewest decisions in the straight rebuy situation and the most in the new-task situation. Over time, new-buy situations become straight rebuys and routine purchase behavior. The buying process passes through several stages: awareness, interest, evaluation, trial, and adoption. Mass media can be most important during the awareness stage;

salespeople often have the greatest impact at the interest stage; and technical sources can be most important during evaluation. Online selling efforts may be useful at all stages.

Many business buyers prefer to buy a total problem solution from one seller. Called *systems buying*, this practice originated with government purchases. In response, many sellers have adopted systems selling or a variant, *systems contracting*, in which one supplier provides the buyer with all MRO (maintenance, repair, and operating) supplies. This lowers procurement costs and allows the seller steady demand and reduced paperwork.

Participants in the Business Buying Process

Who buys the trillions of dollars' worth of goods and services needed by business organizations? Purchasing agents are influential in straight-rebuy and modified-rebuy situations, whereas other employees are more influential in new-buy situations. Engineers are usually influential in selecting product components, and purchasing agents dominate in selecting suppliers.[48]

The Buying Center

Webster and Wind call the decision-making unit of a buying organization *the buying center.* It consists of "all those individuals and groups who participate in the purchasing decision-making process, who share some common goals and the risks arising from the decisions."[49] The buying center includes all organizational members who play any of these roles in the purchase decision process.

1. *Initiators*—Users or others in the organization who request that something be purchased.
2. *Users*—Those who will use the product or service. In many cases, the users initiate the buying proposal and help define the product requirements.
3. *Influencers*—People who influence the buying decision, often by helping define specifications and providing information for evaluating alternatives.
4. *Deciders*—People who decide on product requirements or on suppliers.
5. *Approvers*—People who authorize the proposed actions of deciders or buyers.
6. *Buyers*—People who have formal authority to select the supplier and arrange the purchase terms. Buyers may help shape product specifications, but they play their major role in selecting vendors and negotiating. In more complex purchases, buyers might include high-level managers.
7. *Gatekeepers*—People such as purchasing agents and receptionists who have the power to prevent sellers or information from reaching members of the buying center.

Several people can occupy a given role such as user or influencer, and one person may play multiple roles.[50] A purchasing manager, for example, is often buyer, influencer, and gatekeeper simultaneously, deciding which sales reps can call on others in the organization, what budget and other constraints to place on the purchase, and which firm will actually get the business.

Buying Center Influences

Buying centers usually include participants with differing interests, authority, status, susceptibility to persuasion, and sometimes very different decision criteria. Engineers may want to maximize product performance; production people may want ease of use and reliability of supply; financial staff focus on the economics of the purchase; purchasing may be concerned with operating and replacement costs.

Business buyers also have personal motivations, perceptions, and preferences influenced by their age, income, education, job position, personality, attitudes toward risk, and culture. Webster cautions that ultimately individuals, not organizations, make purchasing decisions.[51] Individuals are motivated by their own needs and perceptions in attempting to maximize the organizational rewards they earn. But organizational needs legitimate the buying process and its outcomes.

Targeting Firms and Buying Centers

Successful business-to-business marketing requires that business marketers know which types of companies to focus on in their selling efforts, as well as whom to concentrate on within the buying centers in those organizations. Finding the market segments with the greatest growth prospects, most profitable customers, and most promising opportunities for the firm is crucial. A slow-growing economy has put a stranglehold on large corporations' purchasing, making small and midsize business markets more attractive for suppliers, as discussed in "Marketing Insight: Big Sales to Small Businesses."

marketing insight   Big Sales to Small Businesses

The Small Business Administration (SBA) defines small businesses as those with fewer than 500 employees for most mining and manufacturing industries and $7 million in annual receipts for most nonmanufacturing industries. Small and midsize businesses present huge marketing opportunities and huge challenges. The market is large but fragmented by industry, size, and number of years in operation. Here are some guidelines for marketing to small businesses:

- **Don't lump small and midsize businesses together.** There's a big gap between $1 million in revenue and $50 million or between a start-up with 10 employees and a mature business with 100 employees. IBM distinguishes its offerings to small and medium-sized businesses on its common Web site for the two.
- **Do keep it simple.** Offer one supplier point of contact for all service problems or one bill for all services and products. AT&T serves millions of businesses with fewer than 100 employees with bundles that include Internet, local phone, long-distance phone, data management, business networking, Web hosting, and teleconferencing.

- **Do use the Internet.** Hewlett-Packard found that time-strapped small-business decision makers prefer to buy, or at least research, purchases online. Its site therefore features extensive advertising, direct mail, e-mail campaigns, catalogs, and events.
- **Don't forget about direct contact.** Even if a small business owner's first point of contact is via the Internet, you still need to be available by phone or in person.
- **Do provide support after the sale.** Small businesses want partners, not pitchmen, and expect service and commitment.
- **Do your homework.** The realities of small or midsize business management are different from those of a large corporation, so understand what target customers need and how they prefer to buy.

Sources: Based on Barnaby J. Feder, "When Goliath Comes Knocking on David's Door," *New York Times,* May 6, 2003; Jennifer Gilbert, "Small but Mighty," *Sales & Marketing Management* (January 2004), pp. 30–35; Kate Maddox, "Driving Engagement with Small Business," *Advertising Age*, November 7, 2011; Christine Birkner, "Big Business Think Small," *Marketing News,* May 15, 2012, pp. 12–16; "IBM Luring SMBs with Expanded Finance Options," *Network World*, September 12, 2011; www.sba.gov; www.openforum.com; www-304.ibm.com /businesscenter/smb/us/en, all accessed May 20, 2014.

Business marketers must figure out: Who are the major decision participants? What decisions do they influence? What evaluation criteria do they use? Small sellers concentrate on reaching the key buying influencers. Larger sellers go for multilevel in-depth selling to reach as many participants as possible. Business marketers should periodically review their assumptions about buying center participants. Traditionally, SAP sold its software to CIOs at large companies. Then a shift to focus on selling to individual corporate units lower down the organizational chart raised the percentage of software sales going to new customers to 40 percent.[52]

Stages in the Business Buying Process

The business buying-decision process includes eight stages called *buyphases*, as identified by Patrick J. Robinson and his associates, in the *buygrid* framework (see Table 5.2).[53] In modified-rebuy or straight-rebuy situations, some stages are compressed or bypassed. For example, the buyer normally has a favorite supplier or a ranked list of suppliers and can skip the search and proposal solicitation stages. Here are some important considerations in each of the eight stages.

Problem Recognition

The buying process begins when someone in the company recognizes a problem or need that can be met by acquiring a good or service. The recognition can be triggered by internal or external stimuli. The internal stimulus might be a decision to develop a new product that requires new equipment and materials or a machine that requires new parts. Externally, the buyer may get new ideas at a trade show, see an ad, receive an e-mail, read a blog, or receive a call from a sales representative who offers a better product or a lower price. Business marketers can stimulate problem recognition by direct marketing in many different ways.

TABLE 5.2	Buygrid Framework: Major Stages (Buyphases) of the Industrial Buying Process in Relation to Major Buying Situations (Buyclasses)		
		Buyclasses	
	New Task	Modified Rebuy	Straight Rebuy
Buyphases	1. Problem recognition	Yes	Maybe	No
	2. General need description	Yes	Maybe	No
	3. Product specification	Yes	Yes	Yes
	4. Supplier search	Yes	Maybe	No
	5. Proposal solicitation	Yes	Maybe	No
	6. Supplier selection	Yes	Maybe	No
	7. Order-routine specification	Yes	Maybe	No
	8. Performance review	Yes	Yes	Yes

Source: Adapted from Patrick J. Johnson, Charles W. Farris, and Yoram Wind, *Industrial Buying and Creative Marketing* (Boston: Allyn & Bacon, 1967), p. 14.

General Need Description and Product Specification

Next, the buyer determines the needed item's general characteristics and required quantity. For standard items, this is simple. For complex items, the buyer will work with others to define characteristics such as reliability, durability, or price. Business marketers can help by describing how their products meet or even exceed the buyer's needs.

The buying organization now develops the item's technical specifications. Often, the company will assign a product-value-analysis engineering team to the project. *Product value analysis (PVA)* is an approach to cost reduction that studies whether components can be redesigned, standardized, or made by cheaper methods of production without adversely affecting product performance. The PVA team will identify overdesigned components, for instance, that last longer than the product itself. Suppliers can use PVA as a tool for positioning themselves to win an account.

Supplier Search

The buyer next tries to identify the most appropriate suppliers through trade directories, contacts with other companies, trade advertisements, trade shows, and the Internet. Companies that purchase online are utilizing electronic marketplaces in several forms (see Table 5.3). Web sites are organized around two types of e-hubs: *vertical hubs* centered on industries (plastics, steel, chemicals, paper) and *functional hubs* (logistics, media buying, advertising, energy management).

Moving into e-procurement means more than acquiring software; it requires changing purchasing strategy and structure. However, the benefits are many. Aggregating purchasing across multiple departments yields larger, centrally negotiated volume discounts, a smaller purchasing staff, and less buying of substandard goods from outside the approved list of suppliers.

The supplier's task is to ensure it is considered when customers are—or could be—in the market and searching for a supplier. Marketing must work with sales to define what makes a "sales ready" prospect and send the right messages via sales calls, trade shows, online activities, PR, events, direct mail, and referrals. After evaluating each company, the buyer will end up with a short list of qualified suppliers.

TABLE 5.3 Electronic Marketplaces for Business Buying

- **Catalog sites.** Companies can order thousands of items through electronic catalogs, such as W. W. Grainger's, distributed by e-procurement software.

- **Vertical markets.** Companies buying industrial products such as plastics or services such as media can go to specialized Web sites called e-hubs, including Plastics.com.

- **"Pure Play" auction sites.** Online auctions can serve business buyers and sellers worldwide. Ritchie Bros. operates the multilingual rbauction.com site, enabling businesses in many nations to buy or sell.

- **Spot (or exchange) markets.** On spot electronic markets, prices change by the minute. IntercontinentalExchange (ICE) is an electronic energy marketplace and soft commodity exchange, for example.

- **Private exchanges.** Hewlett-Packard, IBM, and Walmart operate private online exchanges to link with specially invited groups of suppliers and partners.

- **Barter markets.** In barter markets, participants offer to trade goods or services.

- **Buying alliances.** Several companies buying the same goods can join together to form purchasing consortia and gain deeper discounts on volume purchases. TopSource is an alliance of firms in food-related businesses.

Proposal Solicitation

The buyer next invites qualified suppliers to submit written proposals. After evaluating them, the buyer will invite a few suppliers to make formal presentations. Business marketers must be skilled in researching, writing, and presenting proposals as marketing documents that describe value and benefits in customer terms. Oral presentations must inspire confidence and position the company's capabilities and resources so they stand out from the competition.

Supplier Selection

Before selecting a supplier, members of the buying center will specify and rank desired supplier attributes. To develop compelling value propositions, business marketers need to better understand how these business buyers arrive at their valuations.[54] Further, despite moves toward strategic sourcing and partnering, business buyers still spend a lot of time negotiating price. Suppliers can counter requests for lower price in a number of ways. They may be able to show that their product's life-cycle cost is lower than for competitors' products or cite the value of the services the buyer now receives, especially if it is superior to that offered by competitors.[55] Service support and personal interactions, as well as a supplier's know-how and ability to improve customers' time to market, can be useful differentiators in achieving key-supplier status.[56]

Order-Routine Specification

After selecting suppliers, the buyer negotiates the final order, listing the technical specifications, the quantity needed, the delivery time, warranties, and so on. For maintenance, repair, and operating items, buyers are moving toward blanket contracts under which the supplier promises to resupply the buyer as needed, at agreed-upon prices, over a specified period. Because the seller holds the stock, blanket contracts are sometimes called *stockless purchase plans*. These long-term relationships make it difficult for out-suppliers to break in unless the buyer becomes dissatisfied.

Companies that fear a shortage of key materials are willing to buy and hold large inventories. They will sign long-term contracts with suppliers to ensure a steady flow of materials. Some companies go further and shift the ordering responsibility to their suppliers, using systems called *vendor-managed inventory*. These suppliers are privy to the customer's inventory levels and take responsibility for *continuous replenishment programs*.

Performance Review

The business buyer periodically reviews the performance of the chosen supplier(s) using one of three methods. The buyer may contact end users and ask for their evaluations, rate the supplier on several criteria using a weighted-score method, or aggregate the cost of poor performance to come up with adjusted costs of purchase, including price. This performance review may lead the buyer to continue, modify, or end a supplier relationship.

Managing Business-to-Business Customer Relationships

Business suppliers and customers are exploring different ways to manage their relationships.[57] One key aspect of strong customer relationships between businesses is the concept of vertical coordination.

The Benefits of Vertical Coordination

Much research has advocated greater vertical coordination between buying partners and sellers so they can transcend merely transacting and instead create more value for both parties.[58]

Building trust is a prerequisite to enjoying healthy long-term relationships. A number of forces influence the development of a relationship between business partners, including availability of alternatives, importance of supply, complexity of supply, and supply market dynamism. Based on these we can classify buyer–supplier relationships into eight categories:[59]

1. *Basic buying and selling*—Simple, routine exchanges with moderate levels of cooperation and information exchange.

2. *Bare bones*—These relationships require more adaptation by the seller and less cooperation and information exchange.

3. *Contractual transaction*—Defined by contract, these generally have low levels of trust, cooperation, and interaction.

4. *Customer supply*—In this traditional supply situation, competition rather than cooperation is the dominant form of governance.

5. *Cooperative systems*—Participants are united in operational ways, but neither demonstrates structural commitment through legal means or adaptation.

6. *Collaborative*—Much trust and commitment through collaboration can lead to true partnership.

7. *Mutually adaptive*—Buyers and sellers make many relationship-specific adaptations, but without necessarily achieving strong trust or cooperation.

8. *Customer is king*—In this close, cooperative relationship, the seller adapts to meet the customer's needs without expecting much adaptation or change in exchange.

Risks and Opportunism in Business Relationships

Establishing a customer–supplier relationship creates tension between safeguarding (ensuring predictable solutions) and adapting (allowing for flexibility for unanticipated events). Vertical coordination can facilitate stronger customer–seller ties but may also increase the risk to the customer's and supplier's specific investments.[60] *Specific investments* are expenditures tailored to a particular company and value chain partner (investments in company-specific training, equipment, and operating procedures or systems).[61] They help firms grow profits and achieve their positioning.[62]

When buyers cannot easily monitor supplier performance, the supplier might not deliver the expected value. *Opportunism* is "some form of cheating or undersupply relative to an implicit or explicit contract."[63] It may entail self-serving violation of contractual agreements or an unwillingness to adapt to changing circumstances in satisfying contractual obligations. Opportunism is a concern because firms must devote resources to control and monitoring that would otherwise be allocated to more productive purposes. Contracts may become inadequate to govern supplier transactions when supplier opportunism becomes difficult to detect, when firms make specific investments in assets they cannot use elsewhere, and when contingencies are harder to anticipate. When a supplier has a good reputation, it is more likely to avoid opportunism to protect this valuable intangible asset.

Executive Summary

Consumer behavior is influenced by cultural, social, and personal factors and by four psychological processes: motivation, perception, learning, and memory. The typical consumer buying process follows this sequence: problem recognition, information search, evaluation of alternatives, purchase decision, and postpurchase behavior. The attitudes of others, unanticipated situational factors, and perceived risk may all affect the decision to buy, as will consumers' postpurchase product satisfaction, use and disposal, and the company's actions. Behavioral decision theory helps marketers understand situations in which consumers make seemingly irrational choices.

Organizational buying is the process by which formal organizations establish a need for purchased goods and services, then identify, evaluate, and choose among alternative brands and suppliers. The business market consists of all the organizations that acquire goods and services used in the production of goods or services that are sold, rented, or supplied to others. The institutional market includes schools and other institutions that provide goods and services to people in their care. Governments are also major buyers of goods and services.

Compared to consumer markets, business markets have fewer and larger buyers, closer relationships with suppliers, and more geographically concentrated buyers. Demand in the business market is derived from demand in the consumer market and fluctuates with the business cycle. Three types of buying situations are the straight rebuy, modified rebuy, and new task. The buying center consists of initiators, users, influencers, deciders, approvers, buyers, and gatekeepers. The business buying process consists of eight buyphases: (1) problem recognition, (2) general need description, (3) product specification, (4) supplier search, (5) proposal solicitation, (6) supplier selection, (7) order-routine specification, and (8) performance review. Business marketers seek to form strong relationships with their customers, considering the benefits of vertical coordination and the challenges of opportunism.

Notes

1. Quentin Hardy, "Chambers Challenged," *Forbes*, March 14, 2011, pp. 30–32; Rich Karlgaard, "Cisco's Disruptive (and Cooler) Rival," *Forbes*, July 18, 2011, p. 21; Rich Karlgaard, "Driving Change: Cisco's Chambers," *Forbes*, February 13, 2012; "Charlie Rose Talks to Cisco's John Chambers," *Bloomberg Businessweek*, April 23, 2012, p. 41; Don Clark, "Cisco Makes Like Apple in Push for App Developers," *Wall Street Journal blogs*, July 21, 2014.

2. Michael R. Solomon, *Consumer Behavior: Buying, Having, and Being*, 10th ed. (Upper Saddle River, NJ: Prentice Hall, 2013).

3. Leon G. Schiffman and Leslie Lazar Kanuk, *Consumer Behavior*, 10th ed. (Upper Saddle River, NJ: Prentice Hall, 2010).

4. For some classic perspectives, see Richard P. Coleman, "The Continuing Significance of Social Class to Marketing," *Journal of Consumer Research* 10 (December 1983), pp. 265–80; Richard P. Coleman and Lee P. Rainwater, *Social Standing in America: New Dimension of Class* (New York: Basic Books, 1978).

5. Leon G. Schiffman and Leslie Lazar Kanuk, *Consumer Behavior*, 10th ed. (Upper Saddle River, NJ: Prentice Hall, 2010).

6. Michael Trusov, Anand Bodapati, and Randolph E. Bucklin, "Determining Influential Users in Internet Social Networks," *Journal of Marketing Research* 47 (August 2010), pp. 643–58.

7. Jacqueline Johnson Brown, Peter M. Reingen, and Everett M. Rogers, *Diffusion of Innovations*, 4th ed. (New York: Free Press, 1995); Peter H. Riengen and Jerome B. Kernan, "Analysis of Referral Networks in Marketing: Methods and Illustration," *Journal of Marketing Research* 23 (November 1986), pp. 37–78; Laura J. Kornish and Qiuping Li, "Optimal Referral Bonuses with Asymmetric Information: Firm-Offered and Interpersonal Incentives," *Marketing Science* 29 (January–February 2010), pp. 108–21.

8. Douglas Atkin, *The Culting of Brands: When Customers Become True Believers* (New York: Penguin, 2004); Marian Salzman, Ira Matathia, and Ann O'Reilly, *Buzz: Harness the Power of Influence and Create Demand* (New York: Wiley, 2003).

9. Natasha Singer, "Secret E-Scores Chart Consumers' Buying Power," *New York Times*, August 18, 2012; Erin Griffin, "A Million Little Klouts," *Adweek*, December 12, 2011, p. 18; Jon Swartz, "Klout Says Scoring Parameters Enhanced," *USA Today*, August 15, 2012.

10. Elizabeth S. Moore, William L. Wilkie, and Richard J. Lutz, "Passing the Torch: Intergenerational Influences as a Source of Brand Equity," *Journal of Marketing* 66 (April 2002), pp. 17–37.

11. Kay M. Palan and Robert E. Wilkes, "Adolescent-Parent Interaction in Family Decision Making," *Journal of Consumer Research* 24 (March 1997), pp. 159–69; Sharon E. Beatty and Salil Talpade, "Adolescent

Influence in Family Decision Making: A Replication with Extension," *Journal of Consumer Research* 21 (September 1994), pp. 332–41.

12. Scott I. Rick, Deborah A. Small, and Eli J. Finkel, "Fatal (Fiscal) Attraction: Spendthrifts and Tightwads in Marriage," *Journal of Marketing Research* 48 (April 2011), pp. 228–37.

13. "YouthPulse: The Definitive Study of Today's Youth Generation," *Harris Interactive*, www.harrisinteractive.com, January 29, 2010.

14. Deborah Roedder John, "Consumer Socialization of Children," *Journal of Consumer Research* 26 (December 1999), pp. 183–213; Lan Nguyen Chaplin and Deborah Roedder John, "The Development of Self-Brand Connections in Children and Adolescents," *Journal of Consumer Research* 32 (June 2005), pp. 119–29; Lan Nguyen Chaplin and Deborah Roedder John, "Growing Up in a Material World: Age Differences in Materialism in Children and Adolescents," *Journal of Consumer Research* 34 (December 2007), pp. 480–93; Lan Nguyen Chaplin and Tina M. Lowrey, "The Development of Consumer-Based Consumption Constellations in Children," *Journal of Consumer Research* 36 (February 2010), pp. 757–77.

15. Rex Y. Du and Wagner A. Kamakura, "Household Life Cycles and Lifestyles in the United States," *Journal of Marketing Research* 48 (February 2006), pp. 121–32.

16. Harold H. Kassarjian and Mary Jane Sheffet, "Personality and Consumer Behavior: An Update," Harold H. Kassarjian and Thomas S. Robertson, eds., *Perspectives in Consumer Behavior* (Glenview, IL: Scott Foresman, 1981), pp. 160–80.

17. Jennifer Aaker, "Dimensions of Measuring Brand Personality," *Journal of Marketing Research* 34 (August 1997), pp. 347–56.

18. See Jennifer L. Aaker, Veronica Benet-Martinez, and Jordi Garolera, "Consumption Symbols as Carriers of Culture: A Study of Japanese and Spanish Brand Personality Constructs," *Journal of Personality and Social Psychology* 81 (March 2001), pp. 492–508; and Yongjun Sung and Spencer F. Tinkham, "Brand Personality Structures in the United States and Korea," *Journal of Consumer Psychology* 15 (December 2005), pp. 334–50.

19. Lucia Malär, Harley Krohmer, Wayne D. Hoyer, and Bettina Nyffenegger, "Emotional Brand Attachment and Brand Personality," *Journal of Marketing* 75 (July 2011), pp. 35–52.

20. Timothy R. Graeff, "Image Congruence Effects on Product Evaluations," *Psychology & Marketing* 13 (August 1996), pp. 481–99.

21. Jennifer L. Aaker, "The Malleable Self: The Role of Self-Expression in Persuasion," *Journal of Marketing Research* 36 (February 1999), pp. 45–57.

22. Anne D'Innocenzio, "Frugal Times: Hamburger Helper, Kool-Aid in Advertising Limelight," *Associated Press, Seattle Times*, April 29, 2009; Julie Jargon, "Velveeta Shows Its Sizzle against Hamburger Helper," *Wall Street Journal*, December 29, 2011.

23. Thomas J. Reynolds and Jerry C. Olson, *Understanding Consumer Decision-Making* (Mahwah, NJ: Lawrence Erlbaum, 2001); Brian Wansink, "Using Laddering to Understand and Leverage a Brand's Equity," *Qualitative Market Research* 6 (2003).

24. Clotaire Rapaille, "Marketing to the Reptilian Brain," *Forbes*, July 3, 2006; Clotaire Rapaille, *The Culture Code* (New York: Broadway Books, 2007); Douglas Gantebein, "How Boeing Put the Dream in Dreamliner," *Air and Space*, September 2007; Tom Otley, "The Boeing Dreamliner: A Sneak Preview," *Business Traveller*, June 3, 2009.

25. Abraham Maslow, *Motivation and Personality* (New York: Harper & Row, 1954), pp. 80–106. For an interesting business application, see Chip Conley, *Peak: How Great Companies Get Their Mojo from Maslow* (San Francisco: Jossey Bass 2007).

26. See Frederick Herzberg, *Work and the Nature of Man* (Cleveland: William Collins, 1966); Thierry and Koopman-Iwema, "Motivation and Satisfaction," P. J. D. Drenth, H. Thierry, P. J. Willems, and C. J. de Wolff, eds., *A Handbook of Work and Organizational Psychology* (East Sussex, UK: Psychology Press, 1984), pp. 141–42.

27. Bernard Berelson and Gary A. Steiner, *Human Behavior: An Inventory of Scientific Findings* (New York: Harcourt Brace Jovanovich, 1964), p. 88.

28. Aradhna Krishna, "An Integrative Review of Sensory Marketing: Engaging the Senses to Affect Perception, Judgment and Behavior," *Journal of Consumer Psychology* 22 (July 2012), pp. 332–51.

29. Ed Keller, "Showing Emotion Is the New Black," www.mediabizbloggers.com, October 6, 2011; Jonah Berger and Katherine L. Milkman, "What Makes Online Content Viral?," *Journal of Marketing Research* 49 (April 2012), pp. 192–205.

30. Leonard M. Lodish, Magid Abraham, Stuart Kalmenson, Jeanne Livelsberger, Beth Lubetkin, Bruce Richardson, and Mary Ellen Stevens, "How T.V. Advertising Works: A Meta-Analysis of 389 Real World Split Cable T.V. Advertising Experiments," *Journal of Marketing Research* 32 (May 1995), pp. 125–39.

31. Malcolm Faulds, "Five Tips for Driving Word-of-Mouth—No Matter What Your Product Is," *Advertising*

Age, November 28, 2011, p. 17; Jonah Berger and Eric M. Schwartz, "What Drives Immediate and Ongoing Word of Mouth?," *Journal of Marketing Research* 48 (October 2011), pp. 869–80.

32. For a recent academic examination, see Gerald Häubl, Benedict G. C. Dellaert, and Bas Donkers, "Tunnel Vision: Local Behavioral Influences on Consumer Decisions in Product Search," *Marketing Science* 29 (May–June 2012), pp. 438–55.

33. Janet Schwartz, Mary Frances Luce, and Dan Ariely, "Are Consumers Too Trusting? The Effects of Relationships with Expert Advisers," *Journal of Marketing Research* 48 (Special Issue 2011), pp. S163–S174.

34. Min Ding, John R. Hauser, Songting Dong, Daria Dzyabura, Zhilin Yang, Chenting Su, and Steven Gaskin, "Unstructured Direct Elicitation of Decision Rules," *Journal of Marketing Research* 48 (February 2011), pp. 116–27; Michaela Draganska and Daniel Klapper, "Choice Set Heterogeneity and the Role of Advertising," *Journal of Marketing Research* 48 (August 2011), pp. 653–69; John R. Hauser, Olivier Toubia, Theodoros Evgeniou, Rene Befurt, and Daria Dzyabura, "Disjunctions of Conjunctions, Cognitive Simplicity and Consideration Sets," *Journal of Marketing Research* 47 (June 2010), pp. 485–96; Erjen Van Nierop, Bart Bronnenberg, Richard Paap, Michel Wedel, and Philip Hans Franses, "Retrieving Unobserved Consideration Sets from Household Panel Data," *Journal of Marketing Research* 47 (February 2010), pp. 63–74. For some behavioral perspectives, see Jeffrey R. Parker and Rom Y. Schrift, "Rejectable Choice Sets: How Seemingly Irrelevant No-Choice Options Affect Consumer Decision Processes," *Journal of Marketing Research* 48 (October 2011), pp. 840–54.

35. Benedict G. C. Dellaert and Gerald Häubl, "Searching in Choice Mode: Consumer Decision Processes in Product Search with Recommendations," *Journal of Marketing Research* 49 (April 2012), pp. 277–88. See also Jun B. Kim, Paulo Albuquerque, and Bart J. Bronnenberg, "Mapping Online Consumer Search," *Journal of Marketing Research* 48 (February 2011), pp. 13–27.

36. Paul E. Green and Yoram Wind, *Multiattribute Decisions in Marketing: A Measurement Approach* (Hinsdale, IL: Dryden, 1973), chapter 2; Richard J. Lutz, "The Role of Attitude Theory in Marketing," H. Kassarjian and T. Robertson, eds., *Perspectives in Consumer Behavior* (Lebanon, IN: Scott Foresman, 1981), pp. 317–39.

37. Michael R. Solomon, *Consumer Behavior: Buying, Having, and Being,* 10th ed. (Upper Saddle River, NJ: Prentice Hall, 2013).

38. Martin Fishbein, "Attitudes and Prediction of Behavior," M. Fishbein, ed., *Readings in Attitude Theory and Measurement* (New York: John Wiley & Sons, 1967), pp. 477–92.

39. Margaret C. Campbell and Ronald C. Goodstein, "The Moderating Effect of Perceived Risk on Consumers' Evaluations of Product Incongruity: Preference for the Norm," *Journal of Consumer Research* 28 (December 2001), pp. 439–49; Grahame R. Dowling, "Perceived Risk," Peter E. Earl and Simon Kemp, eds., *The Elgar Companion to Consumer Research and Economic Psychology* (Cheltenham, UK: Edward Elgar, 1999), pp. 419–24; James R. Bettman, "Perceived Risk and Its Components: A Model and Empirical Test," *Journal of Marketing Research* 10 (May 1973).

40. Albert O. Hirschman, *Exit, Voice, and Loyalty* (Cambridge, MA: Harvard University Press, 1970).

41. Leon Schiffman and Leslie Kanuk, *Consumer Behavior,* 10th ed. (Upper Saddle River, NJ: Prentice Hall, 2010); Wayne D. Hoyer, Deborah J. MacInnis, and Rik Pieters, *Consumer Behavior,* 6th ed. (Mason, OH: South-Western College Publishing, 2013).

42. See Richard H. Thaler, "Mental Accounting and Consumer Choice," *Marketing Science* 4 (Summer 1985), pp. 199–214 for a seminal piece; and Richard Thaler, "Mental Accounting Matters," *Journal of Behavioral Decision Making* 12 (September 1999), pp. 183–206 for additional perspectives. For some diverse applications of the theory, see Robin L. Soster, Ashwani Monga, and William O. Bearden, "Tracking Costs of Time and Money: How Accounting Periods Affect Mental Accounting," *Journal of Consumer Research* 37 (December 2010), pp. 712–21; Jonathan Levav and A. Peter McGraw, "Emotional Accounting: How Feelings about Money Influence Consumer Choice," *Journal of Marketing Research* 46 (February 2009), pp. 66–80; John Godek and Kyle B. Murray, "The Effect of Spikes in the Price of Gasoline on Behavioral Intentions: A Mental Accounting Explanation," *Journal of Behavioral Decision Making* 25 (July 2012), pp. 295–302.

43. Frederick E. Webster Jr. and Yoram Wind, *Organizational Buying Behavior* (Upper Saddle River, NJ: Prentice Hall, 1972), p. 2; for a review of some academic literature on the topic, see Håkan Håkansson and Ivan Snehota, "Marketing in Business Markets," Bart Weitz and Robin Wensley, eds., *Handbook of Marketing* (London: Sage Publications, 2002), pp. 513–26; Mark Glynn and Arch Woodside, eds., *Business-to-Business Brand Management: Theory, Research, and Executive Case Study Exercises in Advances in Business Marketing & Purchasing* series, volume 15 (Bingley, UK: Emerald Group Publishing, 2009).

44. Shoe Material, www.bata.com, accessed May 20, 2014. See also www.shoeguide.org/Shoe_Anatomy, accessed May 20, 2014.

45. Jeanne Sahedi, "Cutting Washington Could Hit Main Street," www.money.cnn.com, July 23, 2012.

46. Patrick J. Robinson, Charles W. Faris, and Yoram Wind, *Industrial Buying and Creative Marketing* (Boston: Allyn & Bacon, 1967).

47. Michele D. Bunn, "Taxonomy of Buying Decision Approaches," *Journal of Marketing* 57 (January 1993), pp. 38–56.

48. Jeffrey E. Lewin and Naveen Donthu, "The Influence of Purchase Situation on Buying Center Structure and Involvement," *Journal of Business Research* 58 (October 2005), pp. 1381–90; R. Venkatesh and Ajay K. Kohli, "Influence Strategies in Buying Centers," *Journal of Marketing* 59 (October 1995), pp. 71–82.

49. Frederic E. Webster and Yoram Wind, *Organizational Buying Behavior* (Upper Saddle River, NJ: Prentice Hall, 1972), p. 6.

50. James C. Anderson and James A. Narus, *Business Market Management: Understanding, Creating, and Delivering Value,* 3rd ed. (Upper Saddle River, NJ: Prentice Hall, 2009); Frederick E. Webster Jr. and Yoram Wind, "A General Model for Understanding Organizational Buying Behavior," *Journal of Marketing* 36 (April 1972), pp. 12–19.

51. Frederick E. Webster Jr. and Kevin Lane Keller, "A Roadmap for Branding in Industrial Markets," *Journal of Brand Management* 11 (May 2004), pp. 388–402.

52. Victoria Barret, "SAP Gets a Pit Bull," *Forbes*, February 13, 2012, pp. 38–40.

53. Patrick J. Robinson, Charles W. Faris, and Yoram Wind, *Industrial Buying and Creative Marketing* (Boston, MA: Allyn & Bacon, 1967).

54. Daniel J. Flint, Robert B. Woodruff, and Sarah Fisher Gardial, "Exploring the Phenomenon of Customers' Desired Value Change in a Business-to-Business Context," *Journal of Marketing* 66 (October 2002), pp. 102–17.

55. Wolfgang Ulaga and Werner Reinartz, "Hybrid Offerings: How Manufacturing Firms Combine Goods and Services Successfully," *Journal of Marketing* 75 (November 2011), pp. 5–23.

56. Wolfgang Ulaga and Andreas Eggert, "Value-Based Differentiation in Business Relationships: Gaining and Sustaining Key Supplier Status," *Journal of Marketing* 70 (January 2006), pp. 119–36.

57. For foundational material, see Lloyd M. Rinehart, James A. Eckert, Robert B. Handfield, Thomas J. Page Jr., and Thomas Atkin, "An Assessment of Buyer–Seller Relationships," *Journal of Business Logistics* 25 (2004), pp. 25–62; F. Robert Dwyer, Paul Schurr, and Sejo Oh, "Developing Buyer–Supplier Relationships," *Journal of Marketing* 51 (April 1987), pp. 11–28. For an important caveat, see Christopher P. Blocker, Mark B. Houston, and Daniel J. Flint, "Unpacking What a 'Relationship' Means to Commercial Buyers," *Journal of Consumer Research* 38 (February 2012), pp. 886–908.

58. Das Narayandas and V. Kasturi Rangan, "Building and Sustaining Buyer–Seller Relationships in Mature Industrial Markets," *Journal of Marketing* 68 (July 2004), pp. 63–77.

59. Joseph P. Cannon and William D. Perreault Jr., "Buyer–Seller Relationships in Business Markets," *Journal of Marketing Research* 36 (November 1999), pp. 439–60.

60. Corine S. Noordhoff, Kyriakos Kyriakopoulos, Christine Moorman, Pieter Pauwels, and Benedict G. C. Dellaert, "The Bright Side and Dark Side of Embedded Ties in Business-to- Business Innovation," *Journal of Marketing* 75 (September 2011), pp. 34–52.

61. Akesel I. Rokkan, Jan B. Heide, and Kenneth H. Wathne, "Specific Investment in Marketing Relationships: Expropriation and Bonding Effects," *Journal of Marketing Research* 40 (May 2003), pp. 210–24.

62. Kenneth H. Wathne and Jan B. Heide, "Relationship Governance in a Supply Chain Network," *Journal of Marketing* 68 (January 2004), pp. 73–89; Douglas Bowman and Das Narayandas, "Linking Customer Management Effort to Customer Profitability in Business Markets," *Journal of Marketing Research* 61 (November 2004), pp. 433–47; Mrinal Ghosh and George John, "Governance Value Analysis and Marketing Strategy," *Journal of Marketing* 63 (Special Issue, 1999), pp. 131–45.

63. Kenneth H. Wathne and Jan B. Heide, "Opportunism in Interfirm Relationships: Forms, Outcomes, and Solutions," *Journal of Marketing* 64 (October 2000), pp. 36–51.

Chapter 6

Identifying Market Segments and Targets

In this chapter, we will address the following questions:

1. In what ways can a company divide a consumer or business market into segments? (Page 93)
2. How should a company choose the most attractive target markets? (Page 100)
3. What are the different levels of market segmentation? (Page 101)

Marketing Management at LinkedIn

LinkedIn began operations in 2003, targeting a different audience than most other social networks, with a vision "...to create economic opportunity for every professional in the world." Also separating LinkedIn from other social networks is the fact that it has diverse revenue streams, driven by three customer segments: job seekers who buy premium subscriptions for access to special services; advertisers who rely on its marketing solutions unit; and corporate recruiters who buy special search tools from its talent solutions unit. Today, LinkedIn has more than 300 million users worldwide—including 5 million in China, one of its newer markets—and sees much growth from its mobile users, who in 2013 accounted for more than 30 percent of unique visits to the site. Now LinkedIn's well-targeted and positioned brand faces competition from other online giants, such as Facebook, and from established professional network services overseas, such as Viadeo SA in Europe and elsewhere.[1]

To compete more effectively, many companies are now embracing target marketing. Effective target marketing requires that marketers (1) identify and profile distinct groups of buyers who differ in their needs and wants (market segmentation), (2) select one or more market segments to enter (market targeting), and (3) establish, communicate, and deliver the right benefit(s) to each target segment (market positioning). This chapter focuses on the first two steps; Chapter 7 discusses the third step.

Bases for Segmenting Consumer Markets

Market segmentation divides a market into well-defined slices. A *market segment* consists of a group of customers who share a similar set of needs and wants. The marketer's task is to identify the appropriate number and nature of market segments and decide which one(s) to target.

We use two broad groups of variables to segment consumer markets. Some researchers define segments by looking at descriptive characteristics—geographic, demographic, and psychographic—and asking whether these segments exhibit different needs or product responses. Other researchers define segments by looking at behavioral considerations, such as consumer responses to benefits, usage occasions, or brands, then seeing whether different characteristics are associated with each consumer-response segment.

Regardless of which type of segmentation scheme we use, the key is adjusting the marketing program to recognize customer differences. The major segmentation variables—geographic, demographic, psychographic, and behavioral segmentation—are summarized in Table 6.1.

Geographic Segmentation

Geographic segmentation divides the market into geographical units such as nations, states, regions, counties, cities, or neighborhoods. The company can operate in one or a few areas, or it can operate in all but pay attention to local variations. In that way it can tailor marketing programs to the needs and wants of local customer groups in trading areas, neighborhoods, even individual stores. In a growing trend called *grassroots marketing,* marketers concentrate on making such activities as personally relevant to individual customers as possible.

More and more, regional marketing means marketing right down to a specific zip code. Some approaches combine geographic data with demographic data to yield even richer descriptions of consumers and neighborhoods. Nielsen Claritas has developed a geoclustering approach called PRIZM (Potential Rating Index by Zip Markets) NE that classifies more than half a million U.S. residential neighborhoods into 14 distinct groups and 66 distinct lifestyle segments called PRIZM Clusters.[2] The groupings take into consideration 39 factors in five broad categories: (1) education and affluence, (2) family life cycle, (3) urbanization, (4) race and ethnicity, and (5) mobility. The clusters have descriptive titles such as *Blue Blood Estates, Winner's Circle, Hometown Retired,* and *Back Country Folks.* The inhabitants in a cluster tend to lead similar lives, drive similar cars, have similar jobs, and read similar magazines.

Marketing to microsegments has become possible even for small organizations as database costs decline, software becomes easier to use, and data integration increases. Those who favor such localized marketing see national advertising as wasteful because it is too "arm's length" and fails to address local needs. Those opposed argue that it drives up costs by reducing economies of scale and magnifying logistical problems. A brand's overall image might be diluted if the product and message are too different in different localities.

Demographic Segmentation

One reason demographic variables such as age, family size, family life cycle, gender, income, occupation, education, religion, race, generation, nationality, and social class are so popular with marketers is that they're often associated with consumer needs and wants. Another is that they're easy to measure. Even when we describe the target market in nondemographic terms (say, by personality type), we may need the link back to demographic characteristics in order to estimate the size of the market and the media we should use to reach it efficiently.

Here's how marketers have used certain demographic variables to segment markets.

TABLE 6.1	Major Segmentation Variables for Consumer Markets
Geographic region	Pacific Mountain, West North Central, West South Central, East North Central, East South Central, South Atlantic, Middle Atlantic, New England
City or metro size	Under 5,000; 5,000–20,000; 20,000–50,000; 50,000–100,000; 100,000–250,000; 250,000–500,000; 500,000–1,000,000; 1,000,000–4,000,000; 4,000,000+
Density	Urban, suburban, rural
Climate	Northern, southern
Demographic age	Under 6, 6–11, 12–17, 18–34, 35–49, 50–64, 65+
Family size	1–2, 3–4, 5+
Family life cycle	Young, single; young, married, no children; young, married, youngest child under 6; young; married, youngest child 6 or older; older, married, with children; older, married, no children under 18; older, single; other
Gender	Male, female
Income	Under $10,000; $10,000–$15,000; $15,000–$20,000; $20,000–$30,000; $30,000–$50,000; $50,000–$100,000; $100,000+
Occupation	Professional and technical; managers, officials, and proprietors; clerical sales; craftspeople; forepersons; operatives; farmers; retired; students; homemakers; unemployed
Education	Grade school or less; some high school; high school graduate; some college; college graduate; post college
Religion	Catholic, Protestant, Jewish, Muslim, Hindu, other
Race	White, Black, Asian, Hispanic, Other
Generation	Silent Generation, Baby Boomers, Gen X, Millennials (Gen Y)
Nationality	North American, Latin American, British, French, German, Italian, Chinese, Indian, Japanese
Social class	Lower lowers, upper lowers, working class, middle class, upper middles, lower uppers, upper uppers
Psychographic lifestyle	Culture-oriented, sports-oriented, outdoor-oriented
Personality	Compulsive, gregarious, authoritarian, ambitious
Behavioral occasions	Regular occasion, special occasion
Benefits	Quality, service, economy, speed
User status	Nonuser, ex-user, potential user, first-time user, regular user
Usage rate	Light user, medium user, heavy user
Loyalty status	None, medium, strong, absolute
Readiness stage	Unaware, aware, informed, interested, desirous, intending to buy
Attitude toward product	Enthusiastic, positive, indifferent, negative, hostile

Age and Life-Cycle Stage   Consumer wants and abilities change with age. Toothpaste brands such as Crest offer three main lines of products to target kids, adults, and older consumers. Age segmentation can be even more refined. Pampers divides its market into prenatal, new baby (0–5 months), baby (6–12 months), toddler (13–23 months), and preschooler (24 months+). However, age and life cycle can be tricky variables. The target market for some products may be the *psychologically* young.

Life Stage   People in the same part of the life cycle may still differ in their life stage. **Life stage** defines a person's major concern, such as going through a divorce, going into a second marriage, taking care of an older parent, buying a home, and so on. These life stages present opportunities for marketers who can help people cope with the accompanying decisions. But not everyone goes through that life stage at a certain time—or at all, for that matter. More than a quarter of all U.S. households now consist of only one person—a record high. It's no surprise this $1.9 trillion market is attracting interest from marketers such as Lowe's and DeBeers.

Gender Men and women have different attitudes and behave differently, based partly on genetic makeup and partly on socialization.[3] A research study of shopping found that men often need to be invited to touch a product, whereas women are likely to pick it up without prompting. Men often like to read product information; women may relate to a product on a more personal level. Gender differences are shrinking in some areas as men and women expand their roles. One survey found that more than half of men identified themselves as the primary grocery shoppers in their households, which is why Procter & Gamble now designs some ads with men in mind.

Income Income segmentation is a long-standing practice in such categories as automobiles, clothing, cosmetics, financial services, and travel. However, income does not always predict the best customers for a given product. Many marketers are deliberately going after lower-income groups, in some cases discovering fewer competitive pressures or greater consumer loyalty. Increasingly, companies are finding their markets are hourglass shaped, as middle-market U.S. consumers migrate toward both discount *and* premium products. Recognizing that its channel strategy emphasized retailers selling primarily to the middle class, Levi-Strauss introduced premium lines such as Levi's Made & Crafted to upscale retailers and the less-expensive Signature line to mass market retailers.

Generation Each generation or *cohort* is profoundly influenced by the times in which it grows up—the music, movies, politics, and defining events of that period. The four main U.S. generation cohorts, from youngest to oldest, are Millennials (Gen Y), Gen X, Baby Boomers, and the Silent Generation.[4] Members of each cohort share the same major cultural, political, and economic experiences and often have similar outlooks and values. Marketers may choose to advertise to a cohort by using the icons and images prominent in its experiences. They can also try to develop products and services that uniquely meet the particular interests or needs of a generational target.

- **Millennials (or Gen Y).** Born from 1977 through 1994, the 78 million Millennials are also known as Gen Y or Echo Boomers. Members of this cohort have been wired almost from birth. They may have a sense of entitlement and abundance from growing up during the economic boom, but they are also often socially conscious and concerned about the environment. This cohort may be turned off by overt marketing practices.
- **Generation X.** Born from 1964 through 1978, the 50 million Gen Xers were raised during a period when social diversity and racial diversity were more widely accepted and technology changed the way people lived and worked. This cohort has raised standards in educational achievement, but its members were also the first generation to find surpassing their parents' standard of living a serious challenge. They are pragmatic and individualist, prize self-sufficiency, and view technology as an enabler, not a barrier.
- **Baby Boomers.** Born from 1946 through 1964, the 76 million members of this cohort are interested in products that turn back the hands of time. One study of boomers ages 55 to 64 found a significant number are willing to change brands, spend on technology, use social networking sites, and purchase online.[5]

- **Silent Generation.** Born from 1925 through 1945, the 42 million members of this cohort are defying their advancing age and leading very active lives. Strategies emphasizing seniors' roles as grandparents are well received. They are demanding customers but are also more willing than younger cohorts to pay full price for offerings they value.

Race and Culture   *Multicultural marketing* is an approach recognizing that different ethnic and cultural segments have sufficiently different needs and wants to require targeted marketing activities and that a mass market approach is not refined enough for the diversity of the marketplace. Consider that McDonald's now does 40 percent of its U.S. business with ethnic minorities. Its highly successful "I'm Lovin' It" campaign was rooted in hip-hop culture, but its appeal transcended race and ethnicity.[6] Marketers need to factor the norms, language nuances, buying habits, and business practices of multicultural markets into the initial formulation of their marketing strategy. Diversity also has implications for planning and conducting marketing research.

Psychographic Segmentation

Psychographics is the science of using psychology and demographics to better understand consumers. In *psychographic segmentation,* buyers are divided into groups on the basis of psychological/personality traits, lifestyle, or values. People within the same demographic group can exhibit very different psychographic profiles.

One of the most popular commercially available classification systems based on psychographic measurements is Strategic Business Insight's (SBI) VALS™ framework. VALS is based on psychological traits for people and classifies U.S. adults into eight primary groups based on responses to a questionnaire featuring four demographic and 35 attitudinal questions. The VALS system is continually updated with new data from more than 80,000 surveys per year (see Figure 6.1).[7]

The main dimensions of the VALS segmentation framework are consumer motivation (the horizontal dimension) and consumer resources (the vertical dimension). Consumers are inspired by one of three primary motivations: ideals, achievement, and self-expression. Different levels of resources enhance or constrain a person's expression of his or her primary motivation.

Behavioral Segmentation

In *behavioral segmentation,* marketers divide buyers into groups on the basis of their knowledge of, attitude toward, use of, or response to a product. Behavior variables can include needs or benefits, decision roles, and user and usage.

Needs and Benefits   Not everyone who buys a product has the same needs or wants the same benefits from it. Needs-based or benefit-based segmentation identifies distinct market segments with clear marketing implications.

Decision Roles   People can play five roles in a buying decision: *Initiator, Influencer, Decider, Buyer,* and *User.* For example, assume a wife initiates a purchase by requesting a new treadmill for her birthday. The husband may seek information from many sources, including a friend who has a treadmill and is a key influencer in what models to consider. After presenting the alternative choices to his wife, he purchases her preferred model, which ends up being used by the entire family. Different people are playing different roles, but all are crucial in the decision process and ultimate consumer satisfaction.

FIGURE 6.1 The VALS Segmentation System: An Eight-Part Typology

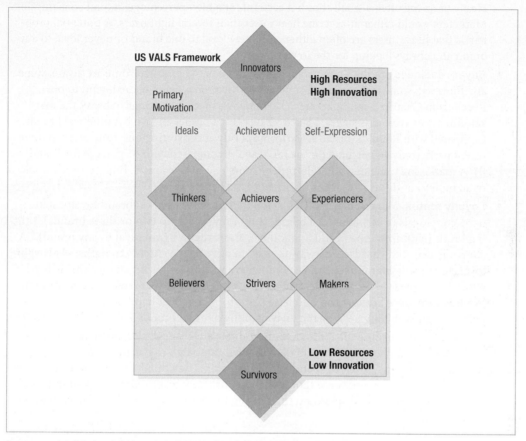

User and Usage-Related Variables   Many marketers believe variables related to users or their usage—occasions, user status, usage rate, buyer-readiness stage, and loyalty status—are good starting points for constructing market segments.

- **Occasions.** Occasions mark a time of day, week, month, year, or other well-defined temporal aspects of a consumer's life. We can distinguish buyers according to the occasions when they develop a need, purchase a product, or use a product. For example, air travel is triggered by occasions related to business, vacation, or family. Occasion segmentation can help expand product usage.

- **User status.** Every product has its nonusers, ex-users, potential users, first-time users, and regular users. The key to attracting potential users, or even possibly nonusers, is understanding the reasons they are not using. Do they have deeply held attitudes, beliefs, or behaviors or just lack knowledge of the product or benefits? Included in the potential-user group are consumers who will become users in connection with some life stage or event. Market-share leaders tend to focus on attracting potential users because they have the most to gain from them. Smaller firms focus on trying to attract current users away from the market leader.

- **Usage rate.** We can segment markets into light, medium, and heavy product users. Heavy users are often a small slice but account for a high percentage of total consumption. Marketers would rather attract one heavy user than several light users. A potential problem is that heavy users are often either extremely loyal to one brand or never loyal to any brand and always looking for the lowest price.

- **Buyer-readiness stage.** Some people are unaware of the product, some are aware, some are informed, some are interested, some desire the product, and some intend to buy. Recall from Chapter 4 that marketers can employ a *marketing funnel* to break the market into buyer-readiness stages. Figure 6.2 displays a funnel for two hypothetical brands. Compared with Brand B, Brand A performs poorly at converting one-time users to more recent users (only 46 percent convert for Brand A compared with 61 percent for Brand B). A marketing campaign could introduce more relevant products, find more accessible retail outlets, or dispel rumors or incorrect brand beliefs.

- **Loyalty status.** Marketers usually envision four groups based on brand loyalty status: hard-core loyals (always buy one brand), split loyals (loyal to two or three brands), shifting loyals (shift from one brand to another), and switchers (not loyal to any brand).[8] A company can study hard-core loyals to help identify the products' strengths; study split loyals to see which brands are most competitive with its own; and study shifting loyals and switchers to identify marketing weaknesses that can be corrected. One caution: What appear to be brand-loyal purchase patterns may reflect habit, indifference, a low price, a high switching cost, or the unavailability of other brands.

- **Attitude.** Five consumer attitudes about products are enthusiastic, positive, indifferent, negative, and hostile. Workers in a political campaign use attitude to determine how much time and effort to spend with each voter. They thank enthusiastic voters and remind them to vote, reinforce those who are positively disposed, try to win the votes of indifferent voters, and spend no time trying to change the attitudes of negative and hostile voters.

FIGURE 6.2 Example of Marketing Funnel

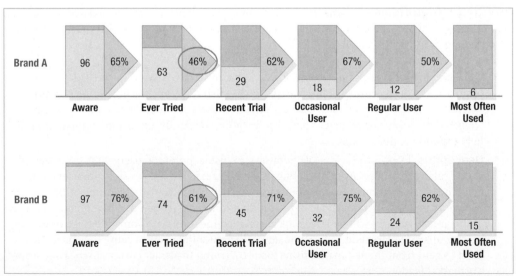

Bases for Segmenting Business Markets

We can segment business markets with some of the same variables we use in consumer markets, such as geography, benefits sought, and usage rate, but business marketers also use other variables (see Table 6.2). The demographic variables are the most important, followed by the operating variables—down to the personal characteristics of the buyer. Within a chosen target industry, a business market can further segment by company size and set up separate operations for selling to large and small customers. A company can segment further by purchase criteria.

Business marketers generally identify segments through a sequential process. Consider an aluminum company: The company first undertook macrosegmentation. It looked at which end-use market to serve: automobile, residential, or beverage containers. It chose the residential market, and it needed to determine the most attractive product application: semifinished material, building components, or aluminum mobile homes. Deciding to focus on building components, it considered the best customer size and chose large. The second stage consisted of microsegmentation. The company distinguished among customers buying on price, service, and quality. Because it had a high-service profile, the firm decided to concentrate on the service-motivated segment of the market.

Business-to-business marketing experts James C. Anderson and James A. Narus have urged marketers to present flexible market offerings to all members of a segment.[9] A *flexible market*

TABLE 6.2   Major Segmentation Variables for Business Markets

Demographic

1. *Industry:* Which industries should we serve?
2. *Company size:* What size companies should we serve?
3. *Location:* What geographical areas should we serve?

Operating Variables

4. *Technology:* What customer technologies should we focus on?
5. *User or nonuser status:* Should we serve heavy users, medium users, light users, or nonusers?
6. *Customer capabilities:* Should we serve customers needing many or few services?

Purchasing Approaches

7. *Purchasing-function organization:* Should we serve companies with a highly centralized or decentralized purchasing organization?
8. *Power structure:* Should we serve companies that are engineering dominated, financially dominated, and so on?
9. *Nature of existing relationship:* Should we serve companies with which we have strong relationships or simply go after the most desirable companies?
10. *General purchasing policies:* Should we serve companies that prefer leasing? Service contract? Systems purchases? Sealed bidding?
11. *Purchasing criteria:* Should we serve companies that are seeking quality? Service? Price?

Situational Factors

12. *Urgency:* Should we serve companies that need quick and sudden delivery or service?
13. *Specific application:* Should we focus on a certain application of our product rather than all applications?
14. *Size or order:* Should we focus on large or small orders?

Personal Characteristics

15. *Buyer-seller similarity:* Should we serve companies whose people and values are similar to ours?
16. *Attitude toward risk:* Should we serve risk-taking or risk-avoiding customers?
17. *Loyalty:* Should we serve companies that show high loyalty to their suppliers?

Source: Adapted from Thomas V. Bonoma and Benson P. Shapiro, *Segmenting the Industrial Market* (Lexington, MA: Lexington Books, 1983).

offering consists of two parts: a *naked solution* containing the product and service elements that all segment members value and *discretionary options* that some segment members value. Each option might carry an additional charge.

Market Targeting

There are many statistical techniques for developing market segments.[10] Once the firm has identified its market-segment opportunities, it must decide how many and which ones to target. Marketers are increasingly combining several variables in an effort to identify smaller, better-defined target groups. Thus, a bank may not only identify a group of wealthy retired adults but within that group distinguish several segments depending on current income, assets, savings, and risk preferences. This has led some market researchers to advocate a *needs-based market segmentation approach*. Roger Best proposed the seven-step approach shown in Table 6.3.

Effective Segmentation Criteria

Not all segmentation schemes are useful. We could divide buyers of table salt into blond and brunette customers, but hair color is irrelevant to the purchase of salt. Furthermore, if all salt buyers buy the same amount of salt each month, believe all salt is the same, and would pay only one price for salt, this market is minimally segmentable from a marketing point of view.

Rating Segments   To be useful, market segments must rate favorably on five key criteria:

- **Measurable.** The size, purchasing power, and characteristics of the segments can be measured.
- **Substantial.** The segments are large and profitable enough to serve. A segment should be the largest possible homogeneous group worth going after with a tailored marketing program.

TABLE 6.3	Steps in the Segmentation Process
	Description
1. Needs-Based Segmentation	Group customers into segments based on similar needs and benefits sought by customers in solving a particular consumption problem.
2. Segment Identification	For each needs-based segment, determine which demographics, lifestyles, and usage behaviors make the segment distinct and identifiable (actionable).
3. Segment Attractiveness	Using predetermined segment attractiveness criteria (such as market growth, competitive intensity, and market access), determine the overall attractiveness of each segment.
4. Segment Profitability	Determine segment profitability.
5. Segment Positioning	For each segment, create a "value proposition" and product-price positioning strategy based on that segment's unique customer needs and characteristics.
6. Segment "Acid Test"	Create "segment storyboard" to test the attractiveness of each segment's positioning strategy.
7. Marketing-Mix Strategy	Expand segment positioning strategy to include all aspects of the marketing mix: product, price, promotion, and place.

Source: Adapted from Roger J. Best, *Market-Based Management,* 6th ed. (Upper Saddle River NJ: Prentice Hall, 2013). ©2013. Printed and electronically reproduced by permission of Pearson Education, Inc. Upper Saddle River, New Jersey.

- **Accessible.** The segments can be effectively reached and served.
- **Differentiable.** The segments are conceptually distinguishable and respond differently to different marketing-mix elements and programs. If married and single women respond similarly to a sale on perfume, they do not constitute separate segments.
- **Actionable.** Effective programs can be formulated for attracting and serving the segments.

Long-Term Segment Attractiveness   Michael Porter has identified five forces that determine the intrinsic long-run attractiveness of a market or market segment: industry competitors, potential entrants, substitutes, buyers, and suppliers.[11] The first is the *threat of intense segment rivalry.* A segment is unattractive if it already contains numerous, strong, or aggressive competitors. It's even more unattractive if it's stable or declining, if plant capacity must be added in large increments, if fixed costs or exit barriers are high, or if competitors have high stakes in staying in the segment.

The second is the *threat of potential entrants.* The most attractive segment is one in which entry barriers are high and exit barriers are low. Few new firms can enter the industry, and poorly performing firms can easily exit. When entry and exit barriers are high, profit potential is high, but firms face more risk because poorer-performing firms stay in and fight it out. When entry and exit barriers are low, firms easily enter and leave the industry, and returns are stable but low. The worst case occurs when entry barriers are low and exit barriers are high: Firms enter during good times but find it hard to leave during bad times.

The third is the *threat of substitutes.* A segment is unattractive when there are actual or potential substitutes for the product. Substitutes place a limit on prices and on profits. If technology advances or competition increases in these substitute industries, prices and profits are likely to fall.

The fourth is the *threat of buyers' growing bargaining power.* A segment is unattractive if buyers possess strong or growing bargaining power. Buyers' bargaining power grows when they become more concentrated or organized, when the product represents a significant fraction of their costs, when the product is undifferentiated, when buyers' switching costs are low, or when they can integrate upstream. To protect themselves, sellers might select buyers who have the least power to negotiate or switch suppliers. A better defense is developing superior offers that strong buyers cannot refuse.

The fifth force is the *threat of suppliers' growing bargaining power.* A segment is unattractive if suppliers are able to raise prices or reduce quantity supplied. Suppliers tend to be powerful when they are concentrated or organized, when they can integrate downstream, when there are few substitutes, when the supplied product is an important input, and when the costs of switching suppliers are high. The best defenses are to build win-win relationships with suppliers or use multiple supply sources.

Evaluating and Selecting Market Segments

In evaluating market segments, the firm must look at two factors: the segment's overall attractiveness and the company's objectives and resources. How well does a potential segment score on the five criteria? Does it have characteristics that make it generally attractive, such as size, growth, profitability, scale economies, and low risk? Does investing in it make sense given the firm's objectives, competencies, and resources? Some attractive segments may not mesh with the company's long-run objectives, or the company may lack one or more competencies necessary to offer superior value.

Marketers have a range or continuum of possible levels of segmentation that can guide their target market decisions. At one extreme is a mass market of essentially one segment; at the other extreme are individuals or segments of one person each. In between are multiple segments and single segments. We describe approaches to each of the four levels next.

Full Market Coverage   Here a firm attempts to serve all customer groups with all the products they might need. Only very large firms such as Microsoft (software market) and Coca-Cola (nonalcoholic beverage market) can undertake a full market coverage strategy, through either differentiated or undifferentiated marketing.

In *undifferentiated* or *mass marketing*, the firm ignores segment differences and goes after the whole market with one offer. It designs a marketing program for a product with a superior image that can be sold to the broadest number of buyers via mass distribution and mass communications. Undifferentiated marketing is appropriate when all consumers have roughly the same preferences and the market shows no natural segments. The narrow product line keeps down the costs of research and development, production, inventory, transportation, marketing communication, and product management. However, many critics point to the increasing splintering of the market and the proliferation of marketing channels and communication, which make it difficult and increasingly expensive to reach a mass audience.

In *differentiated marketing*, the firm sells different products to all the different segments of the market. Differentiated marketing typically creates more total sales than undifferentiated marketing. However, it also increases the costs of doing business. Because differentiated marketing leads to both higher sales and higher costs, no generalizations about its profitability are valid.

Multiple Segment Specialization   With *selective specialization*, a firm selects a subset of all the possible segments, each objectively attractive and appropriate. There may be little or no synergy among the segments, but each promises to be a moneymaker. The multisegment strategy also has the advantage of diversifying the firm's risk. Keeping synergies in mind, companies can try to operate in supersegments rather than in isolated segments. A **supersegment** is a set of segments sharing some exploitable similarity. A firm can also attempt to achieve some synergy with product or market specialization.

- With *product specialization*, the firm sells a certain product to several different market segments. A microscope manufacturer, for instance, sells to university, government, and commercial laboratories, making different instruments for each and building a strong reputation in the specific product area. The risk is that the product may be supplanted by an entirely new technology.
- With *market specialization*, the firm concentrates on serving many needs of a particular customer group, such as by selling an assortment of products only to university laboratories. The firm gains a strong reputation among this customer group and becomes a channel for additional products its members can use. The risk is that the customer group may suffer budget cuts or shrink in size.

Single-Segment Concentration   With single-segment concentration, the firm markets to only one particular segment. Through concentrated marketing, the firm gains deep knowledge of the segment's needs and achieves a strong market presence. It also enjoys operating economies by specializing its production, distribution, and promotion. If it captures segment leadership, the firm can earn a high return on its investment.

A *niche* is a more narrowly defined customer group seeking a distinctive mix of benefits within a segment. Marketers usually identify niches by dividing a segment into subsegments. What does an attractive niche look like? Niche customers have a distinct set of needs; they will pay a premium to the firm that best satisfies them; the niche is fairly small but has size, profit, and growth potential and is unlikely to attract many competitors; and it gains certain economies through specialization. As marketing efficiency increases, niches that seemed too small may become more profitable. See "Marketing Insight: Chasing the Long Tail."

marketing insight

Chasing the Long Tail

The advent of online commerce, made possible by technology and epitomized by Amazon.com, eBay, iTunes, and Netflix, has led to a shift in consumer buying patterns, according to Chris Anderson, author of *The Long Tail*. In most markets, the distribution of product sales conforms to a curve weighted heavily to one side—the "head"—where the bulk of sales are generated by a few products. The curve falls rapidly toward zero and hovers just above it far along the X-axis—the "long tail"—where the vast majority of products generate very little sales. The mass market traditionally focused on generating "hit" products that occupy the head.

Anderson says the Internet is shifting demand "down the tail, from hits to niches" in a number of product categories including music, books, clothing, and movies. His theory is based on three premises: (1) Lower distribution costs make it economically easier to sell products without precise demand predictions; (2) the more products available for sale, the greater the likelihood of tapping into latent demand for niche tastes unreachable through traditional retail channels; and (3) if enough niche tastes are aggregated, a big new market can result. Although some research supports this theory, other research finds very low share products may be so obscure that they disappear before they can be purchased frequently enough to justify their existence. For companies selling physical products, inventory, stocking, and handling costs can outweigh any financial benefits of such products.

Sources: Chris Anderson, *The Long Tail* (New York: Hyperion, 2006); "Reading the Tail," interview with Chris Anderson, *Wired*, July 8, 2006, p. 30; "Wag the Dog: What the Long Tail Will Do," *The Economist*, July 8, 2006, p. 77; John Cassidy, "Going Long," *New Yorker*, July 10, 2006; Erik Brynjolfsson, Yu "Jeffrey" Hu, and Michael D. Smith, "From Niches to Riches: Anatomy of a Long Tail," *MIT Sloan Management Review* (Summer 2006), p. 67; Anita Elberse, "Should You Invest in the Long Tail," *Harvard Business Review*, July–August 2008, pp. 88–96 (with online commentary); Lee Gomes, "Study Refutes Niche Theory Spawned by Web," *Wall Street Journal*, July 2, 2008; Erick Schonfeld, "Poking Holes in the Long Tail Theory," www.techcrunch.com, July 2, 2008; "Rethinking the Long Tail Theory: How to Define 'Hits' and 'Niches,'" *Knowledge@Wharton*, September 16, 2009.

Individual Marketing The ultimate level of segmentation leads to "segments of one," "customized marketing," or "one-to-one marketing."[12] As companies have grown proficient at gathering information about individual customers and business partners and as their factories are being designed more flexibly, they have increased their ability to individualize market offerings, messages, and media. **Mass customization** is the ability of a company to meet each customer's requirements—to prepare on a mass basis individually designed products, services, programs, and communications.[13]

One-to-one marketing is not for every company. It works best for firms that normally collect a great deal of individual customer information and carry a lot of products that can be cross-sold, need periodic replacement or upgrading, and offer high value. For others, the required investment in information collection, hardware, and software may exceed the payout. The cost of goods is raised beyond what the customer is willing to pay.

Legal and Ethical Issues with Market Targets Marketers must target carefully to avoid consumer backlash. Some consumers resist being labeled.[14] Market targeting also can generate public controversy when marketers take unfair advantage of vulnerable groups (such as children) or disadvantaged groups (such as inner-city residents) or when they promote potentially harmful products. A key area of concern for many consumer protection advocates today is the millions of kids who are online.

Not all attempts to target children, minorities, or other special segments draw criticism. Colgate-Palmolive's Colgate Junior toothpaste has special features designed to get children to brush longer and more often. Thus, the issue is not who is targeted, but how and for what purpose. Socially responsible marketing calls for targeting that serves not only the company's interests but also the interests of those targeted.

Executive Summary

Target marketing includes three activities: market segmentation, market targeting, and market positioning. Market segments are large, identifiable, distinct groups within a market who share a similar set of needs and wants. The major segmentation variables for consumer markets are geographic, demographic, psychographic, and behavioral, used singly or in combination. Business marketers use all these variables along with operating variables, purchasing approaches, and situational factors. To be useful, market segments must be measurable, substantial, accessible, differentiable, and actionable.

We can target markets at four main levels: mass, multiple segments, single (or niche) segment, and individuals. A mass market approach, with full market coverage, is adopted only by the biggest firms. A niche is a more narrowly defined group within a segment. More companies now practice individual and mass customization. In evaluating market segments, the firm must look at two factors: the segment's overall attractiveness and the company's objectives and resources. Finally, marketers must choose target markets in a legal and ethical manner.

Notes

1. E. B. Boyd, "After LinkedIn's IPO, What Will It Have to Do to Earn Its $4.3 Billion Valuation," *Fast Company*, May 19, 2011; Evelyn M. Rusli, "LinkedIn Earnings: Profit Soars, but Shares Fall on Weak Outlook," *Wall Street Journal*, May 2, 2013; Alexandra Chang, "LinkedIn Revamps Mobile Apps to Focus on Stories, Updates," *Wired*, April 18, 2013; Russell Flannery, "LinkedIn Members in China Surpass Five Million," Forbes.com, May 26, 2014.

2. By visiting the company's sponsored site, MyBestSegments.com, you can enter in a zip code and discover the top five clusters for that area. Note that another leading supplier of geodemographic data is ClusterPlus (Strategic Mapping).

3. For some consumer behavior findings on gender, see Kristina M. Durante, Vladas Griskevicius, Sarah E. Hill, Carin Perilloux, and Norman P. Li, "Ovulation, Female Competition, and Product Choice: Hormonal Influences on Consumer Behavior," *Journal of Consumer Research* 37 (April 2011), pp. 921–34; Valentyna Melnyk, Stijn M. J. van Osselaer, and Tammo H. A. Bijmolt, "Are Women More Loyal Customers than Men? Gender Differences in Loyalty to Firms and Individual Service Providers," *Journal of Marketing* 73 (July 2009), pp. 82–96; Jane Cunningham and

Philippa Roberts, "What Woman Want," *Brand Strategy*, December 2006–January 2007, pp. 40–41; Robert J. Fisher and Laurette Dube, "Gender Differences in Responses to Emotional Advertising," *Journal of Consumer Research* 31 (March 2005), pp. 850–58.

4. Charles D. Schewe and Geoffrey Meredith, "Segmenting Global Markets by Generational Cohort: Determining Motivations by Age," *Journal of Consumer Behavior* 4 (October 2004), pp. 51–63; Geoffrey E. Meredith and Charles D. Schewe, *Managing by Defining Moments: America's 7 Generational Cohorts, Their Workplace Values, and Why Managers Should Care* (New York: Hungry Minds, 2002); Geoffrey E. Meredith, Charles D. Schewe, and Janice Karlovich, *Defining Markets, Defining Moments* (New York: Hungry Minds, 2001).

5. Amy Chozick, "Television's Senior Moment," *Wall Street Journal*, March 9, 2011.

6. Marissa Miley, "Don't Bypass African-Americans," *Advertising Age*, February 2, 2009.

7. www.strategicbusinessinsights.com/vals/presurvey.shtml, accessed May 20, 2014.

8. This classification was adapted from George H. Brown, "Brand Loyalty: Fact or Fiction?," *Advertising Age*, June 1952–January 1953, a series. See also Peter E. Rossi,

Robert E. McCulloch, and Greg M. Allenby, "The Value of Purchase History Data in Target Marketing," *Marketing Science* 15 (Fall 1996), pp. 321–40.

9. James C. Anderson and James A. Narus, "Capturing the Value of Supplementary Services," *Harvard Business Review,* January–February 1995, pp. 75–83. But also see Frank V. Cespedes, James P. Dougherty, and Ben S. Skinner III, "How to Identify the Best Customers for Your Business," *MIT Sloan Management Review*, Winter 2013, pp. 53–59.

10. For a review of methodological issues in developing segmentation schemes, see William R. Dillon and Soumen Mukherjee, "A Guide to the Design and Execution of Segmentation Studies," Rajiv Grover and Marco Vriens, eds., *Handbook of Marketing Research* (Thousand Oaks, CA: Sage, 2006).

11. Michael E. Porter, *Competitive Strategy* (New York: Free Press, 1980), pp. 22–23.

12. Don Peppers and Martha Rogers, *One-to-One B2B: Customer Development Strategies for the Business-to-Business World* (New York: Doubleday, 2001); Jerry Wind and Arvind Rangaswamy, "Customerization: The Next Revolution in Mass Customization," *Journal of Interactive Marketing* 15 (Winter 2001), pp. 13–32; Itamar Simonson, "Determinants of Customers' Responses to Customized Offers: Conceptual Framework and Research Propositions," *Journal of Marketing* 69 (January 2005), pp. 32–45.

13. James H. Gilmore and B. Joseph Pine II, *Markets of One: Creating Customer-Unique Value through Mass Customization* (Boston: Harvard Business School Press, 2000); B. Joseph Pine II, "Beyond Mass Customization," *Harvard Business Review*, May 2, 2011.

14. Woo Jin Choi and Karen Page Winterich, "Can Brands Move In from the Outside? How Moral Identity Enhances Out-Group Brand Attitudes," *Journal of Marketing* 77 (March 2013), pp. 96–111; Jennifer E. Escales and James R. Bettman, "Self-Construal, Reference Groups, and Brand Meaning," *Journal of Consumer Research* 32 (December 2005), pp. 378–89.

Chapter 7

Crafting the Brand Positioning and Competing Effectively

In this chapter, we will address the following questions:

1. How can a firm develop and establish an effective positioning? (Page 107)
2. How are brands successfully differentiated? (Page 111)
3. How do marketers identify and analyze competition? (Page 112)
4. How can market leaders, challengers, followers, and nichers compete effectively? (Page 116)

Marketing Management at DirecTV

The direct-broadcast satellite service provider DirecTV faces competition from classic cable companies (Comcast), from other direct broadcast satellite service providers (Dish), and from providers of alternate ways to watch television digitally (Hulu, Netflix, and Amazon). DirecTV's positioning reflects its combination of features not easily matched by any competitor. Three pillars of that positioning are captured by its claims to "state-of-the-art technology, unmatched programming, and industry leading customer service." The company puts much emphasis on its sports packages, its wide array of HD channels, and its broadcast platform for enabling customers to access programming on home TVs, laptops, tablets, and cell phones. DirecTV has made a strategic targeting shift to focus on "high quality" subscribers: loyal customers who purchase premium services, pay their bills on time, and rarely call to complain.[1]

Creating a compelling, well-differentiated brand position, as DirecTV has done, requires a keen understanding of consumer needs and wants, company capabilities, and competitive actions. In this chapter, we outline a process by which marketers can uncover the most powerful brand positioning. We also examine the role of competition and how to manage brands based on market position.

Developing and Establishing a Brand Positioning

All marketing strategy is built on segmentation, targeting, and positioning. A company discovers different needs and groups of consumers in the marketplace, targets those it can satisfy in a superior way, and then positions its offerings so the target market recognizes its distinctive offerings. By building customer advantages, companies can deliver high customer value and satisfaction, which lead to high repeat purchases and ultimately to high company profitability.

Understanding Positioning and Value Propositions

Positioning is the act of designing a company's offering and image to occupy a distinctive place in the minds of the target market.[2] The goal is to locate the brand in the minds of consumers to maximize the potential benefit to the firm. A good brand positioning helps guide marketing strategy by clarifying the brand's essence, identifying the goals it helps consumers achieve, and showing how it does so in a unique way.

One result of positioning is the successful creation of a customer-focused *value proposition,* a cogent reason why the target market should buy a product or service. Table 7.1 shows how three companies have defined their value proposition through the years with their target customers.[3]

Deciding on a positioning requires: (1) choosing a frame of reference by identifying the target market and relevant competition, (2) identifying the optimal points-of-parity and points-of-difference brand associations given that frame of reference, including emotional branding, and (3) creating a brand mantra summarizing the brand's positioning and essence.

Choosing a Competitive Frame of Reference

The **competitive frame of reference** defines which other brands a brand competes with and which should thus be the focus of competitive analysis. A good starting point in defining a competitive frame of reference for brand positioning is **category membership**, the products or sets of products with which a brand competes and that function as close substitutes. It would seem a simple task for a company to identify its competitors. PepsiCo knows Coca-Cola's Dasani is a major bottled-water competitor for its Aquafina brand; Wells Fargo knows Bank of America is a major banking competitor.

The range of a company's actual and potential competitors, however, can be much broader. To enter new markets, a brand with growth intentions may need a broader or more aspirational

TABLE 7.1	Examples of Value Propositions	
Company and Product	**Target Customers**	**Value Proposition**
Hertz (car rental)	Busy professionals	Fast, convenient way to rent the right type of car at an airport
Volvo (station wagon)	Safety-conscious upscale families	The safest, most durable wagon in which your family can ride
Domino's (pizza)	Convenience-minded pizza lovers	A delicious hot pizza, delivered promptly to your door

competitive frame. And it may be more likely to be hurt by emerging competitors or new technologies than by current competitors.

We can examine competition from both an industry and a market point of view.[4] An **industry** is a group of firms offering a product or class of products that are close substitutes for one another. Using the market approach, we define *competitors* as companies that satisfy the same customer need. For example, a customer who buys word-processing software really wants "writing ability"—a need that can also be satisfied by pencils, pens, or, in the past, typewriters. Marketers must overcome "marketing myopia" and stop defining competition in traditional category and industry terms.[5]

Once a company has identified its main competitors, and their strengths and weaknesses, it must ask: What is each competitor seeking in the marketplace? What drives each competitor's behavior? Many factors shape a competitor's objectives, including size, history, current management, and financial situation. If the competitor is part of a larger company, it's important to know whether the parent company is running it for growth or for profits or milking it. Based on all this analysis, marketers formally define the competitive frame of reference to guide positioning. In stable markets where little short-term change is likely, it may be fairly easy to define one, two, or perhaps three key competitors. In dynamic categories where competition may exist or arise in different forms, multiple frames of reference may be present.

Marketers should monitor these three variables when analyzing competitors:

1. *Share of market*—The competitor's share of the target market.
2. *Share of mind*—The percentage of customers who named the competitor in responding to the statement "Name the first company that comes to mind in this industry."
3. *Share of heart*—The percentage of customers who named the competitor in responding to the statement "Name the company from which you would prefer to buy the product."

In general, companies that make steady gains in mind share and heart share will inevitably make gains in market share and profitability. Firms such as Timberland, Jordan's Furniture, and Wegmans are all reaping the benefits of providing emotional, experiential, social, and financial value to satisfy customers and all their constituents.[6]

Identifying Potential Points-of-Difference and Points-of-Parity

Once marketers have fixed the competitive frame of reference for positioning by defining the customer target market and the nature of the competition, they can define the appropriate points-of-difference and points-of-parity associations.[7] **Points-of-difference (PODs)** are attributes or benefits that consumers strongly associate with a brand, positively evaluate, and believe they could not find to the same extent with a competitive brand. Strong brands often have multiple points-of-difference. Two examples are Nike (*performance, innovative technology,* and *winning*) and Southwest Airlines (*value, reliability,* and *fun personality*).

Three criteria determine whether a brand association can truly function as a point-of-difference: desirability, deliverability, and differentiability.

1. *Desirable to consumer.* Consumers must see the brand association as personally relevant to them.
2. *Deliverable by the company.* The company must have the resources and commitment to feasibly and profitably create and maintain the brand association in the minds of consumers. The ideal brand association is preemptive, defensible, and difficult to attack.
3. *Differentiating from competitors.* Consumers must see the brand association as distinctive and superior to relevant competitors.

Points-of-parity (POPs) are attribute or benefit associations that are not necessarily unique to the brand but may in fact be shared with other brands.[8] These types of associations come in three basic forms: category, correlational, and competitive.

Category points-of-parity are attributes or benefits that consumers view as essential to a legitimate and credible offering within a certain category, although not necessarily sufficient conditions for brand choice. Category points-of-parity may change over time due to technological advances, legal developments, or consumer trends.

Correlational points-of-parity are potentially negative associations that arise from the existence of positive associations for the brand. One challenge for marketers is that many attributes or benefits that make up their POPs or PODs are inversely related. In other words, if your brand is good at one thing, such as being inexpensive, consumers can't see it as also good at something else, like being "of the highest quality."

Competitive points-of-parity are associations designed to overcome perceived weaknesses of the brand in light of *competitors'* points-of-difference. One good way to uncover key competitive points-of-parity is to role-play competitors' positioning and infer their intended points-of-difference. Competitor's PODs will, in turn, suggest the brand's POPs. For an offering to achieve a point-of-parity on a particular attribute or benefit, a sufficient number of consumers must believe the brand is "good enough" on that dimension.

It is not uncommon for a brand to identify more than one actual or potential competitive frame of reference, if competition widens or the firm plans to expand into new categories. There are two main options with multiple frames of reference. One is to first develop the best possible positioning for each type or class of competitors and then create one combined positioning robust enough to effectively address all. If competition is too diverse, however, it may be necessary to prioritize competitors and choose the most important set as the competitive frame. Try not to be all things to all people—that leads to lowest-common-denominator positioning, which is typically ineffective.

Occasionally, a company will be able to straddle two frames of reference with one set of points-of-difference and points-of-parity. Here the points-of-difference for one category become points-of-parity for the other and vice versa. Subway restaurants are positioned as offering healthy, good-tasting sandwiches. This positioning allows the brand to create a POP on taste and a POD on health with respect to quick-serve restaurants such as McDonald's and Burger King and, at the same time, a POP on health and a POD on taste with respect to health food restaurants and cafés. Straddle positions allow brands to expand their market coverage and potential customer base. If the points-of-parity and points-of-difference are not credible, however, the brand may not be viewed as a legitimate player in either category.

Choosing Specific POPs and PODs

To build a strong brand and avoid the commodity trap, marketers must start with the belief that you can differentiate anything. Michael Porter urged companies to build a sustainable competitive advantage.[9] **Competitive advantage** is a company's ability to perform in one or more ways that competitors cannot or will not match.

Marketers typically focus on brand benefits in choosing the points-of-parity and points-of-difference that make up their brand positioning. Brand attributes generally play more of a supporting role by providing "reasons to believe" or "proof points" as to why a brand can credibly claim it offers certain benefits. Multiple attributes may support a certain benefit, and they may change over time. The obvious, and often the most compelling, means of differentiation for consumers are benefits related to performance. To identify possible means of differentiation, marketers have to match consumers' desire for a benefit with their company's ability to deliver it.

For choosing specific benefits as POPs and PODs to position a brand, perceptual maps may be useful. *Perceptual maps* are visual representations of consumer perceptions and preferences. They provide quantitative pictures of market situations and the way consumers view different products, services, and brands along various dimensions. By overlaying consumer preferences with brand perceptions, marketers can reveal "openings" that suggest unmet consumer needs and marketing opportunities.[10]

For example, Figure 7.1 shows a hypothetical perceptual map for a beverage category. The four brands—A, B, C, and D—vary in terms of how consumers view their taste profile (light versus strong) and personality and imagery (contemporary versus traditional). Also displayed on the map are ideal point "configurations" for three market segments (1, 2, and 3). The ideal points represent each segment's most preferred ("ideal") combination of taste and imagery. Brand A is seen as more balanced in terms of both taste and imagery.

On Figure 7.1 are two possible repositioning strategies for Brand A. By making its image more contemporary, Brand A could move to A' to target consumers in Segment 1 and achieve a point-of-parity on imagery and maintain its point-of-difference on taste profile with respect to Brand B. By changing its taste profile to make it lighter, Brand A could move to A" to target consumers in Segment 2 and achieve a point-of-parity on taste profile and maintain its point-of-difference on imagery with respect to Brand C. Deciding which repositioning is most promising, A' or A", would require detailed consumer and competitive analysis.

FIGURE 7.1 Hypothetical Beverage Perceptual Map

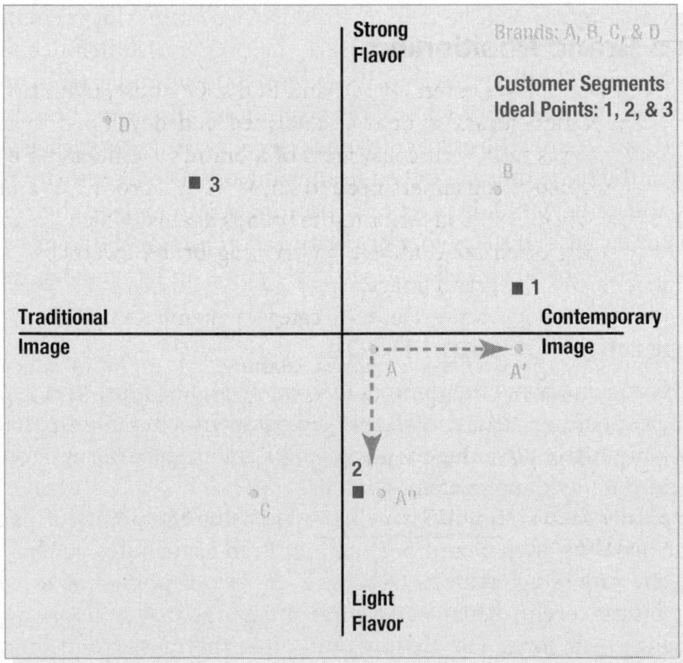

Emotional Branding

Many marketing experts believe a brand positioning should have both rational and emotional components. In other words, it should contain points-of-difference and points-of-parity that appeal to both the head and the heart.[11] A person's emotional response to a brand and its marketing will depend on many factors. An increasingly important one is the brand's authenticity.[12] Brands such as Hershey's, Kraft, Crayola, Kellogg's, and Johnson & Johnson that are seen as authentic and genuine can evoke trust, affection, and strong loyalty.[13]

Authenticity also has functional value. Welch's, owned by 1,150 grape farmers, is seen by consumers as "wholesome, authentic, and real." The brand reinforces those credentials by focusing on its local sourcing of ingredients, increasingly important for consumers who want to know where their foods come from.[14]

Brand Mantras

To further focus brand positioning and guide the way their marketers help consumers think about the brand, firms can define a brand mantra.[15] A *brand mantra* is a three- to five-word articulation of the brand's heart and soul, closely related to other branding concepts like "brand essence" and "core brand promise." Brand mantras must economically communicate what the brand is and what it is *not*. What makes a good brand mantra? McDonald's "Food, Folks, and Fun" captures its brand essence and core brand promise.

A good brand mantra should communicate the category and clarify what is unique about the brand. It should also be vivid and memorable and stake out ground that is personally meaningful and relevant. For brands anticipating rapid growth, it is helpful to define the product or benefit space in which the brand would like to compete, as Nike did with "athletic performance" and Disney with "family entertainment." But for it to be effective, no other brand should singularly excel on all dimensions.

Establishing a Brand Positioning

Often a good positioning will have several PODs and POPs. Of those, often two or three really define the competitive battlefield and should be analyzed and developed carefully. The typical approach to positioning is to inform consumers of a brand's membership before stating its point-of-difference. Presumably, consumers need to know what a product is and what function it serves before deciding whether it is superior to the brands against which it competes. For new products, initial advertising often concentrates on creating brand awareness, and subsequent advertising attempts to create the brand image.

There are three main ways to convey a brand's category membership:

1. *Announcing category benefits*—To reassure consumers that a brand will deliver on the fundamental reason for using a category, marketers frequently use benefits to announce category membership. Thus, industrial tools might claim to have durability.

2. *Comparing to exemplars*—Well-known, noteworthy brands in a category can also help a brand specify its category membership. When Tommy Hilfiger was an unknown, advertising announced his status as a great U.S. designer by associating him with recognized category members like Calvin Klein.

3. *Relying on the product descriptor*—The product descriptor that follows the brand name is often a concise means of conveying category origin.

One common challenge in positioning, as noted above, is that many of the benefits that make up points-of-parity and points-of-difference are negatively correlated. Moreover, individual attributes and benefits often have positive *and* negative aspects. Consider a long-lived brand such as Burberry. The brand's heritage could suggest experience, wisdom, and expertise as well as authenticity, or it could suggest being old-fashioned. Unfortunately, consumers typically want to maximize *both* the negatively correlated attributes or benefits. The best approach clearly is to develop a product or service that performs well on both dimensions.

To address attribute or benefit trade-offs, marketers can: launch two different marketing campaigns, each devoted to a different brand attribute or benefit; link the brand to a person, place, or thing that possesses the right kind of equity to establish an attribute or benefit as a POP or POD; or convince consumers that the negative relationship between attributes and benefits, if they consider it differently, is in fact positive.

Clearly defined POPs and PODs are particularly important to small businesses. See "Marketing Insight: Positioning and Branding for a Small Business" for more on positioning and branding for a small business.

Alternative Approaches to Positioning

Some marketers have proposed other, less-structured approaches in recent years that offer provocative ideas on how to position a brand. These include brand narratives, storytelling, and cultural branding.

Brand Narratives and Storytelling　Rather than outlining specific attributes or benefits, some marketing experts describe positioning a brand as telling a narrative or story. Companies like the richness and imagination they can derive from thinking of the story behind a product or service. Randall Ringer and Michael Thibodeau see *narrative branding* as based on deep metaphors that connect to people's memories, associations, and stories.[16] They identify five elements of narrative branding: (1) the brand story in terms of words and metaphors, (2) the consumer journey or the way consumers engage with the brand over time and touch points where they come into contact with it, (3) the visual language or expression for the brand, (4) the manner in which the narrative is expressed experientially or the brand engages the senses, and (5) the role the brand plays in the lives of consumers.

Patrick Hanlon developed the related concept of "primal branding" that views brands as complex belief systems. According to Hanlon, diverse brands such as Google, MINI Cooper, the U.S. Marine Corps, Starbucks, Apple, UPS, and Aveda all have a "primal code" that resonates with their customers and generates their passion and fervor. Seven assets make up this belief system or primal code: a creation story, creed, icon, rituals, sacred words, a way of dealing with nonbelievers, and a good leader.[17]

Cultural Branding　Douglas Holt believes that for companies to build iconic, leadership brands, they must assemble cultural knowledge, strategize according to cultural branding principles, and hire and train cultural experts.[18] The University of Wisconsin's Craig Thompson views brands as sociocultural templates, citing research investigating brands as cultural resources. For example, American Girl dolls tap into mother–daughter relationships and the cross-generational transfer of femininity.[19] Experts who see consumers actively cocreating brand meaning and positioning refer to this as "Brand Wikification," given that wikis are written by contributors from all walks of life and points of view.[20]

Competitive Strategies for Market Leaders

Suppose a market is occupied by the firms shown in Figure 7.2 (on page 114). Forty percent is in the hands of a *market leader*, another 30 percent belongs to a *market challenger*, and 20 percent is

marketing
insight

marketing insight — Positioning and Branding for a Small Business

Here are some branding guidelines for small businesses with limited resources.

- **Find a compelling performance advantage.** Meaningful differences in product or service performance can be the key to success. The online storage firm Dropbox.com carved out a strong competitive position at the start, partly by virtue of its single-folder approach to accommodate a user's multiple devices.

- **Focus on building one or two strong brands based on one or two key associations.** Small businesses often rely on one or two brands and key associations as points-of-difference, to be reinforced across the marketing program and over time. For example, Volcom has successfully adopted a "Youth Against Establishment" credo to market its music, athletic apparel, and jewelry.

- **Encourage trial in any way possible.** Use sampling, demonstrations, or other methods to engage consumers and encourage trial. See's Candies allows in-store customers to sample the candy of their choice. As one senior executive noted, "That's the best marketing we have, if people try it, they love it."

- **Develop a digital strategy to make the brand "bigger and better."** The Internet and mobile marketing allow small firms to have a big profile. Sales for Rider Shack surf shop in Los Angeles increased when the firm began using Facebook's special features to keep the brand in front of people.

- **Create buzz and a loyal brand community.** Word of mouth is important, as are cost-effective public relations, social networking, promotions, and sponsorships. Evernote has several dozen "power users" who spread the word about the brand.

- **Employ a well-integrated set of brand elements.** Small businesses should develop a distinctive, well-integrated set of brand elements—brand names, logos, packaging—that enhances both awareness and image.

- **Leverage secondary associations.** Secondary associations—any persons, places, or things with potentially relevant associations—are often a cost-effective, shortcut means to build brand equity.

- **Creatively conduct marketing research.** A variety of low-cost marketing research methods can help small businesses connect with customers and study competitors, such as working with students and professors at local colleges and universities.

Sources: Ashlee Vance, "It's a Doc in a Box," *Bloomberg Businessweek*, May 7, 2012, pp. 45–47; Victoria Barret, "Software's Boy Wonder," *Forbes*, March 4, 2013; Daniel Roberts, "The Secrets of See's Candies," *Fortune*, September 3, 2012, pp. 67–72; Jefferson Graham, "How to Ride Facebook's Giant Wave," *USA Today*, May 30, 2013, p. 5B; Rob Walker, "The Cult of Evernote," *Bloomberg Businessweek*, February 28, 2013.

---

claimed by a *market follower* willing to maintain its share and not rock the boat. *Market nichers,* serving small segments larger firms don't reach, hold the remaining 10 percent.

A market leader such as McDonald's has the largest market share and usually leads in price changes, new-product introductions, distribution coverage, and promotional intensity. Although marketers assume well-known brands are distinctive in consumers' minds, unless a dominant firm enjoys a legal monopoly, it must maintain constant vigilance. A powerful product innovation may come along, a competitor might find a fresh marketing angle or commit to a major marketing investment, or the leader's cost structure might spiral upward.

FIGURE 7.2 Hypothetical Market Structure

To stay number one, the firm must find ways to expand total market demand, protect its current share through good defensive and offensive actions, and increase market share, even if market size remains constant.

Expanding Total Market Demand

When the total market expands, the dominant firm usually gains the most. If Heinz can convince more people to use ketchup, or to use ketchup with more meals, or to use more ketchup on each occasion, the firm will benefit considerably because it already sells almost two-thirds of the country's ketchup. In general, the market leader should look for new customers or more usage from existing customers. A company can search for new users among three groups: those who might use it but do not *(market-penetration strategy),* those who have never used it *(new-market segment strategy),* or those who live elsewhere *(geographical-expansion strategy).*

Marketers can try to increase the amount, level, or frequency of consumption. They can sometimes boost the *amount* through packaging or product redesign. Larger package sizes increase the amount of product consumers use at one time.[21] Consumers use more of impulse products such as soft drinks and snacks when the product is made more available. Ironically, some food firms such as Hershey's have developed smaller packaging sizes that have actually increased sales volume through more frequent usage.[22] In general, increasing *frequency* of consumption requires either (1) identifying additional opportunities to use the brand in the same basic way or (2) identifying completely new and different ways to use the brand.

Protecting Market Share

While trying to expand total market size, the dominant firm must actively defend its current business: Boeing against Airbus, and Google against Microsoft.[23] How can the leader do so? The most constructive response is *continuous innovation.* The front-runner should lead the industry in developing new products and customer services, distribution effectiveness, and cost cutting. Comprehensive solutions increase competitive strength and value to customers so they feel appreciative or even privileged to be a customer as opposed to feeling trapped or taken advantage of.[24]

Proactive Marketing In satisfying customer needs, we can draw a distinction between responsive marketing, anticipative marketing, and creative marketing. A *responsive* marketer finds a stated need and fills it. An *anticipative* marketer looks ahead to needs customers may have in the near future. A *creative* marketer discovers solutions customers did not ask for but to which they enthusiastically respond. Creative marketers are proactive *market-driving* firms, not just market-driven ones.[25]

A company needs two proactive skills: (1) *responsive anticipation* to see the writing on the wall, as when IBM changed from a hardware producer to a service business, and (2) *creative anticipation* to devise innovative solutions. Note that *responsive anticipation* is performed before a given change, while *reactive response* happens after the change takes place. Accenture maintains that 10 consumer trends covering areas like e-commerce, social media, and a desire to express individuality will yield market opportunities worth more than $2 trillion between 2013 and 2016.[26]

Defensive Marketing Even when it does not launch offensives, the market leader must not leave any major flanks exposed. The aim of defensive strategy is to reduce the probability of attack, divert attacks to less-threatened areas, and lessen their intensity. A leading firm can use one of six defense strategies.

- **Position defense.** This means occupying the most desirable position in consumers' minds, making the brand almost impregnable. Procter & Gamble "owns" the key functional benefit in many product categories, such as Pampers diapers for dryness.
- **Flank defense.** The market leader should erect outposts to protect a weak front or support a possible counterattack. Procter & Gamble brands such as Gain and Cheer laundry detergent have played strategic offensive and defensive roles in support of Tide.
- **Preemptive defense.** A more aggressive maneuver is to attack first, perhaps with guerrilla action across the market—hitting one competitor here, another there—to keep everyone off balance. Another is to achieve broad market envelopment that signals competitors not to attack.[27] Yet another preemptive defense is to introduce a stream of new products and announce them in advance.
- **Counteroffensive defense.** The market leader can meet the attacker frontally so the rival will have to pull back to defend itself. Another form of counteroffensive is the exercise of economic or political clout. The leader may try to crush a competitor by subsidizing lower prices for a vulnerable product with revenue from its more profitable products, or it may lobby legislators to take political action to inhibit the competition.
- **Mobile defense.** Here the leader stretches its domain over new territories through market broadening and market diversification. *Market broadening* shifts the company's focus from the current product to the underlying generic need, the way "petroleum" companies recast themselves as "energy" companies. *Market diversification* shifts the company's focus into unrelated industries.
- **Contraction defense.** Sometimes large companies can no longer defend all their territory. In *planned contraction* (also called *strategic withdrawal*), they give up weaker markets and reassign resources to stronger ones. P&G sold Pringles to Kellogg for almost $2.7 billion when it decided to focus on its core household and consumer products.[28]

Increasing Market Share

In some markets, one share point can be worth tens of millions of dollars, which is why competition is so fierce. Because the cost of buying higher market share through acquisition may far exceed its revenue value, a company should consider four factors first:

1. *The possibility of provoking antitrust action.* Frustrated competitors are likely to cry "monopoly" and seek legal action if a dominant firm makes further inroads. Microsoft and Intel have had to fend off numerous lawsuits and legal challenges around the world as a result of what some feel are inappropriate or illegal business practices and abuse of market power.

2. *Economic cost.* Figure 7.3 shows that profitability might *fall* with market share gains after some level. In the illustration, the firm's *optimal market share* is 50 percent. The cost of gaining further market share might exceed the value if holdout customers dislike the firm, are loyal to competitors, have unique needs, or prefer dealing with smaller firms. Pushing for higher share is less justifiable when there are unattractive market segments, buyers who want multiple sources of supply, high exit barriers, and few economies of scale.

3. *Pursuing the wrong marketing activities.* Companies successfully gaining share typically outperform competitors in three areas: new-product activity, relative product quality, and marketing expenditures.[29] Companies that attempt to increase market share by cutting prices more deeply than competitors typically don't achieve significant gains because rivals meet the price cuts or offer other values so buyers don't switch.

4. *The effect of increased market share on actual and perceived quality.* Too many customers can put a strain on the firm's resources, hurting product value and service delivery.

Other Competitive Strategies

Firms that are not industry leaders are often called runner-up or trailing firms. Some, such as PepsiCo and Ford, are quite large in their own right. These firms can either attack the leader and other competitors in an aggressive bid for further market share as *market challengers*, or they can choose to not "rock the boat" as *market followers*.

Market-Challenger Strategies

Many market challengers have gained ground or even overtaken the leader. A challenger must first determine a strategic objective (such as to increase market share) and then decide whom to attack. Attacking the market leader is a high-risk but potentially high-payoff strategy if the leader is not serving the market well. The challenger can attack firms its own size that are

FIGURE 7.3 The Concept of Optimal Market Share

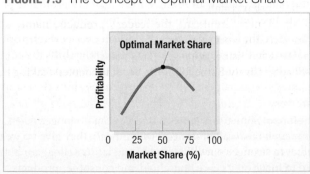

underperforming and underfinanced, have aging products, are charging excessive prices, or are not satisfying customers in other ways. Another option is to attack small local and regional firms. Or a challenger might attack an industry as a whole or a pervasive way of thinking that doesn't adequately address customer needs.

Given clear opponents and objectives, five attack strategies for challengers are:

1. *Frontal attack.* The attacker matches its opponent's product, advertising, price, and distribution. A modified frontal attack, such as cutting price, can work if the market leader doesn't retaliate and if the competitor convinces the market its product is equal to the leader's.

2. *Flank attack.* A flanking strategy is another name for identifying shifts that cause gaps to develop in the market, then rushing to fill the gaps. Flanking is particularly attractive to a challenger with fewer resources and can be more likely to succeed than frontal attacks. With a geographic attack, the challenger spots areas where the opponent is underperforming. Another idea is to serve uncovered market needs.

3. *Encirclement attack.* Encirclement attempts to capture a wide slice of territory by launching a grand offensive on several fronts. It makes sense when the challenger commands superior resources.

4. *Bypass attack.* Bypassing the enemy to attack easier markets offers three lines of approach: diversifying into unrelated products, diversifying into new geographical markets, and leapfrogging into new technologies. In *technological leapfrogging,* the challenger patiently researches and develops the next technology, shifting the battleground to its own territory where it has an advantage.

5. *Guerrilla attack.* Guerrilla attacks consist of small, intermittent attacks, conventional and unconventional, including selective price cuts, intense promotional blitzes, and occasional legal action, to harass the opponent and eventually secure permanent footholds. A guerrilla campaign can be expensive and typically must be backed by a stronger attack to beat the opponent.

Market-Follower Strategies

Theodore Levitt argues that a strategy of *product imitation* might be as profitable as a strategy of *product innovation.*[30] The innovator bears the expense of developing the new product, getting it into distribution, and informing and educating the market. The reward for all this work and risk is normally market leadership. However, another firm can come along and copy or improve on the new product. Although it may not overtake the leader, the follower can achieve high profits because it did not bear any of the innovation expense.

Many companies prefer to follow rather than challenge the market leader, especially in capital-intensive, homogeneous-product industries such as steel, fertilizers, and chemicals. The opportunities for product differentiation and image differentiation are low, service quality is comparable, and price sensitivity runs high. Short-run grabs for market share only provoke retaliation in such situations, so most firms present similar offers to buyers, usually by copying the leader, which keeps market shares stable.

Some followers are cloners, emulating the leader's products, name, and packaging with slight variations. Some are imitators, copying a few things from the leader but differentiating themselves on packaging, advertising, pricing, or location. The leader doesn't mind as long as the imitator doesn't attack aggressively. Some followers become adapters, taking the leader's products and adapting or improving them, perhaps selling them to different markets. Note that these three follower strategies are very different from the illegal and unethical follower strategy of counterfeiting. Counterfeiters duplicate the leader's product and packages and sell them on the black market or through disreputable dealers.

What does a follower earn? Normally, less than the leader. Some follower firms have found success, but in another industry.

TABLE 7.2   Niche Specialist Roles
• **End-user specialist.** The firm specializes in one type of end-use customer.
• **Vertical-level specialist.** The firm specializes at some vertical level of the production-distribution value chain.
• **Customer-size specialist.** The firm concentrates on either small, medium-sized, or large customers.
• **Specific-customer specialist.** The firm limits its selling to one or a few customers.
• **Geographic specialist.** The firm sells only in a certain locality, region, or area of the world.
• **Product or product line specialist.** The firm carries or produces only one product line or product.
• **Product-feature specialist.** The firm specializes in a certain type of product or product feature.
• **Job-shop specialist.** The firm customizes its products for individual customers.
• **Quality-price specialist.** The firm operates at the low- or high-quality end of the market.
• **Service specialist.** The firm offers one or more services not available from other firms.
• **Channel specialist.** The firm specializes in serving only one channel of distribution.

Market-Nicher Strategies

An alternative to being a follower in a large market is to be a leader in a small market, or niche. Smaller firms normally avoid competing with larger firms by targeting small markets of little or no interest to the larger firms. Over time, those markets can sometimes end up being sizable in their own right. The nicher achieves *high margin,* whereas the mass marketer achieves *high volume.* The risk is that the niche might dry up or be attacked, so nichers must seek to create new niches, expand existing niches, and protect their niches. *Multiple niching* can be preferable to *single niching* because strength in two or more niches increases the chances for survival. Table 7.2 shows the specialist roles open to nichers.

Executive Summary

To develop an effective positioning, a company must study competitors as well as actual and potential customers. Developing a positioning requires identifying a frame of reference—by locating the target market and the nature of the competition—and the optimal points-of-parity and points-of-difference brand associations. Industry- and market-based analyses both help uncover competitors and latent competitors. Points-of-difference are those associations unique to the brand that are also strongly held and favorably evaluated by consumers. Points-of-parity are associations not necessarily unique to the brand but perhaps shared with other brands.

Several approaches exist to position a product or service. Less structured, more qualitative approaches are based on concepts such as brand narratives, storytelling, and cultural branding. Market leaders stay number one by expanding total market demand, protecting current share, and increasing market share, even if market size remains constant. Firms that are not leaders can be challengers by attacking the leader and other competitors, or they can be market followers. An alternative to being a follower in a large market is to be a leader in a small market or niche.

Notes

1. Noel Murray, "DirecTV's Ad Campaign Wants to Make You Hate Cable as Much as It Does," www.avclub.com, February 26, 2013; Shalini Ramachandran and Ben Fox Rubin, "DirecTV Profit Rises on Latin America Growth," *Wall Street Journal,* February 14, 2013; Alex Sherman, "DirecTV Profit Lags Estimates after First U.S. Customer Loss," *Bloomberg BusinessWeek,* August 2, 2012.

2. Al Ries and Jack Trout, *Positioning: The Battle for Your Mind, 20th Anniversary Edition* (New York: McGraw-Hill, 2000).

3. Michael J. Lanning and Lynn W. Phillips, "Building Market-Focused Organizations," Gemini Consulting White Paper, 1991.

4. Allan D. Shocker, "Determining the Structure of Product-Markets: Practices, Issues, and Suggestions," Barton A. Weitz and Robin Wensley, eds., *Handbook of Marketing* (London: Sage, 2002), pp. 106–25. See also Bruce H. Clark and David B. Montgomery, "Managerial Identification of Competitors," *Journal of Marketing* 63 (July 1999), pp. 67–83.

5. "What Business Are You In? Classic Advice from Theodore Levitt," *Harvard Business Review,* October 2006, pp. 127–37. See also Theodore Levitt's seminal article, "Marketing Myopia," *Harvard Business Review,* July–August 1960, pp. 45–56.

6. Rajendra S. Sisodia, David B. Wolfe, and Jagdish N. Sheth, *Firms of Endearment: How World-Class Companies Benefit Profit from Passion & Purpose* (Upper Saddle River, NJ: Wharton School Publishing, 2007).

7. Kevin Lane Keller, Brian Sternthal, and Alice Tybout, "Three Questions You Need to Ask about Your Brand," *Harvard Business Review,* September 2002, pp. 80–89.

8. Thomas A. Brunner and Michaela Wänke, "The Reduced and Enhanced Impact of Shared Features on Individual Brand Evaluations," *Journal of Consumer Psychology* 16 (April 2006), pp. 101–11.

9. Michael E. Porter, *Competitive Strategy: Techniques for Analyzing Industries and Competitors* (New York: Free Press, 1980).

10. For a classic analysis of perceptual maps, see John R. Hauser and Frank S. Koppelman, "Alternative Perceptual Mapping Techniques: Relative Accuracy and Usefulness," *Journal of Marketing Research* 16 (November 1979), pp. 495–506. For some contemporary perspectives on measurement techniques for positioning, see Sanjay K. Rao, "Data-Based Differentiation," *Marketing Insights,* Spring 2013, pp. 26–32.

11. Brian Sheehan, *Loveworks: How the World's Top Marketers Make Emotional Connections to Win in the Marketplace* (Brooklyn, NY: powerHouse, 2013).

12. James H. Gilmore and B. Joseph Pine II, *Authenticity: What Consumers Really Want* (Cambridge, MA: Harvard Business School Press, 2007); Lynn B. Upshaw, *Truth: The New Rules for Marketing in a Skeptical World* (New York: AMACOM, 2007).

13. Owen Jenkins, "Gimme Some Lovin'," *Marketing News,* May 15, 2009, p. 19.

14. Jack Neff, "Welch's Local-Sourcing Story Core to Outreach," *Advertising Age,* January 24, 2011.

15. Scott Bedbury, *A New Brand World* (New York: Viking Press, 2002).

16. Randall Ringer and Michael Thibodeau, "A Breakthrough Approach to Brand Creation," *Verse, The Narrative Branding Company,* www.versegroup.com, accessed March 7, 2014.

17. Patrick Hanlon, *Primal Branding: Create Zealots for Your Brand, Your Company, and Your Future* (New York: Free Press, 2006); ThinkTopia, www.thinktopia.com, accessed May 26, 2014.

18. Douglas Holt, *How Brands Become Icons: The Principle of Cultural Branding* (Cambridge, MA: Harvard Business School Press, 2004); Douglas Holt, "Branding as Cultural Activism," www.zibs.com; Douglas Holt, "What Becomes an Icon Most," *Harvard Business Review,* March 2003, pp. 43–49; See also Grant McKracken, *Culture and Consumption II: Markets, Meaning, and Brand Management* (Bloomington, IN: Indiana University Press, 2005).

19. Craig Thompson, "Brands as Culturally Embedded Resources," 43rd AMA Sheth Foundation Doctoral Consortium, University of Missouri, June 6, 2008. See also research by John Sherry and Robert Kozinets, including John F. Sherry Jr., Robert V. Kozinets, Adam Duhachek, Benét DeBerry-Spence, Krittinee Nuttavuthisit and Diana Storm, "Gendered Behavior in a Male Preserve: Role Playing at ESPN Zone Chicago," *Journal of Consumer Psychology* 14, nos. 1 & 2 (2004), pp. 151–58; Stephen Brown, Robert V. Kozinets, and John F. Sherry Jr., "Teaching Old Brands New Tricks: Retro Branding and the Revival of Brand Meaning," *Journal of Marketing* 67 (July 2003), pp. 19–33.

20. Nick Wreden, *Fusion Branding* (Atlanta: Accountability Press, 2002); Fusion Branding, www.fusionbranding.com, accessed May 26, 2014.

21. Priya Raghubir and Eric A. Greenleaf, "Ratios in Proportion: What Should the Shape of the Package Be?," *Journal of Marketing* 70 (April 2006), pp. 95–107;

and Valerie Folkes and Shashi Matta, "The Effect of Package Shape on Consumers' Judgments of Product Volume: Attention as a Mental Contaminant," *Journal of Consumer Research* 31 (September 2004), pp. 390–401.

22. Sarah Nassaur, "The Psychology of Small Packages," *Wall Street Journal*, April 15, 2013.

23. George Stalk Jr. and Rob Lachanauer, "Hardball: Five Killer Strategies for Trouncing the Competition," *Harvard Business Review*, April 2004, pp. 62–71; Richard D'Aveni, "The Empire Strikes Back: Counterrevolutionary Strategies for Industry Leaders," *Harvard Business Review*, November 2002, pp. 66–74.

24. Kyle B. Murray and Gerald Häubl, "Why Dominant Companies Are Vulnerable," *MIT Sloan Management Review*, Winter 2012, pp. 12–14.

25. Nirmalya Kumar, Lisa Sheer, and Philip Kotler, "From Market Driven to Market Driving," *European Management Journal* 18 (April 2000), pp. 129–42.

26. "New Trends Worth \$4.5tr," www.warc.com, January 25, 2013.

27. Michael E. Porter, *Market Signals, Competitive Strategy: Techniques for Analyzing Industries and Competitors* (New York: Free Press, 1998), pp. 75–87; Jaideep Prabhu and David W. Stewart, "Signaling Strategies in Competitive Interaction," *Journal of Marketing Research* 38 (February 2001), pp. 62–72.

28. "P&G Completes Sale of Pringles to Kellogg," *Business Wire*, May 31, 2012.

29. Robert D. Buzzell and Frederick D. Wiersema, "Successful Share-Building Strategies," *Harvard Business Review*, January–February 1981, pp. 135–44.

30. Theodore Levitt, "Innovative Imitation," *Harvard Business Review*, September–October 1966, p. 63. Also see Steven P. Schnaars, *Managing Imitation Strategies: How Later Entrants Seize Markets from Pioneers* (New York: Free Press, 1994).

Chapter 8

Creating Brand Equity and Driving Growth

In this chapter, we will address the following questions:

1. What is a brand, and how does branding work? (Page 122)
2. What is brand equity, and how is it built, measured, and managed? (Page 123)
3. What are the important decisions in developing a branding strategy? (Page 129)
4. Why is it important for companies to grow the core of their business? (Page 133)

Marketing Management at Gatorade

Gatorade was first developed by researchers at the University of Florida to help the school's athletes cope with the hot, humid climate. Its success in pioneering the sports drink category led PepsiCo to acquire its parent company in 2001 and invest in further growth. But when sales declined by $1 billion from 2007 to 2010, PepsiCo decided a change was needed. Gatorade's marketers returned the brand to its roots to focus more on athletes. They repackaged and reformulated three product lines for pre-, during-, and post-workout consumption, targeting three different markets. The G Series line aimed at "performance" athletes active in school or recreational sports; the G Series Fit line targeted 18- to 34-year-olds who exercised three to four times a week; and the G Series Pro line targeted professional athletes. Gatorade's advertising tagline, "Win From Within," reflected the new brand strategy, and the communication budget included a 30 percent digital component.[1]

S*trategic brand management* combines the design and implementation of marketing activities and programs to build, measure, and manage brands to maximize their value. It has four main steps: (1) identifying and establishing brand positioning, (2) planning and implementing brand marketing, (3) measuring and interpreting brand performance, and (4) growing and sustaining brand value.[2] In this chapter, we discuss branding, brand equity, brand strategy, and growing the core business.

How Does Branding Work?

The American Marketing Association defines a **brand** as "a name, term, sign, symbol, or design, or a combination of them, intended to identify the goods or services of one seller or group of sellers and to differentiate them from those of competitors." A brand is thus a product or service whose dimensions differentiate it in some way from other offerings designed to satisfy the same need. These differences may be functional, rational, or tangible—related to product performance of the brand. They may also be more symbolic, emotional, or intangible—related to what the brand represents in a more abstract sense.

The Role of Brands

A brand identifies the maker of a product and allows consumers to assign responsibility for its performance to that maker or distributor. Consumers may evaluate the identical product differently depending on how it is branded.[3] They learn about brands through past experiences with the product and its marketing, finding out which brands satisfy their needs and which do not. As consumers' lives become more rushed and complicated, a brand's ability to simplify decision making and reduce risk becomes invaluable.[4] Brands can also take on personal meaning to consumers and become an important part of their identity.[5] For some consumers, brands can even take on human-like characteristics.[6]

Brands also perform valuable functions for firms.[7] First, they simplify product handling by helping organize inventory and accounting records. In addition, a brand allows the firm legal protection for unique product features.[8] The brand name can be protected through registered trademarks, manufacturing processes can be protected through patents, and packaging can be protected through copyrights and proprietary designs. These intellectual property rights ensure that the firm can safely invest in the brand and reap the benefits. In fact, brands represent enormously valuable pieces of legal property that can influence consumer behavior, be bought and sold, and yield sustained future revenues.[9]

Brand loyalty provides predictability and security of demand for the firm, and it creates barriers to entry that make it difficult for other firms to enter the market. Loyalty also can translate into customer willingness to pay a higher price—often even 20 percent to 25 percent more than competing brands.[10] Although competitors may duplicate manufacturing processes and product designs, they cannot easily match lasting impressions left in the minds of customers by years of favorable product experiences and marketing activity. Thus, branding can be a powerful means to secure a competitive advantage.[11]

The Scope of Branding

Branding is the process of endowing products and services with the power of a brand. It's all about creating differences between products. Marketers need to teach consumers "who" the product is—by giving it a name and other brand elements to identify it—as well as what the product does and why consumers should care. Branding creates mental structures that help consumers organize their knowledge about offerings in a way that clarifies their decision making and, in the process, provides value to the firm.

For branding strategies to be successful and brand value to be created, consumers must be convinced there are meaningful differences among brands in the category. Successful brands are seen as genuine, real, and authentic in what they sell as well as who they are. It's possible to brand a physical good (Ford Focus automobile), a service (Singapore Airlines), a store (Dick's Sporting Goods), a person (actress Angelina Jolie), a place (the country of Iceland), an organization (American Automobile Association), or an idea (free trade).[12]

Defining Brand Equity

Brand equity is the added value endowed to products and services with consumers. It may be reflected in the way consumers think, feel, and act with respect to the brand as well as in the prices, market share, and profitability it commands. Marketers and researchers use various perspectives to study brand equity.[13] Customer-based approaches recognize that the power of a brand lies in what customers have seen, read, heard, learned, thought, and felt about the brand over time.[14]

Customer-Based Brand Equity

Customer-based brand equity is the differential effect brand knowledge has on consumer response to the marketing of that brand.[15] A brand has positive customer-based brand equity when consumers react more favorably to a product and the way it is marketed when the brand is identified than when it is not identified. A brand has negative customer-based brand equity if consumers react less favorably to marketing activity for the brand under the same circumstances.

There are three key ingredients of customer-based brand equity. First, brand equity arises from differences in consumer response. If no differences occur, the brand-name product is essentially a commodity, and competition will probably be based on price. Second, differences in response are a result of consumers' **brand knowledge**, all the thoughts, feelings, images, experiences, and beliefs associated with the brand. Brands must create strong, favorable, and unique brand associations with customers. Third, brand equity is reflected in perceptions, preferences, and behavior related to all aspects of the brand's marketing. Stronger brands earn greater revenue.[16] Table 8.1 summarizes some key benefits of brand equity.

Customers' brand knowledge dictates appropriate future directions for the brand. Consumers will decide, based on what they think and feel about the brand, where (and how) they believe the brand should go and grant permission (or not) to any marketing action. New-product ventures such as Cracker Jack cereal failed because consumers found them inappropriate brand extensions. A **brand promise** is the marketer's vision of what the brand must be and do for consumers.

TABLE 8.1	Marketing Advantages of Strong Brands	
Improved perceptions of product performance		Greater trade cooperation and support
Greater loyalty		Increased marketing communications effectiveness
Less vulnerability to competitive marketing actions		Possible licensing opportunities
Less vulnerability to marketing crises		Additional brand extension opportunities
Larger margins		Improved employee recruiting and retention
More inelastic consumer response to price increases		Greater financial market returns
More elastic consumer response to price decreases		

Brand Equity Models

Models of brand equity offer some differing perspectives on branding. Here we highlight three more established ones.

- **BrandAsset Valuator.** Advertising agency Young and Rubicam (Y&R)'s model of brand equity, the BrandAsset® Valuator (BAV), covers four pillars of brand equity (see Figure 8.1). Strong new brands show higher levels of energized differentiation and energy than relevance, whereas both esteem and knowledge are lower still. Leadership brands show high levels on all pillars, with strength greater than stature. Declining brands show high knowledge, a lower level of esteem, and even lower relevance and energized differentiation.

- **BrandZ and BrandDynamics™.** Marketing research consultants Millward Brown and WPP have developed the BrandZ model of brand strength, at the heart of which is the BrandDynamics model (see Figure 8.2). This model is based on a system of brand associations—meaningful, different, and salient—that builds customer predisposition to buy a brand. The associations have three important outcome measures: power (a prediction of brand volume share), premium (ability to command a price premium), and potential (the probability that a brand will grow value share).

- **Brand Resonance Model.** The brand resonance model views brand building as an ascending series of steps. Enacting these four steps means establishing a pyramid of six "brand building blocks" as illustrated in Figure 8.3. The model emphasizes the duality of brands—the rational route to brand building is on the left side of the pyramid, and the emotional route is on the right side.[17]

FIGURE 8.1 BrandAsset® Valuator Model

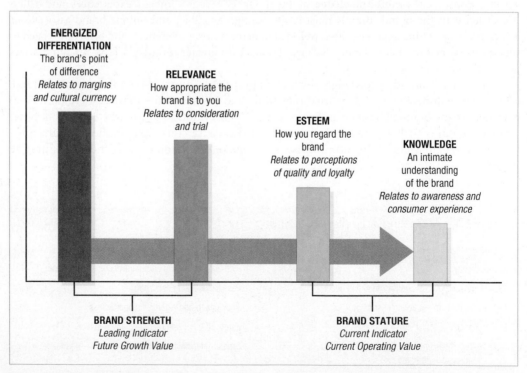

FIGURE 8.2 BrandDynamics™ Model

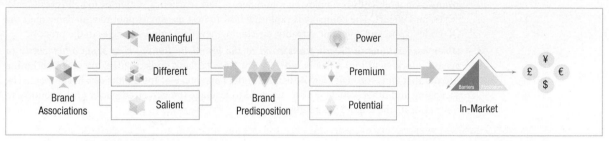

Source: BrandDynamics™ Model. Reprinted with permission of Millward Brown.

Building Brand Equity

Marketers build brand equity by creating the right brand knowledge structures with the right consumers. The success of this process depends on *all* brand-related contacts—whether marketer-initiated or not.[18] From a marketing management perspective, however, there are three main sets of *brand equity drivers:*

1. *The initial choices for the brand elements or identities making up the brand (brand names, URLs, logos, symbols, characters, spokespeople, slogans, jingles, packages, and signage)*—Microsoft chose the name Bing for its new search engine because it felt it unambiguously conveyed search and the "aha" moment of finding what you are looking for. It is also short, appealing, memorable, active, and effective multiculturally.[19]

FIGURE 8.3 Brand Resonance Pyramid

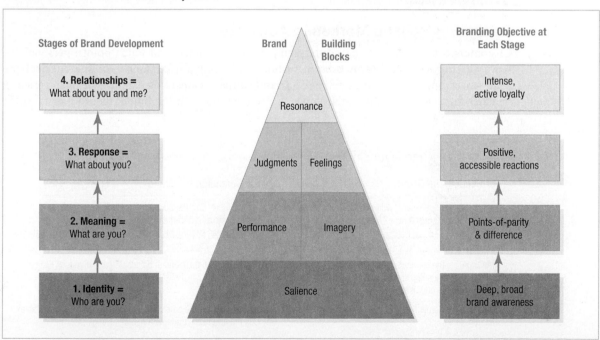

2. *The product and service and all accompanying marketing activities and supporting programs*—General Mills is employing a number of new marketing activities to sell cereals, cake mixes, and yogurt. The company is exploring how to best use smart phones with consumers via QR codes, apps, and augmented reality, developing new packaging strategies in the process.[20]

3. *Other associations indirectly transferred to the brand by linking it to some other entity (a person, place, or thing)*—The brand name of New Zealand vodka 42BELOW refers to both a latitude that runs through New Zealand and the percentage of the drink's alcohol content. The packaging and other visual cues are designed to leverage the perceived purity of the country to communicate the brand's positioning.[21]

Choosing Brand Elements

Brand elements are trademarkable devices that identify and differentiate the brand. Nike has the distinctive "swoosh" logo, the empowering "Just Do It" slogan, and the "Nike" name from the Greek winged goddess of victory. The test of brand building is what consumers would think or feel about the product if the brand element were all they knew. Based on its name alone, for instance, a consumer might expect Panasonic Toughbook laptops to be durable and reliable.

As shown in Table 8.2, there are six criteria for choosing brand elements. The first three—memorable, meaningful, and likable—are brand building. The latter three—transferable, adaptable, and protectable—are defensive and help leverage and preserve brand equity against challenges.

Brand elements can play a number of brand-building roles.[22] If consumers don't examine much information in making product decisions, brand elements should be easy to recall and inherently descriptive and persuasive. The likability of brand elements can increase awareness and associations.[23] Often, the less concrete brand benefits are, the more important that brand elements capture intangible characteristics. Many insurance firms use symbols of strength for their brands (the Rock of Gibraltar for Prudential). Like brand names, slogans are an extremely efficient means to build brand equity.[24] They can help consumers grasp what the brand is and what makes it special, as in "Like a Good Neighbor, State Farm Is There."

Designing Holistic Marketing Activities

Customers come to know a brand through a range of contacts and touch points: personal observation and use, word of mouth, interactions with company personnel, online or telephone experiences, and payment transactions. A **brand contact** is any information-bearing experience, whether positive or negative, a customer or prospect has with the brand, its product category,

TABLE 8.2 Criteria for Choosing Brand Elements	
For Building the Brand	**For Defending the Brand**
Memorable: Is the element easily recalled and recognized at purchase and consumption? Example: Tide	*Transferable:* Can the element introduce new products in the same or different categories? Does it add to brand equity across geographic boundaries and market segments? Example: Amazon.com
Meaningful: Is the element credible and suggestive of the category? Does it suggest something about a product ingredient or a brand user? Example: DieHard	*Adaptable:* Can the element be adapted and updated? Example: Shell logo
Likable: Is the element appealing or playful? Example: Pinterest	*Protectable:* Is the element legally and competitively protectable? Can the firm retain trademark rights? Example: Yahoo!

or its market.[25] The company must put as much effort into managing these experiences as into producing its ads because any brand contact can affect consumers' brand knowledge and the way they think, feel, or act toward the brand.

Integrated marketing is about mixing and matching marketing activities to maximize their individual and collective effects.[26] Marketers need a variety of different marketing activities that consistently reinforce the brand promise, working singularly and in combination. We can evaluate integrated marketing activities in terms of the effectiveness and efficiency with which they affect brand awareness and create, maintain, or strengthen brand associations and image.

Leveraging Secondary Associations

The third and final way to build brand equity is to "borrow" it by linking the brand to other information in memory that conveys meaning to consumers (see Figure 8.4). These "secondary" brand associations can link to sources such as the company itself, countries or other geographical regions, and channels of distribution as well as to other brands, characters (through licensing), spokespeople (through endorsements), sporting or cultural events (through sponsorship), or other third-party sources (through awards or reviews). Leveraging secondary associations can be an efficient and effective way to strengthen a brand. But linking a brand to someone or

FIGURE 8.4 Secondary Sources of Brand Knowledge

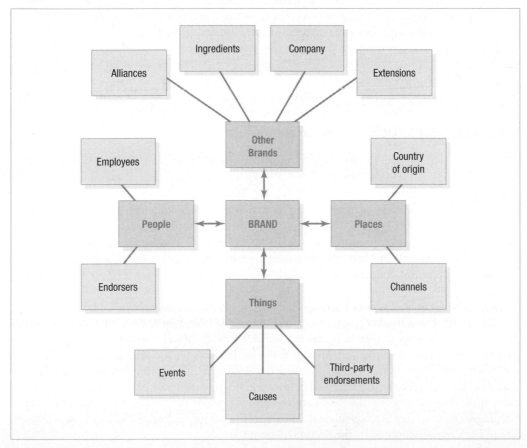

something else can be risky because anything bad that happens to that other entity (such as scandal involving an endorser) can also be linked to the brand.

Internal Branding

Marketers must adopt an *internal* perspective to be sure employees and marketing partners appreciate and understand basic branding notions and how they can help—or hurt—brand equity.[27] *Internal branding* consists of activities and processes that help inform and inspire employees about brands.[28] Holistic marketers go even further and train and encourage distributors and dealers to serve their customers well.

Measuring and Managing Brand Equity

How do we measure brand equity? An *indirect* approach assesses potential sources of brand equity by identifying and tracking consumer brand knowledge structures.[29] A *direct* approach assesses the actual impact of brand knowledge on consumer response to different aspects of the marketing. For brand equity to guide strategy and decisions, marketers need to fully understand (1) the sources of brand equity and how they affect outcomes of interest and (2) how these sources and outcomes change, if at all, over time. Brand audits are important for the former; brand tracking for the latter.

Brand Audits and Brand Tracking

A **brand audit** is a focused series of procedures to assess the health of the brand, uncover its sources of brand equity, and suggest ways to improve and leverage its equity. Conducting brand audits on a regular basis allows marketers to manage brands more proactively and responsively. A good brand audit provides keen insights into consumers, brands, and the relationship between the two. *Brand-tracking studies* use the brand audit as input to collect quantitative data from consumers over time, providing consistent, baseline information about how brands and marketing programs are performing. Tracking studies help us understand where, how much, and in what ways brand value is being created to facilitate day-to-day decision making

Brand Valuation

Marketers should distinguish brand equity from **brand valuation**, which is the job of estimating the total financial value of the brand. In some well-known companies, brand value is typically more than half the total company market capitalization. Top brand-management firm Interbrand has developed a five-step model to estimate the dollar value of a brand and help firms maximize return on brand investment.[30] The first step is market segmentation to determine variations among the brand's different customer groups. The second step is financial analysis to assess purchase price, volume, and frequency and help calculate accurate forecasts of future brand sales and revenues. This step also requires deducting all associated operating costs to derive earnings before interest and tax (EBIT) and deducting taxes and a charge for the capital employed to operate the underlying business. The result is Economic Earnings, the earnings attributed to the branded business.

The third step is market research to assess the role of branding and calculate the percentage of Economic Earnings generated by the brand, which yields Brand Earnings. The fourth step is to assess the brand's strength and determine the likelihood that the forecasted Brand Earnings will be realized. For each segment, Interbrand determines a risk premium for the brand and adds it to the risk-free rate, represented by the yield on government bonds. The Brand Discount Rate, applied to the forecasted Brand Earnings forecast, yields the net present value of the Brand Earnings. The final step is to calculate Brand Value, the net present value (NPV) of the forecasted Brand Earnings, discounted by the Brand Discount Rate.[31]

Managing Brand Equity

Because consumer responses to marketing activity depend on what they know and remember about a brand, short-term marketing actions, by changing brand knowledge, necessarily increase or decrease the long-term success of future marketing actions.

Brand Reinforcement   Marketers can reinforce brand equity by consistently conveying the brand's meaning in terms of (1) what products it represents, what core benefits it supplies, and what needs it satisfies; and (2) how the brand makes products superior and which strong, favorable, and unique brand associations should exist in consumers' minds. Reinforcing brand equity requires that the brand always be moving forward—in the right direction and with new and compelling offerings and ways to market them. While there is little need to deviate from a successful position, many tactical changes may be necessary to maintain the strategic thrust and direction of the brand. When change *is* necessary, marketers should vigorously preserve and defend sources of brand equity.

Brand Revitalization   Any new development in the marketing environment can affect a brand's fortunes. Nevertheless, a number of brands have managed to make impressive comebacks in recent years.[32] After some hard times in the automotive market, Cadillac, Fiat, and Volkswagen have all turned their brand fortunes around to varying degrees. The first step is to understand what the sources of brand equity were to begin with. Are positive associations losing their strength or uniqueness? Have negative associations become linked to the brand? Then decide whether to retain the same positioning or create a new one and, if so, which new one.[33] Sometimes the actual marketing program is the source of the problem because it fails to deliver on the brand promise. Then a "back to basics" strategy may make sense.

In other cases, the old positioning is just no longer viable and a reinvention strategy is necessary. There is obviously a continuum of revitalization strategies, with pure "back to basics" at one end, pure "reinvention" at the other, and many combinations in between. The challenge is to change enough to attract some new customers, but not enough to alienate old customers. Brand revitalization of almost any kind starts with the product.[34]

Devising a Branding Strategy

A firm's **branding strategy**—often called its *brand architecture*—reflects the number and nature of both common and distinctive brand elements. Deciding how to brand new products is especially critical. A firm has three main choices: (1) develop new brand elements for the new product, (2) apply some existing brand elements, or (3) use a combination of new and existing brand elements (see definitions in Table 8.3).

Branding Decisions

Today, hardly anything goes unbranded. Assuming a firm decides to brand its products or services, it must choose which brand names to use. Three general strategies are popular:

- **Individual or separate family brand names.** Companies often use different brand names for different quality lines within the same product class. A major advantage is that if a product fails or appears low quality, the company has not tied its reputation to it.[35]
- **Corporate umbrella or company brand name.** Many firms, such as GE, use their corporate brand as an umbrella brand across their entire range of products.[36] Development costs are lower, and sales of the new product are likely to be strong if the manufacturer's name is good. Corporate-image associations of innovativeness, expertise, and trustworthiness have been shown to directly influence consumer evaluations.[37]

TABLE 8.3	Branding New Products
Concept	Definition
Brand extension	Using an established brand to launch a new product
Sub-brand	Combining a new brand with an existing brand
Parent brand	An existing brand that gives birth to a brand extension or sub-brand
Master (or family) brand	A parent brand that is already associated with multiple products through brand extensions
Line extension	Using a parent brand on a new product within a category it currently serves (such as new flavors or colors)
Category extension	Using a parent brand on a new product to enter a new category, different from the one it currently serves
Brand line	All the products (including line and category extensions) sold under a particular brand
Brand mix	The set of all brand lines sold by a particular seller
Branded variants	Specific brand lines supplied to specific retailers or distribution channels
Licensed product	Using the brand name licensed from one firm on a product made by another firm

- **Sub-brand name.** Sub-brands combine two or more of the corporate brand, family brand, or individual product brand names. Kellogg does this by combining the corporate brand with individual product brands as with Kellogg's Rice Krispies. The company name legitimizes, and the individual name individualizes, the new product.

The use of individual or separate family brand names has been referred to as a "house of brands" strategy, whereas the use of an umbrella corporate or company brand name has been referred to as a "branded house" strategy. These represent two ends of a brand relationship continuum, with the sub-brand strategy falling somewhere between. With a branded house strategy, it is often useful to have a well-defined *flagship product*, one that best represents or embodies the brand as a whole to consumers. It often is the first product by which the brand gained fame, a widely accepted best-seller, or a highly admired or award-winning product.[38]

Brand Portfolios

The **brand portfolio** is the set of all brands and brand lines a particular firm offers for sale in a particular category or market segment. The basic principle is to maximize market coverage so no potential customers are being ignored, but minimize brand overlap so brands are not competing for customer approval. Each brand should be clearly differentiated and appealing to a sizable enough marketing segment to justify its marketing and production costs. Marketers carefully monitor brand portfolios over time to identify weak brands and kill unprofitable ones.[39]

Brands can also play a number of specific roles as part of a portfolio.

- **Flankers.** Flanker or fighter brands are positioned with respect to competitors' brands so that more important (and more profitable) flagship brands can retain their desired positioning. Fighter brands must be neither so attractive that they take sales away from their higher-priced comparison brands nor designed so cheaply that they reflect poorly on them.

- **Cash cows.** Some brands may be kept around despite dwindling sales because they manage to maintain their profitability with virtually no marketing support. Companies can effectively milk these "cash cow" brands by capitalizing on their reservoir of brand equity.
- **Low-end entry level.** The role of a relatively low-priced brand in the portfolio often may be to attract customers to the brand franchise. Retailers like to feature these "traffic builders" because they are able to trade up customers to a higher-priced brand.
- **High-end prestige.** The role of a relatively high-priced brand often is to add prestige and credibility to the entire portfolio.

Brand Extensions

Many firms leverage their most valuable asset by introducing a host of new products under their strongest brand names. Most new products are in fact brand extensions—typically 80 percent to 90 percent in any one year. Moreover, many of the most successful new products, as rated by various sources, are brand extensions.

Advantages of Brand Extensions   Two main advantages of brand extensions are that they can facilitate new-product acceptance and provide positive feedback to the parent brand and company. Consumers form expectations about a new product based on what they know about the parent brand and the extent to which they feel this information is relevant. By setting up positive expectations, extensions reduce risk. It also may be easier to convince retailers to stock and promote a brand extension because of anticipated increased customer demand. An introductory campaign for an extension doesn't need to create awareness of both the brand *and* the new product; it can concentrate on the new product itself.[40]

Extensions can reduce launch costs, important given that establishing a major new brand name for a consumer packaged good in the U.S. marketplace can cost more than $100 million! Extensions also can avoid the difficulty—and expense—of coming up with a new name and allow for packaging and labeling efficiencies. With a portfolio of brand variants within a product category, consumers who want a change can switch to a different product type without having to leave the brand family.

A second advantage is that brand extensions can provide feedback benefits.[41] They can help to clarify the meaning of a brand and its core values or improve consumer loyalty to the company behind the extension.[42] Also, they can renew interest and liking for the brand and benefit the parent brand by expanding market coverage. In fact, a successful category extension may not only reinforce the parent brand and open up a new market but also facilitate even more new category extensions.[43]

Disadvantages of Brand Extensions   On the downside, line extensions may cause the brand name to be less strongly identified with any one product. **Brand dilution** occurs when consumers no longer associate a brand with a specific or highly similar set of products and start thinking less of the brand. If a firm launches extensions consumers deem inappropriate, they may question the integrity of the brand or become confused or even frustrated: Which version of the product is the "right one" for them? Do they know the brand as well as they thought they did? Retailers reject many new products and brands because they don't have the shelf or display space for them. And the firm itself may become overwhelmed. One more disadvantage is that the firm forgoes the chance to create a new brand with its own unique image and equity.

The worst possible scenario is for an extension not only to fail, but to harm the parent brand in the process. Fortunately, such events are rare. "Marketing failures," in which too few consumers are attracted to a brand, are typically much less damaging than "product failures," in which the brand fundamentally fails to live up to its promise. Product failures dilute brand equity only when the extension is seen as very similar to the parent brand. Even if sales of a brand extension meet high targets, the revenue may be coming from consumers switching from existing parent-brand offerings—in effect cannibalizing the parent brand. Yet intrabrand shifts in sales may not be undesirable if they're a form of preemptive cannibalization.

Success Characteristics   Marketers must judge each potential brand extension by how effectively it leverages existing brand equity from the parent brand as well as how effectively, in turn, it contributes to the parent brand's equity. One major mistake in evaluating extension opportunities is failing to take *all* consumers' brand knowledge structures into account and focusing instead on one or a few brand associations as a potential basis of fit.[44]

Customer Equity

We can relate brand equity to one other important marketing concept: *customer equity*. The aim of customer relationship management (CRM) is to produce high customer equity.[45] Although we can calculate it in different ways, one definition is "the sum of lifetime values of all customers."[46] Customer lifetime value is affected by revenue and by the costs of customer acquisition, retention, and cross-selling.[47]

The brand equity and customer equity perspectives share many common themes.[48] Both emphasize the importance of customer loyalty and the notion that we create value by having as many customers as possible pay as high a price as possible. The customer equity perspective focuses on bottom-line financial value. Its clear benefit is its quantifiable measures of financial performance. But it offers limited guidance for go-to-market strategies and ignores some of the important advantages of creating a strong brand. Also, it does not always fully account for competitive moves and counter-moves or for social network effects, word of mouth, and customer-to-customer recommendations.

Brand equity, on the other hand, emphasizes strategic issues in managing brands and creating and leveraging brand awareness and image, providing practical guidance for marketing activities. With a focus on brands, however, managers don't always develop detailed customer analyses in terms of the brand equity they achieve or the resulting long-term profitability they create.[49] Brand equity approaches could benefit from sharper segmentation schemes afforded by customer-level analyses and more consideration of how to develop personalized, customized marketing programs. Nevertheless, both brand equity and customer equity matter. Brands serve as the "bait" that retailers and other channel intermediaries use to attract customers from whom they extract value. Customers are the tangible profit engine for brands to monetize their brand value.

Driving Growth

An important function of marketing is to drive sales and revenue growth. Marketing is especially adept at doing so for a new product with many competitive advantages and much potential. Good marketing can encourage trial and promote word of mouth and diffusion. Marketing in more mature markets can be more challenging.

Growth Strategies

Phil and Milton Kotler stress the following eight growth strategies.[50] Companies can grow by (1) building market share, (2) developing committed customers and stakeholders, (3) building a powerful brand, (4) innovating new offerings and experiences, (5) expanding internationally, (6) arranging acquisitions, mergers, and alliances, (7) building an outstanding reputation for social responsibility, and (8) partnering with government and nongovernmental organizations.

Growing the Core

Some of the best opportunities come from growing the core—focusing on the most successful existing products and markets. Growing the core can be a less risky alternative than expansion into new product categories. It strengthens a brand's credentials as a source of authority and credibility and can yield economies of scale. Through improved revenues and lower costs, growing the core can also lead to greater profits.

UK marketing guru David Taylor advocates three main strategies for growing the core, citing these examples:[51]

1. *Make the core of the brand as distinctive as possible.* Galaxy chocolate has successfully competed with Cadbury by positioning itself as "your partner in chocolate indulgence" and featuring more refined taste and sleeker packaging,

2. *Drive distribution through both existing and new channels.* Costa Coffee, the number-one UK coffee shop chain, has found new distribution routes using drive-through outlets, vending machines, and in-school locations.

3. *Offer the core product in new formats or versions.* WD40 offers a Smart Straw version of its popular multipurpose lubricant with a built-in straw that pops up for use.

A focus on core businesses does not mean foregoing new market opportunities, especially if the core business is not expandable. However, marketers must avoid overestimating the upside of new ventures that stretch the company into uncharted territory. "Marketing Insight: Understanding Double Jeopardy" describes how market leaders can benefit from brand loyalty due to their size.

---

marketing insight — Understanding Double Jeopardy

Double jeopardy was popularized in marketing by the British academic Andrew Ehrenberg. It boils down to the fact that a small-share brand is penalized twice—it has fewer buyers than a large-share brand, and they buy less frequently. As a consequence, most of a brand's market share is explained by its market penetration and the size of its customer base, rather than by customers' repeat purchases. Implicit is the assumption that brands are substitutable and have target segments in common. It is, in fact, most often observed with weakly differentiated brands targeting the same group of people. Exceptions are highly differentiated niche brands that thrive on small shares and high loyalty and seasonal brands that offer unique value and tally cluster purchases in short periods of time.

One implication drawn by double jeopardy proponents is that marketers seeking growth should focus on increasing the size of the customer base rather than on deepening the loyalty of existing customers. Critics of double jeopardy question how inevitable it is and see other implications for marketers. For example, they view new or established brands with a new positioning or message as differentiated enough to avoid double jeopardy's predicted results.

Sources: John Scriven and Gerald Goodhardt, "The Ehrenberg Legacy," *Journal of Advertising Research*, June 2012, pp. 198–202; Byron Sharp, *How Brands Grow: What Marketers Don't Know* (Melbourne, Australia: Oxford University Press, 2010); Nigel Hollis, "The Jeopardy in Double Jeopardy," www.millwardbrown.com, September 2, 2009; Andrew Ehrenberg and Gerald Goodhardt, "Double Jeopardy Revisited, Again," *Marketing Research*, 2002. See also *Andrew Ehrenberg: A Tribute (1926–2010)*, Special Section, *Journal of Advertising Research* 52 (June 2012).

Executive Summary

A brand is a name, term, sign, symbol, or design, or some combination of these elements, intended to identify the goods and services of one seller or group of sellers and to differentiate them from those of competitors. Brands are valuable intangible assets that offer a number of benefits to customers and firms. Brand equity should be defined in terms of marketing effects uniquely attributable to a brand. Building brand equity depends on three main factors: (1) The initial choices for the brand elements or identities making up the brand; (2) the way the brand is integrated into the supporting marketing program; and (3) the associations indirectly transferred to the brand by links to some other entity. Brand audits measure "where the brand has been," and tracking studies measure "where the brand is now."

A branding strategy identifies which brand elements a firm chooses to apply across its various products. In a brand extension, a firm uses an established brand name to introduce a new product. Potential extensions must be judged by how effectively they leverage existing brand equity as well as how effectively they contribute to the equity of the parent brand. Each brand-name product must have a well-defined positioning to maximize coverage, minimize overlap, and thus optimize the portfolio. Customer equity is a concept that is complementary to brand equity and reflects the sum of lifetime values of all customers for a brand. Growing the core—focusing on opportunities with existing products and markets—is often a prudent way to increase sales and profits, less risky than expansion into new product categories.

Notes

1. Jennifer Haderspeck, "Sports and Protein Drinks Share the Glory," *Beverage Industry*, May 2013; Natalie Zmuda, "Why Gatorade Held Big Play for Second Quarter and Print Is Key to New Push," *Advertising Age*, March 25, 2013; Jason Feifer, "How Gatorade Redefined Its Audience and a Flagging Brand," *Fast Company*, June 2012; Duane Stanford, "Gatorade Goes Back to the Lab," *Bloomberg Businessweek*, November 28, 2010; Kate MacArthur, "Gatorade Execs Focus on Sales Gains as Powerade Gulps More of Sports Drink Market," *Chicago Business*, May 30, 2011; Natalie Zmuda, "Morgan Flatley Named CMO of Gatorade, Propel," *Advertising Age*, June 5, 2014.

2. Kevin Lane Keller, *Strategic Brand Management*, 4th ed. (Upper Saddle River, NJ: Pearson, 2013). For other foundational work on branding, see Jean-Noel Kapferer, *The New Strategic Brand Management*, 5th ed. (London, UK: Kogan Page, 2012); Leslie de Chernatony, *From Brand Vision to Brand Evaluation: The Strategic Process of Growing and Strengthening Brands*, 3rd ed. (Oxford, UK: Butterworth-Heinemann, 2010); David A. Aaker and Erich Joachimsthaler, *Brand Leadership* (New York: Free Press, 2000).

3. JoAndrea Hoegg and Joseph W. Alba, "Taste Perception: More than Meets the Tongue," *Journal of Consumer Research* 33 (March 2007), pp. 490–98.

4. Rajneesh Suri and Kent B. Monroe, "The Effects of Time Pressure on Consumers' Judgments of Prices and Products," *Journal of Consumer Research* 30 (June 2003), pp. 92–104.

5. Rosellina Ferraro, Amna Kirmani, and Ted Matherly, "Look at Me! Look at Me! Conspicuous Brand Usage, Self-Brand Connection, and Dilution," *Journal of Marketing Research* 50 (August 2013), pp. 477–88; Alexander Chernev, Ryan Hamilton, and David Gal, "Competing for Consumer Identity: Limits to Self-Expression and the Perils of Lifestyle Branding," *Journal of Marketing* 75 (May 2011).

6. Pankaj Aggrawal and Ann L. McGill, "When Brands Seem Human, Do Humans Act Like Brands? Automatic Behavioral Priming Effects of Brand Anthropomorphism," *Journal of Consumer Research* 39 (August 2012), pp. 307–23. For some related research, see Nicolas Kervyn, Susan T. Fiske, and Chris Malone, "Brands as Intentional Agents Framework: How Perceived Intentions and Ability Can Map Brand Perception," *Journal of Consumer Psychology* 22 (2012), pp. 166–76, as well as commentaries on that article published in that issue.

7. Tilde Heding, Charlotte F. Knudtzen, and Mogens Bjerre, *Brand Management: Research, Theory & Practice* (New York: Routledge, 2009); Rita Clifton and John

Simmons, eds., *The Economist on Branding* (New York: Bloomberg Press, 2004); Rik Riezebos, *Brand Management* (Essex, UK: Pearson Education, 2003); and Paul Temporal, *Advanced Brand Management: From Vision to Valuation* (Singapore: John Wiley & Sons, 2002).

8. Constance E. Bagley, *Managers and the Legal Environment: Strategies for the 21st Century,* 3rd ed. (Cincinnati, OH: South-Western College/West Publishing, 2005); for a marketing academic point of view of some important legal issues, see Judith Zaichkowsky, *The Psychology behind Trademark Infringement and Counterfeiting* (Mahwah, NJ: LEA Publishing, 2006) and Maureen Morrin, Jonathan Lee, and Greg M. Allenby, "Determinants of Trademark Dilution," *Journal of Consumer Research* 33 (September 2006), pp. 248–57.

9. Xueming Luo, Sascha Raithel, and Michael A. Wiles, "The Impact of Brand Rating Dispersion on Firm Value," *Journal of Marketing Research* 50 (June 2013), pp. 399–415.

10. Scott Davis, *Brand Asset Management: Driving Profitable Growth through Your Brands* (San Francisco: Jossey-Bass, 2000); Mary W. Sullivan, "How Brand Names Affect the Demand for Twin Automobiles," *Journal of Marketing Research* 35 (May 1998), pp. 154–65.

11. The power of branding is not without its critics, however, some of whom reject the commercialism associated with branding activities. See Naomi Klein, *No Logo: Taking Aim at the Brand Bullies* (New York: Picador, 2000).

12. For an academic discussion of how consumers become so strongly attached to people as brands, see Matthew Thomson, "Human Brands: Investigating Antecedents to Consumers' Stronger Attachments to Celebrities," *Journal of Marketing* 70 (July 2006), pp. 104–19.

13. Other approaches are based on economic principles of signaling (e.g., Tulin Erdem, "Brand Equity as a Signaling Phenomenon," *Journal of Consumer Psychology* 7 [1998], pp. 131–57) or more of a sociological, anthropological, or biological perspective (e.g., Grant McCracken, *Culture and Consumption II: Markets, Meaning, and Brand Management* (Bloomington: Indiana University Press, 2005)). For a broad view of consumer psychology perspectives on branding, see Bernd Schmitt, "The Consumer Psychology of Brands," *Journal of Consumer Psychology* 22 (2012), pp. 7–17.

14. For an overview of academic research on branding, see Kevin Lane Keller, "Branding and Brand Equity," Bart Weitz and Robin Wensley, eds., *Handbook of Marketing* (London: Sage Publications, 2002), pp. 151–78; Kevin Lane Keller and Don Lehmann, "Brands and Branding: Research Findings and Future Priorities," *Marketing Science* 25 (November–December 2006), pp. 740–59.

15. Keller, *Strategic Brand Management.*

16. Kusum Ailawadi, Donald R. Lehmann, and Scott Neslin, "Revenue Premium as an Outcome Measure of Brand Equity," *Journal of Marketing* 67 (October 2003), pp. 1–17.

17. Kevin Lane Keller, "Building Customer-Based Brand Equity: A Blueprint for Creating Strong Brands," *Marketing Management* 10 (July–August 2001), pp. 15–19.

18. M. Berk Ataman, Carl F. Mela, and Harald J. van Heerde, "Building Brands," *Marketing Science* 27 (November–December 2008), pp. 1036–54.

19. Todd Wasserman, "Why Microsoft Chose the Name 'Bing,'" *Brandweek*, June 1, 2009, p. 33.

20. Jefferson Graham, "General Mills Spoons Up Digital Fun on Cereal Boxes," *USA Today*, January 31, 2013.

21. "No Matter How You 'Like' It, 42BELOW Vodka Encourages Everyone to Celebrate National Coming Out Day," *PR Newswire*, October 7, 2011.

22. Alina Wheeler, *Designing Brand Identity* (Hoboken, NJ: John Wiley & Sons, 2003).

23. Eric A. Yorkston and Geeta Menon, "A Sound Idea: Phonetic Effects of Brand Names on Consumer Judgments," *Journal of Consumer Research* 31 (June 2004), pp. 43–51; Tina M. Lowery and L. J. Shrum, "Phonetic Symbolism and Brand Name Preference," *Journal of Consumer Research* 34 (October 2007), pp. 406–14.

24. For interesting theoretical perspectives, see Claudiu V. Dimofte and Richard F. Yalch, "Consumer Response to Polysemous Brand Slogans," *Journal of Consumer Research* 33 (March 2007), pp. 515–22.

25. Don Schultz and Heidi Schultz, *IMC: The Next Generation* (New York: McGraw-Hill, 2003).

26. Dawn Iacobucci and Bobby Calder, eds., *Kellogg on Integrated Marketing* (New York: John Wiley & Sons, 2003).

27. Scott Davis and Michael Dunn, *Building the Brand-Driven Business* (New York: John Wiley & Sons, 2002).

28. For an interesting application of branding to internal projects, see Karen A. Brown, Richard E. Ettenson, and Nancy Lea Hyer, "Why Every Project Needs a Brand (and How to Create One)," *MIT Sloan Management Review*, Summer 2011, pp. 61–68.

29. Deborah Roedder John, Barbara Loken, Kyeong-Heui Kim, and Alokparna Basu Monga, "Brand Concept Maps: A Methodology for Identifying Brand

Association Networks," *Journal of Marketing Research* 43 (November 2006), pp. 549–63.

30. "The Best Global Brands," *Bloomberg BusinessWeek,* October 2, 2012. For an academic discussion, see V. Srinivasan, Chan Su Park, and Dae Ryun Chang, "An Approach to the Measurement, Analysis, and Prediction of Brand Equity and Its Sources," *Management Science* 51 (September 2005), pp. 1433–48. For a comparison of the Interbrand valuation to a consumer-based brand equity measure, see Johny K. Johansson, Claudiu V. Dimofte, and Sanal K. Mazvancheryl, "The Performance of Global Brands in the 2008 Financial Crisis: A Test of Two Brand Value Measures," *International Journal of Research in Marketing* 29 (September 2012), pp. 235–45.

31. Interbrand, the Interbrand Brand Glossary, and Interbrand's Nik Stucky and Rita Clifton, January 2009. For an alternative brand valuation method, see Millward Brown's BrandZ brand valuation methodology: www.millwardbrown.com/BrandZ /Top_100_Global_Brands/Methodology.aspx.

32. Larry Light and Joan Kiddon, *Six Rules for Brand Revitalization: Learn How Companies Like McDonald's Can Re-Energize Their Brands* (Wharton School Publishing, 2009).

33. Jonathan R. Copulsky, *Brand Resilience: Managing Risk and Recovery in a High Speed World* (New York: Palgrave Macmillan, 2011).

34. Rebecca J. Slotegraaf and Koen Pauwels, "The Impact of Brand Equity and Innovation on the Long-Term Effectiveness of Promotions," *Journal of Marketing Research* 45 (June 2008), pp. 293–306.

35. Jing Lei, Niraj Dawar, and Jos Lemmink, "Negative Spillover in Brand Portfolios: Exploring the Antecedents of Asymmetric Effects," *Journal of Marketing* 72 (May 2008), pp. 111–23.

36. For comprehensive corporate branding guidelines, see James R. Gregory, *The Best of Branding: Best Practices in Corporate Branding* (New York: McGraw-Hill, 2004). For some B-to-B applications, see Atlee Valentine Pope and Ralph Oliva, "Building Blocks: Ten Key Roles of B-to-B Corporate Marketing," *Marketing Management,* Winter 2012, pp. 23–28.

37. Guido Berens, Cees B. M. van Riel, and Gerrit H. van Bruggen, "Corporate Associations and Consumer Product Responses: The Moderating Role of Corporate Brand Dominance," *Journal of Marketing* 69 (July 2005), pp. 35–48; Zeynep Gürhan-Canli and Rajeev Batra, "When Corporate Image Affects Product Evaluations: The Moderating Role of Perceived Risk," *Journal of Marketing Research* 41 (May 2004),

pp. 197–205; Gabriel J. Biehal and Daniel A. Sheinin, "The Influence of Corporate Messages on the Product Portfolio," *Journal of Marketing* 71 (April 2007), pp. 12–25.

38. Deborah Roedder John, Barbara Loken, and Christopher Joiner, "The Negative Impact of Extensions: Can Flagship Products Be Diluted?", *Journal of Marketing* 62 (January 1998), pp. 19–32.

39. Nirmalya Kumar, "Kill a Brand, Keep a Customer," *Harvard Business Review,* December 2003, pp. 87–95.

40. Valarie A. Taylor and William O. Bearden, "Ad Spending on Brand Extensions: Does Similarity Matter?," *Journal of Brand Management* 11 (September 2003), pp. 63–74; Sheri Bridges, Kevin Lane Keller, and Sanjay Sood, "Communication Strategies for Brand Extensions: Enhancing Perceived Fit by Establishing Explanatory Links," *Journal of Advertising* 29 (Winter 2000), pp. 1–11.

41. Subramanian Balachander and Sanjoy Ghose, "Reciprocal Spillover Effects: A Strategic Benefit of Brand Extensions," *Journal of Marketing* 67 (January 2003), pp. 4–13.

42. Bharat N. Anand and Ron Shachar, "Brands as Beacons: A New Source of Loyalty to Multiproduct Firms," *Journal of Marketing Research* 41 (May 2004), pp. 135–50.

43. For consumer processing implications, see Huifung Mao and H. Shanker Krishnan, "Effects of Prototype and Exemplar Fit on Brand Extension Evaluations," *Journal of Consumer Research* 33 (June 2006), pp. 41–49; Byung Chul Shine, Jongwon Park, and Robert S. Wyer Jr., "Brand Synergy Effects in Multiple Brand Extensions," *Journal of Marketing Research* 44 (November 2007), pp. 663–70.

44. Pierre Berthon, Morris B. Holbrook, James M. Hulbert, and Leyland F. Pitt, "Viewing Brands in Multiple Dimensions," *MIT Sloan Management Review* (Winter 2007), pp. 37–43.

45. Roland T. Rust, Valerie A. Zeithaml, and Katherine A. Lemon, "Measuring Customer Equity and Calculating Marketing ROI," Rajiv Grover and Marco Vriens, eds., *Handbook of Marketing Research* (Thousand Oaks, CA: Sage Publications, 2006), pp. 588–601.

46. Robert C. Blattberg and John Deighton, "Manage Marketing by the Customer Equity Test," *Harvard Business Review,* July–August 1996, pp. 136–44.

47. Robert C. Blattberg, Gary Getz, and Jacquelyn S. Thomas, *Customer Equity: Building and Managing Relationships as Valuable Assets* (Boston: Harvard Business School Press, 2001).

48. Much of this section is based on Robert Leone, Vithala Rao, Kevin Lane Keller, Man Luo, Leigh McAlister, and Rajendra Srivatstava, "Linking Brand Equity to Customer Equity," *Journal of Service Research* 9 (November 2006), pp. 125–38.

49. Niraj Dawar, "What Are Brands Good For?," *MIT Sloan Management Review* (Fall 2004), pp. 31–37. See also Florian Stahl, Mark Heitmann, Donald R. Lehmann, and Scott A. Neslin, "The Impact of Brand Equity on Customer Acquisition, Retention, and Profit Margin," *Journal of Marketing* 76 (July 2012), pp. 44–63.

50. Philip Kotler and Milton Kotler, *Market Your Way to Growth: 8 Ways to Win* (Hoboken, NJ: John Wiley & Sons, 2013).

51. David Taylor, *Grow the Core: How to Focus on Your Core Business for Brand Success* (West Sussex, UK: John Wiley & Sons, 2012).

Chapter 9

Setting Product Strategy and Introducing New Offerings

In this chapter, we will address the following questions:

1. What are the characteristics of products, and how do marketers classify products? (Page 139)
2. How can companies differentiate products? (Page 140)
3. How can a company build and manage its product mix and product lines? (Page 142)
4. How can companies use packaging, labeling, warranties, and guarantees as marketing tools? (Page 145)
5. What strategies are appropriate for introducing new offerings and influencing adoption? (Page 146)
6. What strategies are appropriate in different stages of the product life cycle? (Page 152)

Marketing Management at Lexus

Since its inception in 1989, Lexus has emphasized top-notch product quality and customer care, as reflected by its long-time slogan, "The Relentless Pursuit of Perfection." As part of its "Lexus Covenant," it has vowed to "have the finest dealer network in the industry, and treat each customer as we would a guest in our own home." To this end, Lexus built its dealership framework from the ground up, hand-picking dealers committed to providing exceptional experience to customers, a system competitors acknowledge is the industry ideal. With its average buyer in his or her mid-50s, Lexus has set its sights on attracting younger buyers by emphasizing more aggressive styling, handling dynamics, and driver engagement. Social media and other promotions and events also create novel customer experiences around food, fashion, entertainment, and travel.[1]

At the heart of a great brand is a great product offering, which customers judge on three basic elements: product features and quality, service mix and quality, and price. In this chapter we examine product strategy, new product development, and the product life cycle. Chapter 10 explores services, and Chapter 11 discusses price.

Product Characteristics and Classifications

A **product** is anything that can be offered to a market to satisfy a want or need, including physical goods, services, experiences, events, persons, places, properties, organizations, information, and ideas.

Product Levels: The Customer-Value Hierarchy

In planning its market offering, the marketer needs to address five product levels (see Figure 9.1).[2] Each level adds more customer value, and together the five constitute a **customer-value hierarchy.** The fundamental level is the *core benefit*: the service or benefit the customer is really buying. A hotel guest is buying rest and sleep. Marketers must see themselves as benefit providers. At the second level, the marketer must turn the core benefit into a *basic product*. Thus, a hotel room includes a bed, bathroom, and towels. At the third level, the marketer prepares an *expected product*, a set of attributes and conditions buyers normally expect when they purchase this product. Hotel guests expect a clean bed, fresh towels, and so on.

At the fourth level, the marketer prepares an *augmented product* that exceeds customer expectations. In developed countries, brand positioning and competition take place at this level. At the fifth level stands the *potential product*, with all the possible augmentations and transformations the product or offering might undergo in the future. Here companies search for new ways to satisfy customers and distinguish their offering.

Differentiation arises and competition increasingly occurs on the basis of product augmentation. Each augmentation adds cost, however, and augmented benefits soon become expected benefits in the category. As some companies raise the price of their augmented product, others

FIGURE 9.1 Five Product Levels

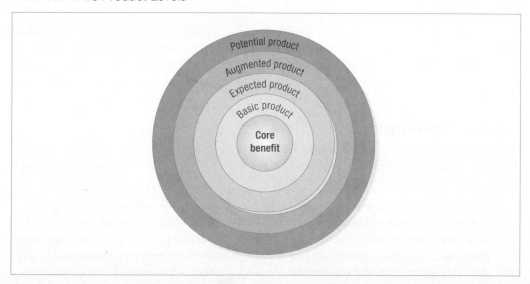

offer a stripped-down version for less. Marketers must be sure, however, that consumers not see lower quality or limited capability versions as unfair.[3]

Product Classifications

Marketers classify products on the basis of durability, tangibility, and use (consumer or industrial). Each type has an appropriate marketing-mix strategy.[4]

- **Durability and tangibility.** *Nondurable goods* are tangible goods (such as shampoo) normally consumed in one or a few uses. Because these are purchased frequently, the appropriate strategy is to make them available in many locations, charge a small markup, and advertise to induce trial and build preference. *Durable goods* are tangible goods (such as refrigerators) that survive many uses, require more personal selling and service, command a higher margin, and require more seller guarantees. *Services* are intangible, inseparable, variable, and perishable products (such as haircuts) that normally require more quality control, supplier credibility, and adaptability.

- **Consumer-goods classification.** Classified on the basis of shopping habits, these include **convenience goods** (such as soft drinks) that are purchased frequently, immediately, and with minimal effort; **shopping goods** (such as furniture) that consumers compare on such bases as suitability, quality, price, and style; **specialty goods** (such as cars) with unique characteristics or brand identification for which enough buyers are willing to make a special purchasing effort; and **unsought goods** (such as smoke detectors) that the consumer does not know about or normally think of buying.

- **Industrial-goods classification.** *Materials and parts* are goods that enter the manufacturer's product completely. *Raw materials* can be either *farm products* (wheat) or *natural products* (iron ore). *Manufactured materials and parts* fall into two categories: component materials (wires) and component parts (small motors). **Capital items** are long-lasting goods that facilitate developing or managing the finished product, including *installations* (factories) and *equipment* (tools). *Supplies and business services* are short-term goods and services that facilitate developing or managing the finished product.

Differentiation

To be branded, product offerings must be differentiated. At one extreme are products that allow little variation: chicken and steel. Yet even here some differentiation is possible: Perdue chickens and India's Tata Steel have carved out distinct identities in their categories. At the other extreme are products capable of high differentiation, such as automobiles, commercial buildings, and furniture.

Product Differentiation

Means for differentiation include form, features, performance quality, conformance quality, durability, reliability, repairability, style, and customization.[5] As discussed below, design is also a means for differentiation.

- **Form. Form** refers to the size, shape, or physical structure of a product. For example, aspirin can be differentiated by dosage size, shape, color, coating, or action time.

- **Features.** Most products can be offered with varying **features** that supplement their basic function. A company can identify and select new features by surveying recent buyers and then calculating *customer value* versus *company cost* for each potential feature. Marketers should consider how many people want each feature, how long it would take to introduce it, and whether competitors could easily copy it.[6]

- **Performance quality. Performance quality** is the level at which the product's primary characteristics operate. Firms should design a performance level appropriate to the target market and competition (not necessarily the highest level possible) and manage performance quality through time.

- **Conformance quality.** Buyers expect a high **conformance quality,** the degree to which all produced units are identical and meet promised specifications. A product with low conformance quality will disappoint some buyers.

- **Durability.** *Durability*, a measure of the product's expected operating life under natural or stressful conditions, is a valued attribute for durable goods. The extra price for durability must not be excessive, and the product must not be subject to rapid technological obsolescence.

- **Reliability.** Buyers normally will pay a premium for *reliability,* a measure of the probability that a product will not malfunction or fail within a specified period.

- **Repairability.** *Repairability* measures the ease of fixing a product when it malfunctions or fails. Ideal repairability would exist if users could fix the product themselves with little cost in money or time.

- **Style.** *Style* describes the product's look and feel to the buyer and creates distinctiveness that is hard to copy, although strong style does not always mean high performance. Style plays a key role in the marketing of many brands, such as Apple's tablets.

- **Customization.** Customized products and marketing allow firms to be highly relevant and differentiating by finding out exactly what a person wants and delivering on that. Customized products include M&M's with specialized messages and Burberry coats with customer-selected fabric and accessories.[7]

Services Differentiation

When the physical product cannot easily be differentiated, the key to competitive success may lie in adding valued services and improving their quality. The main service differentiators are:

- **Ordering ease.** How easy is it for the customer to place an order with the company?

- **Delivery.** How well is the product or service brought to the customer, including speed, accuracy, and care throughout the process?

- **Installation.** How is the product made operational in its planned location? This is a true selling point for buyers of complex products like heavy equipment.

- **Customer training.** How does the supplier teach a customer's employees to use new equipment properly and efficiently?

- **Customer consulting.** What data, information systems, and advice services can companies sell to buyers?

- **Maintenance and repair.** How can companies help customers keep purchased products in good working order? These services are critical in business-to-business settings and with luxury products.

Design Differentiation

As competition intensifies, design offers a potent way to differentiate and position a company's products and services. **Design** is the totality of features that affect the way a product looks, feels, and functions to a consumer. It offers functional and aesthetic benefits and appeals to both our rational and emotional sides.[8] As holistic marketers recognize the emotional power of design and the importance to consumers of look and feel as well as function, design is exerting a stronger influence in categories where it once played a small role. To the company, a well-designed product is easy to manufacture and distribute. To the customer, it is pleasant to look at and easy to open, install, use, repair, and dispose of.

Product and Brand Relationships

Each product can be related to other products to ensure that a firm is offering and marketing the optimal set of products.

The Product Hierarchy

The product hierarchy stretches from basic needs to particular items that satisfy those needs. A **product system** is a group of diverse but related items that function in a compatible manner.[9] A **product mix** (also called a **product assortment**) is the set of all products and items a particular firm offers for sale. A product mix consists of various product lines. As shown in Table 9.1, a company's product mix has a certain width, length, depth, and consistency. The table shows these concepts for selected Procter & Gamble products.

The *width* of a product mix refers to how many different product lines the company carries. Table 9.1 shows a product mix width of five lines (only a portion of what Procter & Gamble offers). The *length* of a product mix refers to the total number of items in the mix. The *depth* of a product mix refers to how many variants are offered of each product in the line. The *consistency* of the product mix describes how closely related the various product lines are in end use, production requirements, distribution channels, or some other way.

These product mix dimensions permit the company to expand its business in four ways. It can add new product lines, thus widening its product mix; lengthen each product line; add more

TABLE 9.1	Product Mix Width and Product Line Length for Procter & Gamble Products (including year of introduction)				
	Product Mix Width				
	Detergents	**Toothpaste**	**Bar Soap**	**Disposable Diapers**	**Paper Products**
	Ivory Snow (1930)	Gleem (1952)	Ivory (1879)	Pampers (1961)	Charmin (1928)
	Dreft (1933)	Crest (1955)	Camay (1926)	Luvs (1976)	Puffs (1960)
Product Line Length	Tide (1946)		Zest (1952)		Bounty (1965)
	Cheer (1950)		Safeguard (1963)		
	Dash (1954)		Oil of Olay (1993)		
	Bold (1965)				
	Gain (1966)				
	Era (1972)				

product variants to deepen its product mix; and pursue more product line consistency. To make these product decisions, marketers conduct product line analysis.

Product Line Analysis

In offering a product line, companies normally develop a basic platform and modules that can be added to meet different customer requirements, the way car manufacturers build vehicles around a basic platform. Product line managers need to know the sales and profits of each item in each line to determine which ones to build, maintain, harvest, or divest.[10] They also need to understand each line's market profile and image.[11] Marketers can use a *product map* to see which competitors' items are competing against their own items and to identify market segments so they can gauge how well their items are positioned to serve the needs of each segment.

Product Line Length

Companies seeking high market share and market growth will generally carry longer product lines. Those emphasizing high profitability will carry shorter lines of carefully chosen items. However, consumers are increasingly weary of dense product lines, overextended brands, and feature-laden products (see "Marketing Insight: When Less Is More").[12]

---

marketing insight When Less Is More

With thousands of new products introduced each year, consumers find it ever harder to navigate store aisles. One study found the average shopper spent 40 seconds or more in the super-market soda aisle, compared with 25 seconds six or seven years ago. Although consumers may think greater product variety increases their likelihood of finding the right product for them, the reality is often different. According to research, when presented with too many options, people "choose not to choose," even if it may not be in their best interests.

Similarly, if product quality in an assortment is high, consumers actually prefer fewer choices. Those with well-defined preferences may benefit from more-differentiated products that offer specific benefits, but others may experience frustration, confusion, and regret. Also, constant product changes and introductions may nudge customers into reconsidering their choices and perhaps switching to a competitor's product. It's not just

product lines making consumer heads spin—many products themselves are too complicated. Technology marketers need to be especially sensitive to the problems of information overload.

Sources: John Davidson, "One Classic Example of When Less Is More," *Financial Review*, April 9, 2013; Carolyn Cutrone, "Cutting Down on Choice Is the Best Way to Make Better Decisions," *Business Insider*, January 10, 2013; Dimitri Kuksov and J. Miguel Villas-Boas, "When More Alternatives Lead to Less Choice," *Marketing Science*, 29 (May/June 2010), pp. 507–24; Kristin Diehl and Cait Poynor, "Great Expectations?! Assortment Size, Expectations, and Satisfaction," *Journal of Marketing Research* 46 (April 2009), pp. 312–22; Joseph P. Redden and Stephen J. Hoch, "The Presence of Variety Reduces Perceived Quantity," *Journal of Consumer Research* 36 (October 2009), pp. 406–17; Alexander Chernev and Ryan Hamilton, "Assortment Size and Option Attractiveness in Consumer Choice Among Retailers," *Journal of Marketing Research* 46 (June 2009), pp. 410–20; Richard A. Briesch, Pradeep K. Chintagunta, and Edward J. Fox, "How Does Assortment Affect Grocery Store Choice," *Journal of Marketing Research* 46 (April 2009), pp. 176–89; Susan M. Broniarczyk, "Product Assortment," Curt P. Haugtvedt, Paul M. Herr, and Frank R. Kardes, eds., *Handbook of Consumer Psychology* (New York: Taylor & Francis, 2008), pp. 755–79.

A company lengthens its product line in two ways: line stretching and line filling. *Line stretching* occurs when a company lengthens its product line beyond its current range. A firm may choose a down-market stretch—introducing a lower-priced line—to attract shoppers who want value-priced goods, battle low-end competitors, or avoid a stagnating middle market. With an up-market stretch, the firm aims to achieve more growth, realize higher margins, or simply position itself as a full-line manufacturer. Companies serving the middle market might stretch their line in both directions.

With *line filling*, a firm lengthens its product line by adding more items within the present range. The goals are to reach for incremental profits, satisfy dealers who complain about lost sales because of items missing from the line, utilize excess capacity, try to become the leading full-line company, and plug holes to keep out competitors.

Line Modernization, Featuring, and Pruning

Product lines need to be modernized. In rapidly changing markets, modernization is continuous. Companies plan improvements to encourage customer migration to higher-value, higher-price items. Marketers want to time improvements so they do not appear too early (damaging sales of the current line) or too late (giving the competition time to establish a strong reputation).[13] The firm typically selects one or a few items in the line to feature, possibly a low-priced item to attract customers or a high-end item for prestige. Multi-brand companies all over the world try to optimize their brand portfolios, ensuring that every product in a line plays a role. This often means focusing on core brand growth and concentrating resources on the biggest and most established brands.

Product Mix Pricing

Marketers must modify their price-setting logic when the product is part of a product mix. In **product mix pricing,** the firm searches for a set of prices that maximizes profits on the total mix. The process is challenging because the various products have demand and cost interrelationships and are subject to different degrees of competition. We can distinguish six situations calling for product mix pricing, as shown in Table 9.2.

TABLE 9.2   Product Mix Pricing Situations

1. ***Product line pricing.*** The seller introduces price steps within a product line and strives to establish perceived quality differences that justify the price differences.

2. ***Optional-feature pricing.*** The seller offers optional products, features, and services with the main product, the way automakers offer different trim levels. The challenge is which options to include in the standard price and which to offer separately.

3. ***Captive-product pricing.*** Some products require the use of ancillary or *captive products.* Manufacturers of razors often price them low and set high markups on razor blades, the captive product. If the captive product is priced too high, however, counterfeiting and substitutions can erode sales.

4. ***Two-part pricing.*** Many service firms charge a fixed fee plus a variable usage fee. Cell phone users often pay a monthly fee plus charges for calls that exceed their allotted minutes. The challenge is deciding how much to charge for basic service and variable usage.

5. ***By-product pricing.*** The production of certain goods (such as meats) often yields by-products that should be priced on their value. Income from the by-products will make it easier for the company to charge less for its main product if competition forces it to do so.

6. ***Product-bundling pricing.*** *Pure bundling* occurs when a firm offers its products only as a bundle. In *mixed bundling,* the seller offers goods both individually and in bundles, normally charging less for the bundle than for the items purchased separately. Savings on the price bundle must be enough to induce customers to buy it.

Co-Branding and Ingredient Branding

Marketers often combine their products with products from other companies in various ways. In **co-branding**—also called dual branding or brand bundling—two or more well-known brands are combined into a joint product or marketed together in some fashion. One form of co-branding is *same-company co-branding,* as when General Mills advertises Trix cereal and Yoplait yogurt. Other forms are *joint-venture co-branding, multiple-sponsor co-branding*, and *retail co-branding.* For co-branding to succeed, the brands must separately have brand equity—adequate brand awareness and a sufficiently positive brand image.

The main advantage of co-branding is that a product can be convincingly positioned by virtue of the multiple brands, generating greater sales from the existing market and opening opportunities for new consumers and channels. It can also reduce the cost of product introduction because it combines two well-known images and speeds adoption. And co-branding may be a valuable means to learn about consumers and how other companies approach them. The potential disadvantages are the risks and lack of control in becoming aligned with another brand. Consumer expectations of co-brands are likely to be high, so unsatisfactory performance could have negative repercussions for both brands. Also, consumers may feel less sure of what they know about the brand.[14]

Ingredient branding is a special case of co-branding.[15] It creates brand equity for materials, components, or parts that are necessarily contained within other branded products. For host products whose brands are not that strong, ingredient brands can provide differentiation and important signals of quality.[16] An interesting take on ingredient branding is *self-branded ingredients* that companies advertise and even trademark.[17] Westin Hotels advertises its own "Heavenly Bed"—an important ingredient for a guest's good night's sleep. Ingredient brands try to create enough awareness and preference so consumers will not buy a host product that doesn't contain it.

What are the requirements for successful ingredient branding?[18]

1. Consumers must believe the ingredient matters to the performance and success of the end product. Ideally, this intrinsic value is easily seen or experienced.

2. Consumers must be convinced that not all ingredient brands are the same and that the ingredient is superior.

3. A distinctive symbol or logo must clearly signal that the host product contains the ingredient. Ideally, this symbol or logo functions like a "seal" and is simple and versatile, credibly communicating quality and confidence.

4. A coordinated "pull" and "push" program must help consumers understand the advantages of the branded ingredient. Channel members must offer full support such as consumer advertising and promotions and—sometimes in collaboration with manufacturers—retail merchandising and promotion programs.

Packaging, Labeling, Warranties, and Guarantees

Many marketers have called packaging a fifth P, along with price, product, place, and promotion. Most, however, treat packaging and labeling as an element of product strategy. Warranties and guarantees can also be an important part of the product strategy.

Packaging

Packaging includes all the activities of designing and producing the container for a product. Packages might have up to three layers: a primary package inside a secondary package, with one or more packaged units sent in a shipping package. Packaging is important because it is the buyer's first encounter with the product. A good package draws the consumer in and encourages product choice. Distinctive packaging like that for Altoids mints is an important part of a brand's equity.

Packaging must achieve a number of objectives: (1) identify the brand, (2) convey descriptive and persuasive information, (3) facilitate product transportation and protection, (4) assist at-home storage, and (5) aid at-home consumption. Functionally, structural design is crucial. Aesthetic considerations relate to a package's size and shape, material, color, text, and graphics. The packaging elements must harmonize with each other and with pricing, advertising, and other parts of the marketing program. Color can define a brand, from Tiffany's blue box to UPS's brown trucks. Packaging updates and redesigns can keep the brand contemporary, relevant, or practical, but they can also have a downside if consumers dislike the new package or confuse it with other brands. Companies must also consider environmental and safety concerns about excess and wasteful packaging.

Labeling

The label can be a simple attached tag or an elaborately designed graphic that is part of the package. A label performs several functions. First, it *identifies* the product or brand—for instance, the name Sunkist stamped on oranges. It might also *grade* the product; canned peaches are grade-labeled A, B, and C. The label might *describe* the product: who made it, where and when, what it contains, how it is to be used, and how to use it safely. Finally, the label might *promote* the product through attractive graphics.

Labels eventually need freshening up. The label on Ivory soap has been redone at least 18 times since the 1890s, with gradual changes in the size and design of the letters. Legal and regulatory requirements must also be considered. For example, processed foods must carry nutritional labeling that clearly states the amounts of protein, fat, carbohydrates, and calories as well as vitamin and mineral content as a percentage of the recommended daily allowance.[19]

Warranties and Guarantees

All sellers are legally responsible for fulfilling a buyer's normal or reasonable expectations. **Warranties** are formal statements of expected product performance by the manufacturer. Products under warranty can be returned to the manufacturer or designated repair center for repair, replacement, or refund. Whether expressed or implied, warranties are legally enforceable. Guarantees reduce the buyer's perceived risk. They suggest that the product is of high quality and the company and its service performance are dependable. They can be especially helpful when the company or product is not well known or when the product's quality is superior to that of competitors.

Managing New Products

A company can add new products through acquisition (buying another firm, buying patents from other firms, licensing or franchising from another firm) or organically through development from within (in its own laboratories, contracting with independent researchers, or hiring a new-product development firm).[20] New products range from new-to-the-world items that create an entirely new market to minor improvements or revisions of existing products. Most new-product activity is devoted to improving existing products. In contrast, new-to-the-world products incur the greatest cost and risk. And while radical innovations can hurt the company's bottom line in the short run, if they succeed they can improve the corporate image, create a greater sustainable competitive advantage than ordinary products, and produce significant rewards.[21]

The Innovation Imperative and New Product Success

In an economy of rapid change, continuous innovation is a necessity. Companies that fail to develop new products leave themselves vulnerable to changing customer needs and tastes, shortened product life cycles, increased domestic and foreign competition, and especially new technologies. Most established companies focus on *incremental innovation*, entering new markets by tweaking products for new customers, using variations on a core product to stay one step ahead of the market, and creating interim solutions for industry-wide problems. Newer companies create *disruptive technologies* that are cheaper and more likely to alter the competitive space.

New-product specialists Robert Cooper and Elko Kleinschmidt found that unique, superior products succeed 98 percent of the time, compared with products that have a moderate advantage (58 percent success) or minimal advantage (18 percent success). Other factors include a well-defined product concept, well-defined target market and benefits, technological and marketing synergy, quality of execution, and market attractiveness.[22]

New products continue to fail at rates estimated as high as 50 percent or even 95 percent in the United States and 90 percent in Europe.[23] The reasons are many: ignored or misinterpreted market research; overestimates of market size; high development costs; poor design or ineffectual performance; incorrect positioning, advertising, or price; insufficient distribution support; competitors who fight back hard; and inadequate ROI or payback.

New Product Development

The stages in new product development are shown in Figure 9.2 and discussed next.

Idea Generation　The new-product development process starts with the search for ideas. Some marketing experts believe we find the greatest opportunities and highest leverage for new

FIGURE 9.2 The New-Product Development Decision Process

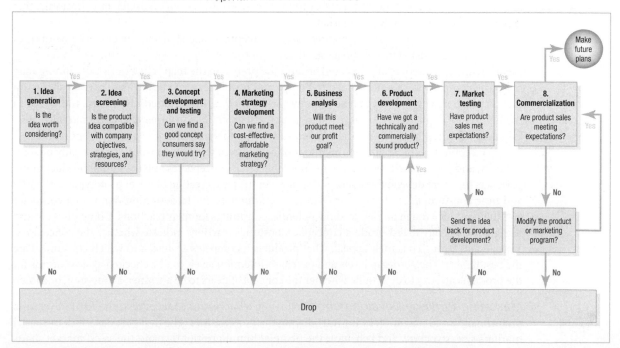

products by uncovering the best possible set of unmet customer needs or technological innovation.[24] Ideas can come from interacting with customers, employees, scientists, and other groups; from using creativity techniques; and from studying competitors. Through Internet-based **crowdsourcing,** paid or unpaid outsiders can offer needed expertise or a different perspective on a new-product project that might otherwise be overlooked. The traditional company-centric approach to product innovation is giving way to a world in which companies cocreate products with consumers. Besides producing new and better ideas, cocreation can help customers feel closer to the company and create favorable word of mouth.[25]

Idea Screening   The purpose of screening is to drop poor ideas as early as possible because product-development costs rise substantially at each successive development stage. Most companies require new-product ideas to be described on a standard form for a committee's review. The description states the product idea, the target market, and the competition and estimates market size, product price, development time and costs, manufacturing costs, and rate of return. The executive committee then reviews each idea against a set of criteria. Does the product meet a need? Would it offer superior value? Can it be distinctively advertised or promoted? Does the company have the necessary know-how and capital? Will the new product deliver the expected sales volume, sales growth, and profit? The committee estimates whether the probability of success is high enough to warrant continued development.

Concept Development and Testing   A *product idea* is a possible product the company might offer to the market. A *product concept* is an elaborated version of the idea expressed in consumer terms. A product idea can be turned into several concepts by asking: Who will use this product? What primary benefit should this product provide? When will people consume or use it? By answering these questions, a company can form several concepts, select the most promising, and create a *product-positioning map* for it. Figure 9.3(a) shows the positioning of a product concept, a low-cost instant breakfast drink, based on the two dimensions of cost and preparation time and compared with other breakfast foods. These contrasts can be useful in communicating and promoting a concept to the market.

Figure 9.3 (b) is a *brand-positioning map*, a perceptual map showing the current positions of three existing brands of instant breakfast drinks (Brands A–C) as seen by consumers in four segments, whose preferences are clustered around the points on the map. The brand-positioning map helps the company decide how much to charge and how calorific to make its drink. As shown on this map, the new brand would be distinctive in the medium-price, medium-calorie market or in the high-price, high-calorie market. There is also a segment of consumers (4) clustered fairly near the medium-price, medium-calorie market, suggesting this may offer the greatest opportunity.

Concept testing means presenting the product concept to target consumers, physically or symbolically, and getting their reactions. The more the tested concepts resemble the final product or experience, the more dependable concept testing is. In the past, creating physical prototypes was costly and time consuming, but today firms can use *rapid prototyping* to design products on a computer and then produce rough models to show potential consumers for their reactions. Companies are also using *virtual reality* to test product concepts. Consumer reactions indicate whether the concept has a broad and strong consumer appeal, what products it competes against, and which consumers are the best targets. The need-gap levels and purchase-intention levels can be checked against norms for the product category to determine whether the concept appears to be a winner, a long shot, or a loser.

Marketing Strategy Development   Following a successful concept test, the firm develops a preliminary three-part strategy for introducing the new product. The first part describes the target market's size, structure, and behavior; the planned brand positioning; and the sales, market share,

FIGURE 9.3 Product and Brand Positioning

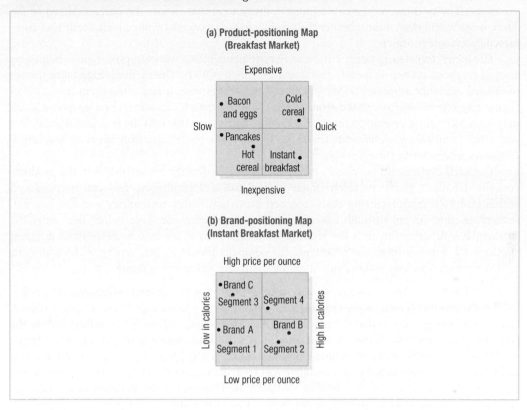

and profit goals sought in the first few years. The second part outlines the planned price, distribution strategy, and marketing budget for the first year. The third part describes the long-run sales and profit goals and marketing-mix strategy over time. This strategy lays a foundation for the business analysis.

Business Analysis   Here the firm evaluates the proposed product's business attractiveness. Management needs to prepare sales, cost, and profit projections to determine whether they satisfy company objectives. If they do, the concept can move to the development stage. As new information comes in, the business analysis will undergo revision and expansion. Sales-estimation methods depend on whether the product is purchased once (such as an engagement ring), infrequently, or often.

For one-time products, sales rise at the beginning, peak, and approach zero as the number of potential buyers becomes exhausted; if new buyers keep entering the market, the curve will not drop to zero. Infrequently purchased products such as automobiles exhibit replacement cycles dictated by physical wear or obsolescence associated with changing styles, features, and performance. Therefore, sales forecasts must estimate first-time sales and replacement sales separately. With frequently purchased products, such as consumer and industrial nondurables, the number of first-time buyers initially increases and then decreases as fewer buyers are left (assuming a fixed population). Repeat purchases occur soon, providing the product satisfies some buyers. The sales curve eventually falls to a plateau of steady repeat-purchase volume; by this time, the product is no longer a new product.

Product Development   Up to now, the product has existed only as a description, drawing, or prototype. The next step represents a jump in investment that dwarfs the costs incurred so far. The company will determine whether the product idea can translate into a technically and commercially feasible product.

The job of translating target customer requirements into a working prototype is helped by a set of methods known as *quality function deployment* (QFD). The methodology takes the list of desired *customer attributes* (CAs) generated by market research and turns them into a list of *engineering attributes* (EAs) that engineers can use. For example, customers of a proposed truck may want a certain acceleration rate (CA). Engineers can turn this into the required horsepower and other engineering equivalents (EAs). QFD improves communication between marketers, engineers, and manufacturing people.[26]

The R&D department develops a prototype that embodies the key attributes in the product-concept statement, performs safely under normal use and conditions, and can be produced within budgeted manufacturing costs, speeded by virtual reality technology and the Internet. Prototypes must be put through rigorous functional and customer tests before they enter the marketplace. *Alpha testing* tests the product within the firm to see how it performs in different applications. After refining the prototype, the company moves to *beta testing* with customers, bringing consumers into a laboratory or giving them samples to use at home.

Market Testing   After management is satisfied with functional and psychological performance, the product is ready to be branded with a name, logo, and packaging and go into a market test. Not all companies undertake market testing. The amount of testing is influenced by the investment cost and risk on the one hand and time pressure and research cost on the other. High-investment–high-risk products, whose chance of failure is high, must be market tested; the cost will be an insignificant percentage of total project cost. Consumer-products tests seek to estimate four variables: *trial*, *first repeat*, *adoption*, and *purchase frequency.* Table 9.3 shows four methods of consumer-goods testing, from the least costly to the most costly.

Expensive industrial goods and new technologies will normally undergo alpha and beta testing. During beta testing, the company's technical people observe how customers use the product,

TABLE 9.3	Methods of Market Testing Consumer Goods
Method	**Description**
Sales-wave research	Consumers who initially try the product at no cost are reoffered it, or a competitor's product, at slightly reduced prices. The offer may be made as many as five times (sales waves), while the company notes how many customers select it again and their reported level of satisfaction.
Simulated test marketing	Thirty to 40 qualified shoppers are asked about brand familiarity and preferences in a specific product category and attend a brief screening of advertising. Consumers receive a small amount of money and are invited into a store to shop. The company notes how many consumers buy the new brand and competing brands and asks consumers why they bought or did not buy. Those who did not buy the new brand are given a free sample and are reinterviewed later to determine attitudes, usage, satisfaction, and repurchase intention.
Controlled test marketing	A research firm delivers the product to a panel of participating stores and controls shelf position, pricing, and number of facings, displays, and point-of-purchase promotions. The company can evaluate sales, the impact of local advertising and promotions, and customers' impressions of the product.
Test markets	The company chooses a few representative cities, implements a full marketing communications campaign, and sells the trade on carrying the product. Marketers must decide how many test cities to use, how long the test will last, and what data will be collected. At the conclusion, they must decide what action to take. Many companies today skip test marketing and rely on faster and more economical testing methods.

a practice that often exposes unanticipated problems of safety and servicing and alerts the company to customer training and servicing requirements. At trade shows the company can observe how much interest buyers show in the new product, how they react to features and terms, and how many express purchase intentions or place orders. In distributor and dealer display rooms, products may stand next to the manufacturer's other products and possibly competitors' products, yielding preference and pricing information in the product's normal selling atmosphere. However, customers who come in might not represent the target market, or they might want to place early orders that cannot be filled.

Commercialization   Commercialization is the costliest stage in the process because the firm will need to contract for manufacture, or it may build or rent a full-scale manufacturing facility. Most new-product campaigns also require a sequenced mix of market communication tools to build awareness and ultimately preference, choice, and loyalty.[27] Market timing is critical.

If a firm learns that a competitor is readying a new product, one choice is *first entry* (for "first mover advantages" of locking up key distributors and customers and gaining leadership). However, this can backfire if the product has not been thoroughly debugged. A second choice is *parallel entry* (timing its entry to coincide with the competitor's entry to gain both products more attention). A third choice is *late entry* (delaying its launch until after the competitor has borne the cost of educating the market). This might reveal flaws the late entrant can avoid and also show the size of the market.

Most companies will develop a planned market rollout over time. In choosing rollout markets, the major criteria are market potential, the company's local reputation, the cost of filling the pipeline, the cost of communication media, the influence of the area on other areas, and competitive penetration. With the Internet connecting far-flung parts of the globe, competition is more likely to cross national borders. Companies are increasingly rolling out new products simultaneously across the globe.

The Consumer-Adoption Process

Adoption is an individual's decision to become a regular user of a product and is followed by the *consumer-loyalty process*. New-product marketers typically aim at early adopters and use the theory of innovation diffusion and consumer adoption to identify them.

Stages in the Adoption Process

An **innovation** is any good, service, or idea that someone *perceives* as new, no matter how long its history. Everett Rogers defines the **innovation diffusion process** as "the spread of a new idea from its source of invention or creation to its ultimate users or adopters."[28] The *consumer-adoption process* is the mental steps through which an individual passes from first hearing about an innovation to final adoption.[29] These five steps are: (1) *awareness* (consumer becomes aware of the innovation but lacks information about it), (2) *interest* (consumer is stimulated to seek information about the innovation), (3) *evaluation* (consumer considers whether to try the innovation), (4) *trial* (consumer tries the innovation to estimate its value), and (5) *adoption* (consumer decides to make full and regular use of the innovation).

Factors Influencing the Adoption Process

Rogers defines a person's level of innovativeness as "the degree to which an individual is relatively earlier in adopting new ideas than the other members of his social system." As Figure 9.4 shows, innovators are the first to adopt something new. After a slow start, an increasing number

FIGURE 9.4 Adopter Categorization on the Basis of Relative Time of Adoption of Innovations

$2\frac{1}{2}$%
Innovators

$13\frac{1}{2}$%
Early adopters

34%
Early majority

34%
Late majority

16%
Laggards

Time of Adoption of Innovations

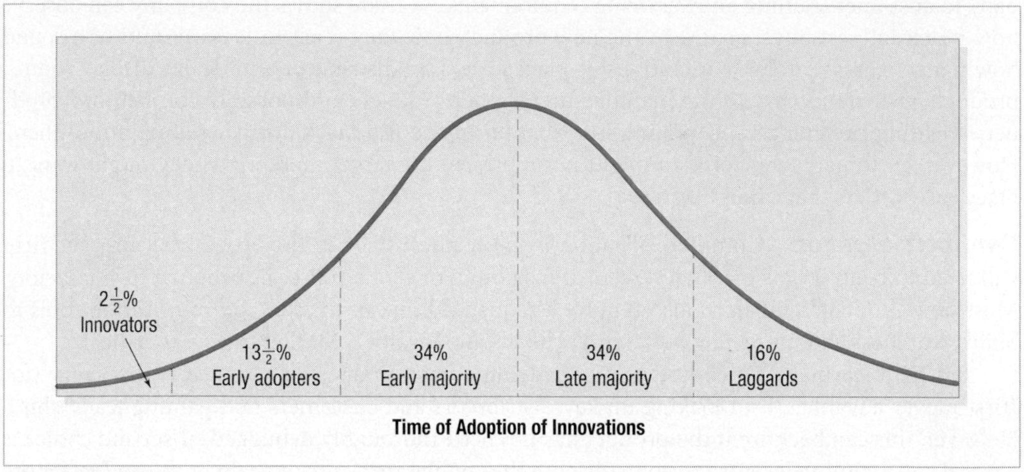

Source: Tungsten, http://en.wikipedia.org/wiki/Everett_Rogers. Based on E. Rogers, *Diffusion of Innovations* (London: Free Press, 1962).

of people adopt the innovation, the number reaches a peak, and then it diminishes as fewer non-adopters remain. The five adopter groups (innovators, early adopters, early majority, late majority, and laggards) differ in their value orientations and their motives for adopting or resisting the new product.[30]

Personal influence, the effect one person has on another's attitude or purchase probability, has greater significance in some situations and for some individuals than others, and it is more important in evaluation than in the other stages. It has more power over late than early adopters and in risky situations.

Five characteristics influence an innovation's rate of adoption. The first is *relative advantage*, the degree to which the innovation appears superior to existing products. The second is *compatibility*, the degree to which the innovation matches consumers' values and experiences. The third is *complexity*, the degree to which the innovation is difficult to understand or use. The fourth is *divisibility*, the degree to which the innovation can be tried on a limited basis. The fifth is *communicability*, the degree to which the benefits of use are observable or describable to others. Other characteristics that influence the rate of adoption are cost, risk and uncertainty, scientific credibility, and social approval.

Finally, adoption is associated with variables in the organization's environment (community progressiveness, community income), the organization itself (size, profits, pressure to change), and the administrators (education level, age, sophistication). Other forces come into play in trying to get a product adopted into organizations that are mostly government-funded, such as public schools. A controversial or innovative product can be squelched by negative public opinion.

Product Life-Cycle Marketing Strategies

A company's positioning and differentiation strategy must change as its product, market, and competitors change over the *product life cycle* (PLC). To say a product has a life cycle is to assert four things: (1) products have a limited life, (2) product sales pass through distinct stages, each posing different marketing challenges and opportunities, (3) profits rise and fall at different stages, and (4) products require different marketing, financial, manufacturing, purchasing, and human resource strategies in each stage.

Product Life Cycles

Most product life cycles are portrayed as bell-shaped curves (see Figure 9.5), typically divided into four stages: introduction, growth, maturity, and decline. In *introduction,* sales grow slowly as the product is introduced; profits are nonexistent because of the heavy introductory expenses. *Growth* is a period of rapid market acceptance and substantial profit improvement. In *maturity,* sales growth slows because the product has achieved acceptance by most potential buyers, and profits stabilize or decline because of increased competition. In *decline,* sales drift downward and profits erode.

Marketing Strategies: Introduction Stage and the Pioneer Advantage

Because it takes time to roll out a new product, work out technical problems, fill dealer pipelines, and gain consumer acceptance, sales growth tends to be slow in the introduction stage. Profits are negative or low, and promotional expenditures are at their highest ratio to sales because of the need to (1) inform potential consumers, (2) induce product trial, and (3) secure distribution.[31]

To be the first to introduce a product can be rewarding, but risky and expensive. Steven Schnaars studied 28 industries in which imitators surpassed the innovators and found several weaknesses among the failing pioneers.[32] These included new products that were too crude, improperly positioned, or launched before strong demand existed; exhaustive product-development costs; a lack of resources to compete against larger entrants; and managerial incompetence or unhealthy complacency. Successful imitators thrived by offering lower prices, continuously improving the product, or using brute market power to overtake the pioneer.

Gerald Tellis and Peter Golder have identified five factors underpinning long-term market leadership: vision of a mass market, persistence, relentless innovation, financial commitment, and asset leverage.[33] One study found Internet companies that realized benefits from moving fast (1) were first movers in large markets, (2) erected barriers of entry against competitors, and (3) directly controlled critical elements necessary for starting a company.[34]

FIGURE 9.5 Sales and Profit Life Cycles

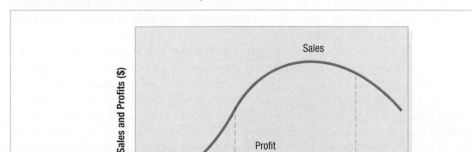

Marketing Strategies: Growth Stage

The growth stage is marked by a rapid climb in sales. Early adopters like the product, and additional consumers start buying it. New competitors enter, introducing new features and expanding distribution, and prices stabilize or fall slightly, depending on how fast demand increases. Companies maintain marketing expenditures or raise them slightly to meet competition, but sales rise much faster than marketing expenditures. Profits increase as marketing costs are spread over a larger volume, and unit manufacturing costs fall faster than price declines. Firms must watch for a change to a decelerating rate of growth in order to prepare new strategies.

To sustain rapid market share growth now, the firm must improve product quality, add new features, and improve styling; add new models and flanker products to protect the main product; enter new segments; increase distribution coverage and enter new channels; shift from awareness and trial communications to preference and loyalty communications; and cut price to attract price-conscious buyers. By spending money on product improvement, promotion, and distribution, the firm can capture a dominant position, trading off maximum current profit for high market share and the hope of greater profits in the next stage.

Marketing Strategies: Maturity Stage

At some point, the rate of sales growth slows. Most products are in this stage of the life cycle, which normally lasts longer than the preceding ones. Three ways to change the course for a brand in the maturity stage are market, product, and marketing program modifications. A firm might try to expand the market by increasing the number of users (converting nonusers, entering new segments, or attracting rivals' customers) and increasing usage rates among users (getting current customers to use the product on more occasions, use more on each occasion, or use the product in new ways). The firm can also try to stimulate sales by improving quality, features, or style. Finally, it might try to stimulate sales by modifying non-product elements—price, distribution, and communications in particular.

Marketing Strategies: Decline Stage

Sales decline for a number of reasons, including technological advances, shifts in consumer tastes, and increased foreign competition. All can lead to overcapacity, increased price cutting, and profit erosion. As sales and profits decline, some firms withdraw. Those remaining may reduce the number of products they offer, exiting smaller segments and weaker trade channels, cutting marketing budgets, and reducing prices further. Unless strong reasons for retention exist, carrying a weak product is often very costly.

A company in an unattractive industry that possesses competitive strength should consider shrinking selectively. A strong competitor in an attractive industry should consider strengthening its investment. Companies that successfully restage or rejuvenate a mature product often do so by adding value to it. Two other options are harvesting and divesting. *Harvesting* calls for gradually reducing a product or business's costs while trying to maintain sales. When a company decides to *divest* a product with strong distribution and residual goodwill, it can probably sell it to another firm. If the company can't find any buyers, it must decide whether to liquidate the brand quickly or slowly.

Critique of the Product Life-Cycle Concept

Table 9.4 summarizes the characteristics, marketing objectives, and marketing strategies in each stage in the product life cycle. The PLC concept helps marketers interpret product and market dynamics, conduct planning and control, and do forecasting. However, critics say that life-cycle

TABLE 9.4	Summary of Product Life-Cycle Characteristics, Objectives, and Strategies			
	Introduction	**Growth**	**Maturity**	**Decline**
Characteristics				
Sales	Low sales	Rapidly rising sales	Peak sales	Declining sales
Costs	High cost per customer	Average cost per customer	Low cost per customer	Low cost per customer
Profits	Negative	Rising profits	High profits	Declining profits
Customers	Innovators	Early adopters	Middle majority	Laggards
Competitors	Few	Growing number	Stable number beginning to decline	Declining number
Marketing Objectives				
	Create product awareness and trial	Maximize market share	Maximize profit while defending market share	Reduce expenditure and milk the brand
Strategies				
Product	Offer a basic product	Offer product extensions, service, warranty	Diversify brands and items	Phase out weak products
Price	Charge cost-plus	Price to penetrate market	Price to match or best competitors'	Cut price
Distribution	Build selective distribution	Build intensive distribution	Build more intensive distribution	Go selective: phase out unprofitable outlets
Communications	Build product awareness and trial among early adopters and dealers	Build awareness and interest in the mass market	Stress brand differences and benefits and encourage brand switching	Reduce to minimal level needed to retain hard-core loyals

Sources: Chester R. Wasson, *Dynamic Competitive Strategy and Product Life Cycles* (Austin, TX: Austin Press, 1978); John A. Weber, "Planning Corporate Growth with Inverted Product Life Cycles," *Long Range Planning* (October 1976), pp. 12–29; Peter Doyle, "The Realities of the Product Life Cycle," *Quarterly Review of Marketing* (Summer 1976).

patterns are too variable to be generalized and that marketers can seldom tell what stage their product is in. A product that appears mature may actually be at a plateau prior to another up-surge. Critics also say that the PLC pattern is the self-fulfilling result of marketing strategies and that skillful marketing can in fact lead to continued growth.[35] Firms also need to visualize a *market's* evolutionary path as it is affected by new needs, competitors, technology, channels, and other developments and change product and brand positioning to keep pace.[36]

Executive Summary

A product is anything that can be offered to a market to satisfy a want or need. The marketer needs to think through the five levels of the product: the core benefit, the basic product, the expected product, the augmented product, and the potential product. Marketers classify products on the basis of durability, tangibility, and use (consumer or industrial). Products may be differentiated by form, features, performance quality, conformance quality, durability, reliability, repairability, style, customization, and design. Service differentiators include ordering ease, delivery, installation, customer training, customer consulting, and maintenance and repair.

A product mix can be classified according to width, length, depth, and consistency, four dimensions for developing the marketing strategy and deciding which product lines to grow, maintain, harvest, and divest. Physical products must be packaged and labeled, may have well-designed packages, and may come with warranties and guarantees. The new-product development process consists of: idea generation, screening, concept development and testing, marketing strategy development, business analysis, product development, market testing, and commercialization. The adoption process—by which customers learn about new products, try them, and adopt or reject them—is influenced by multiple factors. Each product life-cycle stage (introduction, growth, maturity, and decline) calls for different marketing strategies.

Notes

1. Michael McCarthy, "Lexus Makes Big 'Move' to Regain Crown," *Advertising Age*, June 24, 2013; Cheryl Jensen, "Cars More Dependable than Ever, Lexus Tops the Chart while Land Rover Is Least Reliable," *New York Daily News*, April 16, 2013; Matthew de Paula, "Lexus Pursues Hipper Crowd with New Ads for Its LS Sedan," *Forbes*, October 31, 2012; Craig Trudell and Yuki Hagiwara, "Lexus Beating Mercedes Shows U.S. Luxury a 3-Brand Race," *Bloomberg News*, June 6, 2014.

2. This discussion is adapted from a classic article: Theodore Levitt, "Marketing Success through Differentiation: Of Anything," *Harvard Business Review*, January–February 1980, pp. 83–91. The first level, core benefit, has been added to Levitt's discussion.

3. Andrew D. Gershoff, Ran Kivetz, and Anat Keinan, "Consumer Response to Versioning: How Brands' Production Methods Affect Perceptions of Unfairness," *Journal of Consumer Research* 39 (August 2012), pp. 382–98.

4. For some definitions, see *AMA Dictionary* from the American Marketing Association, www.ama.org /resources/Pages/Dictionary.aspx.

5. Some of these bases are discussed in David A. Garvin, "Competing on the Eight Dimensions of Quality," *Harvard Business Review*, November–December 1987, pp. 101–9.

6. Marco Bertini, Elie Ofek, and Dan Ariely, "The Impact of Add-On Features on Product Evaluations," *Journal of Consumer Research* 36 (June 2009), pp. 17–28; Tripat Gill, "Convergent Products: What Functionalities Add More Value to the Base," *Journal of Marketing* 72 (March 2008), pp. 46–62; Robert J. Meyer, Sheghui Zhao, and Jin K. Han, "Biases in Valuation vs. Usage of Innovative Product Features," *Marketing Science* 27 (November–December 2008), pp. 1083–96.

7. Rupal Parekh, "Personalized Products Please but Can They Create Profit," *Advertising Age*, May 20, 2012; www.us.burberry.com/store/bespoke; Paul Sonne,

"Mink or Fox? The Trench Gets Complicated," *Wall Street Journal*, November 3, 2011.

8. Ravindra Chitturi, Rajagopal Raghunathan, and Vijay Mahajan, "Delight by Design: The Role of Hedonic versus Utilitarian Benefits," *Journal of Marketing* 72 (May 2008), pp. 48–63.

9. For branding advantages of a product system, see Ryan Rahinel and Joseph P. Redden, "Brands as Product Coordinators: Matching Brands Make Joint Consumption Experiences More Enjoyable," *Journal of Consumer Research* 39 (April 2013), pp. 1290–99.

10. A. Yesim Orhun, "Optimal Product Line Design when Consumers Exhibit Choice Set-Dependent Preferences," *Marketing Science* 28 (September–October 2009), pp. 868–86; Robert Bordley, "Determining the Appropriate Depth and Breadth of a Firm's Product Portfolio," *Journal of Marketing Research* 40 (February 2003), pp. 39–53; Peter Boatwright and Joseph C. Nunes, "Reducing Assortment: An Attribute-Based Approach," *Journal of Marketing* 65 (July 2001), pp. 50–63.

11. Ryan Hamilton and Alexander Chernev, "The Impact of Product Line Extensions and Consumer Goals on the Formation of Price Image," *Journal of Marketing Research* 47 (February 2010), pp. 51–62.

12. Aner Sela, Jonah Berger, and Wendy Liu, "Variety, Vice and Virtue: How Assortment Size Influences Option Choice," *Journal of Consumer Research* 35 (April 2009), pp. 941–51; Cassie Mogilner, Tamar Rudnick, and Sheena S. Iyengar, "The Mere Categorization Effect: How the Presence of Categories Increases Choosers' Perceptions of Assortment Variety and Outcome Satisfaction," *Journal of Consumer Research* 35 (August 2008), pp. 202–15; John Gourville and Dilip Soman, "Overchoice and Assortment Type: When and Why Variety Backfires," *Marketing Science* 24 (Summer 2005), pp. 382–95.

13. Brett R. Gordon, "A Dynamic Model of Consumer Replacement Cycles in the PC Processor Industry,"

Marketing Science 28 (September–October 2009), pp. 846–67; Raghunath Singh Rao, Om Narasimhan, and George John, "Understanding the Role of Trade-Ins in Durable Goods Markets: Theory and Evidence," *Marketing Science* 28 (September–October 2009), pp. 950–67.

14. Tansev Geylani, J. Jeffrey Inman, and Frenkel Ter Hofstede, "Image Reinforcement or Impairment: The Effects of Co-Branding on Attribute Uncertainty," *Marketing Science* 27 (July–August 2008), pp. 730–44; Ed Lebar, Phil Buehler, Kevin Lane Keller, Monika Sawicka, Zeynep Aksehirli, and Keith Richey, "Brand Equity Implications of Joint Branding Programs," *Journal of Advertising Research* 45 (December 2005).

15. Philip Kotler and Waldemar Pfoertsch, *Ingredient Branding: Making the Invisible Visible* (Heidelberg, Germany: Springer-Verlag, 2011).

16. Simon Graj, "Intel, Gore-Tex and Eastman: The Provenance of Ingredient Branding," *Forbes*, July 10, 2013; Anil Jayaraj, "Solving Ingredient Branding Puzzle," *Business Standard*, August 13, 2012.

17. Kalpesh Kaushik Desai and Kevin Lane Keller, "The Effects of Brand Expansions and Ingredient Branding Strategies on Host Brand Extendibility," *Journal of Marketing* 66 (January 2002), pp. 73–93.

18. Kevin Lane Keller, *Strategic Brand Management,* 4th ed. (Upper Saddle River, NJ: Prentice Hall, 2013). See also Philip Kotler and Waldemar Pfoertsch, *B2B Brand Management* (New York: Springer, 2006).

19. John C. Kozup, Elizabeth H. Creyer, and Scot Burton, "Making Healthful Food Choices," *Journal of Marketing* 67 (April 2003), pp. 19–34; Siva K. Balasubramanian and Catherine Cole, "Consumers' Search and Use of Nutrition Information," *Journal of Marketing* 66 (July 2002), pp. 112–27.

20. Stephen J. Carson, "When to Give Up Control of Outsourced New-Product Development," *Journal of Marketing* 71 (January 2007), pp. 49–66.

21. Thomas Dotzel, Venkatesh Shankar, and Leonard L. Berry, "Service Innovativeness and Firm Value," *Journal of Marketing Research* 50 (April 2013), pp. 259–76; Michael J. Barone and Robert D. Jewell, "The Innovator's License: A Latitude to Deviate from Category Norms," *Journal of Marketing* 77 (January 2013), pp. 120–34; Christine Moorman, Simone Wies, Natalie Mizik, and Fredrika J. Spencer, "Firm Innovation and the Ratchet Effect among Consumer Packaged Goods Firms," *Marketing Science* 31 (November/December 2012), pp. 934–51; Katrijn Gielens, "New Products: The Antidote to Private Label Growth?," *Journal of Marketing Research* 49 (June 2012), pp. 408–23; Gaia Rubera and Ahmet H. Kirca,

"Firm Innovativeness and Its Performance Outcomes: A Meta-Analytic Review and Theoretical Integration," *Journal of Marketing* 76 (May 2012), pp. 130–47; Shuba Srinivasan, Koen Pauwels, Jorge Silva-Risso, and Dominique M. Hanssens, "Product Innovations, Advertising and Stock Returns," *Journal of Marketing* 73 (January 2009), pp. 24–43; Alina B. Sorescu and Jelena Spanjol, "Innovation's Effect on Firm Value and Risk: Insights from Consumer Packaged Goods," *Journal of Marketing* 72 (March 2008), pp. 114–32; Sungwook Min, Manohar U. Kalwani, and William T. Robinson, "Market Pioneer and Early Follower Survival Risks," *Journal of Marketing* 70 (January 2006), pp. 15–33.

22. Robert G. Cooper and Elko J. Kleinschmidt, *New Products: The Key Factors in Success* (Chicago: American Marketing Association, 1990).

23. Elaine Wong, "The Most Memorable Product Launches of 2010," *Forbes*, December 3, 2010; Susumu Ogama and Frank T. Piller, "Reducing the Risks of New-Product Development," *MIT Sloan Management Review* 47 (Winter 2006), pp. 65–71.

24. John Hauser, Gerard J. Tellis, and Abbie Griffin, "Research on Innovation: A Review and Agenda for Marketing Science," *Marketing Science* 25 (November–December 2006), pp. 687–717.

25. Martin Schreier, Christoph Fuchs, and Darren W. Dahl, "The Innovation Effect of User Design: Exploring Consumers' Innovation Perceptions of Firms Selling Products Designed by Users," *Journal of Marketing* 76 (September 2012), pp. 18–32; Patricia Seybold, *Outside Innovation: How Your Customers Will Codesign Your Company's Future* (New York: Collins, 2006).

26. John Hauser, "House of Quality," *Harvard Business Review,* May–June 1988, pp. 63–73; customer-driven engineering is also called "quality function deployment."

27. Alicia Barroso and Gerard Llobet, "Advertising and Consumer Awareness of New, Differentiated Products," *Journal of Marketing Research* 49 (December 2012), pp. 773–92; Norris I. Bruce, Natasha Zhang Foutz, and Ceren Kolsarici, "Dynamic Effectiveness of Advertising and Word of Mouth in Sequential Distribution of New Products," *Journal of Marketing Research* 49 (August 2012), pp. 469–86.

28. The following discussion leans heavily on Everett M. Rogers, *Diffusion of Innovations* (New York: Free Press, 1962). Also see his third edition, published in 1983.

29. Karthik Sridhar, Ram Bezawada, and Minakshi Trivedi, "Investigating the Drivers of Consumer Cross-Category Learning for New Products Using Multiple Data Sets," *Marketing Science* 31 (July/August 2012), pp. 668–88; C. Page Moreau, Donald R. Lehmann, and Arthur B. Markman, "Entrenched Knowledge Structures and

Consumer Response to New Products," *Journal of Marketing Research* 38 (February 2001), pp. 14–29.

30. Everett M. Rogers, *Diffusion of Innovations* (New York: Free Press, 1962), p. 192; Geoffrey A. Moore, *Crossing the Chasm* (New York: HarperBusiness, 1999); for an interesting application with services, see Barak Libai, Eitan Muller, and Renana Peres, "The Diffusion of Services," *Journal of Marketing Research* 46 (April 2009), pp. 163–75.

31. Rajesh J. Chandy, Gerard J. Tellis, Deborah J. MacInnis, and Pattana Thaivanich, "What to Say When: Advertising Appeals in Evolving Markets," *Journal of Marketing Research* 38 (November 2001), pp. 399–414.

32. Steven P. Schnaars, *Managing Imitation Strategies* (New York: Free Press, 1994). See also Jin K. Han, Namwoon Kim, and Hony-Bom Kin, "Entry Barriers: A Dull-, One-, or Two-Edged Sword for Incumbents?," *Journal of Marketing* 65 (January 2001), pp. 1–14.

33. Gerald Tellis and Peter Golder, *Will and Vision: How Latecomers Can Grow to Dominate Markets* (New York:

McGraw-Hill, 2001); Rajesh K. Chandy and Gerald J. Tellis, "The Incumbent's Curse? Incumbency, Size, and Radical Product Innovation," *Journal of Marketing Research* 64 (July 2000), pp. 1–17. See also Dave Ulrich and Norm Smallwood, "Building a Leadership Brand," *Harvard Business Review*, July–August 2007, pp. 93–100.

34. Marty Bates, Syed S. H. Rizvi, Prashant Tewari, and Dev Vardhan, "How Fast Is Too Fast?," *McKinsey Quarterly* no. 3 (2001); see also Stephen Wunker, "Better Growth Decisions: Early Mover, Fast Follower or Late Follower?," *Strategy & Leadership* 40, no. 2 (2012).

35. Youngme Moon, "Break Free from the Product Life Cycle," *Harvard Business Review,* May 2005, pp. 87–94.

36. Hubert Gatignon and David Soberman, "Competitive Response and Market Evolution," Barton A. Weitz and Robin Wensley, eds., *Handbook of Marketing* (London, UK: Sage Publications, 2002), pp. 126–47; Robert D. Buzzell, "Market Functions and Market Evolution," *Journal of Marketing* 63 (Special Issue 1999), pp. 61–63.

Chapter 10

Designing and Managing Services

In this chapter, we will address the following questions:

1. How can services be defined and classified, and how do they differ from goods? (Page 160)
2. What are the new services realities? (Page 162)
3. How can companies manage service quality and achieve excellence in services marketing? (Page 166)
4. How can goods marketers improve customer-support services? (Page 169)

Marketing Management at USAA

USAA Insurance sells auto and other insurance products to current and former members of the military and their families. The company has increased its share of each customer's business by launching a consumer bank, issuing credit cards, opening a discount brokerage, and offering no-load mutual funds. Its legendary service quality has led to the highest customer satisfaction in the industry, resulting in high customer loyalty and significant cross-selling opportunities. It trains its call center reps to answer investment queries as well as insurance-related calls, increasing productivity and reducing the need to transfer customers between agents. A technological leader, USAA was the first bank to allow iPhone deposits for its military customers and to conduct face-to-face video chats with soldiers in the field. Whether a customer is using a tablet, smartphone, or computer or visiting one of its financial centers—located mostly near military bases—USAA is committed to meeting needs by providing exemplary service.[1]

As companies find it harder to differentiate their physical products, they turn to service differentiation, whether that means on-time delivery, better and faster response to inquiries, or quicker resolution of complaints. Because it is critical to understand the special nature of services and what that means to marketers, in this chapter we analyze services and how to market them most effectively.

The Nature of Services

The *government sector,* with its courts, hospitals, military services, police and fire departments, postal service, regulatory agencies, and schools, is in the service business. The *private nonprofit sector*—museums, charities, churches, colleges, and hospitals—is in the service business. A good part of the *business sector,* with its airlines, banks, hotels, insurance companies, law firms, medical practices, and real estate firms, is in the service business. Many workers in the *manufacturing sector,* such as accountants and legal staff, are really service providers, making up a "service factory" providing services to the "goods factory." And those in the *retail sector,* such as cashiers, salespeople, and customer service representatives, are also providing a service.

A **service** is any act or performance one party can offer to another that is essentially intangible and does not result in the ownership of anything. Its production may or may not be tied to a physical product. Increasingly, manufacturers, distributors, and retailers are providing value-added services, or simply excellent customer service, to differentiate themselves. Many pure service firms are now using the Internet to reach customers; some operate purely online.

Categories of Service Mix

The service component can be a minor or a major part of the total offering. We distinguish five categories of offerings:

1. *A pure tangible good* such as soap, toothpaste, or salt with no accompanying services.
2. *A tangible good with accompanying services*, like a car, computer, or cell phone, with a warranty or customer service contract. Typically, the more technologically advanced the product, the greater the need for high-quality supporting services.
3. *A hybrid* offering, like a restaurant meal, of equal parts goods and services.
4. *A major service with accompanying minor goods and services*, like air travel with supporting goods such as snacks and drinks.
5. *A pure service,* primarily an intangible service, such as babysitting, psychotherapy, or massage.

Customers typically cannot judge the technical quality of some services even after they have received them, as shown in Figure 10.1.[2] At the left are goods high in *search qualities*—that is, characteristics the buyer can evaluate before purchase. In the middle are goods and services high in *experience qualities*—characteristics the buyer can evaluate after purchase. At the right are goods and services high in *credence qualities*—characteristics the buyer normally finds hard to evaluate even after consumption.[3]

Because services are generally high in experience and credence qualities, there is more risk in their purchase, with several consequences. First, service consumers generally rely on word of mouth rather than advertising. Second, they rely heavily on price, provider, and physical cues to judge quality. Third, they are highly loyal to service providers who satisfy them. Fourth, because switching costs are high, consumer inertia can make it challenging to entice business away from a competitor.

Distinctive Characteristics of Services

Four distinctive service characteristics greatly affect the design of marketing programs: *intangibility, inseparability, variability,* and *perishability*.

FIGURE 10.1 Continuum of Evaluation for Different Types of Products

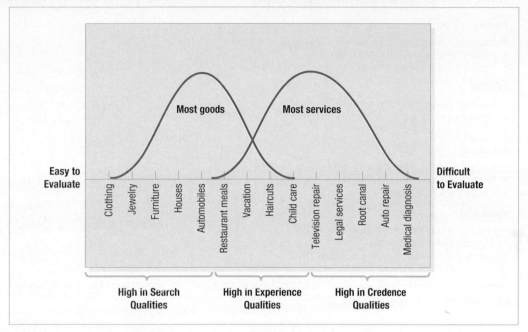

Source: Valarie A. Zeithaml, "How Consumer Evaluation Processes Differ between Goods and Services," James H. Donnelly and William R. George, eds., *Marketing of Services* (Chicago: American Marketing Association, 1981). Reprinted with permission of the American Marketing Association.

Intangibility   Unlike physical products, services cannot be seen, tasted, felt, heard, or smelled before they are bought. A person getting cosmetic surgery cannot see the results before the purchase, for instance. To reduce uncertainty, buyers will look for evidence of quality by drawing inferences from the place, people, equipment, communication material, symbols, and price. Therefore, the service provider's task is to "manage the evidence," to "tangibilize the intangible."[4] Service companies can try to demonstrate their service quality through *physical evidence* and *presentation.*[5] Table 10.1 measures brand experiences in general along sensory, affective, behavioral, and intellectual dimensions; applications to services are clear.

Inseparability   Whereas physical goods are manufactured, then inventoried, then distributed, and later consumed, services are typically produced and consumed simultaneously. Because the client is also often present, provider–client interaction is a special feature of services marketing. Several strategies exist for getting around the limitations of inseparability. When clients have strong provider preferences, the provider can raise its price to ration its limited time. The service provider can also work with larger groups, work faster, or train more providers and build up client confidence.

Variability   Because the quality of services depends on who provides them, when and where, and to whom, services are highly variable. Service buyers are aware of potential variability and often talk to others or go online to collect information before selecting a specific service provider. To reassure customers, some firms offer *service guarantees* that may reduce consumer perceptions of risk.[6] Three steps to increase quality control of services are to (1) invest in good hiring and training procedures, (2) standardize the service-performance process, and (3) monitor

TABLE 10.1   Dimensions of Brand Experience

Sensory

- This brand makes a strong impression on my visual sense or other senses.
- I find this brand interesting in a sensory way.
- This brand does not appeal to my senses.

Affective

- This brand induces feelings and sentiments.
- I do not have strong emotions for this brand.
- This brand is an emotional brand.

Behavioral

- I engage in physical actions and behaviors when I use this brand.
- This brand results in bodily experiences.
- This brand is not action-oriented.

Intellectual

- I engage in a lot of thinking when I encounter this brand.
- This brand does not make me think.
- This brand stimulates my curiosity and problem solving.

Source: Joško Brakus, Bernd H. Schmitt, and Lia Zarantonello, "Brand Experience: What Is It? How Is It Measured? Does It Affect Loyalty?," *Journal of Marketing* 73 (May 2009), pp. 52–68. Reprinted with permission from the *Journal of Marketing*, published by the American Marketing Association.

customer satisfaction. Service firms can also design marketing communication and information programs so consumers learn more about the brand than what their subjective experience alone tells them.

Perishability   Services cannot be stored, so their perishability can be a problem when demand fluctuates. To accommodate rush-hour demand, public transportation companies must own more equipment than if demand was even throughout the day. Demand or yield management is critical—the right services must be available to the right customers at the right places at the right times and right prices to maximize profitability.

Several strategies can produce a better match between service demand and supply.[7] On the demand (customer) side, these include differential pricing to shift some demand to off-peak periods (such as pricing matinee movies lower), cultivating nonpeak demand (the way McDonald's promotes breakfast), offering complementary services as alternatives (the way banks offer ATMs), and using reservation systems to manage demand (airlines do this). On the supply side, strategies include adding part-time employees to serve peak demand, having employees perform only essential tasks during peak periods, increasing consumer participation (shoppers bag their own groceries), sharing services (hospitals can share medical-equipment purchases), and having facilities for future expansion.

The New Services Realities

Although service firms once lagged behind manufacturers in their use of marketing, service firms are now some of the most skilled marketers. However, because U.S. consumers generally have high expectations about service delivery, they often feel their needs are not being adequately met. A 2013 Forrester study asked consumers to rate 154 companies on how well they met their needs and how easy and enjoyable they were to do business with. Almost two-thirds of the companies were rated only "OK," "poor," or "very poor." Retail and hotel companies were rated the highest on average, and Internet, health service, and television service providers were rated the worst.[8] This is just one indicator of the shifting relationship between customers and service providers.

A Shifting Customer Relationship

Savvy services marketers are recognizing the new services realities, such as the importance of the newly empowered customer, customer coproduction, and the need to engage employees as well as customers.

Customer Empowerment Customers are becoming more sophisticated about buying product-support services and are pressing for "unbundled services" so they can select the elements they want. They increasingly dislike having to deal with a multitude of service providers handling different types of products or equipment. Most importantly, the Internet has empowered customers by letting them send their comments around the world with a mouse click. A person who has a good customer experience is more likely to talk about it, but someone who has a bad experience will talk to more people.[9] When a customer complains, most companies are responsive because solving a customer's problem quickly and easily goes a long way toward winning long-term loyal customers.[10]

Customer Coproduction The reality is that customers do not merely purchase and use a service; they play an active role in its delivery. Their words and actions affect the quality of their service experiences and those of others as well as the productivity of frontline employees.[11] This coproduction can put stress on employees, however, and reduce their satisfaction, especially if they differ from customers culturally or in other ways.[12] Moreover, one study estimated that one-third of all service problems are caused by the customer.[13]

Preventing service failures is crucial because recovery is always challenging. One of the biggest problems is attribution—customers often feel the firm is at fault or, even if not, that it is still responsible for righting any wrongs. Unfortunately, although many firms have well-designed and executed procedures to deal with their own failures, they find managing *customer* failures—when a service problem arises from a customer's mistake or lack of understanding—much more difficult. Solutions include: redesigning processes and customer roles to simplify service encounters; using technology to aid customers and employees; enhancing customer role clarity, motivation, and ability; and encouraging customers to help each other.[14]

Satisfying Employees as Well as Customers Excellent service companies know that positive employee attitudes will strengthen customer loyalty.[15] Instilling a strong customer orientation in employees can also increase their job satisfaction and commitment, especially if they have high customer contact. Employees thrive in customer-contact positions when they have an internal drive to (1) pamper customers, (2) accurately read their needs, (3) develop a personal relationship with them, and (4) deliver high-quality service to solve customers' problems.[16] Given the importance of positive employee attitudes to customer satisfaction, service companies must attract the best employees they can find, marketing a career rather than just a job. They must design a sound training program, provide support and rewards for good performance, and reinforce customer-centered attitudes. Finally, they must audit employee job satisfaction regularly.

Achieving Excellence in Services Marketing

The increased importance of the service industry and the new realities have sharpened the focus on what it takes to excel in the marketing of services.[17] In the service sector, excellence

FIGURE 10.2 Three Types of Marketing in Service Industries

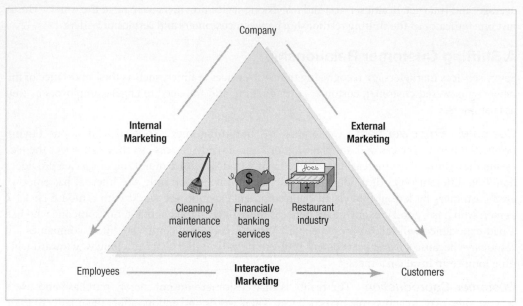

must cover broad areas of marketing: external, internal, and interactive (see Figure 10.2).[18] *External marketing* describes the normal work of preparing, pricing, distributing, and promoting the service to customers. *Internal marketing* describes training and motivating employees to serve customers well. The most important contribution the marketing department can make is to be "exceptionally clever in getting everyone else in the organization to practice marketing."[19]

Interactive marketing describes the employees' skill in serving the client. Clients judge service not only by its *technical quality* (Was the surgery successful?), but also by its *functional quality* (Did the surgeon show concern and inspire confidence?).[20] In interactive marketing, teamwork is often key. Delegating authority to frontline employees can allow for greater service flexibility and adaptability because it promotes better problem solving, closer employee cooperation, and more efficient knowledge transfer.[21]

Companies must avoid pushing technological efficiency so hard, however, that they reduce perceived quality.[22] Some methods lead to too much standardization, but service providers must deliver "high touch" as well as "high tech."[23] Amazon has some of the most innovative technology in online retailing, but it also keeps customers extremely satisfied when a problem arises even if they don't actually talk to an Amazon employee.[24]

Well-managed service companies that achieve marketing excellence have in common a strategic concept, a history of top-management commitment to quality, high standards, profit tiers, and systems for monitoring service performance and resolving customer complaints.

Strategic Concept   Top service companies are "customer obsessed." They have a clear sense of their target customers and their needs and have developed a distinctive strategy for satisfying them.

Top-Management Commitment   Companies such as USAA and Marriott have a thorough commitment to service quality. Their managers look monthly not only at financial performance but also at service performance. USAA, Allstate, Dunkin' Brands, and Oracle have high-level senior executives with titles such as Chief Customer Officer, Chief Client Officer, or Chief Experience Officer, giving these executives the power to improve customer service across every customer interaction.[25]

High Standards   The best service providers set high quality standards. Standards must be set *appropriately* high. A 98 percent accuracy standard may sound good, but it would result in 400,000 incorrectly filled prescriptions daily, 3 million lost pieces of mail each day, and no phone, Internet, or electricity for eight days per year.

Profit Tiers   Firms have decided to coddle big spenders to retain their patronage as long as possible. Customers in high-profit tiers get special discounts, promotional offers, and lots of special service; those in lower-profit tiers who barely pay their way may get more fees, stripped-down service, and voice messages to process their inquiries. Companies that provide differentiated levels of service must be careful about claiming superior service, however—customers who receive lesser treatment will bad-mouth the company and injure its reputation. Delivering services that maximize both customer satisfaction and company profitability can be challenging.

Monitoring Systems   Top firms audit service performance, both their own and competitors', on a regular basis. They collect *voice of the customer (VOC) measurements* to probe customer satisfiers and dissatisfiers and use comparison shopping, mystery or ghost shopping, customer surveys, suggestion and complaint forms, service-audit teams, and customers' letters.

Satisfying Customer Complaints   On average, 40 percent of customers who suffer through a bad service experience stop doing business with the company.[26] Companies that encourage disappointed customers to complain—and also empower employees to remedy the situation on the spot—have been shown to achieve higher revenues and greater profits than companies without a systematic approach for addressing service failures.[27] Customers evaluate complaint incidents in terms of the outcomes they receive, the procedures used to arrive at those outcomes, and the nature of interpersonal treatment during the process.[28] Companies also are increasing the quality of their call centers and their customer service representatives (see "Marketing Insight: Improving Company Call Centers").

Differentiating Services

Marketing excellence requires service marketers to continually differentiate their brands so they are not seen as a commodity. What the customer expects is called the *primary service package.* The provider can also add *secondary service features* to the package. In the hotel industry, various chains have introduced such secondary service features as merchandise for sale, free breakfast buffets, and loyalty programs.

Innovation is as vital in services as in any industry.[29] And it can have big payoffs. When Ticketmaster introduced interactive seat maps that allowed customers to pick their own seats instead of being given one by a "best seat available" function, the conversion rate from potential to actual buyers increased by 25 percent to 30 percent. Persuading a ticket buyer to add an "I'm going …" message to Facebook adds an extra $5 in ticket sales on average; adding reviews of a show on the site doubles the conversion rate.[30]

Improving Company Call Centers

Many firms have learned the hard way that empowered customers will not put up with poor service. After Sprint and Nextel merged, they ran their call centers as cost centers rather than as a means to enhance customer loyalty. Employee rewards were for keeping customer calls short, and when management started to monitor even bathroom trips, morale sank. With customer churn spinning out of control, Sprint Nextel appointed its first chief service officer and started rewarding operators for solving problems on a customer's first call.

Some firms, such as AT&T, JPMorgan Chase, and Expedia, have call centers in the Philippines rather than India because Filipinos speak lightly accented English and are more steeped in U.S. culture. Others are getting smarter about the calls they send to off-shore call centers, *homeshoring* by directing complex calls to highly trained domestic service reps. Some firms are using Big Data to match individual customers with the call center agent best suited to meet their needs. Using something like the methods of online dating sites, advanced analytics technology mines customer transaction and demographic information and examines call center agents' average call handling time and sales efficiency to identify optimal matches in real time.

Sources: Claudia Jasmand, Vera Blazevic, and Ko de Ruyter, "Generating Sales while Providing Service: A Study of Customer Service Representatives' Ambidextrous Behavior," *Journal of Marketing* 76 (January 2012), pp. 20–37; Kimmy Wa Chan and Echo Wen Wan, "How Can Stressed Employees Deliver Better Customer Service?," *Journal of Marketing* 76 (January 2012), pp. 119–37; Joseph Walker, "Meet the New Boss: Big Data," *Wall Street Journal*, September 20, 2012; Vikas Bajaj, "A New Capital of Call Centers," *New York Times*, November 25, 2011; Michael Shroeck, "Why the Customer Call Center Isn't Dead," *Forbes*, March 15, 2011; Michael Sanserino and Cari Tuna, "Companies Strive Harder to Please Customers," *Wall Street Journal*, July 27, 2009, p. B4; Spencer E. Ante, "Sprint's Wake-Up Call," *BusinessWeek*, March 3, 2008, pp. 54–57; Jena McGregor, "Customer Service Champs," *BusinessWeek*, March 5, 2007.

Managing Service Quality

The service quality of a firm is tested at each service encounter. One study identified more than 800 critical behaviors that cause customers to switch services; see the eight categories of those behaviors in Table 10.2.[31] A more recent study honed in on the service dimensions customers would most like companies to measure. Knowledgeable frontline workers and the ability to achieve one-call-and-done rose to the top.[32] Two important considerations in service quality are managing customer expectations and incorporating self-service technologies.

Managing Customer Expectations

Customers form service expectations from many sources, such as past experiences, word of mouth, and advertising. In general, they compare *perceived* service and *expected* service. If the perceived service falls below the expected service, customers are disappointed. Successful companies add benefits to their offering that not only satisfy customers but surprise and delight them by exceeding expectations.[33] The service-quality model in Figure 10.3 on page 168 highlights five gaps that can prevent successful service delivery:[34]

1. *Gap between consumer expectation and management perception*—Management does not always correctly perceive what customers want. Hospital administrators may think patients want better food, but patients may be more concerned with nurse responsiveness.

TABLE 10.2	Factors Leading to Customer Switching Behavior

Pricing
- High price
- Price increases
- Unfair pricing
- Deceptive pricing

Inconvenience
- Location/hours
- Wait for appointment
- Wait for service

Core Service Failure
- Service mistakes
- Billing errors
- Service catastrophe

Service Encounter Failures
- Uncaring
- Impolite
- Unresponsive
- Unknowledgeable

Response to Service Failure
- Negative response
- No response
- Reluctant response

Competition
- Found better service

Ethical Problems
- Cheat
- Hard sell
- Unsafe
- Conflict of interest

Involuntary Switching
- Customer moved
- Provider closed

Source: Susan M. Keaveney, "Customer Switching Behavior in Service Industries: An Exploratory Study," *Journal of Marketing* (April 1995): 71–82. Reprinted with permission from the *Journal of Marketing*, published by the American Marketing Association.

2. *Gap between management perception and service-quality specification*—Management might correctly perceive customers' wants but not set a performance standard. Hospital administrators may tell the nurses to give "fast" service without specifying speed in minutes.

3. *Gap between service-quality specifications and service delivery*—Employees might be poorly trained or incapable of or unwilling to meet the standard; they may be held to conflicting standards, such as taking time to listen to customers and serving them fast.

4. *Gap between service delivery and external communications*—Consumer expectations are affected by statements made by company representatives and ads. If a hospital brochure shows a beautiful room but the patient finds it cheap and tacky-looking, external communications have distorted the customer's expectations.

5. *Gap between perceived service and expected service*—The consumer may misperceive the service quality. The physician may keep visiting the patient to show care, but the patient may interpret this as an indication that something is really wrong.

Based on this service-quality model, researchers identified five determinants of service quality. In descending order of importance, they are reliability, responsiveness, assurance, empathy, and tangibles.[35] The researchers also note there is a *zone of tolerance,* or a range in which a service dimension would be deemed satisfactory, anchored by the minimum level consumers are willing to accept and the level they believe can and should be delivered.

Much work has validated the role of expectations in consumers' interpretations and evaluations of the service encounter and in the relationship they adopt with a firm over time.[36] Consumers are often forward-looking with respect to their decision to keep or drop a service relationship in terms of their likely behavior and interactions with a firm. Any marketing activity that affects current or expected future usage can help to solidify a service relationship.

FIGURE 10.3 Service-Quality Model

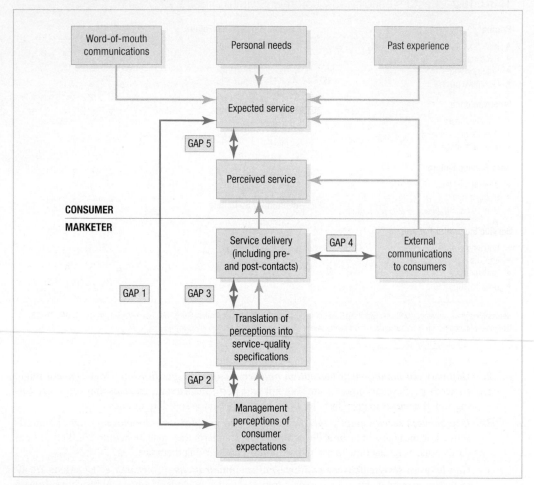

Sources: A. Parasuraman, Valarie A. Zeithaml, and Leonard L. Berry, "A Conceptual Model of Service Quality and Its Implications for Future Research," *Journal of Marketing* (Fall 1985), p. 44. The model is more fully discussed or elaborated in Valarie Zeithaml, Mary Jo Bitner, and Dwayne D. Gremler, *Services Marketing: Integrating Customer Focus across the Firm,* 6th ed. (New York: McGraw-Hill/Irwin, 2013).

Incorporating Self-Service Technologies

Consumers value convenience in services,[37] and many person-to-person service interactions are being replaced by self-service technologies (SSTs) intended to provide that convenience. To traditional vending machines we can add automated teller machines (ATMs), self-pumping at gas stations, self-checkout at hotels, and a variety of activities on the Internet, such as ticket purchasing. Not all SSTs improve service quality, but they can make service transactions more accurate, convenient, and faster. Obviously, they can also reduce costs. One technology firm, Comverse, estimates the cost to answer a query through a call center at $7, but online at only 10 cents.[38]

Successfully integrating technology into the workforce thus requires a comprehensive reengineering of the front office to identify what people do best, what machines do best, and how to deploy them separately and together.[39] Customers must have a clear sense of their roles in the process.

Managing Product-Support Services

Manufacturers of equipment—small appliances, office machines, tractors, mainframes, airplanes—all must provide *product-support services,* now a battleground for competitive advantage. Some equipment companies, such as Caterpillar Tractor and John Deere, make a significant percentage of their profits from these services.[40] In the global marketplace, companies that make a good product but provide poor local service support are seriously disadvantaged.

Identifying and Satisfying Customer Needs

Traditionally, customers have had three specific worries about product service.[41] First, they worry about reliability and *failure frequency.* A farmer may tolerate a combine that will break down once a year, but not one that goes down two or three times a year. Second, they worry about *downtime.* The longer the downtime, the higher the cost, which is why the customer counts on the seller's *service dependability*—the ability to fix the machine quickly or at least provide a loaner. The third issue is *out-of-pocket costs.* How much does the customer have to spend on regular maintenance and repair costs?

A buyer takes all these factors into consideration and tries to estimate the **life-cycle cost**, which is the product's purchase cost plus the discounted cost of maintenance and repair less the discounted salvage value. To provide the best support, a manufacturer must identify the services customers value most and their relative importance. For expensive equipment, manufacturers offer *facilitating services* such as installation, staff training, maintenance and repair services, and financing. They may also add *value-augmenting services* that extend beyond the product's functioning and performance.

A manufacturer can offer, and charge for, product-support services in different ways. One chemical company provides a standard offering plus a basic level of services. If the business customer wants additional services, it can pay extra or increase its annual purchases to a higher level. Many companies offer *service contracts* (also called *extended warranties*), agreeing to provide maintenance and repair services for a specified period at a specified contract price.

Product companies must understand their strategic intent and competitive advantage in developing services. Are service units supposed to support and protect existing product businesses or grow as an independent platform? Are the sources of competitive advantage based on economies of scale (size) or economies of skill (smarts)?[42]

Postsale Service Strategy

The quality of customer service departments varies greatly. At one extreme are those that simply transfer customer calls to the appropriate person for action with little follow-up. At the other extreme are departments eager to receive customer requests, suggestions, and even complaints and handle them expeditiously. Some firms even proactively contact customers to provide service after the sale is complete.[43]

Manufacturers usually start by running their own parts-and-service departments. They want to stay close to the equipment and know its problems. They also find it expensive and time consuming to train others and discover they can make good money from parts and service if they are the only supplier and can charge a premium price. In fact, many equipment manufacturers price their equipment low and compensate by charging high prices for parts and service.

Over time, manufacturers switch more maintenance and repair service to authorized distributors and dealers. These intermediaries are closer to customers, operate in more locations, and can offer quicker service. Still later, independent service firms emerge and offer a lower price or faster service. A significant percentage of auto-service work is now done outside franchised automobile dealerships by independent garages and chains such as Midas Muffler and Sears. Independent service organizations handle mainframes, telecommunications equipment, and a variety of other equipment lines.

Customer-service choices are increasing rapidly, however, and equipment manufacturers increasingly must figure out how to make money on their equipment, independent of service contracts. Some new-car warranties now cover 100,000 miles before customers have to pay for servicing. The increase in disposable or never-fail equipment makes customers less inclined to pay 2 percent to 10 percent of the purchase price every year for service. Some business customers may find it cheaper to have their own service people on-site.

Executive Summary

A service is any act or performance that one party can offer to another that is essentially intangible and does not result in the ownership of anything. It may or may not be tied to a physical product. Five categories of offerings are: (1) pure tangible good, (2) tangible good with accompanying services, (3) hybrid offering of equal parts goods and services, (4) major service with accompanying minor goods and services, and (5) pure service. Services are intangible, inseparable, variable, and perishable. Marketers must find ways to give tangibility to intangibles, to increase service providers' productivity, to increase and standardize the service quality, and to match the supply of services with market demand.

Marketing of services faces new realities due to customer empowerment, customer coproduction, and the need to satisfy employees as well as customers. Achieving excellence in service marketing calls for external marketing, internal marketing, and interactive marketing. Top service companies adopt a strategic concept, have top-management commitment to quality, commit to high standards, establish profit tiers, and monitor service performance and customer complaints. They also differentiate their brands through primary and secondary service features and continual innovation. Superior service delivery requires managing customer expectations and incorporating self-service technologies. Manufacturers of tangible products should identify and satisfy customer needs for service and provide postpurchase service.

Notes

1. John Adams, "How USAA Innovates Online Banking," *American Banker*, September 1, 2012; David Rohde, "In the Era of Greed, Meet America's Good Bank: USAA," *The Atlantic*, January 27, 2012; Jena McGregor, "USAA's Battle Plan," *Bloomberg BusinessWeek*, March 1, 2010; "Customer Service Champs," *BusinessWeek*, March 5, 2007; Allison Enright, "Serve Them Right," *Marketing News*, May 1, 2006; Mike W. Thomas, "USAA Reports Mid-Year Growth," *San Antonio Business Journal*, July 28, 2014, www.bizjournals.com.

2. Valarie A. Zeithaml, "How Consumer Evaluation Processes Differ between Goods and Services," J. Donnelly and W. R. George, eds., *Marketing of Services* (Chicago: American Marketing Association, 1981), pp. 186–90.

3. Jin Sun, Hean Tat Keh, and Angela Y. Lee, "The Effect of Attribute Alignability on Service Evaluation: The Moderating Role of Uncertainty," *Journal of Consumer Research* 39 (December 2012), pp. 831–47.

4. Theodore Levitt, "Marketing Intangible Products and Product Intangibles," *Harvard Business Review*, May–June 1981, pp. 94–102; Leonard L. Berry, "Services Marketing Is Different," *Business*, May–June 1980, pp. 24–29.

5. B. H. Booms and M. J. Bitner, "Marketing Strategies and Organizational Structures for Service Firms," J. Donnelly and W. R. George, eds., *Marketing of Services* (Chicago: American Marketing Association, 1981), pp. 47–51.

6. Rebecca J. Slotegraaf and J. Jeffrey Inman, "Longitudinal Shifts in the Drivers of Satisfaction with

Product Quality: The Role of Attribute Resolvability," *Journal of Marketing Research* 41 (August 2004), pp. 269–80.

7. W. Earl Sasser, "Match Supply and Demand in Service Industries," *Harvard Business Review,* November–December 1976, pp. 133–40.

8. David Roe, "Forrester's Customer Experience Index: The Good, The Bad and the Poor," www.cmswire .com, January 17, 2013; "The Emerging Role of Social Customer Experience in Customer Care," www.lithium .com, May 2013; "The State of Customer Experience, 2012," white paper, Forrester Research, Inc., April 24, 2012; Josh Bernoff, "Numbers Show Marketing Value in Sustaining Good Customer Service," *Advertising Age,* January 17, 2011.

9. Elisabeth Sullivan, "Happy Endings Lead to Happy Returns," *Marketing News,* October 30, 2009, p. 20.

10. Matthew Dixon, Karen Freeman, and Nicholas Toman, "Stop Trying to Delight Your Customers," *Harvard Business Review,* July–August 2010, pp. 116–22.

11. Chi Kin (Bennett) Yim, Kimmy Wa Chan, and Simon S. K. Lam, "Do Customers and Employees Enjoy Service Participation? Synergistic Effects of Self- and Other-Efficacy," *Journal of Marketing* 76 (November 2012), pp. 121–40; Zhenfeng Ma & Laurette Dubé, "Process and Outcome Interdependency in Frontline Service Encounters," *Journal of Marketing* 75 (May 2011), pp. 83–98; Stephen S. Tax, Mark Colgate, and David Bowen, "How to Prevent Your Customers from Failing," *MIT Sloan Management Review* (Spring 2006), pp. 30–38.

12. Kimmy Wa Chan, Chi Kin (Bennett) Yim, and Simon S. K. Lam, "Is Customer Participation in Value Creation a Double-Edged Sword? Evidence from Professional Financial Services Across Cultures," *Journal of Marketing* 74 (May 2010), pp. 48–64.

13. Valarie Zeithaml, Mary Jo Bitner, and Dwayne D. Gremler, *Services Marketing: Integrating Customer Focus across the Firm,* 6th ed. (New York: McGraw-Hill, 2013).

14. Rachel R. Chen, Eitan Gerstner, and Yinghui (Catherine) Yang, "Customer Bill of Rights Under No-Fault Service Failure: Confinement and Compensation," *Marketing Science* 31 (January/February 2012), pp. 157–71; Michael Sanserino and Cari Tuna, "Companies Strive Harder to Please Customers," *Wall Street Journal,* July 27, 2009, p. B4.

15. James L. Heskett, W, Earl Sasser Jr., and Joe Wheeler, *Ownership Quotient: Putting the Service Profit Chain to Work for Unbeatable Competitive Advantage* (Boston, MA: Harvard Business School Press, 2008).

16. D. Todd Donovan, Tom J. Brown, and John C. Mowen, "Internal Benefits of Service Worker Customer Orientation," *Journal of Marketing* 68 (January 2004), pp. 128–46.

17. Frances X. Frei, "The Four Things a Service Business Must Get Right," *Harvard Business Review,* April 2008, pp. 70–80.

18. Christian Gronroos, "A Service-Quality Model and Its Marketing Implications," *European Journal of Marketing* 18 (1984), pp. 36–44.

19. Detelina Marinova, Jun Ye, and Jagdip Singh, "Do Frontline Mechanisms Matter? Impact of Quality and Productivity Orientations on Unit Revenue, Efficiency, and Customer Satisfaction," *Journal of Marketing* 72 (March 2008), pp. 28–45.

20. Christian Gronroos, "A Service-Quality Model and Its Marketing Implications," *European Journal of Marketing* 18 (1984), pp. 36–44.

21. Ad de Jong, Ko de Ruyter, and Jos Lemmink, "Antecedents and Consequences of the Service Climate in Boundary-Spanning Self-Managing Service Teams," *Journal of Marketing* 68 (April 2004), pp. 18–35; Michael D. Hartline and O. C. Ferrell, "The Management of Customer-Contact Service Employees," *Journal of Marketing* 60 (October 1996), pp. 52–70; Christian Homburg, Jan Wieseke, and Torsten Bornemann, "Implementing the Marketing Concept at the Employee-Customer Interface," *Journal of Marketing* 73 (July 2009), pp. 64–81; Chi Kin (Bennett) Yim, David K. Tse, and Kimmy Wa Chan, "Strengthening Customer Loyalty through Intimacy and Passion," *Journal of Marketing Research* 45 (December 2008), pp. 741–56.

22. Roland T. Rust and Ming-Hui Huang, "Optimizing Service Productivity," *Journal of Marketing* 76 (March 2012), pp. 47–66.

23. Linda Ferrell and O.C. Ferrell, "Redirecting Direct Selling: High-touch Embraces High-tech," *Business Horizons* 55 (May 2012), pp. 273–81.

24. Heather Green, "How Amazon Aims to Keep You Clicking," *BusinessWeek,* March 2, 2009, pp. 34–40.

25. Paul Hagen, "The Rise of the Chief Customer Officer," *Forbes,* February 16, 2011.

26. Dave Dougherty and Ajay Murthy, "What Service Customers Really Want," *Harvard Business Review,* September 2009, p. 22; for a contrarian point of view, see Edward Kasabov, "The Compliant Customer," *MIT Sloan Management Review* (Spring 2010), pp. 18–19.

27. Jeffrey G. Blodgett and Ronald D. Anderson, "A Bayesian Network Model of the Customer Complaint Process," *Journal of Service Research* 2 (May 2000), pp. 321–38.

28. Stephen S. Tax, Stephen W. Brown, and Murali Chandrashekaran, "Customer Evaluations of Service

Complaint Experiences: Implications for Relationship Marketing," *Journal of Marketing* 62 (April 1998), pp. 60–76.

29. Thomas Dotzel, Venkatesh Shankar, and Leonard L. Berry, "Service Innovativeness and Firm Value," *Journal of Marketing Research* 50 (April 2013), pp. 259–76.

30. Eric Savitz, "Can Ticketmaster CEO Nathan Hubbard Fix the Ticket Market," *Forbes*, February 18, 2011.

31. Susan M. Keaveney, "Customer Switching Behavior in Service Industries: An Exploratory Study," *Journal of Marketing* 59 (April 1995), pp. 71–82.

32. Dave Dougherty and Ajay Murthy, "What Service Customers Really Want," *Harvard Business Review*, September 2009, p. 22.

33. Roland T. Rust and Richard L. Oliver, "Should We Delight the Customer?," *Journal of the Academy of Marketing Science* 28 (December 2000), pp. 86–94.

34. A. Parasuraman, Valarie A. Zeithaml, and Leonard L. Berry, "A Conceptual Model of Service Quality and Its Implications for Future Research," *Journal of Marketing* 49 (Fall 1985), pp. 41–50. See also Michael K. Brady and J. Joseph Cronin Jr., "Some New Thoughts on Conceptualizing Perceived Service Quality," *Journal of Marketing* 65 (July 2001), pp. 34–49.

35. Leonard L. Berry and A. Parasuraman, *Marketing Services: Competing through Quality* (New York: Free Press, 1991), p. 16.

36. Roland T. Rust and Tuck Siong Chung, "Marketing Models of Service and Relationships," *Marketing Science* 25 (November–December 2006), pp. 560–80; Katherine

N. Lemon, Tiffany Barnett White, and Russell S. Winer, "Dynamic Customer Relationship Management: Incorporating Future Considerations into the Service Retention Decision," *Journal of Marketing* 66 (January 2002), pp. 1–14.

37. Leonard L. Berry, Kathleen Seiders, and Dhruv Grewal, "Understanding Service Convenience," *Journal of Marketing* 66 (July 2002), pp. 1–17.

38. "Help Yourself," *Economist*, July 2, 2009, pp. 62–63.

39. Jeffrey F. Rayport and Bernard J. Jaworski, *Best Face Forward* (Boston: Harvard Business School Press, 2005); Jeffrey F. Rayport, Bernard J. Jaworski, and Ellie J. Kyung, "Best Face Forward," *Journal of Interactive Marketing* 19 (Autumn 2005), pp. 67–80; Jeffrey F. Rayport and Bernard J. Jaworski, "Best Face Forward," *Harvard Business Review,* December 2004, pp. 47–58.

40. Eric Fang, Robert W. Palmatier, and Jan-Benedict E. M. Steenkamp, "Effect of Service Transition Strategies on Firm Value," *Journal of Marketing* 72 (September 2008), pp. 1–14.

41. Mark Vandenbosch and Niraj Dawar, "Beyond Better Products: Capturing Value in Customer Interactions," *MIT Sloan Management Review* 43 (Summer 2002), pp. 35–42.

42. Byron G. Auguste, Eric P. Harmon, and Vivek Pandit, "The Right Service Strategies for Product Companies," *McKinsey Quarterly* 1 (2006), pp. 41–51.

43. Goutam Challagalla, R. Venkatesh, and Ajay K. Kohli, "Proactive Postsales Service: When and Why Does It Pay Off?," *Journal of Marketing* 73 (March 2009), pp. 70–87.

Chapter 11

Developing Pricing Strategies and Programs

In this chapter, we will address the following questions:

1. How do consumers process and evaluate prices? (Page 174)
2. How should a company set prices initially? (Page 176)
3. How should a company adapt prices to meet varying circumstances and opportunities? (Page 184)
4. When and how should a company initiate a price change and respond to a competitor's price changes? (Page 187)

Marketing Management at Ryanair

Profits for discount European air carrier Ryanair have been sky-high thanks to its revolutionary business model. Founder Michael O'Leary thinks like a retailer, charging passengers for almost everything—except their seat. A quarter of Ryanair's seats are free, and O'Leary wants to double that within five years, with the ultimate goal of making all seats free. Passengers currently pay only taxes and fees of about $10 to $24, with an average one-way fare of roughly $52. Everything else is extra: checked luggage ($9.50 per bag) and snacks ($5.50 for a hot dog, $3.50 for water). Other strategies cut costs or generate outside revenue. More than 99 percent of tickets are sold online, and its Web site offers travel insurance, hotels, ski packages, and car rentals. This formula works for Ryanair: The airline flies 58 million people to more than 150 airports each year. Ryanair enjoys net margins of 25 percent, more than three times Southwest's 7 percent. Some industry pundits even refer to Ryanair as "Walmart with wings"![1]

Price is the one element of the marketing mix that produces revenue; the other elements produce costs. Price also communicates the company's intended value positioning of its product or brand. But new economic realities have caused many consumers to reevaluate what they are

173

willing to pay, and companies have had to carefully review their pricing strategies as a result. Pricing decisions must take into account many factors—the company, the customers, the competition, and the marketing environment. In this chapter, we discuss concepts and tools to facilitate the setting of initial prices and adjusting prices over time and markets.

Understanding Pricing

Price is not just a number on a tag. It comes in many forms and performs many functions, whether it's called rent, tuition, fares, fees, rates, tolls, or commissions. Price also has many components. Throughout most of history, prices were set by negotiation between buyers and sellers. Setting one price for all buyers is a relatively modern idea that arose with the development of large-scale retailing at the end of the nineteenth century. Tiffany & Co. and others advertised a "strictly one-price policy" because they carried so many items and supervised so many employees.

Pricing in a Digital World

Traditionally, price has operated as a major determinant of buyer choice. Consumers and purchasing agents who have access to price information and price discounters put pressure on retailers to lower their prices. Retailers in turn put pressure on manufacturers to lower their prices. The result can be a marketplace characterized by heavy discounting and sales promotion.

Downward price pressure from a changing economic environment coincided with some longer-term trends in the technological environment. For some years now, the Internet has been changing the way buyers and sellers interact. Buyers can instantly compare prices from thousands of vendors, check prices at the point of purchase, name their own price, and even get products free. Sellers can monitor customer behavior, tailor offers to individual buyers, and give certain customers access to special prices. Both buyers and sellers can negotiate prices in online auctions and exchanges or in person.

A Changing Pricing Environment

Pricing practices have changed significantly, thanks in part to a severe recession in 2008–2009, a slow recovery, and rapid technological advances. But the new millennial generation also brings new attitudes and values to consumption. Often burdened by student loans and other financial demands, members of this group (born between about 1977 and 1994) are reconsidering just what they really need to own and often choosing to rent, borrow, and share.

Some say these new behaviors are creating a **sharing economy** in which consumers share bikes, cars, clothes, couches, apartments, tools, and skills and extracting more value from what they already own. As one sharing-related entrepreneur noted, "We're moving from a world where we're organized around ownership to one organized around access to assets." In a sharing economy, someone can be both a consumer and a producer, reaping the benefits of both roles.[2] Trust and a good reputation are crucial in any exchange but imperative in a sharing economy. Most platforms that are part of a sharing-related business have some form of self-policing mechanism such as public profiles and community rating systems, sometimes linked with Facebook.

How Companies Price

In small companies, the boss often sets prices. In large companies, division and product line managers do. Even here, top management sets general pricing objectives and policies and often approves lower management's proposals.

Where pricing is a key competitive factor (railroads, oil companies), companies often establish a pricing department to set or assist others in setting appropriate prices. This department reports to the marketing department, finance department, or top management. In B-to-B settings, research suggests that pricing performance improves when pricing authority is spread horizontally across the sales, marketing, and finance units and when there is a balance in centralizing and delegating that authority between individual salespeople and teams and central management.[3]

Common pricing mistakes include not revising price often enough to capitalize on market changes; setting price independently of the rest of the marketing program rather than as an intrinsic element of market-positioning strategy; and not varying price enough for different product items, market segments, distribution channels, and purchase occasions. For any organization, effectively designing and implementing pricing strategies requires a thorough understanding of consumer pricing psychology and a systematic approach to setting, adapting, and changing prices.

Consumer Psychology and Pricing

Marketers recognize that consumers often actively process price information, interpreting it from the context of prior purchasing experience, formal communications (advertising, sales calls, and brochures), informal communications (friends, colleagues, or family members), point-of-purchase or online resources, and other factors.[4] Purchase decisions are based on how consumers perceive prices and what they consider the current actual price to be—*not* on the marketer's stated price. Customers may have a lower price threshold, below which prices signal inferior or unacceptable quality, and an upper price threshold, above which prices are prohibitive and the product appears not worth the money.

Three key topics for understanding how consumers arrive at their perceptions of prices are reference prices, price–quality inferences, and price endings.

- **Reference prices.** Although consumers may have fairly good knowledge of price ranges, surprisingly few can accurately recall specific prices.[5] When examining products, they often employ **reference prices,** comparing an observed price to an internal reference price they remember or an external frame of reference such as a posted "regular retail price."[6] Marketers encourage this thinking by stating a high manufacturer's suggested price, indicating that the price was much higher originally, or pointing to a competitor's high price.[7] Clever marketers try to frame the price to signal the best value possible. For example, a relatively expensive item can look less expensive if the price is broken into smaller units, such as a $500 annual membership for "under $50 a month," even if the totals are the same.[8]

- **Price-quality inferences.** Many consumers use price as an indicator of quality. Image pricing is especially effective with ego-sensitive products such as perfumes, expensive cars, and designer clothing. When information about true quality is available, price becomes a less significant indicator of quality. For luxury-goods customers who desire uniqueness, demand may actually increase price because they then believe fewer other customers can afford the product.[9]

- **Price endings.** Customers perceive an item priced at $299 to be in the $200 range rather than the $300 range; they tend to process prices "left to right" rather than by rounding.[10] Price encoding in this fashion is important if there is a mental price break at the higher, rounded price. Another explanation for the popularity of "9" endings is that they suggest a discount or bargain, so if a company wants a high-price image, it should probably avoid the odd-ending tactic.[11]

Setting the Price

A firm must set a price for the first time when it develops a new product, when it introduces its regular product into a new distribution channel or geographical area, and when it enters bids on new contract work. The firm must decide where to position its product on quality and price.

Firms devise their branding strategies to help convey the price-quality tiers of their products or services to consumers.[12] Having a range of price points allows a firm to cover more of the market and to give any one consumer more choices. "Marketing Insight: Trading Up, Down, and Over" describes how consumers have been shifting their spending in recent years.

The firm must consider many factors in setting its pricing policy.[13] Table 11.1 summarizes the six steps in the process.

Step 1: Selecting the Pricing Objective

Five major pricing objectives are: survival, maximum current profit, maximum market share, maximum market skimming, and product-quality leadership. Companies pursue *survival* as their major objective if they are plagued with overcapacity, intense competition, or changing consumer wants. As long as prices cover variable costs and some fixed costs, the company stays in business. To *maximize current profits,* a firm estimates the demand and costs

---

marketing insight | **Trading Up, Down, and Over**

Michael Silverstein and Neil Fiske, the authors of *Trading Up*, have observed a number of middle-market consumers periodically "trading up" to what they call "New Luxury" products and services "that possess higher levels of quality, taste, and aspiration than other goods in the category but are not so expensive as to be out of reach." Three main types of New Luxury products are:

- *Accessible super-premium products* (such as Kettle gourmet potato chips), which carry a significant price premium but are still relatively low-ticket items in affordable categories.
- *Old Luxury brand extensions* (such as the Mercedes-Benz C-class), which retain their cachet while extending historically high-priced brands down-market.
- *Masstige goods*, such as Kiehl's skin care products, which are "based on emotions" and are priced between average middle-market brands and super-premium Old Luxury brands.

To trade up to brands that offer these emotional benefits, consumers often "trade down" by shopping at discounters for staple items or goods that deliver quality and functionality. The recent economic downturn increased the prevalence of trading down. As the economy improved and consumers tired of putting off discretionary purchases, retail sales picked up. Trading up and down has persisted, however, along with "trading over" or switching spending from one category to another, buying a new home theater system, say, instead of a new car.

Sources: Cotten Timberlake, "U.S. 2 Percenters Trade Down with Post-Recession Angst," www.bloomberg.com, May 15, 2013; Anna-Louise Jackson and Anthony Feld, "Frugality Fatigue Spurs Americans to Trade Up," www.bloomberg.com, April 13, 2012; Walker Smith, "Consumer Behavior: From Trading Up to Trading Off," *Branding Strategy Insider,* January 26, 2012; Bruce Horovitz, "Sale, Sale, Sale: Today Everyone Wants a Deal," *USA Today,* April 21, 2010, pp. 1A–2A; Michael J. Silverstein, *Treasure Hunt: Inside the Mind of the New Consumer* (New York: Portfolio, 2006); Michael J. Silverstein and Neil Fiske, *Trading Up: The New American Luxury* (New York: Portfolio, 2003).

TABLE 11.1	Steps in Setting a Pricing Policy

1. Selecting the Pricing Objective
2. Determining Demand
3. Estimating Costs
4. Analyzing Competitors' Costs, Prices, and Offers
5. Selecting a Pricing Method
6. Selecting the Final Price

associated with alternative prices and chooses the price that produces maximum current profit, cash flow, or rate of return on investment. However, the company may sacrifice long-run performance by ignoring the effects of other marketing variables, competitors' reactions, and legal restraints on price.

Some companies want to *maximize their market share,* believing a higher sales volume will lead to lower unit costs and higher long-run profit. With **market-penetration pricing,** firms set the lowest price, assuming the market is price sensitive. This strategy is appropriate when (1) the market is highly price sensitive and a low price stimulates market growth; (2) production and distribution costs fall with accumulated production experience; and (3) a low price discourages actual and potential competition.

Companies unveiling a new technology favor setting high prices to *maximize market skimming*. **Market-skimming pricing,** in which prices start high and slowly drop over time, makes sense when (1) a sufficient number of buyers have a high current demand; (2) the unit costs of producing a small volume are not so high that they cancel the advantage of charging what the traffic will bear; (3) the high initial price does not attract more competitors to the market; and (4) the high price communicates the image of a superior product.

A company might aim to be the *product-quality leader* in the market.[14] Many brands strive to be "affordable luxuries"—products or services characterized by high levels of perceived quality, taste, and status with a price just high enough not to be out of consumers' reach.

Nonprofit and public organizations may have other pricing objectives. A university aims for *partial cost recovery,* knowing that it must rely on private gifts and public grants to cover its remaining costs. A nonprofit hospital may aim for full cost recovery in its pricing. A nonprofit theater company may price its productions to fill the maximum number of seats.

Step 2: Determining Demand

Each price will lead to a different level of demand and have a different impact on a company's marketing objectives. The normally inverse relationship between price and demand is captured in a demand curve. The higher the price, the lower the demand. For prestige goods, the demand curve sometimes slopes upward. Some consumers take the higher price to signify a better product. However, if the price is too high, demand may fall.

Price Sensitivity   The demand curve shows the market's probable purchase quantity at alternative prices, summing the reactions of many individuals with different price sensitivities. The first step in estimating demand is to understand what affects price sensitivity. Generally speaking, customers are less price sensitive to low-cost items or items they buy infrequently. They are also less price sensitive when (1) there are few or no substitutes or competitors; (2) they do not readily notice the higher price; (3) they are slow to change their buying habits; (4) they think the higher prices are justified; and (5) price is only a small part of the total cost of obtaining, operating, and servicing the product over its lifetime.

A seller can successfully charge a higher price than competitors if it can convince customers that it offers the lowest *total cost of ownership* (TCO). Marketers often treat the service elements in a product offering as sales incentives rather than as value-enhancing augmentations for which they can charge. In fact, pricing expert Tom Nagle believes the most common mistake manufacturers make is to offer services to differentiate their products without charging for them.[15]

Estimating Demand Curves   Most companies attempt to measure their demand curves using several different methods. They may use surveys to explore how many units consumers would buy at different proposed prices. Although consumers might understate their purchase intentions at higher prices to discourage the company from pricing high, they also tend to exaggerate their willingness to pay for new products or services.[16] Price experiments can vary the prices of different products in a store or of the same product in similar territories to see how the change affects sales. Also, statistical analyses of past prices, quantities sold, and other factors can reveal their relationships.

In measuring the price-demand relationship, the market researcher must control for various factors that will influence demand.[17] The competitor's response will make a difference. Also, if the company changes other aspects of the marketing program besides price, the effect of the price change itself will be hard to isolate.

Price Elasticity of Demand   Marketers need to know how responsive, or elastic, demand is to a change in price. If demand hardly changes with a small change in price, we say it is *inelastic*. If demand changes considerably, it is *elastic*. The higher the elasticity, the greater the volume growth resulting from a 1 percent price reduction. If demand is elastic, sellers will consider lowering the price to produce more total revenue. This makes sense as long as the costs of producing and selling more units do not increase disproportionately.

Price elasticity depends on the magnitude and direction of the contemplated price change. It may be negligible with a small price change and substantial with a large price change. It may differ for a price cut versus a price increase, and there may be a band within which price changes have little or no effect. Long-run price elasticity may differ from short-run elasticity. Buyers may continue to buy from a current supplier after a price increase but eventually switch suppliers. The distinction between short-run and long-run elasticity means that sellers will not know the total effect of a price change until time passes.

Consumers tend to be more sensitive to prices during tough economic times, but that is not true across all categories.[18] One comprehensive review of a 40-year period of academic research on price elasticity yielded interesting findings.[19] Price elasticity magnitudes were higher for durable goods than for other goods and higher for products in the introduction/growth stages of the product life cycle than in the mature/decline stages. Also, promotional price elasticities were higher than actual price elasticities in the short run (though the reverse was true in the long run).

Step 3: Estimating Costs

Whereas demand sets a ceiling on the price the company can charge for its product, costs set the floor. The company wants to charge a price that covers its cost of producing, distributing, and selling the product, including a fair return for its effort and risk. Yet when companies price products to cover their full costs, profitability isn't always the net result.

Types of Costs and Levels of Production   A company's costs take two forms, fixed and variable. **Fixed costs,** also known as *overhead*, are costs such as rent and salaries that do not vary with production level or sales revenue. **Variable costs** vary directly with the level of production. For example, each calculator produced by Texas Instruments incurs the cost of plastic, microprocessor chips, and packaging. These costs tend to be constant per unit produced, but they're called *variable* because their total varies with the number of units produced.

Total costs consist of the sum of the fixed and variable costs for any given level of production. **Average cost** is the cost per unit at that level of production; it equals total costs divided by production. Management wants to charge a price that will at least cover the total production costs at a given level of production.

To price intelligently, management needs to know how its costs vary with different levels of production. The cost per unit is high if few units are produced per day. As production increases, the average cost falls because the fixed costs are spread over more units. Short-run average cost *increases* after a certain point, however, because the plant becomes inefficient (due to problems such as machines breaking down). By calculating costs for plants of different sizes, a firm can identify the optimal size and production level. To estimate the real profitability of selling to different types of retailers or customers, the manufacturer needs to use *activity-based cost (ABC)* accounting instead of standard cost accounting.

Accumulated Production Suppose Samsung runs a plant that produces 3,000 tablet computers per day. As the company gains experience producing tablets, its methods improve. Workers learn shortcuts, materials flow more smoothly, and procurement costs fall. The result, as Figure 11.1 shows, is that average cost falls with accumulated production experience. Thus the average cost of producing the first 100,000 tablets is $100 per tablet. When the company has produced the first 200,000 tablets, the average cost has fallen to $90. After its accumulated production experience doubles again to 400,000, the average cost is $80. This decline in the average cost with accumulated production experience is called the **experience curve** or *learning curve*.

Now suppose three firms compete in this particular tablet market, Samsung, A, and B. Samsung is the lowest-cost producer at $80, having produced 400,000 units in the past. If all three firms sell the tablet for $100, Samsung makes $20 profit per unit, A makes $10 per unit, and B breaks even. The smart move for Samsung would be to lower its price to $90. This will drive B out of the market, and even A may consider leaving. Samsung will pick up the business that

FIGURE 11.1 Cost per Unit as a Function of Accumulated Production: The Experience Curve

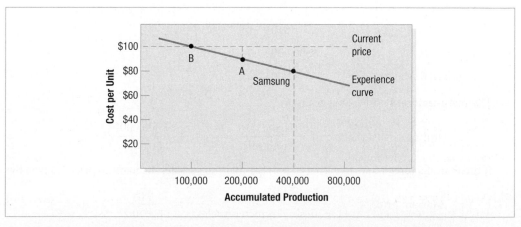

would have gone to B (and possibly A). Furthermore, price-sensitive customers will enter the market at the lower price. As production increases beyond 400,000 units, Samsung's costs will drop still further and faster, more than restoring its profits, even at a price of $90.

Experience-curve pricing nevertheless carries major risks. Aggressive pricing might give the product a cheap image. It also assumes competitors are weak followers. The strategy leads the company to build more plants to meet demand, but a competitor may choose to innovate with a lower-cost technology. The market leader is now stuck with the old technology.

Target Costing   Costs change with production scale and experience. They can also change as a result of a concentrated effort by designers, engineers, and purchasing agents to reduce them through **target costing.** Market research establishes a new product's desired functions and the price at which it will sell, given its appeal and competitors' prices. This price less desired profit margin leaves the target cost the marketer must achieve. The firm must examine each cost element—design, engineering, manufacturing, sales—and bring down costs so the final cost projections are in the target range. Cost cutting cannot go so deep as to compromise the brand promise and value delivered.

Step 4: Analyzing Competitors' Costs, Prices, and Offers

Within the range of possible prices identified by market demand and company costs, the firm must take competitors' costs, prices, and possible reactions into account. If the firm's offer contains features not offered by the nearest competitor, it should evaluate their worth to the customer and add that value to the competitor's price. If the competitor's offer contains some features not offered by the firm, the firm should subtract their value from its own price. Now the firm can decide whether it can charge more, the same, or less than the competitor.[20]

Step 5: Selecting a Pricing Method

The company is now ready to select a price. Figure 11.2 summarizes the three major considerations in price setting: Costs set a floor to the price. Competitors' prices and the price of substitutes provide an orienting point. Customers' assessment of unique features establishes the price ceiling. We will examine seven price-setting methods: markup pricing, target-return pricing, perceived-value pricing, value pricing, EDLP, going-rate pricing, and auction-type pricing.

Markup Pricing   The most elementary pricing method is to add a standard **markup** to the product's cost. Construction companies submit job bids by estimating the total project cost and adding a standard markup for profit. Suppose a toaster manufacturer has the following costs and sales expectations:

Variable cost per unit	$10
Fixed costs	$300,000
Expected unit sales	50,000

The manufacturer's unit cost is given by:

$$\text{Unit cost} = \text{variable cost} + \frac{\text{fixed cost}}{\text{unit sales}} = \$10 + \frac{\$300{,}000}{50{,}000} = \$16$$

If the manufacturer wants to earn a 20 percent markup on sales, its markup price is given by:

$$\text{Markup price} = \frac{\text{unit cost}}{(1 - \text{desired return on sales})} = \frac{\$16}{1 - 0.2} = \$20$$

FIGURE 11.2 The Three Cs Model for Price Setting

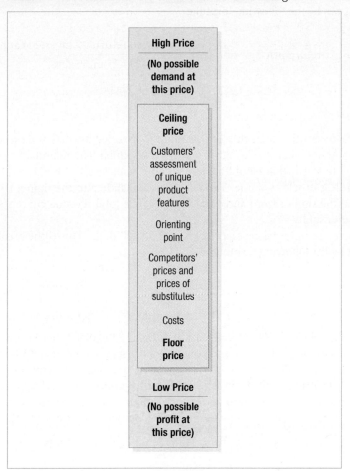

The manufacturer will charge dealers $20 per toaster and make a profit of $4 per unit. If dealers want to earn 50 percent on their selling price, they will mark up the toaster 100 percent to $40.

Generally, the use of standard markups does not make logical sense. Any pricing method that ignores current demand, perceived value, and competition is not likely to lead to the optimal price. Markup pricing works only if the marked-up price actually brings in the expected level of sales. Still, markup pricing remains popular because sellers can determine costs much more easily than they can estimate demand. By tying the price to cost, sellers simplify the pricing task. Also, when all firms in the industry use this pricing method, prices tend to be similar and price competition is minimized. Finally, many people feel cost-plus pricing is fairer to both buyers and sellers.

Target-Return Pricing   In **target-return pricing,** the firm determines the price that yields its target rate of return on investment. Public utilities, which need to make a fair return on investment, often use this method. Suppose the toaster manufacturer has invested $1 million in the business and wants to set a price to earn a 20 percent ROI, specifically $200,000. The target-return price is given by the following formula:

$$\text{Target-return price} = \text{unit cost} + \frac{\text{desired return} \times \text{invested capital}}{\text{unit sales}}$$

$$= \$16 + \frac{.20 \times \$1,000,000}{50,000} = \$20$$

The manufacturer will realize this 20 percent ROI provided its costs and estimated sales turn out to be accurate. But what if sales don't reach 50,000 units? The manufacturer can prepare a break-even chart to learn what would happen at other sales levels (see Figure 11.3). Fixed costs are stable, regardless of sales volume. Variable costs, not shown in the figure, rise with volume. Total costs equal the sum of fixed and variable costs. The total revenue curve starts at zero and rises with each unit sold.

The total revenue and total cost curves cross at 30,000 units. This is the break-even volume. We can verify it by the following formula:

$$\text{Break-even volume} = \frac{\text{fixed cost}}{(\text{price} - \text{variable cost})} = \frac{\$300,000}{\$20 - \$10} = 30,000$$

If the manufacturer sells 50,000 units at $20, it earns $200,000 on its $1 million investment, but much depends on price elasticity and competitors' prices. Unfortunately, target-return pricing tends to ignore these considerations. The manufacturer needs to consider different prices and estimate their probable impacts on sales volume and profits. It should also search for ways to lower its fixed or variable costs because lower costs will decrease its required break-even volume.

Perceived-Value Pricing An increasing number of companies now base their price on the customer's perceived value. *Perceived value* is made up of a host of inputs, such as the buyer's

FIGURE 11.3 Break-Even Chart for Determining Target-Return Price and Break-Even Volume

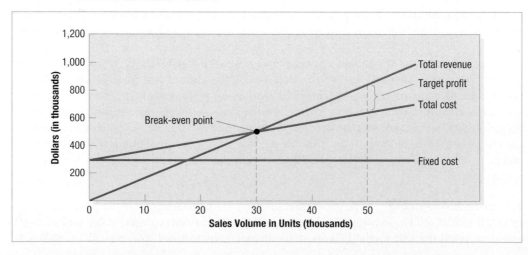

image of product performance, channel deliverables, warranty quality, customer support, and the supplier's reputation. Companies must deliver the value promised by their value proposition, and the customer must perceive this value. Firms use other marketing program elements, such as advertising, the sales force, and the Internet, to communicate and enhance perceived value in buyers' minds.

Even when a company claims its offering delivers more total value, not all customers will respond positively. Some care only about price. But there is also typically a segment that cares about quality. The key to perceived-value pricing is to deliver more unique value than competitors and to demonstrate this to prospective buyers.

Value Pricing   Companies that adopt **value pricing** win loyal customers by charging a fairly low price for a high-quality offering. This requires reengineering the company's operations to become a low-cost producer without sacrificing quality to attract a large number of value-conscious customers.

EDLP   A retailer using **everyday low pricing (EDLP)** charges a constant low price with little or no price promotion or special sales. Constant prices eliminate week-to-week price uncertainty and the high-low pricing of promotion-oriented competitors. In **high-low pricing,** the retailer charges higher prices on an everyday basis but runs frequent promotions with prices temporarily lower than the EDLP level.[21] The most important reason retailers adopt EDLP is that constant sales and promotions are costly and have eroded consumer confidence in everyday prices. Some consumers also have less time and patience for clipping coupons. Yet promotions and sales do create excitement and draw shoppers, so EDLP does not guarantee success and is not for everyone.[22]

Going-Rate Pricing   In **going-rate pricing,** the firm bases its price largely on competitors' prices. Smaller firms "follow the leader," changing their prices when the market leader's prices change. Some may charge a small premium or discount, but they preserve the difference. Going-rate pricing is quite popular. Where costs are difficult to measure or competitive response is uncertain, firms feel it is a good solution because they believe it reflects the industry's collective wisdom.

Auction-Type Pricing   *Auction-type pricing* is growing more popular, especially with electronic marketplaces. *English auctions*, with ascending bids, have one seller and many buyers; bidders raise their offers until the highest bidder gets the item. There are two types of *Dutch auctions*, which feature descending bids. In the first, an auctioneer announces a high price and then slowly decreases the price until a bidder accepts. In the other, the buyer announces something he or she wants to buy, and potential sellers compete to offer the lowest price. In *sealed-bid auctions,* would-be suppliers submit only one bid; they cannot know the other bids. The U.S. government often uses this method to procure supplies. A supplier will not bid below its cost but cannot bid too high for fear of losing the job. The net effect of these two pulls is the bid's *expected profit*.

Step 6: Selecting the Final Price

Pricing methods narrow the range from which the company must select its final price. In selecting that price, the company must consider additional factors, including the impact of other marketing activities, company pricing policies, gain-and-risk-sharing pricing, and the impact of price on other parties.

Impact of Other Marketing Activities   The final price must take into account the brand's quality and advertising relative to the competition. When Paul Farris and David Reibstein examined the relationships among relative price, relative quality, and relative advertising for 227 consumer businesses, they found that brands with average relative quality but high relative advertising budgets could charge premium prices because consumers were willing to pay more for known products.[23] Brands with high relative quality and high relative advertising obtained the highest prices. Conversely, brands with low quality and low advertising charged the lowest prices. For market leaders, the positive relationship between high prices and high advertising held most strongly in the later stages of the product life cycle.

Company Pricing Policies   The price must be consistent with company pricing policies. Although companies may establish pricing penalties under certain circumstances, they should use them judiciously and try not to alienate customers. Many companies set up a pricing department to develop policies and establish or approve decisions. The aim is to ensure salespeople quote prices that are reasonable to customers and profitable to the company.

Gain-and-Risk-Sharing Pricing   Buyers may resist accepting a seller's proposal because they perceive a high level of risk, such as in a big computer hardware purchase or a company health plan. The seller then has the option of offering to absorb part or all the risk if it does not deliver the full promised value. An increasing number of companies, especially B-to-B marketers, may have to stand ready to guarantee any promised savings but also participate in the upside if the gains are much greater than expected.

Impact of Price on Other Parties   How will distributors and dealers feel about the contemplated price?[24] If they don't make enough profit, they may choose not to bring the product to market. Will the sales force be willing to sell at that price? How will competitors react? Will suppliers raise their prices when they see the company's price? Will the government intervene and prevent this price from being charged? For example, it is illegal for a company to set artificially high "regular" prices, then announce a "sale" at prices close to previous everyday prices.

Adapting the Price

Companies usually do not set a single price but rather develop a pricing structure that reflects variations in geographical demand and costs, market-segment requirements, purchase timing, order levels, delivery frequency, guarantees, service contracts, and other factors. As a result of discounts, allowances, and promotional support, a company rarely realizes the same profit from each unit of a product that it sells. Here we will examine several price-adaptation strategies: geographical pricing, price discounts and allowances, promotional pricing, and differentiated pricing.

Geographical Pricing (Cash, Countertrade, Barter)

In geographical pricing, the company decides how to price its products to different customers in different locations and countries. Should the company charge higher prices to distant customers to cover higher shipping costs or a lower price to win additional business? How should it account for exchange rates and the strength of different currencies?

Another question is how to get paid. This issue is critical when buyers lack sufficient hard currency to pay for their purchases. Many want to offer other items in payment, a practice known as **countertrade,** and U.S. companies are often forced to accept if they want the business. One form of countertrade is *barter,* in which the buyer and seller directly exchange goods, with no money and no third party involved. A second form is a *compensation deal,* in which the seller receives some percentage of the payment in cash and the rest in products. A third form is a *buyback agreement,* as when the firm sells a plant, equipment, or technology to a company in another country and agrees to accept as partial payment products manufactured with the supplied equipment. A fourth form of countertrade is *offset,* where the firm receives full payment in cash for a sale overseas but agrees to spend a substantial amount of the money in that country within a stated time period.

Price Discounts and Allowances

Most companies will adjust their list price and give discounts and allowances for early payment, volume purchases, and off-season buying (see Table 11.2). Companies must do this carefully or find their profits much lower than planned.[25] Some product categories self-destruct by always being on sale. Manufacturers should consider the implications of supplying retailers at a discount because they may end up losing long-run profits in an effort to meet short-run volume goals. Upper management should conduct a *net price analysis* to arrive at the "real price" of the offering, which is affected by discounts and other expenses.

Promotional Pricing

Companies can use several pricing techniques to stimulate early purchase:

- **Loss-leader pricing.** Stores often drop the price on well-known brands to stimulate store traffic. This pays if the revenue on the additional sales compensates for the lower loss-leader margins. Manufacturers of loss-leader brands typically object because this practice can dilute the brand image and bring complaints from retailers who charge the list price.
- **Special event pricing.** Sellers establish special prices in certain seasons to draw in more customers, such as back-to-school sales.
- **Special customer pricing.** Sellers offer special prices exclusively to certain customers, such as members of a brand community.

TABLE 11.2	Price Discounts and Allowances
Discount:	A price reduction to buyers who pay bills promptly. A typical example is "2/10, net 30," which means payment is due within 30 days and the buyer can deduct 2 percent by paying within 10 days.
Quantity Discount:	A price reduction to those who buy large volumes. A typical example is "$10 per unit for fewer than 100 units; $9 per unit for 100 or more units." Quantity discounts must be offered equally to all customers and must not exceed the cost savings to the seller. They can be offered on each order placed or on the number of units ordered over a given period.
Functional Discount:	Discount (also called *trade discount*) offered by a manufacturer to trade-channel members if they perform certain functions, such as selling, storing, and record keeping. Manufacturers must offer the same functional discounts within each channel.
Seasonal Discount:	A price reduction to those who buy merchandise or services out of season. Hotels and airlines offer seasonal discounts in slow selling periods.
Allowance:	An extra payment designed to gain reseller participation in special programs. *Trade-in allowances* are granted for turning in an old item when buying a new one. *Promotional allowances* reward dealers for participating in advertising and sales support programs.

- **Cash rebates.** Auto companies and others offer cash rebates to encourage purchase of the manufacturers' products within a specified time period, clearing inventories without cutting the stated list price.
- **Low-interest financing.** Instead of cutting its price, the company can offer low-interest financing.
- **Longer payment terms.** Sellers, especially mortgage banks and auto companies, stretch loans over longer periods and thus lower the monthly payments. Consumers often worry less about the cost (the interest rate) of a loan and more about whether they can afford the monthly payment.
- **Warranties and service contracts.** Companies can promote sales by adding a free or low-cost warranty or service contract.
- **Psychological discounting.** This strategy sets an artificially high price and then offers the product at substantial savings; for example, "Was $359, now $299." The Federal Trade Commission and Better Business Bureau fight illegal discount tactics.

Promotional-pricing strategies are often a zero-sum game. If they work, competitors copy them and they lose their effectiveness. If they don't work, they waste money that could have been put into other marketing tools, such as building up product quality and service or strengthening product image through advertising.

Differentiated Pricing

Companies often adjust their basic price to accommodate differences among customers, products, locations, and so on. **Price discrimination** occurs when a company sells a product or service at two or more prices that do not reflect a proportional difference in costs. In first-degree price discrimination, the seller charges a separate price to each customer depending on the intensity of his or her demand. In second-degree price discrimination, the seller charges less to buyers of larger volumes. In third-degree price discrimination, the seller charges different amounts to different classes of buyers. Examples include: charging students and senior citizens lower prices; pricing different versions of the product differently; pricing the same product at different levels depending on image differences; charging differently for a product sold through different channels; pricing a product differently at different locations; and varying prices by season, day, or time of day.

The airline and hospitality industries use yield management systems and *yield pricing*, offering discounted but limited early purchases, higher-priced late purchases, and the lowest rates on unsold inventory just before it expires. Airlines charge different fares to passengers on the same flight depending on the seating class, the time of day, the day of the week, and so on.

The phenomenon of offering different pricing schedules to different consumers and dynamically adjusting prices is exploding. Online merchants selling their products on Amazon .com are changing their prices on an hourly or even minute-by-minute basis, in part so they can secure the top spot on search results.[26] Even sports teams are adjusting ticket prices to reflect the popularity of the competitor and the timing of the game.[27]

Price discrimination works when (1) the market is segmentable and the segments show different intensities of demand; (2) members in the lower-price segment cannot resell the product to the higher-price segment; (3) competitors cannot undersell the firm in the higher-price segment; (4) the cost of segmenting and policing the market does not exceed the extra revenue derived from price discrimination; (5) the practice does not breed customer resentment and ill will; and (6) the particular form of price discrimination is not illegal.[28]

Initiating and Responding to Price Changes

Companies often need to cut or raise prices.

Initiating Price Cuts

Several circumstances might lead a firm to cut prices. One is *excess plant capacity*: The firm needs additional business and cannot generate it through increased sales effort, product improvement, or other measures. Companies sometimes initiate price cuts in a *drive to dominate the market through lower costs.* Either the company starts with lower costs than its competitors, or it initiates price cuts in the hope of gaining market share and lower costs.

Cutting prices to keep customers or beat competitors often encourages customers to demand price concessions, however, and trains salespeople to offer them.[29] A price-cutting strategy can lead to other possible traps. Consumers might assume quality is low, or the low price buys market share but not market loyalty—because customers switch to lower-priced firms. Also, higher-priced competitors might match the lower prices but have longer staying power because of deeper cash reserves. Finally, lowering prices might trigger a price war.[30]

Initiating Price Increases

A successful price increase can raise profits considerably. If the company's profit margin is 3 percent of sales, a 1 percent price increase will increase profits by 33 percent if sales volume is unaffected. A major circumstance provoking price increases is *cost inflation*. Rising costs unmatched by productivity gains squeeze profit margins and lead companies to regular rounds of price increases. Companies often raise their prices by more than the cost increase, in anticipation of further inflation or government price controls, in a practice called *anticipatory pricing*.

Another factor leading to price increases is *overdemand.* When a company cannot supply all its customers, it can raise its prices, ration supplies, or both. Although there is always a chance a price increase can carry some positive meanings to customers—for example, that the item is "hot" and represents an unusually good value—consumers generally dislike higher prices. To avoid sticker shock and a hostile reaction when prices rise, the firm should give customers advance notice so they can do forward buying or shop around. Sharp price increases also need to be explained in understandable terms.

Anticipating Competitive Responses

How can a firm anticipate a competitor's reactions? One way is to assume the competitor reacts in the standard way to a price being set or changed. Another is to assume the competitor treats each price difference or change as a fresh challenge and reacts according to self-interest at the time. Now the company will need to research the competitor's current financial situation, recent sales, customer loyalty, and corporate objectives. If the competitor has a market share objective, it is likely to match price differences or changes.[31] If it has a profit-maximization objective, it may react by increasing its advertising budget or improving product quality.

Responding to Competitors' Price Changes

In responding to competitive price cuts, the company must consider the product's stage in the life cycle, its importance in the company's portfolio, the competitor's intentions and resources, the market's price and quality sensitivity, the behavior of costs with volume, and the company's alternative opportunities. In markets characterized by high product homogeneity, the firm can enhance its augmented product or meet the price reduction. If the competitor raises its price in a homogeneous product market, other firms might not match it if the increase will not benefit the industry as a whole. Then the leader will need to roll back the increase.

In nonhomogeneous product markets, a firm should consider why the competitor changed the price. Was it to steal the market, to utilize excess capacity, to meet changing cost conditions, or to lead an industry-wide price change? Is the competitor's price change temporary or permanent? What will happen to the company's market share and profits if it does not respond? Are other companies going to respond? And how are competitors and other firms likely to respond to each possible reaction?

Executive Summary

Price is the only marketing element that produces revenue; the others produce costs. Consumers often actively process price information within the context of prior purchasing experience, formal and informal communications, point-of-purchase or online resources, and other factors. In setting pricing policy, a company follows six steps: (1) select the pricing objective; (2) determine demand; (3) estimate costs; (4) analyze competitors' costs, prices, and offers; (5) select a pricing method; and (6) select the final price. Price-adaptation strategies include geographical pricing, price discounts and allowances, promotional pricing, and discriminatory pricing. Price-setting methods include markup pricing, target-return pricing, perceived-value pricing, value pricing, EDLP, going-rate pricing, and auction-type pricing.

A price decrease might be brought about by excess plant capacity, declining market share, a desire to dominate the market through lower costs, or economic recession. A price increase might be brought about by cost inflation or overdemand. Companies must carefully manage customer perceptions when raising prices. Also, they should anticipate competitor price changes and prepare contingent responses, including maintaining or changing price or quality. When facing competitive price changes, the firm should try to understand the competitor's intent and the likely duration of the change.

Notes

1. "Ryanair Food Costs More than Price of Flight," *The Telegraph*, August 28, 2012; Simon Calder, "Ryanair Unveils Its Latest Plan to Save Money: Remove Toilets from the Plane," *The Independent*, October 12, 2011; Peter J. Howe, "The Next Pinch: Fees to Check Bags," *Boston Globe,* March 8, 2007; Kerry Capel, "'Wal-Mart with Wings,'" *BusinessWeek,* November 27, 2006, pp. 44–45; Renee Schultes, "Ryanair Could Hold Altitude in Airline Descent," *Wall Street Journal,* July 6, 2014.

2. Tomio Geron, "The Share Economy," *Forbes*, February 11, 2013.

3. Christian Homburg, Ove Jensen, and Alexander Hahn, "How to Organize Pricing? Vertical Delegation and Horizontal Dispersion of Pricing Authority," *Journal of Marketing* 76 (September 2012), pp. 49–69.

4. For a review of pricing research, see Chezy Ofir and Russell S. Winer, "Pricing: Economic and Behavioral Models," Bart Weitz and Robin Wensley, eds., *Handbook of Marketing* (London: Sage Publications, 2002). For a recent sampling of some research on consumer processing of prices, see Ray Weaver and Shane Frederick, "A Reference Price Theory of the Endowment Effect," *Journal of Marketing Research* 49 (October 2012), pp. 696–707; and Kwanho Suk, Jiheon Lee, and Donald R. Lichtenstein, "The Influence of Price Presentation Order on Consumer Choice," *Journal of Marketing Research* 49 (October 2012), pp. 708–17.

5. Hooman Estalami, Alfred Holden, and Donald R. Lehmann, "Macro-Economic Determinants of Consumer Price Knowledge: A Meta-Analysis of Four Decades of Research," *International Journal of Research in Marketing* 18 (December 2001), pp. 341–55.

6. For a comprehensive review, see Tridib Mazumdar, S. P. Raj, and Indrajit Sinha, "Reference Price Research: Review and Propositions," *Journal of Marketing* 69 (October 2005), pp. 84–102. For a different point of view, see Chris Janiszewski and Donald R. Lichtenstein, "A Range Theory Account of Price Perception," *Journal of Consumer Research* 25 (March 1999), pp. 353–68. For business-to-business applications, see Hernan A. Bruno, Hai Che, and Shantanu Dutta, "Role of Reference Price on Price and Quantity: Insights from Business-to-Business Markets," *Journal of Marketing Research* 49 (October 2012), pp. 640–54.

7. Ritesh Saini, Raghunath Singh Rao, and Ashwani Monga, "Is the Deal Worth My Time? The Interactive Effect of Relative and Referent Thinking on Willingness to Seek a Bargain," *Journal of Marketing* 74 (January 2010), pp. 34–48.

8. John T. Gourville, "Pennies-a-Day: The Effect of Temporal Reframing on Transaction Evaluation," *Journal of Consumer Research* 24 (March 1998), pp. 395–408. See also Anja Lambrecht and Catherine Tucker, "Paying with Money or Effort: Pricing when Customers Anticipate Hassle," *Journal of Marketing Research* 49 (February 2012), pp. 66–82.

9. Wilfred Amaldoss and Sanjay Jain, "Pricing of Conspicuous Goods: A Competitive Analysis of Social Effects," *Journal of Marketing Research* 42 (February 2005), pp. 30–42.

10. Mark Stiving and Russell S. Winer, "An Empirical Analysis of Price Endings with Scanner Data," *Journal of Consumer Research* 24 (June 1997), pp. 57–68.

11. Eric T. Anderson and Duncan Simester, "Effects of $9 Price Endings on Retail Sales: Evidence from Field Experiments," *Quantitative Marketing and Economics* 1 (March 2003), pp. 93–110.

12. Katherine N. Lemon and Stephen M. Nowlis, "Developing Synergies between Promotions and Brands in Different Price-Quality Tiers," *Journal of Marketing Research* 39 (May 2002), pp. 171–85; but see also Serdar Sayman, Stephen J. Hoch, and Jagmohan S. Raju, "Positioning of Store Brands," *Marketing Science* 21 (Fall 2002), pp. 378–97.

13. Shantanu Dutta, Mark J. Zbaracki, and Mark Bergen, "Pricing Process as a Capability: A Resource-Based Perspective," *Strategic Management Journal* 24 (July 2003), pp. 615–30.

14. Wilfred Amaldoss and Chuan He, "Pricing Prototypical Products," *Marketing Science* 32 (September–October 2013), pp. 733–52.

15. Timothy Aeppel, "Seeking Perfect Prices, CEO Tears Up the Rules," *Wall Street Journal,* March 27, 2007.

16. Joo Heon Park and Douglas L. MacLachlan, "Estimating Willingness to Pay with Exaggeration Bias-Corrected Contingent Valuation Method," *Marketing Science* 27 (July–August 2008), pp. 691–98.

17. Thomas T. Nagle, John E. Hogan, and Joseph Zale, *The Strategy and Tactics of Pricing,* 5th ed. (Upper Saddle River, NJ: Pearson, 2011)

18. Brett R. Gordon, Avi Goldfarb, and Yang Li, "Does Price Elasticity Vary with Economic Growth? A Cross-Category Analysis," *Journal of Marketing Research* 50 (February 2013), pp. 4–23. See also Harald J. Van Heerde, Maarten J. Gijsenberg, Marnik G. Dekimpe, and Jan-Benedict E. M. Steenkamp, "Price and Advertising Effectiveness over the Business Cycle," *Journal of Marketing Research* 50 (April 2013), pp. 177–93.

19. Tammo H. A. Bijmolt, Harald J. Van Heerde, and Rik G. M. Pieters, "New Empirical Generalizations on the Determinants of Price Elasticity," *Journal of Marketing Research* 42 (May 2005), pp. 141–56.

20. Marco Bertini, Luc Wathieu, and Sheena S. Iyengar, "The Discriminating Consumer: Product Proliferation and Willingness to Pay for Quality," *Journal of Marketing Research* 49 (February 2012), pp. 39–49.

21. Michael Tsiros and David M. Hardesty, "Ending a Price Promotion: Retracting It in One Step or Phasing It Out Gradually," *Journal of Marketing* 74 (January 2010), pp. 49–64.

22, Paul B. Ellickson, Sanjog Misra, and Harikesh S. Nair, "Repositioning Dynamics and Pricing Strategy," *Journal of Marketing Research* 49 (December 2012), pp. 750–72.

23. Paul W. Farris and David J. Reibstein, "How Prices, Expenditures, and Profits Are Linked," *Harvard Business Review,* November–December 1979, pp. 173–84.

24. Joel E. Urbany, "Justifying Profitable Pricing," *Journal of Product and Brand Management* 10 (2001), pp. 141–57; Charles Fishman, "The Wal-Mart You Don't Know," *Fast Company,* December 2003, pp. 68–80.

25. Kusum L. Ailawadi, Scott A. Neslin, and Karen Gedenk, "Pursuing the Value-Conscious Consumer," *Journal of Marketing* 65 (January 2001), pp. 71–89.

26. "Increasing Revenue and Reducing Workload Using Yield Management Software," *Globe Newswire,* March 12, 2013; Julia Angwin and Dana Mattioli, "Coming Soon: Toilet Paper Priced Like Airline Tickets," *Wall Street Journal*, September 5, 2012.

27. Andrea Rothman, "Greyhound Taps Airline Pricing Models to Boost Profit," www.bloomberg.com, May 21, 2013; Bill Saporito, "This Offer Won't Last! Why

Sellers Are Switching to Dynamic Pricing," *Time*, January 21, 2013, p. 56; Patrick Rishe, "Dynamic Pricing: The Future of Ticket Pricing in Sports," *Forbes*, January 6, 2012.

28. Felix Salmon, "Why the Internet Is Perfect for Price Discrimination," *Reuters*, September 3, 2013. For more information about specific types of price discrimination that are illegal, see Henry Cheeseman, *Business Law*, 8th ed. (Upper Saddle River, NJ: Pearson, 2013).

29. Bob Donath, "Dispel Major Myths about Pricing," *Marketing News*, February 3, 2003, p. 10.

30. Harald J. Van Heerde, Els Gijsbrechts, and Koen Pauwels, "Winners and Losers in a Major Price War," *Journal of Marketing Research* 45 (October 2008), pp. 499–518.

31. Kusum L. Ailawadi, Donald R. Lehmann, and Scott A. Neslin, "Market Response to a Major Policy Change in the Marketing Mix," *Journal of Marketing* 65 (January 2001), pp. 44–61.

Chapter 12

Designing and Managing Integrated Marketing Channels

In this chapter, we will address the following questions:

1. What is a marketing channel system and value network? (Page 192)
2. What work do marketing channels perform? (Page 194)
3. What decisions do companies face in designing, managing, and integrating their channels? (Page 196)
4. What are the key channel issues in e-commerce and m-commerce? (Page 199)

Marketing Management at L.L.Bean

L.L.Bean's founder Leon Leonwood Bean returned from a Maine hunting trip in 1911 with cold, damp feet—and a revolutionary idea for creating a comfortable, functional boot. The shoe was not an initial success. Of the first 100 pairs sold, 90 were returned when the tops and bottoms separated. Bean refunded the purchase price and fixed the problem. The company's guarantee of 100 percent satisfaction is still at the core of its business. Today, it is a $1.5 billion company, selling through its famous catalogs as well as online and in retail stores. L.L.Bean has also expanded globally, with stores in Japan and China. Online it has opened up to customer ratings and reviews, invites customers to chat and e-mail with representatives, and offers a "click and call" system that triggers a customer service call within two minutes. It monitors customer feedback closely and has been ranked number 1 in customer service by Bloomberg Businessweek.[1]

With the advent of *e-commerce* (selling online) and *m-commerce* (selling via mobile phones and tablets), customers are buying in ways they never have before. Companies today must build and manage a continuously evolving and increasingly complex channel system and value network. In this chapter, we consider strategic and tactical issues in integrating marketing channels and developing value networks. Chapter 13 examines marketing channel issues from the perspective of retailers, wholesalers, and physical distribution agencies.

Marketing Channels and Value Networks

Most producers do not sell their goods directly to the final users; between them stands a set of intermediaries performing a variety of functions. These are **marketing channels**, sets of interdependent organizations participating in the process of making a product or service available for use or consumption. They are the set of pathways a product or service follows after production, culminating in purchase and consumption by the final end user.[2]

The Importance of Channels

A **marketing channel system** is the particular set of marketing channels a firm employs, and decisions about it are among the most critical ones management faces. In the United States, channel members as a group have historically earned margins that account for 30 percent to 50 percent of the ultimate selling price. In contrast, advertising typically has accounted for less than 5 percent to 7 percent of the final price.[3] One of the chief roles of marketing channels is to convert potential buyers into profitable customers. Marketing channels must not just *serve* markets, they must also *make* them.[4]

The channels chosen affect all other marketing decisions. The company's pricing depends on whether it uses online discounters or high-quality boutiques. Its sales force and advertising decisions depend on how much training and motivation dealers need. In addition, channel decisions include relatively long-term commitments with other firms as well as a set of policies and procedures. When an automaker signs up independent dealers to sell its automobiles, it cannot buy them out the next day and replace them with company-owned outlets. Holistic marketers ensure that marketing decisions in all these different areas are made to maximize value overall.

In managing its intermediaries, the firm must decide how much effort to devote to push and to pull marketing. A **push strategy** uses the manufacturer's sales force, trade promotion money, or other means to induce intermediaries to carry, promote, and sell the product to end users. This strategy is particularly appropriate when there is low brand loyalty in a category, brand choice is made in the store, the product is an impulse item, and product benefits are well understood. In a **pull strategy** the manufacturer uses advertising, promotion, and other forms of communication to persuade consumers to demand the product from intermediaries, thus inducing the intermediaries to order it. This strategy is particularly appropriate when there is high brand loyalty and high involvement in the category, when consumers are able to perceive differences between brands, and when they choose the brand before they go to the store. Top marketing companies such as Coca-Cola and Nike skillfully employ both push *and* pull strategies.

Multichannel Marketing

Today's successful companies typically employ **multichannel marketing**, using two or more marketing channels to reach customer segments in one market area. HP uses its sales force to sell to large accounts, outbound telemarketing to sell to medium-sized accounts, direct mail with an inbound phone number to sell to small accounts, retailers to sell to still smaller accounts, and the Internet to sell specialty items. Each channel can target a different segment of buyers, or different need states for one buyer, to deliver the right products in the right places in the right way at the least cost.

Research has shown that multichannel customers can be more valuable to marketers.[5] Nordstrom found that its multichannel customers spend four times as much as those who only shop through one channel, though some academic research suggests that this effect is stronger for hedonic products (apparel and cosmetics) than for functional products (office and garden supplies).[6]

Integrating Multichannel Marketing Systems

Most companies today have adopted multichannel marketing. Companies are increasingly employing digital distribution strategies, selling directly online to customers or through e-merchants who have their own Web sites. These firms are seeking to achieve **omnichannel marketing**, in which multiple channels work seamlessly together and match each target customer's preferred ways of doing business, delivering the right product information and customer service regardless of whether customers are online, in the store, or on the phone.

In an **integrated marketing channel system**, the strategies and tactics of selling through one channel reflect the strategies and tactics of selling through one or more other channels. Adding more channels gives companies three important benefits: (1) increased market coverage, (2) lower channel cost, and (3) the ability to do more customized selling. However, new channels typically introduce conflict and problems with control and cooperation. Two or more may end up competing for the same customers.[7] Clearly, companies need to think through their channel architecture and determine which channels should perform which functions.[8]

Value Networks

The company should first think of the target market and then design the supply chain backward from that point. This strategy has been called **demand chain planning**.[9] A broader view sees a company at the center of a **value network**—a system of partnerships and alliances that a firm creates to source, augment, and deliver its offerings. A value network includes a firm's suppliers and its suppliers' suppliers and its immediate customers and their end customers. It also incorporates valued relationships with others such as university researchers and government approval agencies.

Demand chain planning yields several insights.[10] First, the company can estimate whether more money is made upstream or downstream, in case it can integrate backward or forward. Second, the company is more aware of disturbances anywhere in the supply chain that might change costs, prices, or supplies. Third, companies can go online with their business partners to speed communications, transactions, and payments; reduce costs; and increase accuracy.

The Digital Channels Revolution

The digital revolution is profoundly transforming distribution strategies. With customers—both individuals and businesses—becoming more comfortable buying online and the use of smart phones exploding, traditional brick-and-mortar channel strategies are being modified or even replaced. Customers want the advantages of digital—vast product selection, abundant product information, helpful customer reviews and tips—and of physical stores—highly personalized service, detailed physical examination of products, an overall event and experience. They expect seamless channel integration so they can:[11]

- Enjoy helpful customer support in a store, online, or on the phone
- Check online for product availability at local stores before making a trip
- Find out in-store whether a product that is unavailable can be purchased and shipped from another store to home

- Order a product online and pick it up at a convenient retail location
- Return a product purchased online to a nearby store of the retailer
- Receive discounts and promotional offers based on total online and offline purchases

The Role of Marketing Channels

Why does a producer delegate some of the selling job to intermediaries, relinquishing control over how and to whom its products are sold? Through their contacts, experience, specialization, and scale of operation, intermediaries make goods widely available and accessible to target markets, offering more effectiveness and efficiency than the selling firm could achieve on its own.[12] Many producers lack the financial resources and expertise to sell directly on their own. The William Wrigley Jr. Company would not find it practical to establish small retail gum shops throughout the world or to sell gum online or by mail order. It is easier to work through the extensive network of privately owned distribution organizations. Even Ford would be hard-pressed to replace all the tasks done by its thousands of dealer outlets worldwide.

Channel Functions and Flows

A marketing channel performs the work of moving goods from producers to consumers. It overcomes the time, place, and possession gaps that separate goods and services from those who need or want them. Members of the marketing channel perform a number of key functions (see Table 12.1).

Some of these functions (storage and movement, title, and communications) constitute a *forward flow* of activity from the company to the customer; others (ordering and payment) constitute a *backward flow* from customers to the company. Still others (information, negotiation, finance, and risk taking) occur in both directions. Five flows are illustrated in Figure 12.1 for the marketing of forklift trucks. If these flows were superimposed in one diagram, we would see the tremendous complexity of even simple marketing channels.

A manufacturer selling a physical product and services might require three channels: a *sales channel,* a *delivery channel,* and a *service channel.* The question for marketers is not *whether* various channel functions need to be performed—they must be—but, rather, *who* is to perform

TABLE 12.1   Channel Member Functions

- Gather information about potential and current customers, competitors, and other actors and forces in the marketing environment.
- Develop and disseminate persuasive communications to stimulate purchasing.
- Negotiate and reach agreements on price and other terms so that transfer of ownership or possession can be made.
- Place orders with manufacturers.
- Acquire the funds to finance inventories at different levels in the marketing channel.
- Assume risks connected with carrying out channel work.
- Provide for the successive storage and movement of physical products.
- Provide for buyers' payment of bills through banks and other financial institutions.
- Oversee transfer of ownership from one organization or person to another.

FIGURE 12.1 Five Marketing Flows in the Marketing Channel for Forklift Trucks

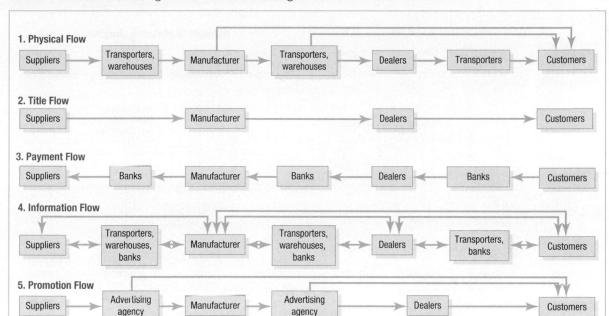

them. All channel functions use up scarce resources; they can often be performed better through specialization; and they can be shifted among channel members. Shifting some functions to intermediaries lowers the producer's costs and prices, but the intermediary must add a charge to cover its work. If the intermediaries are more efficient than the manufacturer, prices to consumers should be lower. If consumers perform some functions themselves, they should enjoy even lower prices.

Channel Levels

The producer and the final customer are part of every channel. We will use the number of intermediary levels to designate the length of a channel. Figure 12.2(a) illustrates several consumer-goods marketing channels, while Figure 12.2(b) illustrates some industrial marketing channels.

A **zero-level channel**, also called a **direct marketing channel**, consists of a manufacturer selling directly to the final customer. The major examples are mail order, online selling, TV selling, telemarketing, door-to-door sales, home parties, and manufacturer-owned stores. A *one-level channel* contains one selling intermediary, such as a retailer. A *two-level channel* contains two intermediaries, typically a wholesaler and a retailer, and a *three-level channel* contains three.

Channels normally describe a forward movement of products from source to user, but *reverse-flow channels* are also important to (1) reuse products or containers (such as refillable chemical-carrying drums), (2) refurbish products for resale (such as circuit boards or computers), (3) recycle products, and (4) dispose of products and packaging. Reverse-flow intermediaries include manufacturers' redemption centers, community groups, trash-collection specialists, recycling centers, trash-recycling brokers, and central processing warehousing.

FIGURE 12.2 Consumer and Industrial Marketing Channels

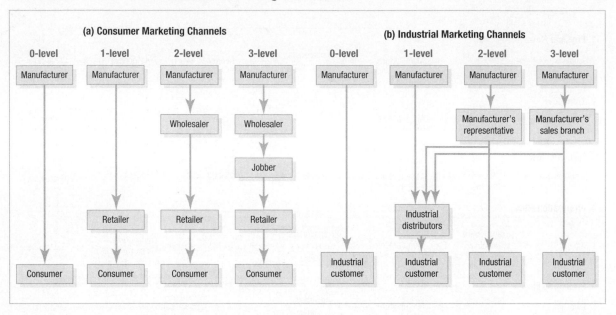

Service Sector Channels

Many of the most successful new banks, insurance and travel companies, and stock brokerages have emerged with strictly or largely online operations, such as Ally banking, Esurance insurance, and Expedia travel. Marketing channels also keep changing for "person marketing." Besides providing live and programmed entertainment, entertainers, musicians, and other artists can reach fans online in many ways—through their own Web sites, on social community sites such as Facebook and Twitter, and through third-party Web sites. Nonprofit service organizations such as schools develop education-dissemination systems, and hospitals develop health-delivery systems. These institutions must figure out agencies and locations for reaching a far-flung population.[13]

Channel-Design Decisions

To design a marketing channel system, marketers analyze customer needs and wants, establish channel objectives and constraints, and identify and evaluate major channel alternatives.

Analyzing Customer Needs and Wants

Consumers may choose the channels they prefer based on price, product assortment, and convenience as well as their own shopping goals (economic, social, or experiential).[14] Channel segmentation exists, and marketers must be aware that different consumers have different needs during the purchase process. Even the same consumer, though, may choose different channels for different reasons.[15] "Marketing Insight: Understanding the Showrooming Phenomena" describes some of the new ways customers are using multiple channels as they make their purchases.

marketing insight

Understanding the Showrooming Phenomena

Consumers have always shopped around to get the best deal or broaden their options, and now selling via mobile phone and tablet offers a new twist. **Showrooming** lets buyers physically examine a product and collect information in a store but make their actual purchase later, from the retailer online or from a different retailer, typically to secure a lower price. One study showed that more than half of U.S. mobile phone users, especially younger ones, have used their phones to ask for purchase advice from a friend, to look at reviews, or to search for lower prices while shopping.

Mobile has become a top priority for many retailers as a means to combat showrooming. Target has expanded its use of mobile media, incorporating QR codes, text-to-buy features, and new checkout scanners to make mobile coupon redemption easier and faster. Many retailers are also making the in-store experience more informative and rewarding. Guess, PacSun, and Aéropostale equip in-store staff with iPads or tablets for sharing in-depth product information with shoppers. One study found that 70 percent of a showrooming audience was more likely to buy from retailers with well-designed Web sites and apps, strong multichannel support, and price comparisons via QR codes.

Sources: "Showrooming Threat Hits Major Chains," www.warc.com, March 1, 2013; Lydia Dishman, "Target's Cartwheel to Bridge the Digital and Brick-and-Mortar Divide," *Forbes*, May 9, 2013; "'Showrooming' Grows in U.S.," www.warc.com, February 4, 2013; "Showrooming to Shape U.S. Holiday Sales," www.warc.com, November 16, 2012; Hadley Malcolm, "Smartphones to Play Bigger Role in Shopping," *USA Today*, November 15, 2012; Maribel López, "Can Omni-Channel Retail Combat Showrooming," *Forbes*, October 22, 2012; Australian School of Business, "Stop Customers Treating Your Business as a Showroom," www.smartcompany.com.au, October 8, 2012.

Channels produce five service outputs:

1. *Desired lot size*—The number of units the channel permits a typical customer to purchase on one occasion. In buying cars for its fleet, Hertz prefers a channel from which it can buy a large lot size; a household wants a channel that permits a lot size of one.

2. *Waiting and delivery time*—The average time customers wait for receipt of goods. Customers increasingly prefer faster delivery channels.

3. *Spatial convenience*—The degree to which the marketing channel makes it easy for customers to purchase the product.

4. *Product variety*—The assortment provided by the marketing channel. Normally, customers prefer a greater assortment because more choices increase the chance of finding what they need, though too many choices can sometimes create a negative effect.[16]

5. *Service backup*—Add-on services (credit, delivery, installation, repairs) provided by the channel.

Providing more service outputs also means increasing channel costs and raising prices. The success of discount stores such as Walmart and Target indicates that many consumers are willing to accept less service if they can save money.

Establishing Objectives and Constraints

Marketers should state their channel objectives in terms of the service output levels they want to provide and the associated cost and support levels. Under competitive conditions, channel members should arrange their functional tasks to minimize costs and still provide desired levels of service. Usually, planners can identify several market segments based on desired service and choose the best channels for each.

Channel objectives vary with product characteristics. Bulky products, such as building materials, require channels that minimize shipping distance and handling. Products requiring installation or maintenance services, such as heating and cooling systems, are usually sold and maintained by the company or franchised dealers. High-unit-value products such as turbines are often sold through a company sales force rather than intermediaries. Legal regulations and restrictions also affect channel design.

Identifying Major Channel Alternatives

Each channel—from sales forces to agents, distributors, dealers, direct mail, telemarketing, and the Internet—has unique strengths and weaknesses. Channel alternatives differ in three ways: the types of intermediaries, the number needed, and the terms and responsibilities of each.

Types of Intermediaries   Some intermediaries—such as wholesalers and retailers—buy, take title to, and resell the merchandise; they are called *merchants*. *Agents*—such as brokers, manufacturers' representatives, and sales agents—search for customers and may negotiate on the producer's behalf but do not take title to the goods. *Facilitators*—transportation companies, independent warehouses, banks, advertising agencies—assist in the distribution process but neither take title nor negotiate purchases or sales. Sometimes a company chooses a new or an unconventional channel because of the difficulty, cost, or ineffectiveness of working with the dominant channel. For instance, Netflix is quickly moving away from the revolutionary channel that brought it much success—renting DVDs by mail—to capitalize on a new one: streaming entertainment online.[17]

Number of Intermediaries   Three strategies based on the number of intermediaries are exclusive, selective, and intensive distribution. **Exclusive distribution** severely limits the number of intermediaries, appropriate when the producer wants more knowledgeable, dedicated resellers. This often includes *exclusive dealing* arrangements, especially in markets increasingly driven by price. **Selective distribution** relies on only some of the intermediaries willing to carry a particular product. The company can gain adequate market coverage with more control and less cost than intensive distribution. **Intensive distribution** places the goods or services in as many outlets as possible, a good strategy for snack foods, soft drinks, newspapers, and gum—products consumers buy frequently or in a variety of locations.

Terms and Responsibilities of Channel Members   The main elements in the "trade relations mix" are price policies, conditions of sale, territorial rights, and specific services to be performed by each party. *Price policy* calls for the producer to establish a price list and schedule of discounts and allowances that intermediaries see as equitable and sufficient. *Conditions of sale* are payment terms and producer guarantees. Most producers grant cash discounts to distributors for early payment. They might also offer a guarantee against defective merchandise or price declines, creating an incentive to buy larger quantities. *Distributors' territorial rights* define the distributors' territories and the terms under which the producer will enfranchise other distributors. *Mutual services and responsibilities* must be carefully spelled out, especially in franchised and exclusive-agency channels.

Evaluating Major Channel Alternatives

Each channel alternative needs to be evaluated against economic, control, and adaptive criteria.

FIGURE 12.3 The Value-Adds versus Costs of Different Channels

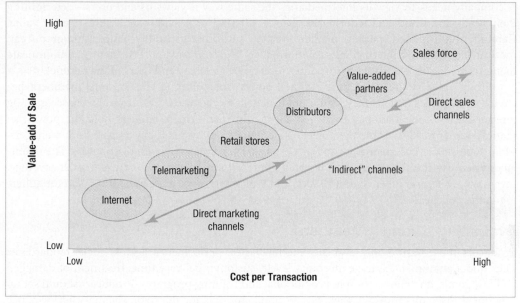

Source: Oxford Associates, adapted from Dr. Rowland T. Moriarty, Cubex Corp.

Figure 12.3 shows how six different sales channels stack up in terms of the value added per sale and the cost per transaction. The first step is to estimate the dollar volume of sales each alternative will likely generate. Sellers try to replace high-cost channels with low-cost channels as long as the value added per sale is sufficient. To develop a channel, members must commit to each other for a specified period. Yet these commitments invariably reduce the producer's ability to respond to change and uncertainty. Using a sales agency can pose a control problem. Agents may concentrate on the customers who buy the most, not necessarily those who buy the manufacturer's goods. They might not master the technical details of the company's product or handle its promotion materials effectively.

Channel-Management Decisions

After a company has chosen a channel system, it must select, train, motivate, and evaluate intermediaries for each channel. It must also modify channel design and arrangements over time.

Selecting Channel Members

To customers, the channels are the company. Consider the negative impression customers would get if a Mercedes-Benz dealer appeared dirty, inefficient, or unpleasant. Producers should determine what characteristics distinguish the better intermediaries—number of years in business, other lines carried, growth and profit record, financial strength, cooperativeness, and service reputation. If the intermediaries are sales agents, producers should evaluate the number and character of other lines carried and the size and quality of the sales force. If the intermediaries want exclusive distribution, consider their locations, future growth potential, and type of clientele.

Training and Motivating Channel Members

A company needs to view its intermediaries the same way it views its end users—determining their needs and wants and tailoring its channel offering to provide them with superior value. Carefully implemented training, market research, and other capability-building programs can motivate and improve intermediaries' performance. The company must constantly communicate that intermediaries are crucial partners in a joint effort to satisfy end users of the product.

Producers vary greatly in their **channel power**, the ability to alter channel members' behavior so they take actions they would not have taken otherwise.[18] Most producers see gaining intermediaries' cooperation as a huge challenge. In many cases, retailers hold the power, so manufacturers need to know the acceptance criteria used by retail buyers and store managers. More sophisticated companies try to forge a long-term partnership with distributors. The manufacturer clearly communicates what it wants from its distributors in the way of market coverage, inventory levels, and other channel issues, and it may introduce a compensation plan for adhering to the policies.

Evaluating Channel Members

Producers must periodically evaluate intermediaries' performance against such standards as sales-quota attainment, average inventory levels, customer delivery time, treatment of damaged and lost goods, and cooperation in promotional and training programs. Producers should set up functional discounts in which they pay specified amounts for the trade channel's performance of each agreed-upon service. Underperformers need to be counseled, retrained, motivated, or terminated.

Modifying Channel Design and Arrangements

A new firm typically starts as a local operation selling in a fairly circumscribed market, using a few existing intermediaries. Here the problem is often to convince the available intermediaries to handle the firm's line. If the firm is successful, it might branch into new markets with different channels. However, no channel strategy remains effective over the whole product life cycle. The distribution channel may not work as planned, consumer buying patterns change, the market expands, new competition arises, innovative distribution channels emerge, and the product moves into later stages in the product life cycle.[19] To add or drop individual channel members, the company needs to make an incremental analysis. What would the firm's sales and profits look like with and without this intermediary?

Global Channel Considerations

International markets pose distinct challenges, including variations in customers' shopping habits and the need to gain social acceptance or legitimacy among others, but opportunities do exist.[20] The first step in global channel planning is to get close to customers. To adapt its clothing lines to European tastes, Philadelphia-based Urban Outfitters set up a separate design and merchandising unit in London before it opened its first store in Europe. Although it increased costs, the distinctive blend of U.S. and European looks helped the retailer stand out, and it was one of the few fashion retailers to build strength during the recent recession.[21]

Channel Integration and Systems

In addition to multichannel marketing systems, discussed earlier, two other channel developments are vertical and horizontal marketing systems.

Vertical Marketing Systems

A *conventional marketing channel* consists of an independent producer, wholesaler(s), and retailer(s). Each is a separate business seeking to maximize its own profits, even if this goal reduces profit for the system as a whole. No channel member has complete or substantial control over other members.

A **vertical marketing system (VMS)**, by contrast, includes the producer, wholesaler(s), and retailer(s) acting as a unified system. One channel member, the *channel captain*, sometimes called a *channel steward*, owns or franchises the others or has so much power that they all cooperate. Stewards accomplish channel coordination without issuing commands or directives by persuading channel partners to act in the best interest of all.[22] A channel steward might be the maker of the product or service (Procter & Gamble or American Airlines), the maker of a key component (microchip maker Intel), the supplier or assembler (Dell), the distributor (W.W. Grainger), or the retailer (Walmart).

VMSs have become the dominant mode of distribution in the U.S. consumer marketplace. There are three types: corporate, administered, and contractual. A *corporate VMS* combines successive stages of production and distribution under single ownership, the way Sherwin-Williams makes paint but also owns and operates retail outlets. An *administered VMS* coordinates successive stages of production and distribution through the size and power of one of the members, the way Frito-Lay and other big brands secure strong reseller cooperation and support. A *contractual VMS* consists of independent firms at different levels of production and distribution integrating their programs on a contractual basis to obtain more economies or sales impact than they could achieve alone.[23] Table 12.2 describes three types of contractual VMSs.

Horizontal Marketing Systems

In a **horizontal marketing system**, two or more unrelated companies put together resources or programs to exploit an emerging marketing opportunity. Each company lacks the capital, know-how, production, or marketing resources to venture alone, or it is afraid of the risk. The companies might work together on a temporary or permanent basis or create a joint venture company. For example, many supermarket chains have arrangements with local banks to offer in-store banking.

TABLE 12.2 Contractual Vertical Marketing Systems	
Type of Contractual VMS	**Description**
Wholesaler-sponsored voluntary chains	Wholesalers organize voluntary chains of independent retailers to help standardize their selling practices and achieve buying economies in competing with large chain organizations.
Retailer cooperatives	Retailers organize a new business entity to carry on wholesaling and possibly some production. Members concentrate their purchases through the retailer co-op and plan their advertising jointly, sharing in profits in proportion to their purchases.
Franchise organizations	A *franchisor* links several successive stages in the production-distribution process. Such arrangements include: manufacturer-sponsored retailer franchises (Ford and its dealers), manufacturer-sponsored wholesaler franchises (Coca-Cola and its bottlers), and service-firm-sponsored retailer franchises (McDonald's).

E-Commerce and M-Commerce Marketing Practices

As noted earlier, the digital channels revolution is affecting distribution strategies. **E-commerce** uses a Web site to transact or facilitate the sale of products and services online; *m-commerce* is selling via mobile devices such as smart phones and tablets. Online retailers can predictably provide convenient, informative, and personalized experiences for vastly different types of consumers and businesses. By saving the cost of retail floor space, staff, and inventory, e-commerce marketers can profitably sell low-volume products to niche markets. While consumers often go online to try to find lower prices,[24] online retailers in fact compete in three key aspects of a transaction: (1) customer interaction with the Web site, (2) delivery, and (3) ability to address problems when they occur.[25]

Pure-click companies have launched a Web site without any previous existence as a firm, whereas **brick-and-click** companies are existing companies that have added an online site for information or e-commerce.

E-Commerce and Pure-Click Companies

There are several kinds of pure-click companies: search engines, Internet service providers (ISPs), commerce sites, transaction sites, content sites, and enabler sites. Customer service is critical for pure-click companies, and their Web sites must be fast, simple, and easy to use. Something as simple as enlarging product images on screen can increase perusal time and the amount customers buy.[26] Some of the larger e-commerce firms such as eBay and Amazon are offering same-day delivery in major markets.[27] A good return policy is also crucial.[28] Ensuring security and privacy online remains important. Customers must find the Web site trustworthy.

B-to-B sites make markets more efficient, giving buyers easy access to a great deal of information from (1) supplier Web sites; (2) *infomediaries,* third parties that add value by aggregating information about alternatives; (3) *market makers,* third parties that link buyers and sellers; and (4) *customer communities*, where buyers can swap stories about products and services.[29] Firms are using B-to-B auction sites, spot exchanges, online product catalogs, barter sites, and other online resources to obtain better prices, with the result that prices are now more transparent.

E-Commerce and Brick-and-Click Companies

Although many brick-and-mortar companies once hesitated to open an e-commerce channel for fear of conflict with their channel partners, most have added the Internet after seeing how much business was generated online. Even Procter & Gamble is selling some big brands such as Tide via its P&G e-store, in part to examine consumer shopping habits more closely.[30]

Managing the online and offline channels has thus become a priority for many firms.[31] To gain acceptance from intermediaries, marketers are (1) offering different brands or products online and offline; (2) offering offline partners higher commissions to cushion the negative impact on sales; or (3) taking orders online but having retailers deliver and collect payment.

M-Commerce Marketing

Mobile channels and media can keep consumers as connected and interacting with a brand as they choose. By mid-2013, more than half of all online U.S. buyers had made a purchase on a mobile device, and m-commerce accounted for more than 11 percent of all e-commerce.[32] Tablets are expected to overtake smart phones for mobile shopping, and one estimate says tablets will make up more than 70 percent of mobile retail sales by 2017.[33]

In some parts of the world, m-commerce is very well established. Asian consumers use their mobile phones as their main computers and benefit from a well-developed mobile infrastructure. In the United States, mobile marketing is becoming more prevalent and taking all forms. Companies are trying to give their customers more control over their shopping experiences by bringing Web technologies into the store, especially via mobile apps.

Advertising, Promotions, and M-commerce Given the small screen and fleeting attention paid, fulfilling advertising's traditional role of informing and persuading is more challenging for m-commerce marketers. On the plus side, consumers are more engaged and attentive with their smart phones than when they are online.[34] Nevertheless, a number of m-commerce companies are eliminating ads to allow consumers to make purchases with as few clicks as possible.[35] Promotions are a different story. Consumers often use their smart phones to find deals or capitalize on them: The redemption rate for mobile coupons (10 percent) far exceeds that of paper coupons (1 percent).[36] According to research, mobile promotions can get consumers to travel greater distances within a store and make more unplanned purchases.[37]

Geofencing, Privacy, and M-commerce The idea of *geofencing* is to target customers with a mobile promotion when they are within a defined geographical space, typically near or in a store. The local-based service requires just an app and GPS coordinates, but consumers have to opt in. For example, cosmetics retailer Kiehl's uses geofencing around its freestanding stores and kiosks within other stores, offering a free lip balm to customers who enroll. It limits texts to three per month to avoid being intrusive.[38]

The fact that a company can pinpoint a customer's or employee's location with GPS technology raises privacy issues. Many consumers are happy to tolerate cookies, profiles, and other online tools that let e-commerce businesses know who they are and when and how they shop, but they are nevertheless concerned when such tracking occurs in the store. When Nordstrom informed shoppers it was testing new technology to follow the Wi-Fi signals from customers' smart phones, some consumers objected, leading Nordstrom to drop the experiment.[39]

Channel Conflict, Cooperation, and Competition

No matter how well channels are designed and managed, there will be some conflict, if only because the interests of independent business entities do not always coincide. **Channel conflict** is generated when one channel member's actions prevent another channel from achieving its goal. Software giant Oracle Corp., plagued by conflict between its high-powered sales force and its vendor partners, has tried a number of solutions, including rolling out new "All Partner Territories" where all deals except for specific strategic accounts go through select Oracle partners and allowing partners to secure bigger $1 billion-plus accounts.[40]

Channel coordination occurs when channel members are brought together to advance the goals of the channel instead of their own potentially incompatible goals.[41] Here we examine three questions: What types of conflict arise in channels? What causes conflict? What can marketers do to resolve it?

Types of Conflict and Competition

Horizontal channel conflict occurs between channel members at the same level. *Vertical channel conflict* occurs between different levels of the channel. Greater retailer consolidation—the 10 largest U.S. retailers account for more than 80 percent of the average manufacturer's business—has led to increased price pressure and influence from retailers.[42] Walmart, for example, is the principal buyer for many manufacturers, including Disney, and can command reduced prices or quantity discounts from suppliers.[43] *Multichannel conflict* exists when the manufacturer has established two or more channels that sell to the same market.[44] It's likely to be especially intense when the members of one channel get a lower price (based on larger-volume purchases) or work with a lower margin.

Causes of Channel Conflict

One cause of channel conflict is *goal incompatibility*. The manufacturer may want to achieve rapid market penetration through a low-price policy, but the dealers prefer to work with high margins for short-run profitability. Another cause is *unclear roles and rights,* including issues of territory boundaries and credit for sales. A third cause is *differences in perception,* as when a producer is optimistic about the economy and wants dealers to carry higher inventory, but its dealers are pessimistic. Finally, channel conflict can emerge from intermediaries' *dependence* on the manufacturer. For example, the fortunes of exclusive dealers, such as auto dealers, are profoundly affected by the manufacturer's product and pricing decisions.

Managing Channel Conflict

Some channel conflict can be constructive and lead to better adaptation to a changing environment, but too much is dysfunctional.[45] The challenge is not to eliminate all conflict but to manage it better through mechanisms such as: *strategic justification* (showing channels or members how each serves distinctive segments); *dual compensation* (paying existing channels for sales made through new channels); *superordinate goals* (for mutual benefit); *employee exchange* (between channel levels); *joint memberships* (in trade groups); *co-optation* (including leaders in advisory councils and other groups); *diplomacy, mediation, and arbitration* (when conflict is chronic or acute); and *legal recourse* (if nothing else proves effective).[46]

Dilution and Cannibalization

Marketers must be careful not to dilute their brands through inappropriate channels. This is particularly important for luxury brands whose images rest on exclusivity and personalized service. Given the lengths to which they go to pamper store customers—including doormen and extravagant surroundings—luxury brands have had to work hard to provide a high-quality digital experience. To reach affluent customers who work long hours and have little time to shop, many high-end fashion brands such as Dior, Louis Vuitton, and Fendi have unveiled e-commerce sites for researching items before visiting a store—and as a means to combat fakes sold online.

Legal and Ethical Issues in Channel Relations

The law seeks to prevent only exclusionary tactics that might keep competitors from using a channel. Here we briefly consider the legality of certain practices, including exclusive dealing, exclusive territories, tying agreements, and dealers' rights. With *exclusive distribution*, only certain outlets are allowed to carry a seller's products. Requiring these dealers not to handle competitors' products is called *exclusive dealing*. The seller obtains more loyal and dependable outlets, and the dealer gets a steady supply of special products and strong support. Exclusive arrangements are legal as long as they are voluntary and do not substantially lessen competition or tend to create a monopoly.

Producers of a strong brand sometimes sell it to dealers only if they will take some or all of the rest of the line, a practice called *full-line forcing*. Such *tying agreements* are not necessarily illegal, but they do violate U.S. law if they tend to lessen competition substantially. In general, sellers can drop dealers "for cause," but not if, for example, a dealer refuses to cooperate in a doubtful legal arrangement, such as exclusive dealing or tying agreements.

Executive Summary

Most producers do not sell their goods directly to final users. Between producers and final users stands one or more marketing channels, marketing intermediaries performing a variety of functions. Companies use intermediaries when they lack the financial resources for direct marketing, when direct marketing is not feasible, and when they can earn more by doing so. The most important functions performed by intermediaries are information, promotion, negotiation, ordering, financing, risk taking, physical possession, payment, and title.

Manufacturers can sell direct or use one-, two-, or three-level channels, depending on customer needs, channel objectives, and the major alternatives, including the types and numbers of intermediaries involved in the channel. Effective channel management calls for selecting intermediaries and training and motivating them to build a profitable partnership. Three key channel trends are the growth of vertical marketing systems, horizontal marketing systems, and multichannel marketing systems. More companies have adopted "brick-and-click" channel systems for e-commerce; m-commerce (selling via smart phones and tablets) is also gaining in importance. All marketing channels have the potential for conflict and competition resulting from goal incompatibility, poorly defined roles and rights, perceptual differences, and interdependent relationships. Among the legal and ethical issues to be considered when planning channel strategies are exclusive dealing or territories, tying agreements, and dealers' rights.

Notes

1. L.L.Bean, www.llbean.com; Shelley Banjo, "Firms Take Online Reviews to Heart," *Wall Street Journal*, July 29, 2012; Michael Arndt, "L.L.Bean Follows Its Shoppers to the Web," *Bloomberg Businessweek*, February 18, 2010; Darren Fishell, "L.L.Bean's First Chief Executive from Outside the Founding Family to Retire in 2016," *Bangor Daily News (Maine)*, May 19, 2014.

2. Anne T. Coughlan, Erin Anderson, Louis W. Stern, and Adel I. El-Ansary, *Marketing Channels,* 7th ed. (Upper Saddle River, NJ: Prentice Hall, 2007).

3. Louis W. Stern and Barton A. Weitz, "The Revolution in Distribution: Challenges and Opportunities," *Long Range Planning* 30 (December 1997), pp. 823–29.

4. For a summary of academic research, see Erin Anderson and Anne T. Coughlan, "Channel Management: Structure, Governance, and Relationship Management," Bart Weitz and Robin Wensley, eds., *Handbook of Marketing* (London: Sage, 2001), pp. 223–47.

5. V. Kumar and Rajkumar Venkatesan, "Who Are Multichannel Shoppers and How Do They Perform?," *Journal of Interactive Marketing* 19 (Spring 2005), pp. 44–61.

6. Tarun Kushwaha and Venkatesh Shankar, "Are Multichannel Customers Really More Valuable? The Moderating Role of Product Category Characteristics," *Journal of Marketing* 77 (July 2013), pp. 67–85.

7. For a detailed conceptual model, see Jill Avery, Thomas J. Steenburgh, John Deighton, and Mary Caravella, "Adding Bricks to Clicks: Predicting the Patterns of Cross-Channel Elasticities over Time," *Journal of Marketing* 76 (May 2012), pp. 96–111.

8. Peter C. Verhoef, Scott A. Neslin, and Björn Vroomen, "Multichannel Customer Management: Understanding the Research-Shopper Phenomenon," *International Journal of Research in Marketing* 24, no. 2 (2007), pp. 129–48.

9. Chekitan S. Dev and Don E. Schultz, "In the Mix: A Customer-Focused Approach Can Bring the Current Marketing Mix into the 21st Century," *Marketing Management* 14 (January–February 2005).

10. Robert Shaw and Philip Kotler, "Rethinking the Chain," *Marketing Management* (July/August 2009), pp. 18–23.

11. "E-commerce Sales to Rise in U.S.," www.warc.com, March 15, 2013; Lucia Moses, "Data Points: Spending It," *Adweek*, April 16, 2012, pp. 24–25; Darrell Rigby, "The Future of Shopping," *Harvard Business Review*, December 2011.

12. Anderson and Coughlan, "Channel Management: Structure, Governance, and Relationship Management," *Handbook of Marketing*, pp. 223–47.

13. www.clevelandclinic.org, December 9, 2010; Geoff Colvin, "The Cleveland Clinic's Delos Cosgrove," *Fortune*, March 1, 2010, pp. 38–45.

14. Asim Ansari, Carl F. Mela, and Scott A. Neslin, "Customer Channel Migration," *Journal of Marketing Research* 45 (February 2008), pp. 60–76; Jacquelyn S. Thomas and Ursula Y. Sullivan, "Managing Marketing Communications," *Journal of Marketing* 69 (October 2005), pp. 239–51; Sridhar Balasubramanian, Rajagopal Raghunathan, and Vijay Mahajan, "Consumers in a Multichannel Environment," *Journal of Interactive Marketing* 19 (Spring 2005), pp. 12–30; Edward J. Fox, Alan L. Montgomery, and Leonard M. Lodish, "Consumer Shopping and Spending across Retail Formats," *Journal of Business* 77 (April 2004), pp. S25–S60.

15. Sara Valentini, Elisa Montaguti, and Scott A. Neslin, "Decision Process Evolution in Customer Channel Choice," *Journal of Marketing* 75 (November 2011), pp. 72–86.

16. Susan Broniarczyk, "Product Assortment," Curtis Haugtvedt, Paul Herr, and Frank Kardes, eds., *Handbook of Consumer Psychology* (New York: Lawrence Erlbaum Associates, 2008), pp. 755–79; Alexander Chernev and Ryan Hamilton, "Assortment Size and Option Attractiveness in Consumer Choice among Retailers," *Journal of Marketing Research* 46 (June 2009), pp. 410–20; Richard A. Briesch, Pradeep K. Chintagunta, and Edward J. Fox, "How Does Assortment Affect Grocery Store Choice," *Journal of Marketing Research* 46 (April 2009), pp. 176–89.

17. Janko Roettgers, "Netflix May Ditch DVDs Sooner Rather than Later," *Bloomberg Businessweek*, October 21, 2013; Ashlee Vance, "Netflix, Reed Hastings Survive Missteps to Join Silicon Valley's Elite," *Bloomberg Businessweek*, May 9, 2013; Ronald Grover, Adam Satariano, and Ari Levy, "Honest, Hollywood, Netflix Is Your Friend," *Bloomberg Businessweek*, January 11, 2010, pp. 54–55.

18. Anderson and Coughlan, "Channel Management: Structure, Governance, and Relationship Management," *Handbook of Marketing*, pp. 223–47; Michaela Draganska, Daniel Klapper, and Sofia B. Villa-Boas, "A Larger Slice or a Larger Pie? An Empirical Investigation of Bargaining Power in the Distribution Channel," *Marketing Science* 29 (January–February 2010), pp. 57–74.

19. Xinlei Chen, George John, and Om Narasimhan, "Assessing the Consequences of a Channel Switch," *Marketing Science* 27 (May–June 2008), pp. 398–416.

20. Rajdeep Grewal, Alok Kumar, Girish Mallapragada, and Amit Saini, "Marketing Channels in Foreign Markets: Control Mechanisms and the Moderating Role of Multinational Corporation Headquarters–Subsidiary Relationship," *Journal of Marketing Research* 50 (June 2013), pp. 378–98; Zhilin Yang, Chenting Su, and Kim-Shyan Fam, "Dealing with Institutional Distances in International Marketing Channels: Governance Strategies That Engender Legitimacy and Efficiency," *Journal of Marketing* 76 (May 2012), pp. 41–55.

21. Harriett Walker, "Bright Sparks: Urban Outfitters," *The Independent*, January 23, 2012; Michael Arndt, "Urban Outfitters Grow-Slow Strategy," *Bloomberg Businessweek*, March 1, 2010, p. 56; Michael Arndt, "How to Play It: Apparel Makers," *Bloomberg Businessweek*, March 1, 2010, p. 61.

22. V. Kasturi Rangan, *Transforming Your Go-to-Market Strategy: The Three Disciplines of Channel Management* (Boston: Harvard Business School Press, 2006).

23. Arnt Bovik and George John, "When Does Vertical Coordination Improve Industrial Purchasing Relationships," *Journal of Marketing* 64 (October 2000), pp. 52–64.

24. "Low Prices Key to E-commerce," www.warc.com, March 6, 2013.

25. Joel C. Collier and Carol C. Bienstock, "How Do Customers Judge Quality in an E-tailer," *MIT Sloan Management Review* (Fall 2006), pp. 35–40.

26. Jeff Borden, "The Right Tools," *Marketing News*, April 15, 2008, pp. 19–21.

27. Geg Bensinger, "Order It Online, and … Voilá," *Wall Street Journal*, December 3, 2012.

28. Amanda B. Bower and James G. Maxham III, "Return Shipping Policies of Online Retailers: Normative Assumptions and the Long-Term Consequences of Fee and Free Returns," *Journal of Marketing* 76 (September 2012), pp. 110–24.

29. Ronald Abler, John S. Adams, and Peter Gould, *Spatial Organizations: The Geographer's View of the World* (Upper Saddle River, NJ: Prentice Hall, 1971), pp. 531–32.

30. Anjali Cordeiro, "Procter & Gamble Sees Aisle Expansion on the Web," *Wall Street Journal*, September 2, 2009, p. B6A; Anjali Cordeiro and Ellen Byron, "Procter & Gamble to Test Online Store to Study Buying Habits," *Wall Street Journal*, January 15, 2010.

31. Xubing Zhang, "Retailer's Multichannel and Price Advertising Strategies," *Marketing Science* 28 (November–December 2009), pp. 1080–94.

32. "How Mobile Coupons Are Driving an Explosion in Mobile Commerce," *Business Insider,* August 12, 2013; "New York Startup Launches First Stand-Alone Mobile Commerce Solution for Small and Medium-Sized Businesses," *PRNewswire,* June 27, 2013.

33. Lucia Moses, "Data Points: Mobile Shopping," *Adweek*, May 20, 2013, pp. 20–21.

34. Christopher Heine, "The Top 7 Reasons Mobile Ads Don't Work," *Adweek*, October 17, 2013.

35. Farhan Thawar, "2013: The Breakout Year for Mobile Commerce," *Wired,* March 15, 2013.

36. "How Mobile Coupons Are Driving an Explosion in Mobile Commerce," *Business Insider,* August 12, 2013.

37. Sam K. Hui, J. Jeffrey Inman, Yanliu Huang, and Jacob Suher, "The Effect of In-Store Travel Distance on Unplanned Spending: Applications to Mobile Promotion Strategies," *Journal of Marketing* 77 (March 2013), pp. 1–16.

38. Lauren Brousel, "5 Things You Need to Know about Geofencing," *CIO*, August 28, 2013; Dana Mattioli and Miguel Bustillo, "Can Texting Save Stores?," *Wall Street Journal*, May 8, 2012.

39. Stephanie Clifford, "Attention, Shoppers: Store Is Tracking Your Cell," *New York Times*, July 14, 2013.

40. Rick Whiting, "Oracle Says Recent Initiatives Are Reducing Channel Conflict," www.crn.com, October 14, 2009; Barbara Darow, "Oracle's New Partner Path," *CRN,* August 21, 2006, p. 4.

41. Anne Coughlan and Louis Stern, "Marketing Channel Design and Management," Dawn Iacobucci, ed., *Kellogg on Marketing* (New York: John Wiley & Sons, 2001), pp. 247–69.

42. Matthew Boyle, "Brand Killers," *Fortune,* August 11, 2003, pp. 51–56; for an opposing view, see Anthony J. Dukes, Esther Gal-Or, and Kannan Srinivasan, "Channel Bargaining with Retailer Asymmetry," *Journal of Marketing Research* 43 (February 2006), pp. 84–97.

43. Jerry Useem, Julie Schlosser, and Helen Kim, "One Nation under Wal-Mart," *Fortune* (Europe), March 3, 2003. For a more thorough academic examination that shows the benefits to suppliers from Walmart expanding their market, see Qingyi Huang, Vincent R. Nijs, Karsten Hansen, and Eric T. Anderson, "Wal-Mart's Impact on Supplier Profits," *Journal of Marketing Research* 49 (April 2012), pp. 131–43.

44. Sreekumar R. Bhaskaran and Stephen M. Gilbert, "Implications of Channel Structure for Leasing or Selling Durable Goods," *Marketing Science* 28 (September–October 2009), pp. 918–34.

45. For some examples of when conflict can be viewed as helpful, see Anil Arya and Brian Mittendorf, "Benefits of Channel Discord in the Sale of Durable Goods," *Marketing Science* 25 (January–February 2006), pp. 91–96; and Nirmalya Kumar, "Living with Channel Conflict," *CMO Magazine,* October 2004.

46. This section draws on Coughlan et al., *Marketing Channels,* chapter 9. See also Jonathan D. Hibbard, Nirmalya Kumar, and Louis W. Stern, "Examining the Impact of Destructive Acts in Marketing Channel Relationships," *Journal of Marketing Research* 38 (February 2001), pp. 45–61; Kersi D. Antia and Gary L. Frazier, "The Severity of Contract Enforcement in Interfirm Channel Relationships," *Journal of Marketing* 65 (October 2001), pp. 67–81; James R. Brown, Chekitan S. Dev, and Dong-Jin Lee, "Managing Marketing Channel Opportunism: The Efficiency of Alternative Governance Mechanisms," *Journal of Marketing* 64 (April 2000), pp. 51–65; Alberto Sa Vinhas and Erin Anderson, "How Potential Conflict Drives Channel Structure: Concurrent (Direct and Indirect) Channels," *Journal of Marketing Research* 42 (November 2005), pp. 507–15.

Chapter 13

Managing Retailing, Wholesaling, and Logistics

In this chapter, we will address the following questions:

1. What major types of marketing intermediaries occupy this sector, and what marketing decisions do they face? (Page 209)
2. What does the future hold for private-label brands? (Page 213)
3. What are some of the important issues in wholesaling and logistics? (Page 214)

Marketing Management at Warby Parker

Started by four Wharton MBA graduates, e-commerce start-up Warby Parker is challenging eyewear mammoth Luxottica with a marketing strategy that cleverly combines fashion, value, customer experience, and social responsibility. With material for frames from a family-owned Italian company, assembly in China, and no middleman, it promises quality comparable to that of well-known designers at a fraction of the cost. Warby Parker eyeglasses sell for a flat $95 (or $145 for titanium frames) with free shipping and free returns. To assess fit, customers can use a virtual try-on tool employing facial recognition technology or have up to five sample pairs shipped to try on in person. Promoting "eyewear with a purpose," Warby Parker donates one pair for every pair sold. To expand reach and engagement beyond its Web site, the company has launched shops within shops in selected cities and operates a flagship store in New York City.[1]

Retailers, wholesalers, and logistical organizations are forging their own marketing strategies in a rapidly changing world. Successful intermediaries segment their markets, improve their market targeting and positioning, and connect with customers through memorable experiences, relevant and timely information, and the right products and services. In this chapter, we consider marketing excellence in retailing, wholesaling, and logistics.

Retailing

Retailing includes all the activities in selling goods or services directly to final consumers for personal, nonbusiness use. A **retailer** or *retail store* is any business enterprise whose sales volume comes primarily from retailing. Any organization selling to final consumers—whether it is a manufacturer, wholesaler, or retailer—is doing retailing. It doesn't matter *how* the goods or services are sold (in person, by mail, by telephone, by vending machine, or online) or *where* (in a store, on the street, or in the consumer's home).

Types of Retailers

Consumers today can shop for goods and services at store retailers, nonstore retailers, and retail organizations, as shown in Table 13.1. Different formats of store retailers will have different competitive and price dynamics. Discount stores, for example, historically have competed much more directly with each other than with other formats, though that is changing.[2]

Retailers can position themselves as offering one of four levels of service:

1. *Self-service*—Self-service is the cornerstone of all discount operations. Many customers are willing to carry out their own "locate-compare-select" process to save money.
2. *Self-selection*—Customers find their own goods, though they can ask for assistance.
3. *Limited service*—These retailers carry more shopping goods and services such as credit and merchandise-return privileges. Customers need more information and assistance.
4. *Full service*—Salespeople are ready to assist in every phase of the "locate-compare-select" process. The high staffing cost and many services, along with the higher proportion of specialty goods and slower-moving items, result in high-cost retailing.

TABLE 13.1   Major Types of Store Retailers

Specialty store: Narrow product line. The Limited, The Body Shop.

Department store: Several product lines. Macy's, Bloomingdale's.

Supermarket: Large, low-cost, low-margin, high-volume, self-service store designed to meet total needs for food and household products. Kroger, Safeway.

Convenience store: Small store in residential area, often open 24/7, limited line of high-turnover convenience products plus takeout. 7-Eleven, Circle K.

Drug store: Prescription and pharmacies, health and beauty aids, other personal care, small durable, miscellaneous items. CVS, Walgreens.

Discount store: Standard or specialty merchandise; low-price, low-margin, high-volume stores. Walmart, Kmart.

Extreme value or hard-discount store: A more restricted merchandise mix than discount stores but at even lower prices. Aldi, Dollar General.

Off-price retailer: Leftover goods, overruns, irregular merchandise sold at less than retail. Factory outlets; independent off-price retailers such as TJ Maxx; warehouse clubs such as Costco.

Superstore: Huge selling space, routinely purchased food and household items, plus services (laundry, shoe repair, check cashing). Category killer (deep assortment in one category) such as Staples; combination store such as Jewel-Osco; hypermarket (huge stores that combine supermarket, discount, and warehouse retailing) such as Carrefour in France.

Catalog showroom: Broad selection of high-markup, fast-moving, brand-name goods sold by catalog at a discount. Customers pick up merchandise at the store. Inside Edge Ski and Bike.

Source: Data from www.privatelabelmag.com.

Nonstore retailing has been growing much faster than store retailing, as shown in the rise of e-commerce and m-commerce. Nonstore retailing falls into four major categories: (1) *direct marketing* (including telemarketing, direct mail, catalog marketing, and online shopping); (2) *direct selling*, also called *multilevel selling* and *network marketing*, in which companies sell door to door or through at-home sales parties; (3) *automatic vending* for impulse goods such as soft drinks and other products such as cosmetics; and (4) *buying service*, a storeless retailer serving a specific clientele—usually employees of large organizations—who are entitled to discounts in return for membership.

An increasing number are part of a *corporate retailing* organization (see Table 13.2). These organizations achieve economies of scale, greater purchasing power, wider brand recognition, and better-trained employees than independent stores can usually gain alone.

The Modern Retail Marketing Environment

The retail marketing environment is dramatically different today from what it was just a decade or so ago. To better satisfy customers' need for convenience, a variety of new retail forms have emerged. Retailers are experimenting with "pop-up" stores that let them create buzz through interactive experiences and promote brands for a few weeks in busy areas. Also, giant retailers such as Walmart are using information systems, logistical systems, and buying power to deliver good service and immense volumes of product to masses of consumers at appealing prices. Middle-market retailers are in decline as discount retailers improve both quality and image and some retailers move even further upscale. Department stores can't worry just about other department stores now that discount chains such as Walmart and Tesco are expanding into product areas such as clothing, health, beauty, and electrical appliances.[3]

An important trend in fashion retailing in particular, but with broader implications, is the emergence of fast retailing. Here retailers such as Zara and Uniqlo develop completely different supply chain and distribution systems to allow them to offer consumers constantly changing product choices. Critics, however, pan fast fashion for its planned obsolescence and the resulting disposability and waste.[4]

Technology is profoundly affecting the way retailers conduct virtually every facet of their business. Almost all now use technology to produce forecasts, control inventory costs, and order from suppliers, reducing the need to discount and run sales to clear out languishing products.

TABLE 13.2	Major Types of Corporate Retail Organizations

Corporate chain store: Two or more outlets owned and controlled, employing central buying and merchandising, and selling similar lines of merchandise. Gap, Pottery Barn.

Voluntary chain: A wholesaler-sponsored group of independent retailers engaged in bulk buying and common merchandising. Independent Grocers Alliance (IGA).

Retailer cooperative: Independent retailers using a central buying organization and joint promotion efforts. ACE Hardware.

Consumer cooperative: A retail firm owned by its customers. Members contribute money to open their own store, vote on its policies, elect a group to manage it, and receive dividends. Local cooperative grocery stores can be found in many markets.

Franchise organization: Contractual association between a franchisor and franchisees, popular in a number of product and service areas. Dunkin' Donuts, Marriott, The UPS Store.

Merchandising conglomerate: A corporation that combines several diversified retailing lines and forms under central ownership, with some integration of distribution and management. Macy's operates Macy's and other retailers such as Bloomingdale's.

Technology is also directly affecting the consumer shopping experience inside the store, including experiments with virtual shopping screens, audio/video presentations, and other applications. **Shopper marketing** is the way manufacturers and retailers use stocking, displays, and promotions to influence consumers actively shopping for a product. "Marketing Insight: The Growth of Shopper Marketing" describes the important role technology is taking in the aisles.

Social media are especially important for retailers during the holiday season when shoppers are seeking information and sharing successes. Beyond the holidays, many retailers are linking to customer photos supporting their brands on Instagram, Pinterest, and other sites to create social engagement.[5]

Retailer Marketing Decisions

With this new retail environment as a backdrop, we now examine retailers' marketing decisions in some key areas: target market, channels, product assortment, procurement, prices, services, store atmosphere, store activities and experiences, communications, and location.

Target Market Until it defines and profiles the target market, the retailer cannot make consistent decisions about product assortment, store decor, advertising messages and media, price, and

---

marketing insight   The Growth of Shopper Marketing

Buoyed by research suggesting that more than half of all purchase decisions are made inside the store, firms are increasingly recognizing the importance of influencing consumers at the point of purchase, via shopper marketing. Procter & Gamble observed the power of displays in a Walmart project designed to boost sales of premium diapers such as Pampers. By creating the first baby center in which infant products were united in a single aisle, the new shelf layout encouraged parents to linger longer and spend more money, increasing Pampers sales.

Retailers are also using technology to research shopping behavior and influence customers as they shop. Some supermarkets are employing mobile phone apps or "smart shopping carts" that help customers locate items in the store, find out about sales and special offers, and pay more easily. Academic research shows that unplanned purchases increase the more a product is touched, the longer a purchase is considered, the closer a customer is to the shelf, the fewer the shelf displays in sight, and the more quickly shoppers can

reference external information. Even the simple act of touching a product on a tablet screen has been shown to increase purchase intent.

Sources: Megan Woolhouse, "Tablets Facilitate Impulse Shopping for Many," *Boston Globe*, December 18, 2013; Elizabeth Dwoskin and Greg Bensinger, "Tracking Technology Sheds Light on Shopper Habits," *Wall Street Journal*, December 9, 2013; S. Adam Brasel and Jim Gips, "Tablets, Touchscreens, and Touchpads: How Varying Touch Interfaces Trigger Psychological Ownership and Endowment," *Journal of Consumer Psychology* 24 (April 2014), pp. 226–33; Koert van Ittersum, Brian Wansink, Joost M. E. Pennings, and Daniel Sheehan, "Smart Shopping Carts: How Real-Time Feedback Influences Spending," *Journal of Marketing* 77 (November 2013), pp. 21–36; Noreen O'Leary, "Shopper Marketing Goes Mainstream," *Adweek*, May 20, 2013, p. 19; Yanliu Huang, Sam K. Hui, J. Jeffrey Inman, and Jacob A. Suher, "Capturing the 'First Moment of Truth': Understanding Point-of-Purchase Drivers of Unplanned Consideration and Purchase," MSI Report 12-101, www.msi.org, 2012; Pat Lenius, "P&G Leverages Facebook to Enhance Promotions in Walmart," www.cpgmatters.com, November 2011; Venkatesh Shankar, "Shopper Marketing: Current Insights, Emerging Trends, and Future Directions," *MSI Relevant Knowledge Series Book*, www.msi.org, 2011; Anthony Dukes and Yunchuan Liu, "In-Store Media and Distribution Channel Coordination," *Marketing Science* 29 (January–February 2010), pp. 94–107.

service levels. Retailers are slicing the market into ever-finer segments and introducing new lines of stores to exploit niche markets with more relevant offerings, the way Gymboree launched Janie and Jack to sell apparel and gifts for babies and toddlers.

Channels   Based on a target market analysis and other considerations discussed in Chapter 12, retailers must decide which channels to employ to reach their customers. Increasingly, the answer is multiple channels. Staples sells through its traditional retail brick-and-mortar channel, a direct-response Internet site, virtual malls, and thousands of links on affiliated sites. Although some experts predicted otherwise, catalogs have actually grown in an Internet world as more firms have revamped them to use them as branding devices and to complement online activity.[6]

Product Assortment   The retailer's product assortment must match the target market's shopping expectations in *breadth* and *depth*.[7] A restaurant can offer a narrow and shallow assortment (small lunch counters), a narrow and deep assortment (delicatessen), a broad and shallow assortment (cafeteria), or a broad and deep assortment (large restaurant). *Destination categories* play an important role because they have the greatest impact on where households choose to shop (for fresh produce, for instance) and how they view a particular retailer. Another challenge is to develop a product-differentiation strategy by featuring brands not available at competing stores, featuring mostly private-label merchandise, presenting distinctive merchandise events, changing merchandise frequently or offering surprise items, featuring new merchandise, offering customizing services, or offering a highly targeted assortment.

Procurement   Stores are using **direct product profitability (DPP)** to measure a product's handling costs (receiving, moving to storage, paperwork, selecting, checking, loading, and space cost) from the time it reaches the warehouse until a customer buys it in the retail store. Sometimes they find that a product's gross margin bears little relationship to the direct product profit. Some high-volume products may have such high handling costs that they are less profitable and deserve less shelf space than low-volume products, at least unless customers buy enough other, more profitable products to justify the loss involved in pushing the high-volume products.

Prices   Prices are a key positioning factor and must be set in relationship to the target market, product-and-service assortment mix, and competition.[8] Most retailers fall into the *high-markup, lower-volume* group (fine specialty stores) or the *low-markup, higher-volume* group (discount stores). Most retailers will put low prices on some items to serve as traffic builders (or loss leaders) or to signal their pricing policies.[9] A store's average price level and discounting policies will affect its price image with consumers, but non-price-related factors such as store atmosphere and levels of service also matter.[10]

Services   Retailers must decide on the *services mix* to offer customers. Prepurchase services include accepting telephone and mail orders, advertising, window and interior display, fitting rooms, shopping hours, fashion shows, and trade-ins. Postpurchase services include shipping and delivery, gift wrapping, adjustments and returns, alterations and tailoring, installations, and engraving. Ancillary services include general information, check cashing, parking, restaurants, repairs, interior decorating, and credit.

Store Atmosphere   Every store has a look and a physical layout that makes it hard or easy to move around. Kohl's floor plan is modeled after a racetrack loop and is designed to convey customers smoothly past all the merchandise in the store. It includes a middle aisle that hurried shoppers can use as a shortcut and yields higher spending levels than many competitors.[11]

Store Activities and Experiences The growth of e-commerce has forced traditional brick-and-mortar retailers to respond. In addition to their natural advantages, such as products that shoppers can actually see, touch, and test; real-life customer service; and no delivery lag time for most purchases, stores also provide a shopping experience as a strong differentiator. The store atmosphere should match shoppers' basic motivations—if customers are likely to be in a task-oriented and functional mind-set, then a simpler, more restrained in-store environment may be better.[12] On the other hand, some retailers are creating in-store entertainment to attract customers who want fun and excitement.

Communications Retailers use a wide range of communication tools to generate traffic and purchases, including advertising, special sales, money-saving coupons, e-mail promotions, frequent-shopper-reward programs, and in-store food sampling. Many work with manufacturers to design point-of-sale materials that reflect both their images. Retailers are also using interactive and social media to pass on information and create communities around their brands. They study the way consumers respond to their e-mails, not only where and how messages are opened but also which words and images led to a click.

Location The three keys to retail success are "location, location, and location." Retailers can place their stores in the following locations:

- **Central business districts.** The oldest and most heavily trafficked city areas, often known as "downtown."
- **Regional shopping centers.** Large suburban malls containing 40 to 200 stores, typically featuring one or two nationally known anchor stores or a combination of big-box stores and smaller stores.
- **Community shopping centers.** Smaller malls with one anchor store and 20 to 40 smaller stores.
- **Shopping strips.** A cluster of stores, usually in one long building, serving a neighborhood's needs for groceries, hardware, laundry, and more.
- **A location within a larger store.** Concession spaces taken by well-known retailers like Starbucks inside larger stores, airports, or schools; or "store-within-a-store" specialty retailers located within a department store.
- **Stand-alone stores.** Freestanding storefronts not connected directly to other retail stores.

Private Labels

A **private-label brand** (also called a reseller, store, house, or distributor brand) is a brand that retailers and wholesalers develop. In grocery stores in Europe and Canada, store brands account for as much as 40 percent of the items sold. In Britain, roughly half of what Sainsbury and Tesco, the largest food chains, sell is store-label goods. Germany and Spain are also European markets with a high percentage of private-label sales.[13] According to the Private Label Manufacturers' Association, store brands now account for one of every five items sold in U.S. supermarkets, drug chains, and mass merchandisers. The stakes in private-label marketing are high. A one-percentage-point shift from national brands to private labels in food and beverages is estimated to add $5.5 billion in revenue for supermarket chains.[14]

Private labels are rapidly gaining ground in a way that has many manufacturers of name brands running scared. Recessions increase private-label sales, and once some consumers switch to a private label, they don't always go back.[15] But some experts believe 50 percent is the natural limit on how much private-label volume to carry because consumers prefer certain national brands, and many product categories are not feasible or attractive on a private-label basis.

Role of Private Labels

Why do intermediaries sponsor their own brands? First, these brands can be more profitable. Intermediaries may be able to use manufacturers with excess capacity that will produce private-label goods at low cost. Other costs, such as research and development, advertising, sales promotion, and physical distribution, are also much lower, so private labels can generate a higher profit margin.[16] Retailers also develop exclusive store brands to differentiate themselves from competitors.

Generics are unbranded, plainly packaged, less expensive versions of common products such as spaghetti, paper towels, and canned peaches. They offer standard or lower quality at a price that may be as much as 20 percent to 40 percent lower than nationally advertised brands and 10 percent to 20 percent lower than the retailer's private-label brands.

Private-Label Success Factors

In the battle between manufacturers' and private labels, retailers have increasing market power. Because shelf space is scarce, many supermarkets charge a *slotting fee* for accepting a new brand; retailers also charge for special display space and in-store advertising space. They typically give more prominent display to their own brands and make sure they are well stocked.

Although retailers get credit for the success of private labels, the growing power of store brands has also benefited from the weakening of national brands. Many consumers have become more price sensitive, a trend reinforced by the continuous barrage of coupons and price specials that has trained a generation to buy on price. Competing manufacturers and national retailers copy and duplicate the quality and features of the best brands in a category, reducing physical product differentiation. A steady stream of brand extensions and line extensions has blurred brand identity at times and led to a confusing amount of product proliferation.

Bucking these trends, many manufacturers are fighting back by investing in R&D to bring out new brands, line extensions, features, and quality improvements. They are also investing in strong "pull" advertising programs to maintain high brand recognition and consumer preference and to overcome the in-store marketing advantage private labels can enjoy. Experts suggest that manufacturers compete against or collaborate with private labels by fighting selectively, partnering effectively, innovating, and creating winning value propositions.[17]

Wholesaling

Wholesaling includes all the activities in selling goods or services to those who buy for resale or business use. It excludes manufacturers and farmers because they are engaged primarily in production, and it excludes retailers. The major types of wholesalers are described in Table 13.3.

Wholesalers (also called *distributors*) differ from retailers in a number of ways. First, wholesalers pay less attention to promotion, atmosphere, and location because they are dealing with business customers rather than final consumers. Second, wholesale transactions are usually larger than retail transactions, and wholesalers usually cover a larger trade area than retailers. Third, wholesalers and retailers are subject to different legal regulations and taxes.

TABLE 13.3	Major Wholesaler Types

Merchant wholesalers: Independently owned businesses that take title to the merchandise they handle. They are full-service and limited-service jobbers, distributors, and mill supply houses.

Full-service wholesalers: Carry stock, maintain a sales force, offer credit, make deliveries, and provide management assistance. Wholesale merchants sell primarily to retailers; industrial distributors sell to manufacturers and also provide services such as credit and delivery.

Limited-service wholesalers: *Cash and carry wholesalers* sell a limited line of fast-moving goods to small retailers for cash. *Truck wholesalers* sell and deliver a limited line of semiperishable goods to supermarkets, grocery stores, hospitals, restaurants, and hotels. *Drop shippers* serve bulk industries such as coal, lumber, and heavy equipment. They assume title and risk from the time an order is accepted to its delivery. *Rack jobbers* serve grocery retailers in nonfood items, setting up displays, pricing goods, and keeping inventory records; they retain title and bill retailers only for goods sold. *Producers' cooperatives* assemble farm produce to sell in local markets. *Mail-order wholesalers* send catalogs to retail, industrial, and institutional customers; orders are filled and sent by mail, rail, plane, or truck.

Brokers and agents: Facilitate buying and selling, working on commission; limited functions; generally specialize by product line or customer type. *Brokers* bring buyers and sellers together and assist in negotiation, paid by the party hiring them. *Agents* represent buyers or sellers on a more permanent basis. Most agents are small businesses with a few skilled salespeople. Selling agents are authorized to sell a manufacturer's entire output; purchasing agents make purchases for buyers and often receive, inspect, warehouse, and ship merchandise; commission merchants take physical possession of products and negotiate sales.

Manufacturers' and retailers' branches and offices: Wholesaling operations conducted by sellers or buyers themselves rather than through independent wholesalers. Separate branches and offices are dedicated to sales or purchasing.

Specialized wholesalers: Agricultural assemblers (buy the agricultural output of many farms), petroleum bulk plants and terminals (consolidate the output of many wells), and auction companies (auction cars, equipment, etc., to dealers and other businesses).

Wholesaling Functions

Why use wholesalers at all? In general, wholesalers can more efficiently perform one or more of the following functions:

- **Selling and promoting.** Wholesalers' sales forces help manufacturers reach many small business customers at a relatively low cost.
- **Buying and assortment building.** Wholesalers are able to select items and build the assortments their customers need.
- **Bulk breaking.** Wholesalers achieve savings for customers by buying large carload lots and breaking the bulk into smaller units.
- **Warehousing.** Wholesalers hold inventories, thereby reducing inventory costs and risks to suppliers and customers.
- **Transportation.** Wholesalers can often provide quicker delivery to buyers because they are closer to the buyers.
- **Financing.** Wholesalers finance customers by granting credit and finance suppliers by ordering early and paying bills on time.
- **Risk bearing.** Wholesalers absorb some risk by taking title and bearing the cost of theft, damage, spoilage, and obsolescence.
- **Market information.** Wholesalers supply information to suppliers and customers regarding competitors' activities, new products, price developments, and so on.
- **Management services and counseling.** Wholesalers often help retailers improve their operations by training sales clerks, helping with store layouts and displays, and setting up accounting and inventory-control systems.

Trends in Wholesaling

Wholesaler-distributors have faced mounting pressures in recent years from new sources of competition, demanding customers, new technologies, and more direct-buying programs by large industrial, institutional, and retail buyers. Manufacturers' major complaints against wholesalers are: They don't aggressively promote the manufacturer's product line and they act more like order takers; they don't carry enough inventory and therefore don't fill customers' orders fast enough; they don't supply the manufacturer with up-to-date market, customer, and competitive information; they don't attract high-caliber managers to bring down their own costs; and they charge too much for their services.

Savvy wholesalers are adding value to the channel by adapting their services to meet their suppliers' and target customers' changing needs. They're increasing asset productivity by better managing inventories and receivables. They're also reducing operating costs by investing in more advanced materials-handling technology, information systems, and the Internet. Finally, they're improving their strategic decisions about target markets, product assortment and services, price, communications, and distribution. Yet the wholesaling industry remains vulnerable to one of the most enduring trends—fierce resistance to price increases and the winnowing out of suppliers based on cost and quality.

Market Logistics

Physical distribution starts at the factory. Managers choose a set of warehouses (stocking points) and transportation carriers that will deliver the goods to final destinations in the desired time or at the lowest total cost. Physical distribution has now been expanded into the broader concept of **supply chain management (SCM)**. Supply chain management starts before physical distribution and includes strategically procuring the right inputs (raw materials, components, and capital equipment), converting them efficiently into finished products, and dispatching them to the final destinations. The supply chain perspective can help a company identify superior suppliers and distributors, improve productivity, and reduce costs. Some companies choose to partner with third-party logistics specialists for help with transportation planning, distribution center management, and other valued-added services that go beyond shipping and storing.[18]

Market logistics includes planning the infrastructure to meet demand, then implementing and controlling the physical flows of materials and final goods from points of origin to points of use to meet customer requirements at a profit. Market logistics planning has four steps:[19]

1. Deciding on the company's value proposition to its customers. (What on-time delivery standard should we offer? What levels should we attain in ordering and billing accuracy?)
2. Selecting the best channel design and network strategy for reaching the customers. (Should we serve customers directly or through intermediaries? How many warehouses should we maintain, and where should we locate them?)
3. Developing operational excellence in sales forecasting, warehouse management, transportation management, and materials management.
4. Implementing the solution with the best information systems, equipment, policies, and procedures.

Integrated Logistics Systems

The market logistics task calls for **integrated logistics systems (ILS)**, which include materials management, material flow systems, and physical distribution, aided by information technology. Market logistics encompass several activities. The first is sales forecasting, on the basis of which the company schedules distribution, production, and inventory levels. Production plans indicate the materials the purchasing department must order. These materials arrive through inbound transportation, enter the receiving area, and are stored in raw-material inventory. Raw materials are converted into finished goods. Finished-goods inventory is the link between customer orders and manufacturing activity. Customers' orders draw down the finished-goods inventory level, and manufacturing activity builds it up. Finished goods flow off the assembly line and pass through packaging, in-plant warehousing, shipping-room processing, outbound transportation, field warehousing, and delivery and service.

Firms are concerned about the total cost of market logistics, which can amount to as much as 30 percent to 40 percent of the product's cost. Many experts call market logistics "the last frontier for cost economies." Lowering these costs yields lower prices, higher profit margins, or both. Even though the cost of market logistics can be high, a well-planned program can be a potent tool in competitive marketing.

Market-Logistics Objectives

Many companies state their market-logistics objective as "getting the right goods to the right places at the right time for the least cost." Unfortunately, no system can simultaneously maximize customer service and minimize distribution cost. Maximum customer service implies large inventories, premium transportation, and multiple warehouses, all of which raise market-logistics costs. Given that market-logistics activities require trade-offs, managers must make decisions on a total-system basis. The starting point is to study what customers require and what competitors are offering. Customers want on-time delivery, help meeting emergency needs, careful handling of merchandise, and quick return and replacement of defective goods. The company must also consider competitors' service standards. It will normally want to match or exceed these, but the objective is to maximize profits, not sales.

Market-Logistics Decisions

The firm must make four major decisions about its market logistics: (1) How should we handle orders (order processing)? (2) Where should we locate our stock (warehousing)? (3) How much stock should we hold (inventory)? and (4) How should we ship goods (transportation)?

Order Processing   Most companies try to shorten the *order-to-payment cycle*—the time between an order's receipt, delivery, and payment. This cycle has many steps, including order transmission by the salesperson, order entry and customer credit check, inventory and production scheduling, order and invoice shipment, and receipt of payment. The longer this cycle takes, the lower the customer's satisfaction and the lower the company's profits.

Warehousing   Every company must store finished goods until they are sold because production and consumption cycles rarely match. More stocking locations mean goods can be delivered to customers more quickly but warehousing and inventory costs are higher. To reduce these costs, the company might centralize its inventory in one place and use fast transportation to fill orders. To better manage inventory, many department stores such as Nordstrom and Macy's now ship online orders from individual stores.[20]

Inventory   Salespeople would like their companies to carry enough stock to fill all customer orders immediately. However, this is not cost effective. Inventory cost increases at an accelerating rate as the customer-service level approaches 100 percent. Management needs to know how much sales and profits would increase as a result of carrying larger inventories and promising faster order fulfillment times and then make a decision.

As inventory draws down, management must know at what stock level to place a new order. This stock level is called the *order (or reorder) point*. An order point of 20 means reordering when the stock falls to 20 units. The order point should balance the risks of stock-out against the costs of overstock. The other decision is how much to order. The larger the quantity ordered, the less frequently an order needs to be placed. The company needs to balance order-processing costs and inventory-carrying costs. *Order-processing costs* for a manufacturer consist of *setup costs* and *running costs* (operating costs when production is running) for the item. If setup costs are low, the manufacturer can produce the item often; if setup costs are high, the firm can reduce the average cost per unit by producing a long run and carrying more inventory.

Order-processing costs must be compared with *inventory-carrying costs,* which include storage charges, cost of capital, taxes and insurance, and depreciation and obsolescence. The larger the average stock carried, the higher the inventory-carrying costs. This means marketing managers who want to carry larger inventories need to show that incremental gross profits will exceed incremental carrying costs.

We can determine the optimal order quantity by observing how order-processing costs and inventory-carrying costs add up at different order levels. Figure 13.1 shows that the order-processing cost per unit decreases as the number of units ordered increases because the order costs are spread over more units. Inventory-carrying charges per unit increase with the number of units ordered because each unit remains longer in inventory. We sum the two cost curves vertically into a total-cost curve and project the lowest point of the total-cost curve on the horizontal axis to find the optimal order quantity Q^*.[21]

Companies are reducing their inventory costs by keeping slow-moving items in a central location and carrying fast-moving items in warehouses closer to customers. They are also considering inventory strategies that give them flexibility should anything go wrong, whether a dock strike in California, an earthquake in Japan, or political turmoil in North Africa. The ultimate answer to carrying *near-zero inventory* is to build for order, not for stock.

Transportation   Transportation choices affect product pricing, on-time delivery performance, and the condition of the goods when they arrive, all of which affect customer satisfaction. In shipping goods to its warehouses, dealers, and customers, a company can choose rail, air, truck,

FIGURE 13.1 Determining Optimal Order Quantity

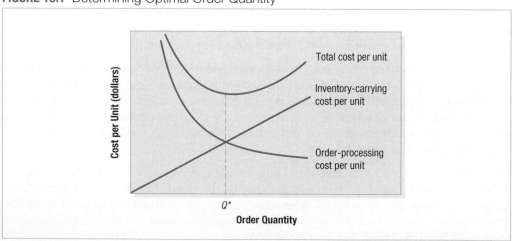

waterway, or pipeline. Shippers consider such criteria as speed, frequency, dependability, capability, availability, traceability, and cost. For speed, the prime contenders are air, rail, and truck. If the goal is low cost, then the choice is water or pipeline.

Shippers are increasingly combining two or more transportation modes, thanks to **containerization**, putting the goods in boxes or trailers that are easy to transfer between two transportation modes. *Piggyback* describes the use of rail and trucks; *fishyback,* water and trucks; *trainship,* water and rail; and *airtruck,* air and trucks. Each coordinated mode offers specific advantages. For example, piggyback is cheaper than trucking alone yet provides flexibility and convenience.

Shippers can choose private, contract, or common carriers. If the shipper owns its own truck or air fleet, it becomes a *private carrier.* A *contract carrier* is an independent organization selling transportation services to others on a contract basis. A *common carrier* provides services between predetermined points on a scheduled basis and is available to all shippers at standard rates. To reduce costly handing at arrival, some firms are putting items into shelf-ready packaging. To reduce damage in shipping, the size, weight, and fragility of the item must be reflected in the crating technique used and the density of foam cushioning.[22] With logistics, every little detail must be reviewed to see how it might be changed to improve productivity and profitability.

Executive Summary

Retailing includes all the activities in selling goods or services directly to final consumers for personal, nonbusiness use. Retailers can be store retailers, nonstore retailers, and retail organizations. Nonstore retailing is growing and includes direct selling, direct marketing, automatic vending, and buying services. As new retail forms have emerged, competition between them has increased, the rise of giant retailers has been matched by the decline of middle-market retailers, investment in technology has grown, and shopper marketing has become a priority. Like all marketers, retailers must make decisions about target markets, channels, product assortment and procurement, prices, services, store atmosphere, store activities and experiences, communications, and location. A private-label brand is one that retailers and wholesalers develop. Private labels are rapidly gaining ground, creating marketing challenges for manufacturers' and national brands.

Wholesaling includes all the activities in selling goods or services to those who buy for resale or business use. Wholesalers can perform functions better and more cost-effectively than the manufacturer can. These functions include selling and promoting, buying and assortment building, bulk breaking, warehousing, transportation, financing, risk bearing, dissemination of market information, and provision of management services and consulting. The most successful are those that adapt their services to meet suppliers' and target customers' needs. Producers of physical products and services must decide on market logistics—the best way to store and move goods and services to market destinations and to coordinate the activities of suppliers, purchasing agents, manufacturers, marketers, channel members, and customers.

Notes

1. Mike O'Toole, "Warby Parker, One Million Eyeglasses, and the Next Generation of Brands," *Forbes,* July 22, 2013; Knowledge@Wharton, "The Consumer Psychology behind Warby Parker's $95 Pricing for Eyeglasses," *Time,* May 23, 2013; Sheila Shayon, "Warby Parker's Long-Term Vision: From the Web to the Street, NYC to the World," *Brandchannel,* September 11, 2012; "Warby Parker Revolutionizes Eyewear Market by Borrowing from Apple, Zappos," *Advertising Age,* November 27, 2011; James Surowiecki, "The Financial Page: Companies with Benefits," *New Yorker,* August 4, 2014, p. 23.

2. Karsten Hansen and Vishal Singh, "Market Structure across Retail Formats," *Marketing Science* 28 (July–August 2009), pp. 656–73.

3. Mark Vroegrijk, Els Gijsbrechts, and Katia Campo, "Close Encounter with the Hard Discounter: A Multiple-Store Shopping Perspective on the Impact of Local Hard-Discounter Entry," *Journal of Marketing Research* 50 (October 2013), pp. 606–26.

4. Jim Zarroli, "In Trendy World of Fast Fashion, Styles Aren't Made to Last," www.npr.org, March 11, 2013; "Zara, H&M Are Top UK Fashion Brands," www.warc.com, December 17, 2012; "Fast Retailing Prioritizes Innovation," www.warc.com, October 15, 2012.

5. Christopher Heine, "Social Pics Help Retailers Get Real," *Adweek,* September 16, 2013, p. 11.

6. Jillian Berman, "Retailers Try to Get Creative with Their Catalogs during Tough Times," *USA Today,* July 19, 2010.

7. Robert P. Rooderkerk, Harald J. van Heerde, and Tammo H. A. Bijmolt, "Optimizing Retail Assortment," *Marketing Science* 32 (September–October 2013), pp. 699–715.

8. Venkatesh Shankar and Ruth N. Bolton, "An Empirical Analysis of Determinants of Retailer Pricing Strategy," *Marketing Science* 23 (Winter 2004), pp. 28–49.

9. Paul W. Miniard, Shazad Mustapha Mohammed, Michael J. Barone, and Cecilia M. O. Alvarez, "Retailers' Use of Partially Comparative Pricing: From Across-Category to Within-Category Effects," *Journal of Marketing* 77 (July 2013), pp. 33–48; Jiwoong Shin, "The Role of Selling Costs in Signaling Price Image," *Journal of Marketing Research* 42 (August 2005), pp. 305–12.

10. For a comprehensive framework of the key image drivers of price image formation for retailers, see Ryan Hamilton and Alexander Chernev, "Low Prices Are Just the Beginning: Price Image in Retail Management," *Journal of Marketing* 77 (November 2013), pp. 1–20.

11. Ilaina Jones, "Kohl's Looking at Spots in Manhattan," *Reuters,* August 19, 2009; Cametta Coleman, "Kohl's Retail Racetrack," *Wall Street Journal,* March 1, 2000.

12. Velitchka D. Kaltcheva and Barton Weitz, "When Should a Retailer Create an Exciting Store Environment?," *Journal of Marketing* 70 (January 2006), pp. 107–18.

13. "Private Label Sales Rise in Europe," www.warc.com, October 19, 2012.

14. Matthew Boyle, "Even Better than the Real Thing," *Bloomberg Businessweek,* November 28, 2011.

15. Lien Lamey, Barbara Deleersnyder, Jan-Benedict E. M. Steenkamp, and Marnik G. Dekimpe, "The Effect of Business-Cycle Fluctuations on Private-Label Share: What Has Marketing Conduct Got to Do with It?," *Journal of Marketing* 76 (January 2012), pp. 1–19.

16. Anne ter Braak, Marnik G. Dekimpe, and Inge Geyskens, "Retailer Private-Label Margins: The Role of Supplier and Quality-Tier Differentiation," *Journal of Marketing* 77 (July 2013), pp. 86–103.

17. Nirmalya Kumar and Jan-Benedict E. M. Steenkamp, *Private Label Strategy* (Boston: Harvard Business School Press, 2007); Nirmalya Kumar, "The Right Way to Fight for Shelf Domination," *Advertising Age,* January 22, 2007.

18. "The Supply Chain Evolution," *Fortune,* Special Advertising Section, March 8, 2012.

19. William C. Copacino, *Supply Chain Management* (Boca Raton, FL: St. Lucie Press, 1997); Robert Shaw and Philip Kotler, "Rethinking the Chain: Making Marketing Leaner, Faster, and Better," *Marketing Management* (July/August 2009), pp. 18–23.

20. Dana Mattioli, "Macy's Regroups in Warehouse Wars," *Wall Street Journal,* May 14, 2012.

21. The optimal order quantity is given by the formula $Q^* = 2DS/IC$, where D = annual demand, S = cost to place one order, and I = annual carrying cost per unit. Known as the economic-order quantity formula, it assumes a constant ordering cost, a constant cost of carrying an additional unit in inventory, a known demand, and no quantity discounts.

22. Perry A. Trunick, "Nailing a Niche in Logistics," *Logistics Today,* March 4, 2008.

Chapter 14

Designing and Managing Integrated Marketing Communications

In this chapter, we will address the following questions:

1. What is the role of marketing communications? (Page 222)
2. What are the major steps in developing effective communications? (Page 224)
3. What is the marketing communications mix, and how should it be set and evaluated? (Page 229)
4. What is an integrated marketing communications program? (Page 232)

Marketing Management at Mondelēz International

Through carefully crafted communications in different markets, Mondelēz International's Oreo brand is establishing a strong global positioning as "milk's favorite cookie" and associations with "moments of togetherness." In the United States, the highly successful "Celebrate the Kid Inside" campaign was buoyed by celebrations of the brand's 100th anniversary. Ads and in-store contests created a party atmosphere and focused on the "twist, lick, and dunk" method of eating Oreos with milk. The 100-day "Daily Twist" promotion paired the brand in online and print ads with various cultural images, icons, and events, such as Elvis Presley week, the Mars Rover, Gay Pride week, and Bastille Day. The Oreo birthday page on Facebook received 25 million likes, and U.S. sales increased 25 percent. In India, launch ads featured a father and son in the "twist, lick, and dunk" ritual. An Oreo Togetherness Bus roamed the country, providing a platform for parents and children to catch fun family moments.[1]

In addition to developing a good product, pricing it attractively, and making it accessible, companies like Mondelēz International must communicate with stakeholders and the general public. This chapter describes how communications work, what they can do for a company, and how holistic marketers combine and integrate marketing communications. Chapter 15 examines mass communications including advertising, sales promotion, and public relations; Chapter 16 looks at digital communications like online, social media, and mobile marketing; and Chapter 17 explores personal communications.

The Role of Marketing Communications

Marketing communications are the means by which firms attempt to inform, persuade, and re-mind consumers—directly or indirectly—about the products and brands they sell. Communications represent the voice of the company and its brands; they are a means by which the firm can establish a dialogue and build relationships with consumers. By strengthening customer loyalty, they can contribute to customer equity.

Marketing communications also work by showing consumers how and why a product is used, by whom, where, and when. Consumers can learn who makes the product and what the company and brand stand for, and they can become motivated to try or use it. Marketing communications allow companies to link their brands to other people, places, events, brands, experiences, feelings, and things. They can contribute to brand equity—by establishing the brand in memory and creat-ing a brand image—as well as drive sales and even affect shareholder value.[2]

Technology and other factors have profoundly changed the way consumers process communi-cations and even whether they choose to process them at all. The rapid diffusion of powerful smart phones, broadband and wireless Internet connections, and ad-skipping digital video recorders (DVRs) has eroded the effectiveness of the mass media. In 1960, a company could reach 80 percent of U.S. women with one 30-second commercial aired simultaneously on three TV networks: ABC, CBS, and NBC. Today, the same ad would have to run on 100 channels or more to achieve this marketing feat.

Another challenge is rampant commercial clutter. The average city dweller is exposed to an estimated 3,000 to 5,000 ad messages a day. Short-form video content and ads appear at gas sta-tions, grocery stores, doctors' offices, and big-box retailers. Marketing communications in almost every medium and form have been on the rise, and some consumers feel they are increasingly invasive. Marketers must be creative in using technology but not intrude in consumers' lives.

The Marketing Communications Mix

In this new communication environment, although advertising is often a central element of a marketing communications program, it is usually not the only one—or even the most important one—for sales and building brand and customer equity. The **marketing communications mix** consists of eight major modes of communication:[3]

1. *Advertising*—Any paid form of nonpersonal presentation and promotion of ideas, goods, or services by an identified sponsor via print media (newspapers and magazines), broadcast media (radio and television), network media (telephone, cable, satellite, wireless), electronic media (audiotape, videotape, videodisk, CD-ROM, Web page), and display media (billboards, signs, posters).

2. *Sales promotion*—Short-term incentives to encourage trial or purchase of a product or service including consumer promotions (such as samples, coupons, and premiums), trade promotions (such as advertising and display allowances), and business and sales force promotions (contests for sales reps).

3. *Events and experiences*—Company-sponsored activities and programs designed to create brand-related interactions with consumers, including sports, arts, entertainment, and cause events as well as less formal activities.

4. *Public relations and publicity*—Programs directed internally to employees of the company or externally to consumers, other firms, the government, and media to promote or protect a company's image or individual product communications.

5. *Online and social media marketing*—Online activities and programs to engage customers or prospects and directly or indirectly raise awareness, improve image, or elicit sales.

6. *Mobile marketing*—A special form of online marketing that places communications on consumer's cell phones, smart phones, or tablets.

7. *Direct and database marketing*—Use of mail, telephone, fax, e-mail, or Internet to communicate directly with or solicit response or dialogue from specific customers and prospects.

8. *Personal selling*—Face-to-face interaction with prospective purchasers for the purpose of making presentations, answering questions, and procuring orders.

Table 14.1 lists examples of these platforms. However, company communication goes beyond these platforms. Every *brand contact* delivers an impression that can strengthen or weaken a customer's view of a company.[4]

TABLE 14.1 Examples of the Eight Common Communication Platforms

Advertising	Sales Promotion	Events and Experiences	Public Relations and Publicity	Online and Social Media Marketing	Mobile Marketing	Direct and Database Marketing	Personal Selling
Print and broadcast ads	Contests, games, sweepstakes, lotteries	Sports	Press kits	Web sites	Text messages	Catalogs	Sales presentations
Packaging—outer	Premiums and gifts	Entertainment	Speeches	E-mail	Online marketing	Mailings	Sales meetings
Packaging inserts	Sampling	Festivals	Seminars	Search ads	Social media marketing	Telemarketing	Incentive programs
Cinema	Fairs and trade shows	Arts	Annual reports	Display ads		Electronic shopping	Samples
Brochures and booklets	Exhibits	Causes	Charitable donations	Company blogs		TV shopping	Fairs and trade shows
Posters and leaflets	Demonstrations	Factory tours	Publications	Third-party chat rooms, forums, and blogs		Fax	
Directories	Coupons	Company museums	Community relations	Facebook and Twitter messages, YouTube channels and videos		Catalogs	
Reprints of ads	Rebates	Street activities	Lobbying				
Billboards	Low-interest financing		Identity media				
Display signs	Trade-in allowances		Company magazine				
Point-of-purchase displays	Continuity programs						
DVDs	Tie-ins						

FIGURE 14.1 Elements in the Communications Process

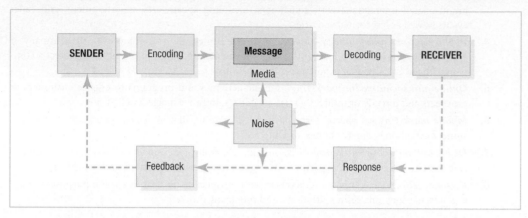

As Chapter 1 noted, communication options appear in paid media (traditional outlets such as TV, print, direct mail), owned media (company-controlled options such as Web sites, blogs, mobile apps), and earned media (virtual or real-world word of mouth, press coverage).

Communications Process Models

Marketers should understand the fundamental elements of effective communications. Two models are useful: a macromodel and a micromodel. Figure 14.1 shows a macromodel with nine key factors in effective communication. Two represent the major parties—*sender* and *receiver*. Two represent the major tools—*message* and *media*. Four represent major communication functions—*encoding, decoding, response,* and *feedback*. The last element in the system is *noise*, random and competing messages that may interfere with the intended communication.

Micromodels of marketing communications concentrate on consumers' specific responses to communications.[5] Figure 14.2 summarizes four classic *response hierarchy models*. These models assume the buyer passes through cognitive, affective, and behavioral stages in that order. This "learn-feel-do" sequence is appropriate when the audience has high involvement with a product category perceived to have high differentiation, such as an automobile. An alternative sequence, "do-feel-learn," is relevant when the audience has high involvement but perceives little or no differentiation within the product category, such as airline tickets. A third sequence, "learn-do-feel," is relevant when the audience has low involvement and perceives little differentiation, such as with salt. By choosing the right sequence, the marketer can do a better job of planning communications.

Developing Effective Communications

Figure 14.3 on page 226 shows the eight steps in developing effective communications. We begin with the basics: identifying the target audience, setting the communications objectives, designing the communications, selecting the communication channels, and establishing the total marketing communications budget.

Identify the Target Audience

The process must start with a clear target audience in mind: potential buyers of the company's products, current users, deciders, or influencers as well as individuals, groups, particular publics,

FIGURE 14.2 Response Hierarchy Models

Stages	AIDA Model[a]	Hierarchy-of-Effects Model[b]	Innovation-Adoption Model[c]	Communications Model[d]
		Models		
Cognitive Stage	Attention	Awareness ↓ Knowledge	Awareness	Exposure ↓ Reception ↓ Cognitive response
Affective Stage	Interest ↓ Desire	Liking ↓ Preference ↓ Conviction	Interest ↓ Evaluation	Attitude ↓ Intention
Behavior Stage	Action	Purchase	Trial ↓ Adoption	Behavior

Sources: [a]E. K. Strong, *The Psychology of Selling* (New York: McGraw-Hill, 1925), p. 9; [b]Robert J. Lavidge and Gary A. Steiner, "A Model for Predictive Measurements of Advertising Effectiveness," *Journal of Marketing* (October 1961), p. 61; [c]Everett M. Rogers, *Diffusion of Innovation* (New York: Free Press, 1962), pp. 79–86; [d]various sources.

or the general public. The target audience is a critical influence on decisions about what to say, how, when, where, and to whom.

Though we can profile the target audience in terms of any of the market segments identified in Chapter 6, it's often useful to do so in terms of usage and loyalty. Is the target new to the category or a current user? Is the target loyal to the brand, loyal to a competitor, or someone who switches between brands? If a brand user, is he or she a heavy or light user? Communication strategy will differ depending on the answers. We can also conduct *image analysis* by profiling the target audience's brand knowledge.

Set the Communications Objectives

John Rossiter and Larry Percy identify four possible objectives:[6]

1. ***Establish need for category***—Establishing a product or service category as necessary for removing or satisfying a perceived discrepancy between a current motivational state and a desired motivational state. A new-to-the-world product such as electric cars will always begin with a communications objective of establishing category need.

2. ***Build brand awareness***—Fostering the consumer's ability to recognize or recall the brand in sufficient detail to make a purchase. Brand recall is important outside the store, whereas brand recognition is important inside the store. Brand awareness provides a foundation for brand equity.

FIGURE 14.3 Steps in Developing Effective Communications

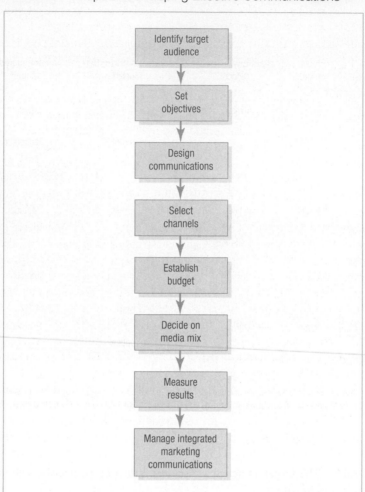

3. ***Build brand attitude***—Helping consumers evaluate the brand's perceived ability to meet a currently relevant need. Relevant brand needs may be negatively oriented (problem removal, problem avoidance, incomplete satisfaction, normal depletion) or positively oriented (sensory gratification, intellectual stimulation, or social approval).

4. ***Influence brand purchase intention***—Moving consumers to decide to purchase the brand or take purchase-related action.

Design the Communications

Formulating the communications to achieve the desired response requires answering three questions: what to say (message strategy), how to say it (creative strategy), and who should say it (message source).

Message Strategy   In selecting message strategy, management searches for appeals, themes, or ideas that will tie in to the brand positioning and help establish points-of-parity or points-of-difference. Some of these appeals or ideas may relate directly to product or service performance (the quality, economy, or value of the brand); others may relate to more extrinsic considerations (the brand as being contemporary, popular, or traditional). Researcher John C. Maloney felt buyers expected one of four types of reward from a product: rational, sensory, social, or ego satisfaction.[7] They might visualize these rewards from results-of-use experience, product-in-use experience, or incidental-to-use experience. Crossing the four types of rewards with the three types of experience generates 12 types of messages.

Creative Strategy   *Creative strategies* are the way marketers translate their messages into a specific communication. We can broadly classify them as either *informational* or *transformational* appeals.[8] An **informational appeal** elaborates on product or service attributes or benefits. Examples in advertising are problem-solution ads (Aleve offers the longest-lasting pain relief), product demonstration ads (Thompson Water Seal withstands intense rain or snow), product comparison ads (AT&T offers the largest 4G mobile network), and testimonials from unknown or celebrity endorsers (NBA star LeBron James pitching McDonald's and other brands).

The best informational appeals ask questions and allow readers and viewers to form their own conclusions.[9] You might expect one-sided presentations that praise a product to be more effective than two-sided arguments that also mention shortcomings. Yet two-sided messages may be more appropriate, especially when negative associations must be overcome.[10] Two-sided messages are more effective with more educated audiences and those who are initially opposed.[11] Finally, the order in which arguments are presented is important.[12]

A **transformational appeal** elaborates on a nonproduct-related benefit or image. It might depict what kind of person uses a brand (VW advertised to active, youthful people with its "Drivers Wanted" campaign) or what kind of experience results from use (Pringles advertised "Once You Pop, the Fun Don't Stop"). Transformational appeals often attempt to stir up emotions that will motivate purchase.[13] Communicators use negative appeals such as fear, guilt, and shame to get people to do things (brush their teeth) or stop doing things (smoking). Communicators also use positive emotional appeals such as humor, love, pride, and joy. Motivational or "borrowed interest" devices—such as cute babies or frisky puppies—are used to attract attention and raise involvement with an ad. However, attention-getting tactics may detract from comprehension, wear out their welcome fast, or overshadow the product.

Message Source   Research has shown that the source's credibility is crucial to a message's acceptance. The three most often identified sources of credibility are expertise, trustworthiness, and likability.[14] *Expertise* is the specialized knowledge the communicator possesses to back the claim. *Trustworthiness* describes how objective and honest the source is perceived to be. Friends are trusted more than strangers or salespeople, and people who are not paid to endorse a product are viewed as more trustworthy than people who are paid. *Likability* describes the source's attractiveness, measured in terms of candor, humor, and naturalness. Messages delivered by attractive or popular sources can achieve higher attention and recall, which is why some advertisers use celebrity spokespeople. On the other hand, some advertisements include ordinary people to add realism and overcome consumer skepticism.

If a person has a positive attitude toward a source and a message or a negative attitude toward both, a state of *congruity* is said to exist. But what happens if a consumer hears a likable celebrity praise a brand she dislikes? Charles Osgood and Percy Tannenbaum believe attitude change will take place that increases the amount of congruity between the two evaluations.[15] The consumer will end up respecting the celebrity somewhat less or the brand somewhat more. If she encounters the same celebrity praising other disliked brands, she will eventually develop a negative view of the celebrity and maintain negative attitudes toward the brands. The **principle**

of congruity implies that communicators can use their good image to reduce some negative feelings toward a brand but in the process might lose some esteem with the audience.

Select the Communications Channels

Communications channels may be personal and nonpersonal. Within each are many subchannels.

Personal Communications Channels   **Personal communications channels** let two or more persons communicate face to face or person to audience through a phone, surface mail, or e-mail. They derive their effectiveness from individualized presentation and feedback and include direct marketing, personal selling, and word of mouth. We can draw a further distinction between advocate, expert, and social communications channels. *Advocate channels* consist of company salespeople contacting buyers in the target market. *Expert channels* consist of independent experts making statements to target buyers. *Social channels* consist of neighbors, friends, family members, and associates talking to target buyers.

A study by Burson-Marsteller and Roper Starch Worldwide found that one influential person's word of mouth tends to affect the buying attitudes of two other people, on average. That circle of influence jumps to eight online. Personal influence carries especially great weight (1) when products are expensive, risky, or purchased infrequently and (2) when products suggest something about the user's status or taste. People often ask others to recommend a doctor, hotel, lawyer, accountant, architect, or financial consultant. If we have confidence in the recommendation, we normally act on the referral. Consumers use *word of mouth* to talk about dozens of brands each day. Positive word of mouth sometimes happens organically with little advertising, but, as Chapter 16 discusses, it can also be managed and facilitated.[16]

Nonpersonal (Mass) Communications Channels   Nonpersonal channels are communications directed to more than one person and include advertising, sales promotions, events and experiences, and public relations. Events marketers who once favored sports events are now using other venues such as art museums, zoos, and ice shows to entertain clients and employees. Events can create attention, though whether they have a lasting effect on brand awareness, knowledge, or preference will vary considerably depending on the quality of the product, the event itself, and its execution. Some companies are creating their own events to surprise the public and create a buzz. "Marketing Insight: Playing Tricks to Build a Brand" describes two clever marketing promotions.

Integration of Communications Channels   Although personal communication is often more effective than mass communication, mass media might be the major means of stimulating it. Mass communications affect personal attitudes and behavior through a two-step process. Ideas often first flow from radio, television, and print to opinion leaders or consumers highly engaged with media and then from these influencers to less media-involved population groups.[17]

This two-step flow has several implications. First, the influence of mass media on public opinion is not as direct, powerful, and automatic as marketers have supposed. It is mediated by opinion leaders and media mavens, people who track new ideas and whose opinions others seek or who carry their opinions to others. Second, the two-step flow challenges the notion that consumption styles are primarily influenced by a "trickle-down" or "trickle-up" effect from mass media. People interact primarily within their own social groups and acquire ideas from others in their groups. Third, mass communicators should direct messages specifically to opinion leaders and others engaged with media if possible and let them carry the message to others.

marketing insight

Playing Tricks to Build a Brand

Some marketers are taking advantage of viral videos and other digital forms of expression to develop creative stunts or "reality pranks" to promote their brands. For example, LG shot a hidden-camera prank commercial in Chile to demonstrate the high-resolution picture quality of its Ultra HD TVs. In an office in a high-rise building, the company replaced the large window overlooking the city with one of its Ultra HD TVs showing the same scene. Then it filmed unsuspecting job seekers talking with an actor posing as an interviewer. All is well until the middle of the interview when a large meteor is shown crashing into the city with a monstrous dust cloud rushing toward the building. The interviewees try to remain calm until the realistic images eventually overwhelm them and they react in panic.

To demonstrate the eye-tracking feature of its Galaxy S4 smart phone, Samsung ran a "Stare Down" challenge contest. Anyone who could sustain eye contact with an S4 handset for a full hour in a busy public setting would win the phone free. The phone was placed at eye level, but as time went on, increasingly attention-getting distractions would appear: police holding back a barking German shepherd, a motorcycle crashing into a flower stand, and so on. There was a consolation prize too. The longer a participant was able to stare at the S4, the bigger the discount for purchasing one. Both videos became viral sensations with millions of views, entertainingly reinforcing key benefits that made up the brand positioning.

Sources: Will Burns, "Samsung 'Stare Down' the Latest Great Reality Prank," *Forbes*, May 31, 2013; "An Eye to Eye Phone Competition," www.feishmanhillard.com, accessed March 30, 2014; Will Burns, "LG Ultra HDTV: A Product Demo for the Ages," *Forbes*, September 5, 2013; Salvador Rodriguez, "LG Hidden-Camera Prank Ad for Its Ultra HD TV Goes Viral," *Los Angeles Times*, September 7, 2013.

Establish the Total Marketing Communications Budget

Industries and companies vary considerably in how much they spend on marketing communications. Expenditures might be 40 percent to 45 percent of sales in the cosmetics industry, but only 5 percent to 10 percent in the industrial-equipment industry. As shown in Table 14.2, four common methods for deciding on a budget are: the affordable method, the percentage-of-sales method, the competitive-parity method, and the objective-and-task method.

Marketing communications budgets tend to be higher when there is low channel support, the marketing program changes greatly over time, many customers are hard to reach, customer decision making is complex, products are differentiated and customer needs are nonhomogeneous, and purchases are frequent and quantities small.[18] In theory, marketers should establish the total communications budget so the marginal profit from the last communication dollar just equals the marginal profit from the last dollar in the best noncommunication use. Implementing this economic principle can be a challenge, however.

Selecting the Marketing Communications Mix

Companies must allocate their marketing communications budget over the eight major modes of communication. Within the same industry, companies can differ considerably in their media and channel choices. Companies are always searching for ways to gain efficiency by substituting one communications tool for others. Many are replacing some field sales activity with ads, direct

TABLE 14.2	Four Methods of Budgeting for Marketing Communications	
Budgeting method	Description	Advantages/Disadvantages
Affordable method	Setting the communications budget at what managers think they can afford.	Disadvantages: This ignores the role of marketing communications as an investment and the immediate impact on sales volume. Also, it leads to an uncertain annual budget, which makes long-range planning difficult.
Percentage-of-sales method	Setting expenditures at a specified percentage of current or anticipated sales or of the sales price.	Disadvantages: This views sales as the determiner of communications rather than as the result, leading to a budget set by funds availability rather than by market opportunities. It discourages experimentation with countercyclical communication or aggressive spending, and its dependence on year-to-year sales fluctuations interferes with long-range planning. There is no logical basis for choosing the specific percentage, and the budget does not identify what each product and territory deserves.
Competitive-parity method	Setting communications budgets to achieve share-of-voice parity with competitors.	Disadvantages: There are no grounds for believing competitors know better. Company reputations, resources, opportunities, and objectives differ significantly. Also, there is no evidence that budgets based on competitive parity discourage communication wars.
Objective-and-task method	Setting the budget by defining specific objectives, identifying the tasks that must be performed to achieve the objectives, and estimating the costs of performing them.	Advantage: This method requires management to spell out its assumptions about the relationship among dollars spent, exposure levels, trial rates, and regular usage.

mail, and telemarketing. Substitutability among communications tools explains why marketing functions need to be coordinated.

Characteristics of the Marketing Communications Mix

Each communication tool has its own unique characteristics and costs. We will briefly review them here and then discuss them in more detail in Chapters 15, 16, and 17.

- *Advertising* reaches geographically dispersed buyers. It can build up a long-term image for a product (Coca-Cola ads) or trigger quick sales (a Macy's ad for a weekend sale). It can be pervasive, offers opportunities for dramatizing brands and products, and enables the advertiser to focus on specific aspects of the brand or product.

- *Sales promotion* uses tools such as coupons, contests, premiums, and the like to draw a stronger and quicker buyer response. Three key benefits are that sales promotion draws attention to the product, provides an incentive that gives value to the customer, and invites the customer to engage in the transaction now.

- *Events and experiences* can be seen as highly relevant because the consumer is often personally invested in the outcome. Also, they are more actively engaging for consumers and are typically an indirect soft sell.

- *Public relations and publicity* can be extremely effective when coordinated with the other communications-mix elements. The appeal is based on high credibility, the ability to reach prospects who avoid mass media and targeted promotions, and the ability to tell the story of a company, brand, or product.

- *Online and social media marketing,* which can take many forms, shares three characteristics. It can be information- or entertainment-rich, it can be changed or updated depending on response, and the message can be prepared and diffused quickly.

- *Mobile marketing* is distinguished by its ability to be time-sensitive, reflecting when and where a consumer is. Also, it can reach and influence consumers as they are making a purchase decision. Because consumers carry their phones everywhere, mobile communications are always at their fingertips.

- *Direct and database marketing*, including "Big Data," allows for more personal and relevant marketing communications. Key characteristics are that messages can be personalized for recipients, used to create attention and inform consumers with a call to action included, and offer information that helps other communications.

- *Personal selling* is the most effective tool at later stages of the buying process, particularly in building up buyer preference, conviction, and action. Three notable qualities are that it can be customized for individuals, it is relationship-oriented, and it is response-oriented.

Factors in Setting the Marketing Communications Mix

Companies must consider several factors in developing their communications mix: type of product market, consumer readiness to make a purchase, and stage in the product life cycle.

First, consumer marketers tend to spend comparatively more on sales promotion and advertising; business marketers tend to spend comparatively more on personal selling. Even in business markets, advertising still plays a significant role in introducing the firm and its products, explaining product features, reminding customers of offerings, generating leads for sales follow-up, legitimizing the firm, and reassuring customers about purchases. In consumer markets, a trained company sales force can help persuade dealers to take more stock and allocate more shelf space to the brand. Sales reps can also build dealer enthusiasm, sign up more dealers, and increase sales at existing accounts.

Second, communication tools vary in cost-effectiveness at different stages of buyer readiness (see Figure 14.4). Advertising and publicity play the most important roles in the awareness-building stage. Customer comprehension is primarily affected by advertising and publicity. Customer conviction is influenced mostly by personal selling. Personal selling and sales promotion are most helpful in closing the sale. Reordering is also affected mostly by personal

FIGURE 14.4 Cost-Effectiveness of Three Different Communication Tools at Different Buyer-Readiness Stages

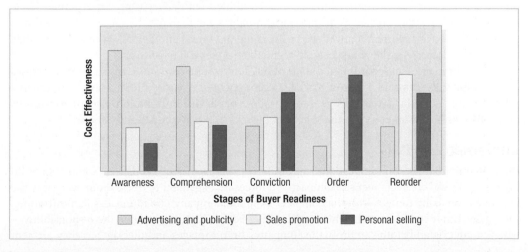

selling and sales promotion and somewhat by reminder advertising. Note too that online activities can affect virtually any stage.

Third, communication tools vary in cost effectiveness at different stages of the product life cycle. In the introduction stage, advertising, events and experiences, and publicity have the highest cost-effectiveness, followed by personal selling to gain distribution coverage and sales promotion and direct marketing to induce trial. In the growth stage, demand has its own momentum through word of mouth and interactive marketing. Advertising, events and experiences, and personal selling become more important in the maturity stage. In the decline stage, sales promotion continues strong, other communication tools are reduced, and salespeople give the product only minimal attention.

Measuring Communication Results

After implementing the communications plan, the firm must measure its impact by asking members of the target audience whether they recognize or recall the message, how many times they saw it, what points they recall, how they felt about the message, and what are their previous and current attitudes toward the product and company. The communicator should also collect behavioral measures of audience response, such as how many people bought the product, liked it, and talked to others about it.

Managing the Integrated Marketing Communications Process

The American Marketing Association defines **integrated marketing communications (IMC)** as "a planning process designed to assure that all brand contacts received by a customer or prospect for a product, service, or organization are relevant to that person and consistent over time." This planning process evaluates the strategic roles of a variety of communications disciplines and combines them seamlessly to provide clarity, consistency, and maximum impact of messages.

Coordinating Media

Media coordination can occur across and within media types, but marketers should combine personal and nonpersonal communications channels through *multiple-vehicle, multiple-stage campaigns* to achieve maximum impact and increase message reach and impact. Promotions and online solicitations can be more effective when combined with advertising, for example.[19] The awareness and attitudes created by advertising campaigns can increase the success of more direct sales pitches. Advertising can convey the positioning of a brand and benefit from online display advertising or search engine marketing that sends a stronger call to action.[20]

Most companies are coordinating their online and offline communications. Web addresses in ads (especially print ads) and on packages allow people to more fully explore a company's products, find store locations, and get more product or service information. Even if consumers don't order online, marketers can use Web sites in ways that drive buyers into stores.

Implementing IMC

Integrated marketing communications can produce stronger message consistency and help build brand equity and create greater sales impact.[21] It forces management to think about every way the customer comes in contact with the company, how the company communicates its positioning, the relative importance of each vehicle, and timing issues. It gives someone the responsibility—where none existed before—to unify the company's brand images and messages as they are sent through thousands of company activities. IMC should improve the company's ability to reach the right customers with the right messages at the right time and in the right place.[22]

Executive Summary

The marketing communications mix includes advertising, sales promotion, public relations and publicity, events and experiences, online and social media marketing, mobile marketing, direct and database marketing, and personal selling. The communications process consists of sender, receiver, message, media, encoding, decoding, response, feedback, and noise. Developing effective communications requires eight steps: (1) identify the target audience, (2) choose the communications objectives, (3) design the communications, (4) select the communications channels, (5) set the total communications budget, (6) choose the communications mix, (7) measure the communications results, and (8) manage the integrated marketing communications process. Designing the communication involves decisions about message strategy, creative strategy, and message source.

Communications channels can be personal or nonpersonal. The objective-and-task method of setting the communications budget is typically most desirable. In choosing the marketing communications mix, marketers must examine the advantages and costs of each tool and the company's market rank as well as the type of product market, purchase readiness, and product life-cycle stage. To measure effectiveness, marketers ask members of the target audience whether they recognize or recall the communication, how many times they saw it, what they recall, how they felt about it, and what are their previous and current attitudes toward the firm, brand, and product. Integrated marketing communications (IMC) recognizes the added value of a comprehensive plan to evaluate the strategic roles of a variety of communications disciplines and combines these disciplines to provide clarity, consistency, and maximum impact through the seamless integration of discrete messages.

Notes

1. Tim Nudd, "Inside Oreo's Adorable Triple Play for Father's Day," *Adweek*, June 10, 2013; T. L. Stanley, "Brand Genius: Lisa Mann, VP Cookies, Mondelēz International," *Adweek*, October 29, 2012; Stuart Elliott, "For Oreo Campaign Finale, a Twist on Collaboration," *New York Times*, September 24, 2012; Rohit Nautiyal, "Cookie Time," *The Financial Express*, June 28, 2011; Rae Ann Ferra, "An Oreo Experiment Reveals Mondelēz's Approach to Innovation," *Fast Company Create*, March 19, 2014.

2. Ernst C. Osinga, Peter S. H. Leeflang, Shuba Srinivasan, and Jaap E. Wieringa, "Why Do Firms Invest in Consumer Advertising with Limited Sales Response? A Shareholder Perspective," *Journal of Marketing* 75 (January 2011), pp. 109–24; Xueming Luo and Naveen Donthu, "Marketing's Credibility: A Longitudinal Investigation of Marketing Communication Productivity and Shareholder Value," *Journal of Marketing* 70 (October 2006), pp. 70–91.

3. Some of these definitions are adapted from the *AMA Dictionary* from the American Marketing Association, www.ama.org/resources/Pages/Dictionary.aspx.

4. Tom Duncan, *Principles of Advertising and IMC,* 2nd ed. (New York: McGraw-Hill/Irwin, 2005).

5. Norris I. Bruce, Kay Peters, and Prasad A. Naik, "Discovering How Advertising Grows Sales and Builds Brands," *Journal of Marketing Research* 49 (December 2012), pp. 793–806.

6. This section is based on the excellent text, John R. Rossiter and Larry Percy, *Advertising and Promotion Management,* 2nd ed. (New York: McGraw-Hill, 1997).

7. James F. Engel, Roger D. Blackwell, and Paul W. Minard, *Consumer Behavior,* 9th ed. (Fort Worth, TX: Dryden, 2001).

8. John R. Rossiter and Larry Percy, *Advertising and Promotion Management,* 2nd ed. (New York: McGraw-Hill, 1997).

9. Roger D. Blackwell, Paul W. Miniard, and James F. Engel, *Consumer Behavior,* 10th ed. (Mason, OH: South-Western Publishing, 2006).

10. Ayn E. Crowley and Wayne D. Hoyer, "An Integrative Framework for Understanding Two-Sided Persuasion," *Journal of Consumer Research* 20 (March 1994), pp. 561–74.

11. C. I. Hovland, A. A. Lumsdaine, and F. D. Sheffield, *Experiments on Mass Communication,* vol. 3 (Princeton, NJ: Princeton University Press, 1949).

12. H. Rao Unnava, Robert E. Burnkrant, and Sunil Erevelles, "Effects of Presentation Order and Communication Modality on Recall and Attitude," *Journal of Consumer Research* 21 (December 1994), pp. 481–90.

13. Gillian Naylor, Susan Bardi Kleiser, Julie Baker, and Eric Yorkston, "Using Transformational Appeals to Enhance the Retail Experience," *Journal of Retailing* 84 (April 2008), pp. 49–57.

14. Herbert C. Kelman and Carl I. Hovland, "Reinstatement of the Communication in Delayed Measurement of Opinion Change," *Journal of Abnormal and Social Psychology* 48 (July 1953), pp. 327–35.

15. C. E. Osgood and P. H. Tannenbaum, "The Principles of Congruity in the Prediction of Attitude Change," *Psychological Review* 62 (January 1955), pp. 42–55.

16. Robert V. Kozinets, Kristine de Valck, Andrea C. Wojnicki, and Sarah J. S. Wilner, "Networked Narratives: Understanding Word-of-Mouth Marketing in Online Communities," *Journal of Marketing* 74 (March 2010), pp. 71–89; David Godes and Dina Mayzlin, "Firm-Created Word-of-Mouth Communication," *Marketing Science* 28 (July–August 2009), pp. 721–39.

17. Norris I. Bruce, Natasha Zhang Foutz, and Ceren Kolsarici, "Dynamic Effectiveness of Advertising and Word of Mouth in Sequential Distribution of New Products," *Journal of Marketing Research* 49 (August 2012), pp. 469–86. See also Shyam Gopinath, Jacquelyn Thomas, and Lakshman Krishnamurthi, "Investigating the Relationship between the Content of Online Word of Mouth, Advertising and Brand Performance," *Marketing Science* 33 (March–April 2014), pp. 241–58.

18. Thomas C. Kinnear, Kenneth L. Bernhardt, and Kathleen A. Krentler, *Principles of Marketing,* 6th ed. (New York: HarperCollins, 1995).

19. Scott Neslin, *Sales Promotion*, MSI Relevant Knowledge Series (Cambridge, MA: Marketing Science Institute, 2002).

20. Markus Pfeiffer and Markus Zinnbauer, "Can Old Media Enhance New Media?," *Journal of Advertising Research* (March 2010), pp. 42–49.

21. Sreedhar Madhavaram, Vishag Badrinarayanan, and Robert E. McDonald, "Integrated Marketing Communication (IMC) and Brand Identity as Critical Components of Brand Equity Strategy," *Journal of Advertising* 34 (Winter 2005), pp. 69–80; Mike Reid, Sandra Luxton, and Felix Mavondo, "The Relationship between Integrated Marketing Communication, Market Orientation, and Brand Orientation," *Journal of Advertising* 34 (Winter 2005), pp. 11–23.

22. Don E. Schultz and Heidi Schultz, *IMC, The Next Generation: Five Steps for Delivering Value and Measuring Financial Returns* (New York: McGraw-Hill, 2003).

Chapter 15

Managing Mass Communications: Advertising, Sales Promotions, Events and Experiences, and Public Relations

In this chapter, we will address the following questions:

1. What steps are required in developing an advertising program? (Page 236)
2. How should sales promotion decisions be made? (Page 241)
3. What are the guidelines for effective brand-building events and experiences? (Page 244)
4. How can companies exploit the potential of public relations? (Page 246)

Marketing Management at Procter & Gamble

After its sponsorship of the U.S. national team at the 2010 Winter Olympics led to an estimated $100 million in increased revenue, Procter & Gamble (P&G) signed up to be an official Olympic sponsor for Summer and Winter Games from 2012 to 2020. Targeting women in their roles as "caregivers and family anchors," the company launched a multimedia "Thank You Mom" global marketing campaign for the 2012 Summer Olympics in London, portraying the crucial roles played by mothers of Olympic champions. Each ad included P&G's corporate logo and some of its billion-dollar-plus brands, such as Pampers, Gillette, and Bounty. The campaign also combined promotions, PR, cause marketing, and other communications to "immerse the consumer with the brands and the message *at every level, on every platform, from smartphones to stores in 204 international markets." P&G marketers estimated the campaign brought in an additional $200 million in sales. Building on this success, they launched a campaign for the 2014 Winter Olympics in Sochi, Russia, that "paid homage to moms of athletes from across the globe, bringing to life the daily lessons all mom teach . . . and the unconditional love moms give kids no matter what."*[1]

P&G has found great success with its multimedia Olympics campaigns, while other marketers are still coming to grips with how to best use mass media in the evolving communication environment. In this chapter, we examine the nature and use of four mass-communication tools—advertising, sales promotion, events and experiences, and public relations and publicity.

Developing and Managing an Advertising Program

Advertising can be a cost-effective way to disseminate messages, whether to build a brand preference or to educate people. Even in today's challenging media environment, good ads can pay off, as they did for P&G.

In developing an advertising program, marketing managers start by identifying the target market and buyer motives. Then they can make the five major decisions known as "the five Ms": *Mission*: What are our advertising objectives? *Money*: How much can we spend, and how do we allocate our spending across media types? *Message*: What should the ad campaign say? *Media*: What media should we use? *Measurement*: How should we evaluate the results? These decisions are summarized in Figure 15.1 and described in the following sections.

Setting the Advertising Objectives

An **advertising objective** (or goal) is a specific communications task and achievement level to be accomplished with a specific audience in a specific period of time.[2] We classify advertising

FIGURE 15.1 The Five Ms of Advertising

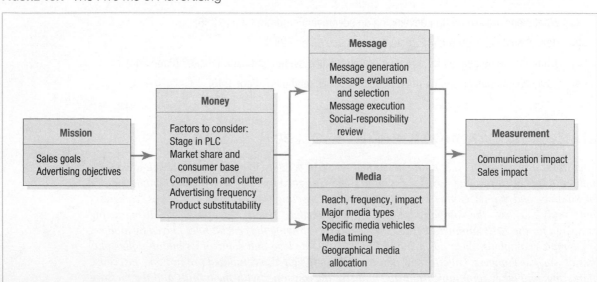

objectives according to whether they aim to inform, persuade, remind, or reinforce. These goals correspond to stages in the *hierarchy-of-effects* model discussed in Chapter 14.

Informative advertising aims to create brand awareness and knowledge of new products or new features of existing products.[3] *Persuasive advertising* aims to create liking, preference, conviction, and purchase of a product or service. Some persuasive advertising is comparative advertising, which explicitly compares the attributes of two or more brands. This works best when it elicits cognitive and affective motivations simultaneously and when consumers are processing advertising in a detailed, analytical mode.[4] *Reminder advertising* aims to stimulate repeat purchase of products and services. *Reinforcement advertising* aims to convince current purchasers they made the right choice. Automobile ads often depict satisfied customers enjoying special features of their new car.

The advertising objective should emerge from a thorough analysis of the current marketing situation. If the product class is mature, the company is the market leader, and brand usage is low, the objective is to stimulate more usage. If the product class is new, the company is not the market leader, and the brand is superior to the leader, the objective is to convince the market of the brand's superiority.

Deciding on the Advertising Budget

Here are five specific factors to consider when setting the advertising budget:[5]

1. *Stage in the product life cycle*—New products typically merit large advertising budgets to build awareness and gain consumer trial. Established brands usually are supported by lower advertising budgets, measured as a ratio to sales.

2. *Market share and consumer base*—High-market-share brands usually require less advertising expenditure as a percentage of sales to maintain share. Building share by increasing market size requires larger expenditures.

3. *Competition and clutter*—In a market with a large number of competitors and high advertising spending, a brand must advertise more heavily to be heard. Even advertisements not directly competitive to the brand create clutter and a need for heavier advertising.

4. *Advertising frequency*—The number of repetitions needed to put the brand's message across to consumers has an obvious impact on the advertising budget.

5. *Product substitutability*—Brands in less-differentiated or commodity-like product classes (beer, soft drinks, banks, and airlines) require heavy advertising to establish a unique image.

Developing the Advertising Campaign

Advertisers employ both art and science to develop the *message strategy* or positioning of an ad—*what* it attempts to convey about the brand—and its *creative strategy*—*how* the ad expresses the brand claims. They use three steps: message generation and evaluation, creative development and execution, and social-responsibility review.

Message Generation and Evaluation   A good ad normally focuses on one or two core selling propositions. As part of refining the brand positioning, the advertiser should conduct market research to determine which appeal works best with its target audience and then prepare a *creative brief*. This is an elaboration of the positioning strategy and includes considerations such as key message, target audience, communications objectives (to do, to know, to believe), key brand benefits, supports for the brand promise, and media. The more themes explored, the higher the probability of finding an excellent one. Marketers can also cut the cost of creative dramatically by using consumers as their creative team, a strategy sometimes called "open sourcing" or "crowdsourcing."[6]

Creative Development and Execution　The ad's impact depends not only on what it says but, often more important, on *how* it says it. Creative execution can be decisive.[7] Every advertising medium has advantages and disadvantages. For example, television reaches a broad spectrum of consumers at low cost per exposure. It can vividly demonstrate product attributes and explain their benefits as well as dramatically portray brand personality and other intangibles. Print advertising—which has declined in recent years—can provide detailed product information and effectively communicate user and usage imagery.[8] Radio, a flexible and inexpensive medium, reaches 93 percent of the U.S. population age 12 and older, both at home and away from home.

Legal and Social Issues　To break through clutter, some advertisers believe they have to push the boundaries of advertising. They must be sure, however, not to overstep social and legal norms or offend consumers. A substantial body of U.S. laws and regulations governs advertising. Advertisers must not make false claims, use false demonstrations, or create ads with the capacity to deceive, even if no one is actually deceived. Also, bait-and-switch advertising that attracts buyers under false pretenses is illegal. "Marketing Insight: Off-Air Ad Battles" describes one legal dispute about what should be permissible in a brand's advertising.

Advertising can play a more positive broader social role. The Ad Council is a nonprofit organization that uses top-notch industry talent to produce and distribute public service announcements for nonprofits and government agencies.

Choosing Media

After choosing the message, the advertiser's next task is to select media to carry it. The steps here are deciding on desired reach, frequency, and impact; choosing among major media types;

---

marketing insight　　Off-Air Ad Battles

In a highly competitive environment, not everyone sees eye to eye on what is suitable advertising. For example, Splenda's tagline for its artificial sweetener was "Made from sugar, so it tastes like sugar," with "but it's not sugar" in small writing almost as an afterthought. McNeil Nutritionals, Splenda's manufacturer, does begin production of Splenda with pure cane sugar but burns it off in the manufacturing process.

Merisant, maker of Equal, claimed that Splenda's advertising confused consumers who were likely to conclude that a product "made from sugar" is healthier than one made from aspartame, Equal's main ingredient. A document from McNeil's own files and used in court says consumers' perception of Splenda as "not an artificial sweetener" was one of the biggest triumphs of the company's marketing campaign.

Splenda became the leader in the sugar-substitute category with 60 percent of the market, leaving roughly 14 percent each to Equal and Sweet'N Low. Although McNeil eventually settled the lawsuit and paid Merisant an undisclosed but "substantial" award (and changed its advertising), it may have been too late to change consumers' perception of Splenda as something sugary *and* sugar-free.

Sources: Sarah Hills, "McNeil and Sugar Association Settle Splenda Dispute," *Food Navigator-usa.com*, www.foodnavigator-usa.com, November 18, 2008; James P. Miller, "Bitter Sweets Fight Ended," *Chicago Tribune*, May 12, 2007; Avery Johnson, "How Sweet It Isn't: Maker of Equal Says Ads for J&J's Splenda Misled," *Wall Street Journal*, April 6, 2007. For a discussion of the possible role of corrective advertising, see Peter Darke, Laurence Ashworth, and Robin J. B. Ritchie, "Damage from Corrective Advertising: Causes and Cures," *Journal of Marketing* 72 (November 2008), pp. 81–97.

selecting specific media vehicles; and setting media timing and geographical allocation. Then the marketer evaluates the results of these decisions.

Reach, Frequency, and Impact **Media selection** is finding the most cost-effective media to deliver the desired number and type of exposures to the target audience. The advertiser seeks a specified advertising objective and response from the target audience—for example, a target level of product trial. This level depends on, among other things, level of brand awareness. The effect of exposures on audience awareness depends on the exposures' reach, frequency, and impact:

- **Reach (R).** The number of different persons or households exposed to a particular media schedule at least once during a specified time period
- **Frequency (F).** The number of times within the specified time period that an average person or household is exposed to the message
- **Impact (I).** The qualitative value of an exposure through a given medium (thus, a food ad will have a higher impact in *Bon Appetit* than in *Fortune* magazine)

Reach is most important when launching new products, flanker brands, extensions of well-known brands, and infrequently purchased brands or when going after an undefined target market. Frequency is most important where there are strong competitors, a complex story to tell, high consumer resistance, or a frequent-purchase cycle.[9] More repetition is needed when a brand, product category, or message is associated with a higher forgetting rate. Advertisers should not coast on a tired ad but insist on fresh executions by their ad agency.[10]

Choosing Among Major Media Types The media planner must know the capacity of the major advertising media types to deliver reach, frequency, and impact. The major advertising media along with their costs, advantages, and limitations are profiled in Table 15.1. Media planners make their choices by considering factors such as target audience media habits, product characteristics, message requirements, and cost.

Place Advertising Options **Place advertising,** or out-of-home advertising, is a broad category including many creative and unexpected forms to grab consumers' attention where they work, play, and shop. Popular options include billboards (including 3D images), public spaces (such as on movie screens and on fitness equipment), product placement (in movies and television), and **point of purchase (P-O-P),** reaching consumers where buying decisions are made through ads on shopping carts, in-store demonstrations, and live sampling.[11] Mobile marketing reaches consumers via smart phones when in store. P-O-P radio provides FM-style programming and commercial messages to thousands of food stores and drugstores nationwide. Video screens in some stores, such as Walmart, play TV-type ads.[12]

Evaluating Alternate Media Nontraditional media can often reach a very precise and captive audience in a cost-effective manner, with ads anywhere consumers have a few seconds to notice them. The message must be simple and direct. Unique ad placements designed to break through clutter may also be perceived as invasive and obtrusive, however, especially in traditionally ad-free spaces such as in schools, on police cruisers, and in doctors' waiting rooms.

Selecting Specific Media Vehicles Media planners select the most cost-effective vehicles within each chosen media type, relying on measurement services that estimate audience size, composition, and media cost and then calculate the cost per thousand persons reached. They also consider audience quality, audience-attention probability, the medium's editorial quality, and extra services. Media planners are using more sophisticated measures of effectiveness and employing them in mathematical models to arrive at the best media mix.[13]

TABLE 15.1	Profiles of Major Media Types	
Medium	Advantages	Limitations
Newspapers	Flexibility; timeliness; good local market coverage; broad acceptance; high believability	Short life; poor reproduction quality; small "pass-along" audience
Television	Combines sight, sound, and motion; appealing to the senses; high attention; high reach	High absolute cost; high clutter; fleeting exposure; less audience selectivity
Direct mail	Audience selectivity; flexibility; no ad competition within the same medium; personalization	Relatively high cost; "junk mail" image
Radio	Mass use; high geographic and demographic selectivity; low cost	Audio presentation only; lower attention than television; nonstandardized rate structures; fleeting exposure
Magazines	High geographic and demographic selectivity; credibility and prestige; high-quality reproduction; long life; good pass-along readership	Long ad purchase lead time; some waste in circulation
Outdoor	Flexibility; high repeat exposure; low cost; low competition	Limited audience selectivity; creative limitations
Yellow Pages	Excellent local coverage; high believability; wide reach; low cost	High competition; long ad purchase lead time; creative limitations
Newsletters	Very high selectivity; full control; interactive opportunities; relative low costs	Costs could run away
Brochures	Flexibility; full control; can dramatize messages	Overproduction could lead to runaway costs
Telephone	Many users; opportunity to give a personal touch	Relative high cost; increasing consumer resistance

Selecting Media Timing and Allocation   In choosing media, the advertiser makes both a macroscheduling and a microscheduling decision. The *macroscheduling decision* relates to seasons and the business cycle. Suppose 70 percent of a product's sales occur between June and September. The firm can vary its advertising expenditures to follow the seasonal pattern, to oppose the seasonal pattern, or to be constant throughout the year. The *microscheduling decision* calls for allocating advertising expenditures within a short period to obtain maximum impact. Advertising can be concentrated ("burst" advertising), dispersed continuously throughout the month, or dispersed intermittently.

In launching a new product, the advertiser must choose among continuity, concentration, flighting, and pulsing. *Continuity* means exposures appear evenly throughout a given period. Generally, advertisers use continuous advertising in expanding markets, with frequently purchased items, and in tightly defined buyer categories. *Concentration* calls for spending all the advertising dollars in a single period, which makes sense for products with one selling season or related holiday. *Flighting* calls for advertising during a period, followed by a period with no advertising, followed by a second period of advertising activity. It is useful when funding is limited, the purchase cycle is relatively infrequent, or items are seasonal. *Pulsing* is continuous advertising at low levels, reinforced periodically by waves of heavier activity, to help the audience learn the message more thoroughly at a lower cost to the firm.[14]

Evaluating Advertising Effectiveness

Most advertisers try to measure the communication effect of an ad—that is, its potential impact on awareness, knowledge, or preference. They would also like to measure its sales effect. **Communication-effect research,** called *copy testing*, seeks to determine whether an ad is

FIGURE 15.2 Formula for Measuring Different Stages in the Sales Impact of Advertising

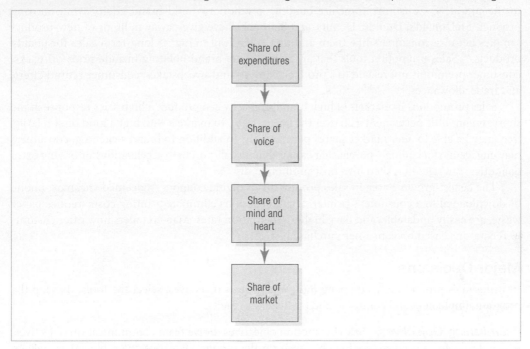

communicating effectively. Marketers should perform this test both before an ad is put into media and after it is printed or broadcast. Many advertisers use posttests to assess the overall impact of a completed campaign.

One way a company can find out whether it is overspending or underspending on advertising is to work with the formula in Figure 15.2. A company's *share of advertising expenditures* produces a *share of voice* (proportion of company advertising of that product to all advertising of that product) that earns a *share of consumers' minds and hearts* and, ultimately, a *share of market*.

Researchers can measure sales impact with the *historical approach,* which uses advanced statistical techniques to correlate past sales to past advertising expenditures.[15] Other researchers use *experimental data* to measure advertising's sales impact. A growing number of researchers measure the sales effect of advertising expenditures instead of settling for communication-effect measures.[16]

Sales Promotion

Sales promotion, a key ingredient in marketing campaigns, consists of a collection of incentive tools, mostly short term, designed to stimulate quicker or greater purchase of particular products or services by consumers or the trade.[17] Whereas advertising offers a *reason* to buy, sales promotion offers an *incentive.*

Advertising versus Promotion

Although sales promotion expenditures increased as a percentage of budget expenditure for a number of years, their growth has recently slowed, in part because consumers began to tune out promotions. Some sales promotion tools are *consumer franchise building*, imparting a selling message along with the deal (such as free samples, frequency awards, and premiums related to the product). Consumer franchise-building promotions build brand equity while moving product. McDonald's, Dunkin' Donuts, and Starbucks have given away millions of new-product samples because consumers like them and they often lead to higher long-term sales for quality products.[18] Sales promotion tools that are typically *not* brand building include price-off packs, consumer premiums not related to a product, contests and sweepstakes, consumer refund offers, and trade allowances.

Sales promotions in markets of high brand similarity can produce a high sales response in the short run but little permanent gain over the longer term. In markets with high brand dissimilarity, they may be able to alter market shares permanently. In addition to brand switching, consumers may engage in stockpiling—purchasing earlier than usual (purchase acceleration) or buying extra quantities. But sales may then hit a post-promotion dip.[19]

The fastest-growing area in sales promotions is digital coupons, redeemed via smart phone or downloaded to a consumer's printer. Digital coupons eliminate printing costs, reduce paper waste, are easily updatable, and have higher redemption rates. Many retailers now offer customized coupons based on consumer purchase histories.[20]

Major Decisions

In using sales promotion, a company must establish its objectives, select the tools, develop the program, implement and control it, and evaluate the results.

Establishing Objectives Sales promotion objectives derive from communication objectives, which derive from basic marketing objectives for the product. For *consumers*, objectives include encouraging more frequent purchases or purchase of larger-sized units among users, building trial among nonusers, and attracting switchers away from competitors' brands. Ideally, consumer promotions have short-run sales impact and long-run brand equity effects.[21] For *retailers*, objectives include persuading retailers to carry new items and more inventory, encouraging off-season buying, encouraging stocking of related items, offsetting competitive promotions, building brand loyalty, and gaining entry into new retail outlets. For the *sales force*, objectives of promotion include encouraging support of a new product or model, encouraging more prospecting, and stimulating off-season sales.

Selecting Consumer Promotion Tools The main consumer promotion tools are summarized in Table 15.2. *Manufacturer promotions* in the auto industry, for instance, are rebates, gifts to motivate test drives and purchases, and high-value trade-in credit. *Retailer promotions* include price cuts, feature advertising, retailer coupons, and retailer contests or premiums.[22]

Selecting Trade Promotion Tools Manufacturers use a number of trade promotion tools (see Table 15.3).[23] They award money to the trade (1) to persuade the retailer or wholesaler to carry the brand; (2) to persuade the retailer or wholesaler to carry more units than the normal amount; (3) to induce retailers to promote the brand by featuring, display, and price reductions; and (4) to stimulate retailers and their sales clerks to push the product.

Selecting Business and Sales Force Promotion Tools Companies spend billions of dollars on business and sales force promotion tools (see Table 15.4 on page 244) to gather leads, impress and reward customers, and motivate the sales force.[24] They typically develop budgets for tools that remain fairly constant from year to year. For many new businesses that want to make a splash to a targeted audience, especially in the B-to-B world, trade shows are an important tool, but the cost per contact is the highest of all communication options.

TABLE 15.2 Major Consumer Promotion Tools

Samples: Offer of a free amount of a product or service delivered door to door, sent in the mail, picked up in a store, attached to another product, or featured in an advertising offer.

Coupons: Certificates entitling the bearer to a stated saving on the purchase of a specific product: mailed, enclosed in other products or attached to them, or inserted in magazine and newspaper ads.

Cash Refund Offers (rebates): Provide a price reduction after purchase rather than at the retail shop: Consumer sends a specified "proof of purchase" to the manufacturer who "refunds" part of the purchase price by mail.

Price Packs (cents-off deals): Offers to consumers of savings off the regular price of a product, flagged on the label or package. A *reduced-price pack* is a single package sold at a reduced price (such as two for the price of one). A *banded pack* is two related products banded together (such as a toothbrush and toothpaste).

Premiums (gifts): Merchandise offered at a relatively low cost or free as an incentive to purchase a particular product. A *with-pack premium* accompanies the product inside or on the package. A *free in-the-mail premium* is mailed to consumers who send in a proof of purchase. A *self-liquidating premium* is sold below its normal retail price to consumers who request it.

Frequency Programs: Programs providing rewards related to the consumer's frequency and intensity in purchasing the company's products or services.

Prizes (contests, sweepstakes, games): *Prizes* are offers of the chance to win cash, trips, or merchandise as a result of purchasing something. A *contest* calls for consumers to submit an entry to be examined by a panel of judges who will select the best entries. A *sweepstakes* asks consumers to submit their names in a drawing. A *game* presents consumers with something every time they buy—bingo numbers, missing letters—which might help them win a prize.

Patronage Awards: Values in cash or in other forms that are proportional to patronage of a certain vendor or group of vendors.

Free Trials: Inviting prospective purchasers to try the product without cost in the hope that they will buy.

Product Warranties: Explicit or implicit promises by sellers that the product will perform as specified or that the seller will fix it or refund the customer's money during a specified period.

Tie-in Promotions: Two or more brands or companies team up on coupons, refunds, and contests to increase pulling power.

Cross-Promotions: Using one brand to advertise another noncompeting brand.

Point-of-Purchase (P-O-P) Displays and Demonstrations: P-O-P displays and demonstrations that take place at the point of purchase or sale.

Developing the Program   In deciding to use a particular incentive, marketers must determine the *size* of the incentive, the *conditions* for participation, the *duration* of the promotion, the *distribution vehicle,* the *timing,* and the *total sales promotion budget.* Next, the marketing manager establishes the *timing* of the promotion and, finally, the *total sales promotion budget.* The cost of a particular promotion consists of the administrative cost (printing, mailing, and promoting the deal) and the incentive cost (cost of premium or cents-off, including redemption costs),

TABLE 15.3 Major Trade Promotion Tools

Price-Off (off-invoice or off-list): A straight discount off the list price on each case purchased during a stated time period.

Allowance: An amount offered in return for the retailer's agreeing to feature the manufacturer's products in some way. An *advertising allowance* compensates retailers for advertising the manufacturer's product. A *display allowance* compensates them for carrying a special product display.

Free Goods: Offers of extra cases of merchandise to intermediaries who buy a certain quantity or who feature a certain flavor or size.

TABLE 15.4	Major Business and Sales Force Promotion Tools

Trade Shows and Conventions: Industry associations organize annual trade shows and conventions. Participating vendors can generate new sales leads, maintain customer contacts, introduce new products, meet new customers, sell more to present customers, and educate customers with publications, videos, and other audiovisual materials.

Sales Contests: A sales contest aims at inducing the sales force or dealers to increase sales results over a stated period, with prizes (money, trips, gifts, or points) going to those who succeed.

Specialty Advertising: Specialty advertising consists of useful, low-cost items bearing the company's name and address, and sometimes an advertising message, that salespeople give to prospects and customers. Common items are ballpoint pens, calendars, key chains, flashlights, tote bags, and memo pads.

multiplied by the expected number of units sold. The cost of a coupon deal recognizes that only a fraction of consumers will redeem the coupons.

Implementing and Evaluating the Program   For each promotion, implementation and control plans must cover *lead time* (for preparation before launch) and *sell-in time* (beginning at launch and ending when 95 percent of the deal merchandise is in consumers' hands). Manufacturers can evaluate the program using sales data (including scanner data showing who bought and later behavior toward the brand), consumer surveys (about recall, attitudes, and behavior), and experiments (varying incentive value, duration, or distribution media).

Events and Experiences

Becoming part of a personally relevant moment in consumers' lives through sponsored events and experiences can broaden and deepen a company's or brand's relationship with the target market. Daily encounters with brands may also affect consumers' brand attitudes and beliefs. *Atmospheres* are "packaged environments" that create or reinforce leanings toward product purchase. For example, a five-star hotel will use elegant chandeliers, marble columns, and other tangible signs of luxury.

Events Objectives

Marketers report a number of reasons to sponsor events:

1. *To identify with a particular target market or lifestyle*—Customers can be targeted geographically, demographically, psychographically, or behaviorally according to events. Old Spice sponsors college sports—including its college basketball Old Spice Classic—to highlight product relevance and sample among 16- to 24-year-old males.

2. *To increase salience of company or product name*—Sponsorship offers sustained exposure for a brand, a necessary condition for reinforcing brand salience. Top-of-mind awareness for soccer World Cup sponsors McDonald's and Castrol is a benefit from repeated brand and ad exposure over the month-long tournament.

3. *To create or reinforce perceptions of key brand image associations*—Events themselves have associations that help to create or reinforce brand associations.[25] To toughen its image and appeal to the heartland, Toyota Tundra sponsors B.A.S.S. fishing tournaments.

4. *To enhance corporate image*—Sponsorship can improve perceptions that the company is likable and prestigious. Although Visa views its long-standing Olympic sponsorship as a means of enhancing international brand awareness and increasing usage and volume, it also engenders patriotic goodwill and taps into the emotional Olympic spirit.

5. *To create experiences and evoke feelings*—The feelings engendered by an exciting or rewarding event may indirectly link to the brand. Audi vehicles featured prominently in the 2010 blockbuster movie *Iron Man 2*. After a month-long marketing blitz, positive word of mouth doubled for the brand.[26]

6. *To express commitment to the community or on social issues*—Cause-related marketing sponsors nonprofit organizations and charities. Firms such as Stonyfield Farms, Home Depot, American Express, and Tom's of Maine have made their support of causes an important cornerstone of their marketing programs.

7. *To entertain key clients or reward key employees*—Many events include lavish hospitality tents and other special services or activities only for sponsors and their guests to build goodwill and establish valuable business contacts. From an employee perspective, events can also build participation and morale or serve as an incentive.

8. *To permit merchandising or promotional opportunities*—Many marketers tie contests or sweepstakes, in-store merchandising, direct response, or other marketing activities with an event.

Despite these potential advantages, the result of an event can still be unpredictable and beyond the sponsor's control. And although many consumers credit sponsors for providing the financial assistance to make an event possible, some may resent its commercialization.

Major Sponsorship Decisions

Making sponsorships successful requires choosing the appropriate events, designing the optimal sponsorship program, and measuring the effects of sponsorship.

- **Choosing event opportunities.** The event must meet the brand's marketing objectives and communication strategy, match the target market, have sufficient awareness and favorable attributions, possess the desired image, and be able to create the desired effects. An ideal event also is unique but not encumbered with many sponsors, lends itself to ancillary marketing activities, and reflects or enhances the sponsor's brand or corporate image.[27]

- **Designing sponsorship programs.** Many marketers believe the marketing program accompanying an event sponsorship ultimately determines its success. At least two to three times the amount of the sponsorship expenditure should be spent on related marketing activities. *Event creation* is a particularly important skill in publicizing fund-raising drives for nonprofit organizations.

- **Measuring sponsorship activities.** The *supply-side* method for measuring an event's success assesses media coverage; for example, the number of seconds the brand is clearly visible on a television screen. The *demand-side* method identifies the sponsorship's effect on consumers' brand knowledge. Although supply-side methods provide quantifiable measures, equating media coverage with advertising exposure ignores the content of the respective communications.

Creating Experiences

A large part of local, grassroots marketing is *experiential marketing*, which not only communicates features and benefits but also connects a product or service with unique and interesting experiences. Consumers seem to appreciate that effort. In one survey, four of five respondents found participating in a live event was more engaging than all other forms of communication. The vast majority also felt experiential marketing gave them more information than other forms of communication and would make them more likely to tell others about the experience and be receptive to other marketing for the brand.[28]

Public Relations

Not only must the company relate constructively to customers, suppliers, and dealers, it must also relate to a large number of interested publics. A **public** is any group that has an actual or potential interest in or impact on a company's ability to achieve its objectives. **Public relations (PR)** includes a variety of programs to promote or protect a company's image or individual products.

The wise company takes concrete steps to manage successful relationships with its key publics. Most have a public relations department that monitors the attitudes of the organization's publics and distributes information and communications to build goodwill. The best PR departments counsel top management to adopt positive programs and eliminate questionable practices so negative publicity doesn't arise in the first place. They perform the following five functions:

1. *Press relations*—Presenting news and information about the organization in the most positive light
2. *Product publicity*—Sponsoring efforts to publicize specific products
3. *Corporate communications*—Promoting understanding of the organization through internal and external communications
4. *Lobbying*—Dealing with legislators and government officials to promote or defeat legislation and regulation
5. *Counseling*—Advising management about public issues as well as company positions and image during good times and bad

Marketing Public Relations

Many companies use **marketing public relations (MPR)** to support corporate or product promotion and image making. MPR, like financial PR and community PR, serves a special constituency, the marketing department. The old name for MPR was **publicity,** the task of securing editorial space—as opposed to paid space—in print and broadcast media to promote or hype a product, service, idea, place, person, or organization. MPR goes beyond simple publicity and plays an important role in the following tasks:

- **Launching new products.** The amazing commercial success of toys such as Silly Bandz owes a great deal to strong publicity.
- **Repositioning mature products.** New York City had extremely bad press in the 1970s until the "I Love New York" campaign.
- **Building interest in a product category.** Companies and trade associations have used MPR to rebuild interest in declining commodities such as eggs and milk and to expand consumption of such products as tea and pork.
- **Influencing specific target groups.** McDonald's sponsors special neighborhood events in Latino and African American communities to build goodwill.
- **Defending products that have encountered public problems.** PR professionals must be adept at managing crises, such as those weathered by such well-established brands as Toyota and BP.
- **Building the corporate image in a way that reflects favorably on its products.** The late Steve Jobs's Macworld keynote speeches helped to create an innovative, iconoclastic image for Apple Corporation.

As the power of mass advertising weakens, marketing managers are turning to MPR to build awareness and brand knowledge for both new and established products. MPR is also effective in blanketing local communities and reaching specific groups, and it can be more cost-effective

TABLE 15.5	Major Tools in Marketing PR

Publications: Companies rely extensively on published materials to reach and influence their target markets via annual reports, brochures, articles, newsletters and magazines, and audiovisual materials.

Events: Companies can draw attention to new products or other activities by arranging and publicizing special events such as news conferences, seminars, trade shows, exhibits, contests and competitions, and celebrations that will reach the target publics.

Sponsorships: Companies can promote their brands and corporate name by sponsoring and publicizing sports and cultural events and highly regarded causes.

News: One of the major tasks of PR professionals is to find or create favorable news about the company, its products, and its people.

Speeches: Increasingly, company executives must field questions from the media or give talks at trade associations or sales meetings, and these appearances can build the company's image.

Public Service Activities: Companies can build goodwill by contributing money and time to good causes.

Identity Media: Companies need a visual identity that the public immediately recognizes. The visual identity is carried by company logos, stationery, brochures, business cards, buildings, uniforms, and dress codes.

than advertising. Increasingly, MPR takes place online, but it must be planned jointly with advertising and other marketing communications.[29]

Major Decisions in Marketing PR

In considering when and how to use MPR, management must establish the marketing objectives, choose the PR messages and vehicles, implement the plan, and evaluate the results. The main tools of MPR are described in Table 15.5.

In setting MPR objectives, a firm can seek to build *awareness* by placing stories in the media to bring attention to a product, service, person, organization, or idea. It can build *credibility* by communicating the message in an editorial context. It can help boost sales force and dealer *enthusiasm* with stories about a new product before launch. It can hold down *promotion cost* because MPR costs less than direct-mail and media advertising.

Next, the firm will search for interesting stories or develop stories about the product or brand. Whereas PR practitioners reach their target publics through the mass media, MPR is increasingly borrowing the techniques and technology of online and direct-response marketing to reach target-audience members one on one. The firm may have difficulty assessing MPR's contribution to the bottom line because MPR is used along with other promotional tools. The easiest gauge of its effectiveness is the number of *exposures* carried by the media. A better measure is the *change in product awareness, comprehension, or attitude* resulting from the MPR campaign (after accounting for the effect of other promotional tools as well as possible).

Executive Summary

Advertising is any paid form of nonpersonal presentation and promotion of ideas, goods, or services by an identified sponsor. Developing an advertising program is a five-step process: (1) set advertising objectives, (2) establish a budget, (3) choose the advertising message and creative strategy, (4) decide on the media, and (5) evaluate communication and sales effects. Sales promotion consists of mostly short-term incentive tools, designed to stimulate quicker or greater purchase of particular products or services by consumers or the trade. In using sales promotion, a company must establish its objectives, select the tools, develop the program, implement and control it, and evaluate the results.

Events and experiences are a means to become part of special and more personally relevant moments in consumers' lives. Well-managed events can broaden and deepen the sponsor's relationship with its target market. Public relations (PR) includes a variety of programs designed to promote or protect a company's image or its individual products. Marketing public relations (MPR), to support the marketing department in corporate or product promotion and image making, can affect public awareness at a fraction of the cost of advertising and is often much more credible.

Notes

1. Alexander Coolidge, "P&G Aims for Moms' Heart with Latest 'Thank You' Ad," *USA Today*, January 8, 2013; Emma Bazilian, "Ad of the Day: P&G Has a Winner with Latest Big Tearjerker Spot for Moms," *Adweek*, January 7, 2014; "Procter & Gamble Brands Unite to Kick Off Sochi 2014 Olympic Winter Games," www.pg.com, October 28, 2013; "In 2013, Once Again: Marketing Art Meets Science—Best in Show Winners of the Advertising Research Foundation's David Ogilvy Awards," *Journal of Advertising Research* 53, no. 3 (2013); Katy Bachman, "Brought to You by the Moms of the World," *Adweek*, August 19, 2013; Dan Monk, "Procter & Gamble Company Aims to Win by Marketing 'Like a Girl,'" *WCPO (Cincinnati),* July 3, 2014, www.wcpo.com/money.

2. Russell H. Colley, *Defining Advertising Goals for Measured Advertising Results* (New York: Association of National Advertisers, 1961).

3. Alicia Barroso and Gerard Llobet, "Advertising and Consumer Awareness of New, Differentiated Products," *Journal of Marketing Research* 49 (December 2012), pp. 773–92; Wilfred Amaldoss and Chuan He, "Product Variety, Informative Advertising, and Price Competition," *Journal of Marketing Research* 47 (February 2010), pp. 146–56.

4. Debora Viana Thompson and Rebecca W. Hamilton, "The Effects of Information Processing Mode on Consumers' Responses to Comparative Advertising," *Journal of Consumer Research* 32 (March 2006), pp. 530–40.

5. Rajesh Chandy, Gerard J. Tellis, Debbie MacInnis, and Pattana Thaivanich, "What to Say When: Advertising Appeals in Evolving Markets," *Journal of Marketing Research* 38 (November 2001), pp. 399-414; Gerard J. Tellis, Rajesh Chandy, and Pattana Thaivanich, "Decomposing the Effects of Direct Advertising: Which Brand Works, When, Where, and How Long?," *Journal of Marketing Research* 37 (February 2000), pp. 32–46;

Peter J. Danaher, André Bonfrer, and Sanjay Dhar, "The Effect of Competitive Advertising," *Journal of Marketing Research* 45 (April 2008), pp. 211–25.

6. Debora V. Thompson and Prashant Malaviya, "Consumer-Generated Ads: Does Awareness of Advertising Co-Creation Help or Hurt Persuasion?," *Journal of Marketing* 77 (May 2013), pp. 33–47; Benjamin Lawrence, Susan Fournier, and Frederic Brunel, "When Companies Don't Make the Ad: A Multi-Method Inquiry into the Differential Effectiveness of Consumer-Generated Advertising," *Journal of Advertising* 42, no. 4 (2013), pp. 292–307; Rosie Baker, "McDonald's Preps Crowdsourced Olympic Ads," *Marketing Week*, August 3, 2012; Eric Pfanner, "When Consumers Help, Ads Are Free," *New York Times*, June 22, 2009, p. B6; Elisabeth Sullivan, "H. J. Heinz: Consumers Sit in the Director's Chair for Viral Effort," *Marketing News*, February 10, 2008, p. 10; Louise Story, "The High Price of Creating Free Ads," *New York Times*, May 26, 2007. See also the Special Issue on the Emergence and Impact of User-Generated Content, *Marketing Science* 31 (May–June 2012).

7. Werner Reinartz and Peter Saffert, "Creativity in Advertising: When It Works and When It Doesn't," *Harvard Business Review*, June 2013, pp. 107–12.

8. "Newspapers: By the Numbers," The State of the News Media 2013, www.stateofthemedia.org.

9. Schultz et al., *Strategic Advertising Campaigns* (Chicago: NTC/Contemporary Publishing Company, September 1994), p. 340.

10. Prashant Malaviya, "The Moderating Influence of Advertising Context on Ad Repetition Effects: The Role of Amount and Type of Elaboration," *Journal of Consumer Research* 34 (June 2007), pp. 32–40.

11. Ram Bezawada, S. Balachander, P. K. Kannan, and Venkatesh Shankar, "Cross-Category Effects of Aisle and Display Placements: A Spatial Modeling Approach and Insights," *Journal of Marketing* 73 (May 2009),

pp. 99–117; Pierre Chandon, J. Wesley Hutchinson, Eric T. Bradlow, and Scott H. Young, "Does In-Store Marketing Work? Effects of the Number and Position of Shelf Facings on Brand Attention and Evaluation at the Point of Purchase," *Journal of Marketing* 73 (November 2009), pp. 1–17.

12. www.walmartsmartnetwork.info, accessed March 27, 2014; Bob Greenberg, "Reinventing Retail; E-commerce Impacts the Brick-and-Mortar Store Experience," *Adweek*, February 15, 2010; Bill Yackey, "Walmart Reveals 18-Month Results for SMART Network," *Digital Signage Today*, February 23, 2010.

13. Chen Lin, Sriram Venkataraman, and Sandy Jap, "Media Multiplexing Behavior: Implications," *Marketing Science*, 32 (March–April 2013), pp. 310–24.

14. Marshall Freimer and Dan Horsky, "Periodic Advertising Pulsing in a Competitive Market," *Marketing Science* 31 (July–August 2012), pp. 637–48.

15. David B. Montgomery and Alvin J. Silk, "Estimating Dynamic Effects of Market Communications Expenditures," *Management Science* (June 1972), pp. 485–501; Kristian S. Palda, *The Measurement of Cumulative Advertising Effect* (Upper Saddle River, NJ: Prentice Hall, 1964), p. 87.

16. Peter J. Danaher and Tracey S. Dagger, "Comparing the Relative Effectiveness of Advertising Channels: A Case Study of a Multimedia Blitz Campaign," *Journal of Marketing Research* 50 (August 2013), pp. 517–34; Gerard J. Tellis, Rajesh K. Chandy, and Pattana Thaivanich, "Which Ad Works, When, Where, and How Often? Modeling the Effects of Direct Television Advertising," *Journal of Marketing Research* 37 (February 2000), pp. 32–46.

17. From Robert C. Blattberg and Scott A. Neslin, *Sales Promotion: Concepts, Methods, and Strategies* (Upper Saddle River, NJ: Prentice Hall, 1990). This text provides a detailed, analytical treatment of sales promotion. A comprehensive review of academic work on sales promotions can be found in Scott Neslin, "Sales Promotion," Bart Weitz and Robin Wensley, eds., *Handbook of Marketing* (London: Sage, 2002), pp. 310–38.

18. Emily Bryson York and Natalie Zmuda, "Sampling: The New Mass Media," *Advertising Age*, May 12, 2008, pp. 3, 56.

19. Harald J. Van Heerde, Sachin Gupta, and Dick Wittink, "Is 75% of the Sales Promotion Bump due to Brand Switching? No, Only 33% Is," *Journal of Marketing Research* 40 (November 2003), pp. 481–91.

20. Rajkumar Venkatesan and Paul W. Farris, "Measuring and Managing Returns from Retailer-Customized Coupon Campaigns," *Journal of Marketing* 76 (January 2012), pp. 76–94.

21. Rebecca J. Slotegraaf and Koen Pauwels, "The Impact of Brand Equity Innovation on the Long-Term Effectiveness of Promotions," *Journal of Marketing Research* 45 (June 2008), pp. 293–306.

22. Kusum L. Ailawadi, Bari A. Harlam, Jacques Cesar, and David Trounce, "Promotion Profitability for a Retailer: The Role of Promotion, Brand, Category, and Store Characteristics," *Journal of Marketing Research* 43 (November 2006), pp. 518–36.

23. Miguel Gomez, Vithala Rao, and Edward McLaughlin, "Empirical Analysis of Budget and Allocation of Trade Promotions in the U.S. Supermarket Industry," *Journal of Marketing Research* 44 (August 2007); Norris Brucc, Preyas S. Desai, and Richard Staelin, "The Better They Are, the More They Give: Trade Promotions of Consumer Durables," *Journal of Marketing Research* 42 (February 2005), pp. 54–66.

24. IBIS World USA, www.ibisworld.com; Noah Lim, Michael J. Ahearne, and Sung H. Ham, "Designing Sales Contests: Does the Prize Structure Matter?," *Journal of Marketing Research* 46 (June 2009), pp. 356–71.

25. Bettina Cornwell, Michael S. Humphreys, Angela M. Maguire, Clinton S. Weeks, and Cassandra Tellegen, "Sponsorship-Linked Marketing: The Role of Articulation in Memory," *Journal of Consumer Research* 33 (December 2006), pp. 312–21.

26. "Brands Suit Up for 'Iron Man 2'," *Adweek*, May 14, 2010.

27. T. Bettina Cornwell, Clinton S. Weeks, and Donald P. Roy, "Sponsorship-Linked Marketing: Opening the Black Box," *Journal of Advertising* 34 (Summer 2005).

28. "2006 Experiential Marketing Study," *Jack Morton,* www.jackmorton.com.

29. "Do We Have a Story for You!," *Economist*, January 21, 2006, pp. 57–58; Al Ries and Laura Ries, *The Fall of Advertising and the Rise of PR* (New York: HarperCollins, 2002).

Chapter 16

Managing Digital Communications: Online, Social Media, and Mobile

In this chapter, we will address the following questions:

1. What are the pros and cons of online marketing? (Page 251)
2. How can companies carry out effective social media campaigns? (Page 253)
3. What are some tips for enjoying positive word of mouth? (Page 254)
4. What are important guidelines for mobile marketing? (Page 256)

Marketing Management at PepsiCo

PepsiCo has been an early champion of digital marketing. For its Mountain Dew soft drink, its first "Dewmocracy" contest had consumers go online to determine the flavor, color, packaging, and name of a new Mountain Dew product. The winning flavor, Voltage, generated several hundred million dollars in revenue for the company in its first year. For its Doritos brand, PepsiCo runs the annual "Crash the Super Bowl" contest, giving contestants a chance to develop an ad to be run during the game broadcast and win $1 million. In 2014, anyone from Doritos's 35 global markets was allowed to enter the competition. The winning ad, "Time Machine," cost only $200 to make and one day to film, but it was one of the most positively received Super Bowl ads by viewers that year. During the contest, Doritos always enjoys a healthy uptick in Twitter, Facebook, and other social media activity.[1]

The newest and fastest-growing channels for communicating and selling directly to customers are digital, providing opportunities for greater *interaction* and *individualization*. Companies like PepsiCo are asking not only "How should we reach our customers?" but also "How should our customers reach us?" and "How can our customers reach each other?" In this chapter, we consider how marketers can use online marketing, social media, and mobile marketing to create loyal customers, build strong brands, and generate profits. We also consider the broader topic of word-of-mouth marketing.

Online Marketing

As described in Chapter 1, marketers distinguish paid and owned media from earned (or free) media. *Paid media* includes company-generated advertising, publicity, and other promotional efforts. *Earned media* is all the PR and word-of-mouth benefits a firm receives without having directly paid for anything—all the news stories, blogs, and social network conversations that deal with a brand.[2] Social media play a key role in earned media. A large part of *owned media* consists of online marketing communications, which we review next.

Advantages and Disadvantages of Online Marketing Communications

Online marketing communications allow companies to offer or send tailored information or messages that engage consumers by reflecting their special interests and behavior. A firm can easily trace the effects by noting how many unique visitors click on a page or ad, how long they spend with it, what they do on it, and where they go afterward. The Internet also offers the advantage of *contextual placement,* buying ads on sites related to the marketer's own offerings. And a firm can place advertising based on keywords typed into search engines to reach people when they've actually started the buying process.

Going online has some disadvantages. Consumers can effectively screen out most messages. Marketers may think their ads are more effective than they really are if bogus clicks are generated by software-powered Web sites.[3] Finally, advertisers lose some control over their online messages, which can be hacked or vandalized.

But the pros clearly can outweigh the cons, and marketers must go where the customers are—increasingly, that means online. Of the time U.S. adults spend with all media, almost half is spent online (see Figure 16.1).[4] Customers define the rules of engagement, however, and insulate themselves with the help of agents and intermediaries if they so choose.

Online Marketing Communication Options

A company chooses which forms of online marketing will be most cost-effective in achieving communication and sales objectives.[5] The options include Web sites, search ads, display ads, and e-mail.

Web Sites   Companies must design Web sites that embody or express their purpose, history, products, and vision and that are attractive on first viewing and interesting enough to encourage repeat visits.[6] Jeffrey Rayport and Bernard Jaworski propose that effective sites feature seven design elements (see Figure 16.2).[7] Visitors will judge a site's performance on ease of use (quick downloads, first page easy to understand, easy navigation) and physical attractiveness (pages clean and not crammed, text readable, good use of color and sound).[8] Companies must also be sensitive to online security and privacy-protection issues.

Besides their Web sites, companies may employ **microsites**, individual Web pages or clusters of pages that function as supplements to a primary site. They're particularly relevant for companies selling low-interest products. People rarely visit an insurance company's Web site, for example, but the company can create a microsite on used-car sites that offers advice for buyers of used cars and a good insurance deal at the same time.

FIGURE 16.1 Share of Time Spent per Day with Major Media by U.S. Adults, 2014 (hrs:mins)

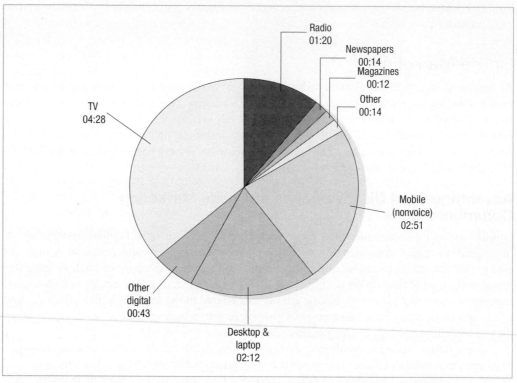

Source: eMarketer, April 2014, accessed at http://www.emarketer.com/Article/Digital-Set-Surpass-TV-Time-Spent-with-USMedia/1010096.

Search Ads   An important component of online marketing is **paid search** or **pay-per-click ads**. In paid search, marketers bid on search terms that serve as a proxy for the consumer's product or consumption interests. When a consumer searches for any of those words with Google, Yahoo!, or Bing, the marketer's ad may appear above or next to the results, depending on the amount the company bids and an algorithm the search engines use to determine an ad's relevance to a particular search.[9] Advertisers pay only if people click, but marketers believe consumers who have already expressed interest by engaging in search are prime prospects.

FIGURE 16.2 Seven Key Design Elements of an Effective Web Site

- *Context.* Layout and design
- *Content.* Text, pictures, sound, and video the site contains
- *Community.* How the site enables user-to-user communication
- *Customization.* Site's ability to tailor itself to different users or to allow users to personalize the site
- *Communication.* How the site enables site-to-user, user-to-site, or two-way communication
- *Connection.* Degree that the site is linked to other sites
- *Commerce.* Site's capabilities to enable commercial transactions

Source: Jeffrey F. Rayport and Bernard J. Jaworski, *e-commerce* (New York: McGraw-Hill, 2001), p. 116.

Search engine optimization (SEO) describes activities designed to improve the likelihood that a link for a brand is as high as possible in the rank order of all nonpaid links when consumers search for relevant terms. A number of guidelines have been suggested as part of SEO as well as paid search.[10] Broader search terms are useful for general brand building; more specific ones identifying a particular product model or service are useful for generating and converting sales leads. Be sure to spotlight search terms on the marketer's Web site so search engines can easily identify them. Any one product can usually be identified by means of multiple keywords, but marketers must bid on each keyword according to its likely return on revenue. Marketers should collect data to track the effects of paid search.

Display Ads   **Display ads** or **banner ads** are small, rectangular boxes containing text and perhaps a picture that companies pay to place on relevant Web sites.[11] The larger the audience, the higher the cost. Given that Internet users spend only 5 percent of their time online actually searching for information, display ads still hold great promise compared to popular search ads. But ads need to be more attention-getting and influential, better targeted, and more closely tracked.[12] **Interstitials** are advertisements, often with video or animation, that pop up between page changes within a Web site or across Web sites. Because consumers find such pop-up ads intrusive and distracting, many use software to block them.

E-mail   E-mail allows marketers to inform and communicate with customers at a fraction of the cost of direct mail. E-mails can be very productive selling tools. The rate at which they prompt purchase has been estimated to be at least three times that of social media ads, and the average order value is thought to be 17 percent higher.[13] Consumers are besieged by e-mails, though, and many employ spam filters to halt the flow. Some firms are asking consumers to say whether and when they would like to receive e-mails. E-mails must be timely, targeted, and relevant. The Gilt Groupe sends more than 3,000 variations of its daily e-mail for its flash-sale site based on recipient's past click-throughs, browsing history, and purchase history.[14]

Social Media

Social media are a means for consumers to share text, images, audio, and video information with each other and with companies, and vice versa. Social media allow marketers to establish a public voice and presence online. They can cost-effectively reinforce other communication activities. Because of their day-to-day immediacy, they can also encourage companies to stay innovative and relevant. Marketers can build or tap into online communities, inviting participation from consumers and creating a long-term marketing asset in the process.

Social Media Platforms

There are three main platforms for social media: (1) online communities and forums, (2) blogs (individual blogs and blog networks such as Sugar and Gawker), and (3) social networks (like Facebook, Twitter, and YouTube).

Online Communities and Forums   Many online communities and forums are created by consumers or groups of consumers with no commercial interests or company affiliations. Others are sponsored by companies whose members communicate with the company and with each other through postings, text messaging, and chat discussions about special interests related to the company's products and brands. Information flow in online communities and forums is two-way and can provide companies with useful, hard-to-get customer information and insights.

Blogs   *Blogs*, regularly updated online journals or diaries, have become an important outlet for word of mouth. One obvious appeal of blogs is that they bring together people with common interests. Blog networks such as Gawker Media offer marketers a portfolio of choices. Corporations are creating their own blogs and carefully monitoring those of others.[15] Popular blogs are creating influential opinion leaders. Because many consumers examine product information and reviews contained in blogs, the Federal Trade Commission has also taken steps to require bloggers to disclose their relationship with marketers whose products they endorse. At the other extreme, some consumers use blogs and videos as a means of getting retribution for a company's bad service or faulty products.

Social Networks   Social networks have become an important force in both business-to-consumer and business-to-business marketing. Major ones include Facebook, one of the world's biggest; LinkedIn, which focuses on career-minded professionals; and Twitter, with its 140-character "tweets." Marketers are still learning how to best tap into social networks and their huge, well-defined audiences.[16] Given networks' noncommercial nature—users are generally there looking to connect with others—attracting attention and persuading are more challenging. Also, given that users generate their own content, ads may find themselves appearing beside inappropriate or even offensive material.[17] Advertising is only one avenue, however. Like any individual, companies can also join social groups and actively participate. Having a Facebook page has become a virtual prerequisite for many companies.[18]

Using Social Media

Social media are rarely the sole source of marketing communications for a brand.[19] First, social media may not be as effective in attracting new users and driving brand penetration. Also, research by DDB suggests that brands and products vary widely in how social they are online. Consumers are most likely to engage with media, charities, and fashion and least likely to engage with consumer goods.[20] Finally, although consumers may use social media to get useful information or deals or to enjoy brand-created content, a much smaller percentage want to engage in two-way "conversations" with brands. In short, marketers must recognize that when it comes to social media, only *some* consumers want to engage with *some* brands and, even then, only *some* of the time.

Word of Mouth

Social media are one example of online word of mouth. Word of mouth (WOM) is a powerful marketing tool, as discussed next.

Forms of Word of Mouth

Contrary to popular opinion, most WOM is *not* generated online. Research and consulting firm Keller Fay notes that 90 percent occurs offline, specifically 75 percent face to face and 15 percent over the phone. Keller Fay also notes how advertising and WOM are inextricably linked: "WOM has proven to be highly credible and linked to sales; advertising has proven to help spark conversation."[21]

Viral marketing is a form of online WOM or "word of mouse," that encourages consumers to pass along company-developed products and services or audio, video, or written information to others online.[22] With user-generated content sites such as YouTube, Vimeo, and Google Video, consumers and advertisers can upload ads and videos to be shared by millions of people.[23]

Creating Word-of-Mouth Buzz

Although more interesting brands are more likely to be talked about online, whether a brand is seen as novel, exciting, or surprising has little effect on whether it is discussed in face-to-face, oral communications.[24] Brands discussed offline are often those that are salient and visible and come easily to mind.[25] Research has shown that consumers tend to generate positive WOM themselves and share information about their *own* positive consumption experiences. They tend to only transmit negative WOM and pass on information they heard about *others'* negative consumption experiences.[26]

It's worth remembering that much online content is not necessarily naturally shared and does not go viral. One study found that only 4 percent of content "cascaded" to more than one person beyond the initial recipient.[27] In deciding whether to contribute to social media, consumers can be motivated by intrinsic factors such as whether they are having fun or learning, but more often they are swayed by extrinisic factors such as social and self-image considerations.[28]

Companies can help create buzz for their products or services, and media and advertising are not always necessary for it to occur. Procter & Gamble (P&G) has enrolled more than half a million mothers in Vocalpoint, a group built on the premise that certain highly engaged individuals want to learn about products, receive samples and coupons, share their opinions with companies, and, of course, talk up their experiences with others. The Vocalpoint moms have big social networks and generally speak to 25 to 30 other women during the day, compared with an average of five for other moms. A campaign for P&G's Secret Clinical Strength Deodorant resulted in 42,000 click-throughs to an opt-in coupon redemption and 50,000 strong product reviews on the brand's Web site.

Ultimately, the success of any viral or WOM buzz campaign depends on the willingness of consumers to talk to other consumers.[29] Customer reviews can be especially influential.[30] A recent Nielsen survey found that online customer reviews were the second-most trusted source of brand information (after recommendations from friends and family).[31] Many review sites are now using a Facebook login that attaches a review posted by someone to his or her Facebook profile. By attaching their reviews to their Facebook pages, users can find out what friends or noteworthy celebrities deem positive or negative about a brand.[32]

Although many WOM effects are beyond marketers' control, certain steps can improve the likelihood of starting positive buzz:[33]

- **Identify influential individuals and companies and devote extra effort to them.** Companies can trace online activity to identify more influential users who may function as opinion leaders, such as industry analysts and journalists, selected policy makers, and early adopters.

- **Supply key people with product samples.** Chevrolet gave a free three-day rental of its electric Chevy Volt car to 900 people with a Klout online influence score of more than 50 (out of a possible 100), resulting in 46,000 tweets and more than 20.7 million largely positive blog posts.

- **Work through community influentials.** Ford's prelaunch "Fiesta Movement" campaign invited 100 young Millennials to drive the Fiesta car for six months. Drivers were chosen based on the size and quality of their online social network as well as a video they submitted about their desire for adventure. The campaign attracted 4.3 million YouTube views, more than 500,000 Flickr views, more than 3 million Twitter impressions, and 50,000 potential customers, 97 percent of whom were not already Ford owners.[34]

- **Develop word-of-mouth referral channels to build business.** Professionals will often encourage clients to recommend their services.
- **Provide compelling information that customers want to pass along.** Make it easy and desirable for a customer to borrow elements from an e-mail message or blog.

Measuring the Effects of Word of Mouth

Many marketers concentrate on the online effects of WOM given the ease of tracking them through advertising, PR, and digital agencies. Through demographic information or proxies for that information and cookies, firms can monitor when customers blog, comment, post, share, link, upload, friend, stream, write on a wall, or update a profile. "Marketing Insight: Tracking Online Buzz" describes some company efforts in this area.

Mobile Marketing

Given the presence of smart phones and tablets everywhere and marketers' ability to personalize messages based on demographics and other characteristics, the appeal of mobile marketing as a communication tool is obvious.

---

marketing insight   Tracking Online Buzz

Marketers have to decide *what* they are going to track online as well as *how* they are going to track it. DuPont employs measures of online word of mouth such as scale (how far the campaign reached), speed (how fast it spread), share of voice in that space, share of voice in that speed, whether it achieved positive lift in sentiment, whether the message was understood, whether it was relevant, whether it had sustainability (and was not a one-shot deal), and how far it moved from its source. Other researchers focus on characterizing the source of word of mouth according to relevance, sentiment, and authority.

More firms are directing their online tracking efforts from a specific location. To monitor the Gatorade brand on social networks around the clock, PepsiCo created a "Mission Control Center" in its Chicago headquarters. Four full-time people handle the operations, with six big monitors providing data visualizations and dashboards. The Gatorade team reviews blog conversations, tracks sentiment, and, based on feedback, makes appropriate changes to the company's marketing. The team also decides when to intervene in an online conversation. Any post that includes a query directly about the brand or that reflects a misunderstanding is usually an opportunity for the team to weigh in, but as one team member notes, "If they want to talk about working out, we let them have that conversation."

Sources: Wendy W. Moe and David A. Schweidel, *Social Media Intelligence* (New York: Cambridge University Press, 2014); Ryan Holmes, "NASA-Style Mission Control Centers for Social Media Are Taking Off," www.tech.fortune.cnn.com, October 25, 2012; Lionel Menchaca, Donna L. Hoffman and Marek Fodor, "Can You Measure the ROI of Your Social Media Marketing," *MIT Sloan Management Review*, Fall 2010, pp. 41–49; "Valerie Bauerlin, "Gatorade's 'Mission': Sell More Drinks," *Wall Street Journal*, September 13, 2010; Adam Ostrow, "Inside Gatorade's Social Media Command Center," www.mashable.com, June 15, 2010; Rick Lawrence, Prem Melville, Claudia Perlich, Vikas Sindhwani, Steve Meliksetian, Pei-Yun Hsueh, and Yan Liu, "Social Media Analytics," *OR/MS Today*, February 2010, pp. 26–30; "Is There a Reliable Way to Measure Word-of-Mouth Marketing?" *Marketing NPV* 3 (2006), www.marketingnpv.com, pp. 3–9.

The Scope of Mobile Marketing

Six of every 10 U.S. consumers owned a smart phone in 2014, creating a major opportunity for advertisers to reach consumers on the "third screen" (TV and the computer are the first and second).[35] Perhaps not surprisingly, U.S. consumers spend a considerable amount of time on mobile—more than on radio, magazines, and newspapers combined (an average of two hours and 51 minutes versus one hour and 46 minutes).[36]

Much recent interest has been generated in **mobile apps**—bite-sized software programs that can be downloaded to smart phones. Apps can perform useful functions—adding convenience, social value, incentives, and entertainment and making consumers' lives a little or a lot better.[37] Smart phones are also conducive to boosting loyalty programs in which customers can track their visits to and purchases from a merchant and receive rewards. By tracking the whereabouts of receptive customers who opt in to receive communications, retailers can send them location-specific promotions when they are near shops or outlets.[38] Sonic Corp. used GPS data and proximity to cell towers in Atlanta to identify when customers who had signed up for company communications were near one of roughly 50 Sonic restaurants in the area. At that point, the company sent such customers a text message with a discount offer or an ad to entice them to visit the restaurant.[39]

Although the cookies that allow firms to track online activity don't typically work in wireless applications, technological advances are making it easier to track users across their smart phones and tablets too. With user privacy safeguards in place, marketers' greater knowledge of cross-screen identities (online and mobile) can permit more relevant, targeted ads.[40]

Developing Effective Mobile Marketing Programs

Marketers are wise to design simple, clear, and clean sites, paying even greater attention than usual to user experience and navigation.[41] Being concise is critical with mobile messaging.[42] For example, mobile ad copy should occupy only 50 percent of the screen, logos should be in a corner of the frame, and calls to action should be highlighted with a bright color.

Mobile Marketing across Markets

In developed Asian markets such as Hong Kong, Japan, Singapore, and South Korea, mobile marketing is fast becoming a central component of customer experiences.[43] In developing markets, high smart-phone penetration also makes mobile marketing attractive. A pioneer in China, Coca-Cola created a national campaign asking Beijing residents to send text messages guessing the high temperature in the city every day for just over a month for a chance to win a one-year supply of Coke products. The campaign attracted more than 4 million messages over the course of 35 days.[44]

Executive Summary

Online marketing provides marketers with opportunities for much greater interaction and individualization through well-designed and executed Web sites, search ads, display ads, and e-mails. However, consumers can effectively screen out most messages, bogus clicks may be a problem, and advertisers lose some control over online messages. Social media come in many forms: online communities and forums, blogs, and social networks such as Facebook, Twitter, and YouTube. Social media offer marketers the opportunity to have a public voice and online presence for their brands and to reinforce other communications. Marketers can build or tap into online communities, inviting participation from consumers and creating a long-term marketing asset. Social media are rarely the sole source of marketing communications for a brand.

Word-of-mouth marketing finds ways to engage customers so they will talk positively with others about products, services, and brands. Viral marketing encourages people to exchange online information related to a product or service. Mobile marketing is an increasingly important form of interactive marketing by which marketers can use text messages, software apps, and ads to connect with consumers via their smart phones and tablets.

Notes

1. Thomas Leskin, "Schuylkill Native Part of Winning Doritos Super Bowl Commercial," *The Morning Call*, February 4, 2014; Jennifer Rooney, "Doritos Again Asks Fans to 'Crash the Super Bowl'—This Time from Around the World," *Forbes*, September 12, 2013; Elaine Wong, "What Mountain Dew Learned from 'DEWmocracy,'" *Adweek*, June 16, 2010; Natalie Zmuda, "New Pepsi 'Dewmocracy' Push Threatens to Crowd Out Shops," *Advertising Age*, November 2, 2009.

2. Andrew T. Stephen and Jeff Galak, "The Effects of Traditional and Social Earned Media on Sales: A Study of a Microlending Marketplace," *Journal of Marketing Research* 49 (October 2012), pp. 624–39.

3. Kenneth C. Wilbur and Yi Zhu, "Click Fraud," *Marketing Science* 28 (March–April 2009), pp. 293–308.

4. "Mobile Continues to Steal Share of US Adults' Daily Time Spent with Media," *eMarketer*, April 22, 2014.

5. Hans Risselada, Peter C. Verhoef, and Tammo H.A. Bijmolt, "Dynamic Effects of Social Influence and Direct Marketing on the Adoption of High-Technology Products," *Journal of Marketing* 78 (March 2014), pp. 52–68; Zsolt Katona, Peter Pal Zubcsek, and Miklos Sarvary, "Network Effects and Personal Influences: The Diffusion of an Online Social Network," *Journal of Marketing Research* 48 (June 2011), pp. 425–43; Allen P. Adamson, *Brand Digital* (New York: Palgrave Macmillan, 2008).

6. John R. Hauser, Glen L. Urban, Guilherme Liberali, and Michael Braun, "Website Morphing," *Marketing Science* 28 (March–April 2009), pp. 202–23; Peter J. Danaher, Guy W. Mullarkey, and Skander Essegaier, "Factors Affecting Web Site Visit Duration: A Cross-Domain Analysis," *Journal of Marketing Research* 43 (May 2006), pp. 182–94; Philip Kotler, *According to Kotler* (New York: American Management Association, 2005).

7. Jeffrey F. Rayport and Bernard J. Jaworski, *e-commerce* (New York: McGraw-Hill, 2001), p. 116.

8. Jan-Benedict E. M. Steenkamp and Inge Geyskens, "How Country Characteristics Affect the Perceived Value of Web Sites," *Journal of Marketing* 70 (July 2006), pp. 136–50.

9. Emily Steel, "Marketers Take Search Ads Beyond Search Engines," *Wall Street Journal*, January 19, 2009.

10. Ron Berman and Zsolt Katona, "The Role of Search Engine Optimization in Search Marketing," *Marketing Science* 32 (July–August 2013), pp. 644–51; Oliver J. Rutz, Randolph E. Bucklin, and Garrett P. Sonnier, "A Latent Instrumental Variables Approach to Modeling Keyword Conversion in Paid Search Advertising," *Journal of Marketing Research* 49 (June 2012), pp. 306–19; Oliver J. Rutz and Randolph E. Bucklin, "From Generic to Branded: A Model of Spillover in Paid Search Advertising," *Journal of Marketing Research* 48 (February 2011), pp. 87–102; Paula Andruss, "How to Win the Bidding Wars," *Marketing News*, April 1, 2008, p. 28; Jefferson Graham, "To Drive Traffic to Your Site, You Need to Give Good Directions," *USA Today*, June 23, 2008.

11. Peter J. Danaher, Janghyuk Lee, and Laoucine Kerbache, "Optimal Internet Media Selection," *Marketing Science* 29 (March–April 2010), pp. 336–47; Puneet Manchanda, Jean-Pierre Dubé, Khim Yong Goh, and Pradeep K. Chintagunta, "The Effects of Banner Advertising on Internet Purchasing," *Journal of Marketing Research* 43 (February 2006), pp. 98–108.

12. Glen Urban, Guilherme (Gui) Liberali, Erin Macdonald, Robert Bordley, and John Hauser, "Morphing Banner Advertising," *Marketing Science* 33 (January–February 2014), pp. 27–46; Jan H. Schumann, Florian von Wangenheim, and Nicole Groene, "Targeted Online Advertising: Using Reciprocity Appeals to Increase Acceptance among Users of Free Web Services," *Journal of Marketing* 78 (January 2014), pp. 59–75; Michael Braun and Wendy Moe, "Online Display Advertising: Modeling the Effects of Multiple Creatives and Individual Impression Histories," *Marketing Science* 32 (September/October 2013), pp. 753–67; Anja Lambrecht and Catherine

Tucker, "When Does Retargeting Work? Information Specificity in Online Advertising," *Journal of Marketing Research* 50 (October 2013), pp. 561–76.

13. Nora Aufreiter, Julien Boudet and Vivien Weng, "Why Marketers Keep Sending You E-mails," *McKinsey Quarterly*, January 2014.

14. Aurfreiter, Boudet and Weng, "Why Marketers Keep Sending You E-mails."

15. For an academic discussion of chat rooms, recommendation sites, and customer review sections online, see Dina Mayzlin, "Promotional Chat on the Internet," *Marketing Science* 25 (March–April 2006), pp. 155–63; and Judith Chevalier and Dina Mayzlin, "The Effect of Word of Mouth on Sales: Online Book Reviews," *Journal of Marketing Research* 43 (August 2006), pp. 345–54.

16. Jae Young Lee and David R. Bell, "Neighborhood Social Capital and Social Learning for Experience Attributes of Products," *Marketing Science* 32 (November–December 2013), pp. 960–76.

17. "Profiting from Friendship," *Economist*, January 30, 2010, pp. 9–12.

18. Rebecca Walker Naylor, Cait Poynor Lamberton, and Patricia M. West, "Beyond the 'Like' Button: The Impact of Mere Virtual Presence on Brand Evaluations and Purchase Intentions in Social Media Settings," *Journal of Marketing* 76 (November 2012), pp. 105–20.

19. David Taylor, "Can Social Media Show You the Money," *Brandgym Research Paper* 6, September 2012.

20. Christian Schulze, Lisa Scholer, and Bernd Skiera, "Not All Fun and Games: Viral Marketing for Utilitarian Products," *Journal of Marketing* 78 (January 2014), pp. 1–19.

21. Ed Keller and Brad Fay, "Word of Mouth Advocacy: A New Key to Advertising Effectiveness," *Journal of Advertising Research*, 52 (December 2012), pp. 459–64.

22. Barak Libai, Eitan Muller, and Renana Peres, "Decomposing the Value of Word-of-Mouth Seeding Programs: Acceleration Versus Expansion," *Journal of Marketing Research* 50 (April 2013), pp. 161–76, Oliver Hinz, Bernd Skiera, Christian Barrot, and Jan U. Becker, "Seeding Strategies for Viral Marketing: An Empirical Comparison," *Journal of Marketing* 75 (November 2011), pp. 55–71; Ralf van der Lans, Gerrit van Bruggen, Jehoshua Eliashberg, and Berend Wierenga, "A Viral Branching Model for Predicting the Spread of Electronic Word of Mouth," *Marketing Science* 29 (March–April 2010), pp. 348–65.

23. Thales Teixeira, "How to Profit from 'Lean' Advertising," *Harvard Business Review*, June 2013, pp. 23–25.

24. Jonah Berger and Raghuram Iyengar, "Communication Channels and Word of Mouth: How the Medium Shapes the Message," *Journal of Consumer Research* 40 (October 2013), pp. 567–79. See also Mitch Lovett, Renana Peres, and Roni Shachar, "On Brands and Word of Mouth," *Journal of Marketing Research* 50 (August 2013), pp. 427–44; Amar Cheema and Andrew M. Kaikati, "The Effect of Need for Uniqueness on Word of Mouth," *Journal of Marketing Research* 47 (June 2010), pp. 553–63.

25. Jonah Berger and Eric M. Schwartz, "What Drives Immediate and Ongoing Word of Mouth?," *Journal of Marketing Research* 48 (October 2011), pp. 869–80.

26. Matteo De Angelis, Andrea Bonezzi, Alessandro M. Peluso, Derek D. Rucker, and Michele Costabile, "On Braggarts and Gossips: A Self-Enhancement Account of Word-of-Mouth Generation and Transmission," *Journal of Marketing Research* 49 (August 2012), pp. 551–63; Sha Yang, Mantian Hu, Russ Winer, Henry Assael, and Xiaohong Chen, "An Empirical Study of Word-of-Mouth Generation and Consumption," *Marketing Science* 31 (November–December 2012), pp. 952–63. See also Yinlong Zhang, Lawrence Feick, and Vikas Mittal, "How Males and Females Differ in Their Likelihood of Transmitting Negative Word of Mouth," *Journal of Consumer Research* 40 (April 2014), pp. 1097–108; David Dubois, Derek D. Rucker, and Zakary L. Tormala, "From Rumors to Facts, and Facts to Rumors: The Role of Certainty Decay in Consumer Communications," *Journal of Marketing Research* 48 (December 2011), pp. 1020–32.

27. Sharad Goel, Duncan J. Watts, and Daniel G. Goldstein, "The Structure of Online Diffusion Networks," *Proceedings of the 13th ACM Conference on Electronic Commerce (EC'12)*, Valencia, Spain, June 4–8, 2012, pp. 623–38.

28. Olivier Toubia and Andrew T. Stephen, "Intrinsic vs. Image-Related Utility in Social Media: Why Do People Contribute Content to Twitter?," *Marketing Science* 32 (May–June 2013), pp. 368–92.

29. Amar Cheema and Andrew M. Kaikati, "The Effect of Need for Uniqueness on Word of Mouth," *Journal of Marketing Research* 47 (June 2010), pp. 553–63.

30. Stephan Ludwig, Ko de Ruyter, Mike Friedman, Elisabeth C. Brüggen, Martin Wetzels, and Gerard Pfann, "More than Words: The Influence of Affective Content and Linguistic Style Matches in Online Reviews on Conversion Rates," *Journal of Marketing* 77 (January 2013), pp. 87–103; Yi Zhao, Sha Yang, Vishal Narayan, and Ying Zhao, "Modeling Consumer Learning from Online Product Reviews," *Marketing Science* 32 (January–February 2013), pp. 153–69; Rebecca Walker Naylor, Cait Poynor Lamberton, and David A. Norton, "Seeing Ourselves in Others:

Reviewer Ambiguity, Egocentric Anchoring, and Persuasion," *Journal of Marketing Research* 48 (June 2011), pp. 617–31.

31. "Nielsen: Global Consumers' Trust in 'Earned' Advertising Grows in Importance," April 10, 2012. See also Itamar Simonson and Emanuel Rosen, *Added Value* (New York: Harper Collins, 2014).

32. Ekaterina Walter, "When Co-creation Becomes the Beating Heart of Marketing, Companies Win," *Fast Company*, November 29, 2012.

33. Beth Saulnier, "It's Complicated," *Cornell Alumni Magazine*, September/October 2013, pp. 45-49; Olga Kharif, "Finding a Haystack's Most Influential Needles," *Bloomberg Businessweek*, October 22, 2012; Michael Trusov, Anand V. Bodapati, and Randolph E. Bucklin, "Determining Influential Users in Internet Social Networks," *Journal of Marketing Research* 47 (August 2010), pp. 643–58; Matthew Dolan, "Ford Takes Online Gamble with New Fiesta," *Wall Street Journal*, April 8, 2009; Sarit Moldovan, Jacob Goldenberg, and Amitava Chattopadhyay, "What Drives Word of Mouth? The Roles of Product Originality and Usefulness," *MSI Report No. 06-111* (Cambridge, MA: Marketing Science Institute, 2006); Karen J. Bannan, "Online Chat Is a Grapevine That Yields Precious Fruit," *New York Times*, December 25, 2006.

34. Keith Barry, "Fiesta Stars in Night of the Living Social Media Campaign," *Wired*, May 21, 2010; Matthew Dolan, "Ford Takes Online Gamble with New Fiesta," *Wall Street Journal*, April 8, 2009.

35. "Mobile Marketing Facts 2014," *Advertising Age*, April 14, 2014.

36. "Mobile Continues to Steal Share of US Adults' Daily Time Spent with Media," *eMarketer*, April 22, 2014.

37. Sunil Gupta, "For Mobile Devices, Think Apps, Not Ads," *Harvard Business Review*, March 2013, pp. 71–75.

38. Peter DaSilva, "Cellphone in New Role: Loyalty Card," *New York Times*, May 31, 2010.

39. Diana Ransom, "When the Customer Is in the Neighborhood," *Wall Street Journal*, May 17, 2010.

40. Spencer E. Ante, "Online Ads Can Follow You Home," *Wall Street Journal*, April 29, 2013.

41. Piet Levy, "Set Your Sites on Mobile," *Marketing News*, April 30, 2010, p. 6; Tom Lowry, "Pandora: Unleashing Mobile-Phone Ads," *BusinessWeek*, June 1, 2009, pp. 52–53.

42. Christopher Heine, "Agencies and Cannes Judges Say Less Is More for Mobile," *Adweek*, June 17, 2013.

43. Elisabeth Sullivan, "The Tao of Mobile Marketing," *Marketing News*, April 30, 2010, pp. 16–20.

44. Loretta Chao, "Cell Phone Ads Are Easier Pitch in China Interactive Campaigns," *Wall Street Journal*, January 4, 2007.

Chapter 17

Managing Personal Communications: Direct and Database Marketing and Personal Selling

In this chapter, we will address the following questions:

1. How can companies conduct direct marketing for competitive advantage? (Page 262)
2. What are the advantages and disadvantages of database marketing? (Page 264)
3. What decisions do companies face in designing and managing a sales force? (Page 265)
4. How can salespeople improve their selling, negotiating, and relationship marketing skills? (Page 271)

Marketing Management at "Obama for President"

After database marketing proved a key to winning the presidential election in 2008, the Obama campaign team vowed to exploit it even more during his 2012 reelection campaign. By merging Democratic voter files with other information, as well as social media and mobile contacts, the team created one comprehensive database. Data analytics helped raise $1 billion and fine-tune the use of TV ads, phone calls, direct mail, door-to-door campaigning, and social media. Much of the $690 million raised online resulted from carefully targeted and tested e-mails. Every day, the campaign tested as many as 18 different versions of e-mails varying in subject line, amounts requested, and sender. The campaign also broke new ground with a Facebook campaign in which *people who downloaded an app were sent messages with pictures of their friends in swing states and asked to click a button to urge those targeted voters to register to vote or get to the polls. As a result of all these efforts, 1.25 million more 18- to 24-year-old voters supported President Obama in 2012 than in 2008.*[1]

Personalizing communications and saying and doing the right thing for the right person at the right time are critical for marketing effectiveness, as marketers for the Obama campaign recognized. In this chapter, we consider how organizations can personalize their marketing communications for more impact. We begin by evaluating direct and database marketing, then move on to consider personal selling and the sales force.

Direct Marketing

Direct marketing is the use of consumer-direct channels to reach and deliver goods and services to customers without using marketing middlemen. Direct marketers can use a number of channels to reach individual prospects and customers: direct mail, catalog marketing, telemarketing, interactive TV, kiosks, Web sites, and mobile devices. They often seek a measurable response, typically a customer order, through **direct-order marketing**. Direct marketing has been a fast-growing avenue, partly in response to the high and increasing costs of reaching business markets through a sales force. Direct marketing has been outpacing U.S. retail sales. It produced $2.05 trillion in sales in 2012, accounting for approximately 8.7 percent of GDP.[2]

The Benefits of Direct Marketing

Consumers short of time and tired of traffic and parking headaches appreciate toll-free phone numbers, always-open Web sites, next-day delivery, and direct marketers' commitment to customer service. In addition, many chain stores have dropped slower-moving specialty items, creating an opportunity for direct marketers to promote these to interested buyers instead. Direct marketers benefit as well: They can buy a list containing the names of almost any group (left-handed people, millionaires), customize and personalize messages to build customer relationships, reach interested prospects at the right moment, easily test alternative media and messages, and measure responses to determine profitability.

Direct Mail

Direct-mail marketing means sending an offer, announcement, reminder, or other item to an individual consumer. Using highly selective mailing lists, direct marketers send out millions of mail pieces each year—letters, fliers, foldouts, and other "salespeople with wings." Direct mail is popular because it permits target market selectivity, can be personalized, is flexible, and allows early testing and response measurement. Although the cost per thousand is higher than for mass media, the people reached are much better prospects.

In constructing an effective direct-mail campaign, direct marketers must choose their objectives, target markets and prospects, offer elements, means of testing the campaign, and measures of campaign success.

- **Objectives.** Marketers judge a campaign's success by the response rate. An order-response rate for letter-sized direct mail averages 3.4 percent to an internal company list and 1.3 percent to a general public list, depending on the product, price, and nature of the offering. This is much higher than e-mails' average response rates of 0.12 percent and 0.03 percent, respectively.[3] Other objectives may include generating leads, strengthening customer relationships, informing and educating customers, reminding customers of offers, and reinforcing purchase decisions.

- **Target markets and prospects.** Direct marketers apply the RFM (*recency, frequency, monetary amount*) formula to select customers according to how much time has passed since their last purchase, how many times they have purchased, and how much they have spent since becoming a customer.[4] Marketers also identify prospects on the basis of age, sex, income, education, previous mail-order purchases, and occasion. In B-to-B direct marketing, the prospect is often a group or committee of decision makers and decision influencers.

- **Offer elements.** The offer strategy has five elements—the *product,* the *offer,* the *medium,* the *distribution method,* and the *creative strategy.*[5] The direct-mail marketer also must choose five components of the mailing itself: the outside envelope, sales letter, circular, reply form, and reply envelope. Often, direct mail is followed up by e-mail.

- **Testing elements.** One of the great advantages of direct marketing is the ability to test, under real marketplace conditions, different elements of an offer strategy, such as products, product features, copy platform, mailer type, envelope, prices, or mailing lists. Response rates typically understate a campaign's long-term impact. To better estimate a promotion's impact, some companies measure the impact of direct marketing on awareness, intention to buy, and word of mouth.

- **Measuring success: lifetime value.** By adding up the planned campaign costs, the direct marketer can determine the needed break-even response rate (net of returns and bad debts). A specific campaign may fail to break even in the short run but can still be profitable in the long run if customer lifetime value is factored in.

Catalog Marketing

In catalog marketing, companies may send full-line merchandise catalogs, specialty consumer catalogs, and business catalogs, usually in print form but also as DVDs or online. Catalogs are a huge business—the Internet and catalog retailing industry includes 20,000 companies with combined annual revenue of $350 billion.[6]

Successful catalog marketing depends on managing customer lists carefully to avoid duplication or bad debts, controlling inventory, offering good-quality merchandise so returns are low, and projecting a distinctive image. Some companies add literary or information features, send swatches of materials, operate a special online or telephone hotline to answer questions, send gifts to their best customers, and donate a percentage of profits to good causes. Putting their entire catalog online also provides business marketers with better access to global consumers, saving printing and mailing costs.

Telemarketing

Telemarketing is the use of the telephone and call centers to attract prospects, sell to existing customers, and provide service by taking orders and answering questions. Companies use call centers for *inbound telemarketing*—receiving calls from customers—and *outbound telemarketing*—initiating calls to prospects and customers. Since the establishment of the National Do Not Call Registry in 2003, consumer telemarketing has lost much of its effectiveness, although business-to-business telemarketing is increasing.

Other Media for Direct-Response Marketing

Direct marketers use all the major media. Newspapers and magazines carry ads offering books, clothing, appliances, vacations, and other goods and services that individuals can order via toll-free numbers. Radio ads present offers 24 hours a day. Some companies prepare 30- and 60-minute *infomercials* to combine the selling power of television commercials with the draw of information and entertainment. Infomercials promote products that are complicated or technologically advanced or that require a great deal of explanation. At-home shopping channels are dedicated to selling goods and services through a toll-free number or via the Internet for speedy delivery.

Customer Databases and Database Marketing

Some observers believe a proprietary *customer database* can provide a company with a significant competitive advantage.[7] In general, companies can use their databases in five ways for direct marketing:

1. *To identify prospects*—Many companies generate sales leads by advertising their product or service and including a response feature, such as a link to a home page, a business reply card, or a toll-free phone number, and building a database from customer responses. The company sorts through the database to identify the best prospects, then contacts them by mail, e-mail, or phone to try to convert them into customers.

2. *To decide which customers should receive a particular offer*—Companies interested in selling, up-selling, and cross-selling set up criteria describing the ideal target customer for a particular offer. Then they search their customer databases for those who most closely resemble the ideal. By noting response rates, a company can improve its targeting precision.

3. *To deepen customer loyalty*—Companies can build interest and enthusiasm by remembering customer preferences and sending appropriate gifts, discount coupons, and interesting reading material.

4. *To reactivate customer purchases*—Automatic mailing programs (automatic marketing) can send out birthday or anniversary cards, holiday shopping reminders, or off-season promotions.

5. *To avoid serious customer mistakes*—Capturing all transactions and communications in a customer database can save companies from mistakes such as making conflicting offers to one customer and not providing proper service to good customers.

On the other hand, five main problems can prevent a firm from effectively using database marketing.

1. *Some situations are just not conducive to database marketing.* Building a customer database may not be worthwhile when: (1) the product is a once-in-a-lifetime purchase (a grand piano); (2) customers show little loyalty to a brand (there is a lot of customer churn); (3) the unit sale is very small (a candy bar) so customer lifetime value is low; (4) the cost of gathering information is too high; and (5) there is no direct contact between the seller and ultimate buyer.

2. *Building and maintaining a customer database require a large investment.* Computer hardware, database software, analytical programs, communication links, and skilled staff can be costly. It's difficult to collect the right data, especially to capture all the occasions of company interaction with individual customers.

3. *Employees may resist becoming customer-oriented and using the available information.* Employees find it far easier to carry on traditional transaction marketing than to practice CRM. Effective database marketing requires managing and training employees as well as dealers and suppliers.

4. *Not all customers want a relationship with the company.* Some may resent knowing the company has collected that much personal information about them. Online companies should explain their privacy policies and give consumers the right not to have their information stored. European countries do not look favorably on database marketing and are protective of

consumers' private information. The European Union passed a law handicapping the growth of database marketing in its 27 member countries.

5. *The assumptions behind CRM may not always hold true.*[8] High-volume customers often know their value to a company and can leverage it to extract premium service and/or price discounts, so it may not cost the firm less to serve them. Loyal customers may also be jealous of attention lavished on other customers and may not necessarily be the best ambassadors for the brand.

Public and Ethical Issues in Direct Marketing

Direct marketers and their customers usually enjoy mutually rewarding relationships. Occasionally, however, a darker side emerges. Many people don't like hard-sell direct marketing solicitations or unwanted junk mail. Some direct marketers take advantage of impulsive or less sophisticated buyers, prey on the vulnerable, or design mailers and copy to mislead. Critics worry that marketers may know too much about consumers' lives and they may take unfair advantage.[9] However, most direct marketers want what consumers want: honest and well-designed marketing offers targeted only to those who appreciate receiving them.

Personal Selling and the Sales Force

The original and oldest form of direct marketing is the field sales call. To locate prospects, develop them into customers, and grow the business, most industrial companies rely heavily on a professional sales force or hire manufacturers' representatives and agents. Many consumer companies such as Allstate and Mary Kay use a direct-selling force. In asserting that selling is the core function of every company, Boston Beer founder Jim Koch notes, "Without sales, there is no business to manage."[10] Not surprisingly, companies are trying to increase sales force productivity through better selection, training, supervision, motivation, and compensation.[11]

Selling increasingly calls for teamwork and the support of others, such as top management, especially when national accounts or major sales are at stake; technical people, who supply information and service before, during, and after product purchase; customer service representatives, who provide installation, maintenance, and other services; and office staff, consisting of sales analysts, order expediters, and assistants.[12]

Types of Sales Representatives

The term *sales representative* covers six positions, ranging from the least to the most creative types of selling:[13]

1. *Deliverer*—A salesperson whose major task is the delivery of a product (water, fuel).
2. *Order taker*—An inside order taker (standing behind the counter) or outside order taker (calling on store managers).
3. *Missionary*—A salesperson not permitted to take an order but expected rather to build goodwill or educate the actual or potential user (the medical "detailer" representing a pharmaceutical firm).
4. *Technician*—A salesperson with a high level of technical knowledge (the engineering salesperson who is primarily a consultant to client companies).
5. *Demand creator*—A salesperson who relies on creative methods for selling tangible products (vacuum cleaners) or intangibles (advertising services).
6. *Solution vendor*—A salesperson whose expertise is solving a customer's problem, often with a system of the company's products and services (for example, communications systems).

Personal Selling and Relationship Marketing

Companies now spend millions of dollars each year to train sales reps in methods of analysis and customer management and to transform them from passive order takers into active order getters. The six major steps in any effective sales process are shown in Table 17.1.[14] Note that application of these selling practices can vary in different parts of the world. Pfizer has to sell very differently in Latin America than in North America.[15]

The principles of personal selling and negotiation are largely transaction-oriented because their purpose is to close a specific sale. But in many cases the company seeks not an immediate sale but rather a long-term supplier–customer relationship. Today's customers prefer suppliers who can sell and deliver a coordinated set of products and services to many locations, who can quickly solve problems in different locations, and who can work closely with customer teams to improve products and processes.[16]

Salespeople working with key customers must do more than call only when they think customers might be ready to place orders. They should call or visit at other times and make useful suggestions about the business to create value. They should monitor key accounts, know customers' problems, and be ready to serve them in a number of ways, adapting and responding to different customer needs or situations.[17] Relationship marketing is not effective in all situations. But when it is the right strategy and is properly implemented, the organization will focus as much on managing its customers as on managing its products.

TABLE 17.1	Six Major Steps In Effective Selling
Sales Step	**Application in Industrial Selling**
Prospecting and qualifying	Firms generate leads and qualify them by mail or phone to assess their level of interest and financial capacity. The purpose is to allow salespeople to use their expensive time doing what they do best: selling.
Preapproach	The sales rep researches what the prospect needs, how the buying process operates, who is involved in buying, and buyers' personal characteristics and buying styles. The rep also sets call objectives to qualify the prospect, gather information, or make an immediate sale; decides on the best contact approach—a personal visit, phone call, e-mail, or letter; plans the timing of the approach; and sets overall sales strategy for the account.
Presentation and demonstration	The salesperson tells the product "story" to the buyer, using a features, advantages, benefits, and value approach. Reps should be engaging and avoid spending too much time on features and not enough on benefits and value.
Overcoming objections	Salespeople must handle objections raised by buyers by maintaining a positive approach, asking buyers to clarify the objections, asking questions in such a way that buyers answer their own objections, denying the validity of the objection, or turning it into a reason for buying.
Closing	Reps can ask for the order, recapitulate points of agreement, offer to write up the order, ask whether the buyer wants A or B, get the buyer to make minor choices such as color or size, or indicate what the buyer will lose by not ordering now. The rep might offer specific inducements to close, such as an additional service.
Follow-up and maintenance	To ensure customer satisfaction and repeat business, the rep salesperson should confirm details about delivery, purchase terms, and other matters important to the customer. Also, the rep should schedule a follow-up call to ensure proper installation, instruction, and servicing and to detect any problems, assure the buyer of his or her interest, and reduce any cognitive dissonance. Each account needs a maintenance and growth plan as well.

Designing the Sales Force

Salespeople are the company's personal link to its customers. In designing a sales force, the company must develop sales force objectives, strategy, structure, size, and compensation (see Figure 17.1).

Sales Force Objectives and Strategy   Sales reps need to know how to diagnose a customer's problem and propose a solution that can help improve the customer's profitability. The best

FIGURE 17.1 Designing a Sales Force

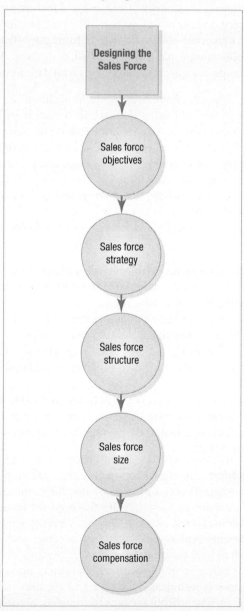

salespeople go beyond the customer's stated problems to offer fresh insights into the customer's business and identify unrecognized needs and unstated problems.[18] In performing their jobs, salespeople will complete one or more specific tasks, including prospecting, targeting, communicating about products and services, selling to prospects and customers, servicing customers, information gathering for marketing research, and allocating products when supplies are scarce.

To manage costs, most companies are choosing a *leveraged sales force* that focuses reps on selling the company's more complex and customized products to large accounts and uses inside salespeople and online ordering for low-end selling. To maintain a market focus, salespeople should know how to analyze sales data, measure market potential, gather market intelligence, and develop marketing strategies and plans.

Once the company chooses its strategy, it can use a direct or a contractual sales force. A **direct (company) sales force** consists of full- or part-time paid employees who work exclusively for the company. Inside salespeople conduct business from the office and receive visits from prospective buyers, and field salespeople travel and visit customers. A **contractual sales force** consists of manufacturers' reps, sales agents, and brokers who earn a commission based on sales.

Sales Force Structure   The sales force strategy has implications for its structure. A company that sells one product line to one end-using industry with customers in many locations would use a territorial structure. A company that sells many products to many types of customers might need a product or market structure. Some companies need a more complex structure and adopt some combination of four types of sales force: (1) a strategic market sales force assigned to major accounts (see below); (2) a geographic sales force for customers in different territories; (3) a distributor sales force calling on and coaching distributors; and (4) an inside sales force marketing and taking orders online and via phone.

"Marketing Insight: Major Account Management" discusses a specialized form of sales force structure.

Sales Force Size   Once the company establishes the number of customers it wants to reach, it can use a *workload approach* to establish sales force size, following five steps: (1) group customers into size classes according to annual sales volume; (2) establish call frequencies (number of calls on an account per year); (3) multiply the number of accounts in each size class by the call frequency to arrive at the total workload, in sales calls per year; (4) determine the average number of calls a sales representative can make per year; (5) divide the total annual calls (calculated in step 3) by the average annual calls made by a sales rep (calculated in step 4) to arrive at the number of sales reps needed.

Suppose the company estimates it has 1,000 A accounts and 2,000 B accounts. A accounts require 36 calls a year, and B accounts require 12, so the company needs a sales force that can make 60,000 sales calls (36,000 + 24,000) a year. If the average full-time rep can make 1,000 calls a year, the company needs 60 reps.

Sales Force Compensation   To attract top-quality reps, the company must develop an attractive compensation package. The company must quantify four components of sales force compensation. The *fixed amount,* a salary, satisfies the need for income stability. The *variable amount,* whether commissions, bonus, or profit sharing, serves to stimulate and reward effort.[19] *Expense allowances* enable sales reps to meet the costs of travel and entertaining on the company's behalf. *Benefits,* such as paid vacations, provide security and job satisfaction.

Fixed compensation is common in jobs with a high ratio of nonselling to selling duties and in jobs where the selling task is technically complex and requires teamwork. Such compensation plans provide a secure income, encourage reps to complete nonselling activities, and reduce

marketing insight

Major Account Management

Marketers typically single out for attention major accounts (also called key accounts, national accounts, global accounts, or house accounts). These are important customers with multiple divisions in many locations that use uniform pricing and coordinated service for all divisions. The typical salesperson alone might not have the skill, authority, or coverage to sell effectively to such large buyers. A major account manager (MAM) usually reports to the national sales manager and supervises field reps calling on customer plants within their territories. MAMs act as the single point of contact, develop and grow customer business, understand customer decision processes, identify added-value opportunities, provide competitive intelligence, negotiate sales, and orchestrate customer service.

Procter & Gamble has a strategic account management team of 300 staffers to work with Walmart in its Bentonville, Arkansas, headquarters, with more stationed at Walmart headquarters in Europe, Asia, and Latin America. Many major accounts look for added value more than a price advantage. They appreciate having a single point of dedicated contact, single billing, special warranties, electronic links, priority shipping, early information releases, customized products, and efficient maintenance, repair, and upgraded service.

Sources: Noel Capon, Dave Potter, and Fred Schindler, *Managing Global Accounts: Nine Critical Factors for a World-Class Program*, 2nd ed. (Bronxville, NY: Wessex Press, 2008); Peter Cheverton, *Global Account Management: A Complete Action Kit of Tools and Techniques for Managing Key Global Customers* (London, UK: Kogan Page, 2008); Malcolm McDonald and Diana Woodburn, *Key Account Management: The Definitive Guide*, 2nd ed. (Oxford, UK: Butterworth-Heinemann, 2007); Jack Neff, "Bentonville or Bust," *Advertising Age*, February 24, 2003. More information can be obtained from SAMA (Strategic Account Management Association) and the *Journal of Selling and Major Account Management*.

incentive to overstock customers. For the firm, these plans deliver administrative simplicity and lower turnover. Variable compensation works best where sales are cyclical or depend on individual initiative. These plans attract higher performers, provide more motivation, require less supervision, and control selling costs, although they emphasize getting the sale over building the relationship.

Plans that combine fixed and variable pay link the variable portion to a wide variety of strategic goals. One current trend deemphasizes sales volume in favor of gross profitability, customer satisfaction, and customer retention. Other companies reward reps partly on sales team or even company-wide performance, motivating them to work together for the common good.

Managing the Sales Force

Various policies and procedures guide the firm in recruiting, selecting, training, supervising, motivating, and evaluating sales representatives to manage its sales force (see Figure 17.2).

Recruiting and Selecting Representatives

At the heart of any successful sales force are appropriately selected representatives. It's a great waste to hire the wrong people. The average annual turnover rate of sales reps for all industries is almost 20 percent. Sales force turnover leads to lost sales, the expense of finding and training replacements, and often pressure on existing salespeople to pick up the slack.[20]

FIGURE 17.2 Managing the Sales Force

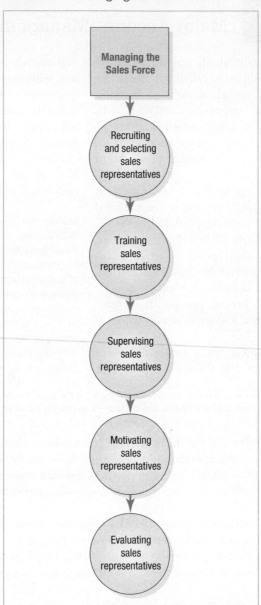

Studies have not always shown a strong relationship between sales performance on one hand and background and experience variables, current status, lifestyle, attitude, personality, and skills on the other. More effective predictors of high performance in sales are composite tests and assessment centers that simulate the working environment and assess applicants in an environment similar to the one in which they would work.[21] Although scores from formal tests are only one element in a set that includes personal characteristics, references, past employment history, and interviewer reactions, they have been weighted quite heavily by companies such as IBM.

Training and Supervising Sales Representatives

Today's customers expect salespeople to have deep product knowledge, add ideas to improve operations, and be efficient and reliable. These demands have required companies to make a much greater investment in sales training. New reps may spend a few weeks to several months in training. The median training period is 28 weeks in industrial-products companies, 12 in service companies, and 4 in consumer-products companies. Training time varies with the complexity of the selling task and the type of recruit.

Sales Rep Productivity

How many calls should a company make on a particular account each year? Some research suggests today's sales reps spend too much time selling to smaller, less profitable accounts instead of focusing on larger, more profitable ones.[22] Companies therefore often specify how much time reps should spend prospecting for new accounts.[23] Some companies rely on a missionary sales force to create new interest and open new accounts.

The best sales reps manage their time efficiently. *Time-and-duty analysis* and hour-by-hour breakdowns of activities help them understand how they spend their time and how they might increase their productivity. To cut costs, reduce time demands on their outside sales force, and leverage technological innovations, many firms have increased the size and responsibilities of their inside sales force. The inside sales force frees outside reps to spend more time selling to major accounts, identifying and converting new major prospects, and obtaining more blanket orders and systems contracts.

Inside selling is less expensive and growing faster than in-person selling. Each contact made by an inside salesperson might cost a company $25 to $30 compared with $300 to $500 for a field staff person with travel expenses. Virtual meeting software such as WebEx, communication tools such as Skype, and social media sites make it easier to sell with few if any face-to-face meetings. And inside sellers don't even need to be in the office—a growing percentage work at home.[24]

Today's salesperson has truly gone electronic. Not only is sales and inventory information transferred much more quickly, but specific computer-based decision support systems have been created for sales managers and sales representatives. Going online with a tablet or laptop, salespeople can prime themselves on backgrounds of clients, call up prewritten sales letters, transmit orders and resolve customer-service issues on the spot, and send samples, pamphlets, brochures, and other materials to clients. Social networking is useful in "front end" prospecting and lead qualification as well as in "back end" relationship building and management.

Motivating Sales Representatives

The majority of sales representatives require encouragement and special incentives, especially those in the field who encounter daily challenges.[25] Most marketers believe that the higher the salesperson's motivation, the greater the effort and the resulting performance, rewards, and satisfaction—all of which in turn further increase motivation. One research study found the employee reward with the highest value was pay, followed by promotion, personal growth, and sense of accomplishment.[26] Least valued were liking and respect, security, and recognition. In other words, salespeople are highly motivated by pay and the chance to get ahead and satisfy their intrinsic needs, and they may be less motivated by compliments and security.

Many companies set annual sales quotas, based on the annual marketing plan, for dollar sales, unit volume, margin, selling effort or activity, or product type. Compensation is often tied to quota fulfillment, yet setting sales quotas can create problems. If the company underestimates and the sales reps easily achieve their quotas, it has overpaid them. If it overestimates sales potential, the salespeople will find it very hard to reach their quotas and be frustrated or quit. Another downside is that quotas can drive reps to get as much business as possible—often ignoring the service side of the business. The company gains short-term results at the cost of long-term customer satisfaction. For these reasons, some companies are dropping quotas.

Evaluating Sales Representatives

We have been describing the *feed-forward* aspects of sales supervision—how management communicates what the sales reps should be doing and motivates them to do it. But good feed-forward requires good *feedback,* which means getting regular information about reps to evaluate their performance. Information about reps can come from sales reports and salesperson self-reports, personal observation, customer comments, customer surveys, and conversations with other reps.

Many firms require representatives to develop an annual territory-marketing plan in which they outline their program for developing new accounts and increasing business from existing accounts. Sales reps write up completed activities on *call reports.* They also submit expense reports, new-business reports, lost-business reports, and reports on local business and economic conditions. These reports provide raw data from which sales managers can extract key indicators of sales performance: (1) average number of sales calls per salesperson per day, (2) average sales call time per contact, (3) average revenue per sales call, (4) average cost per sales call, (5) entertainment cost per sales call, (6) percentage of orders per hundred sales calls, (7) number of new customers per period, (8) number of lost customers per period, and (9) sales force cost as a percentage of total sales.

Even if effective in producing sales, the rep may not rate highly with customers. Success may come because competitors' salespeople are inferior, the rep's product is better, or new customers are always found to replace those who dislike the rep. Sales performance could be related to internal factors (effort, ability, and strategy) and/or external factors (task and luck).[27]

Executive Summary

Direct marketing is an interactive marketing system that uses one or more media to effect a measurable response or transaction at any location. Direct marketers plan campaigns by deciding on objectives, target markets and prospects, offers, and prices. Next, they test and establish measures to determine campaign success. Major channels for direct marketing include face-to-face selling, direct mail, catalog marketing, telemarketing, interactive TV, kiosks, Web sites, and mobile devices. Companies often build a customer database to help with identifying prospects, deciding which customers receive which offers, deepening customer loyalty, reactivating customer buying, and avoiding customer mistakes. However, not all situations are conducive to this database marketing; building a database is expensive and difficult; employees may resist using the database; not all customers want a relationship with the firm; and assumptions behind relationship management may not always hold true.

Designing the sales force requires choosing objectives, strategy, structure, size, and compensation. The five steps in managing the sales force are: (1) recruiting and selecting sales representatives; (2) training the representatives in sales techniques and in the company's products, policies, and customer-satisfaction orientation; (3) supervising the sales force and helping reps to use their time efficiently; (4) motivating the sales force and balancing quotas, monetary rewards, and supplementary motivators; and (5) evaluating individual and group sales performance. Personal selling entails six steps: prospecting and qualifying customers, preapproach, presentation and demonstration, overcoming objections, closing, and follow-up and maintenance.

Notes

1. Joshua Green, "The Science behind Those Obama Campaign E-Mails," *Bloomberg Businessweek*, November 29, 2012; Michael Scherer, "Inside the Secret World of the Data Crunchers Who Helped Obama Win," *Time*, November 7, 2012; David Jackson, "How Obama Won Re-Election," *USA Today*, November 9, 2012; Joshua Green, "Corporations Want Obama's Winning Formula," *Bloomberg Businessweek*, November 26, 2012, pp. 37–39.

2. Ira Kalb, "How to Do Direct Marketing That's Not Annoying," *Business Insider*, November 12, 2013.

3. Allison Schiff, "DMA: Direct Response Rates Beat Digital," *Direct Marketing News*, June 14, 2012.

4. For an intriguing variation based on the timing involved with RFM, see Y. Zhang, Eric T. Bradlow, and Dylan S. Small, "Capturing Clumpiness when Valuing Customers: From RFM to RFMC," working paper, 2014, Wharton School of Business.

5. Edward L. Nash, *Direct Marketing: Strategy, Planning, Execution*, 4th ed. (New York: McGraw-Hill, 2000).

6. "Internet & Mail-Order Retail Industry Profile," www.firstresearch.com, March 3, 2014.

7. Christopher R. Stephens and R. Sukumar, "An Introduction to Data Mining," Rajiv Grover and Marco Vriens, eds., *Handbook of Marketing Research* (Thousand Oaks, CA: Sage Publications, 2006), pp. 455–86; Pang-Ning Tan, Michael Steinbach, and Vipin Kumar, *Introduction to Data Mining* (Upper Saddle River, NJ: Addison Wesley, 2005); Michael J. A. Berry and Gordon S. Linoff, *Data Mining Techniques: For Marketing, Sales, and Customer Relationship Management*, 2nd ed. (Hoboken, NJ: Wiley Computer, 2004); James Lattin, Doug Carroll, and Paul Green, *Analyzing Multivariate Data* (Florence, KY: Thomson Brooks/Cole, 2003).

8. Werner Reinartz and V. Kumar, "The Mismanagement of Customer Loyalty," *Harvard Business Review*, July 2002, pp. 86–94; Susan M. Fournier, Susan Dobscha, and David Glen Mick, "Preventing the Premature Death of Relationship Marketing," *Harvard Business Review*, January–February 1998, pp. 42–51.

9. Steve Kroft, "The Data Brokers: Selling Your Personal Information," www.cbsnews.com, March 9, 2014.

10. "The View from the Field," *Harvard Business Review*, July–August 2012, pp. 101–9.

11. Shrihari Sridhar, Murali K. Mantrala, and Sönke Albers, "Personal Selling Elasticities: A Meta-Analysis," *Journal of Marketing Research* 47 (October 2010).

12. Michael Ahearne, Scott B. MacKenzie, Philip M. Podsakoff, John E. Mathieu, and Son K. Lam, "The Role of Consensus in Sales Team Performance," *Journal of Marketing Research* 47 (June 2010), pp. 458–69.

13. Adapted from Robert N. McMurry, "The Mystique of Super-Salesmanship," *Harvard Business Review*, March–April 1961, p. 114. Also see William C. Moncrief III, "Selling Activity and Sales Position Taxonomies for Industrial Sales Forces," *Journal of Marketing Research* 23 (August 1986), pp. 261–70.

14. Some of the following discussion is based on a classic analysis in W. J. E. Crissy, William H. Cunningham, and Isabella C. M. Cunningham, *Selling: The Personal Force in Marketing* (New York: Wiley, 1977), pp. 119–29. For some contemporary perspective and tips, see Jia Lynn Yang, "How to Sell in a Lousy Economy," *Fortune*, September 29, 2008, pp. 101–6; and Jessi Hempel, "IBM's All-Star Salesman," *Fortune*, September 29, 2008, pp. 110–19.

15. "The View from the Field," *Harvard Business Review*, July August 2012, pp. 101–9.

16. Brent Adamson, Matthew Dixon, and Nicholas Toman, "Dismantling the Sales Machine," *Harvard Business Review*, November 2013, pp. 103–9.

17. V. Kumar, Rajkumar Venkatesan, and Werner Reinartz, "Performance Implications of Adopting a Customer-Focused Sales Campaign," *Journal of Marketing* 72 (September 2008), pp. 50–68; George R. Franke and Jeong Eun Park, "Salesperson Adaptive Selling Behavior and Customer Orientation," *Journal of Marketing Research* 43 (November 2006), pp. 693–702; Richard G. McFarland, Goutam N. Challagalla, and Tasadduq A. Shervani, "Influence Tactics for Effective Adaptive Selling," *Journal of Marketing* 70 (October 2006), pp. 103–17.

18. Brent Adamson, Matthew Dixon, and Nicholas Toman, "The End of Solution Sales," *Harvard Business Review*, July–August 2012, pp. 60–68.

19. For distinctions between bonuses and commissions, see Sunil Kishore, Raghunath Singh Rao, Om Narasimhan, and George John, "Bonuses versus Commissions: A Field Study," *Journal of Marketing Research* 50 (June 2013), pp. 317–33.

20. Tony Ritigliano and Benson Smith, *Discover Your Sales Strengths* (New York: Random House Business Books, 2004).

21. Sonke Albers, "Sales-Force Management—Compensation, Motivation, Selection, and Training," Bart Weitz and Robin Wensley, eds., *Handbook of Marketing* (London: Sage, 2002), pp. 248–66.

22. Michael R. W. Bommer, Brian F. O'Neil, and Beheruz N. Sethna, "A Methodology for Optimizing Selling

Time of Salespersons," *Journal of Marketing Theory and Practice* (Spring 1994), pp. 61–75. See also Lissan Joseph, "On the Optimality of Delegating Pricing Authority to the Sales Force," *Journal of Marketing* 65 (January 2001), pp. 62–70.

23. Gaurav Sabnis, Sharmila C. Chatterjee, Rajdeep Grewal, and Gary L. Lilien, "The Sales Lead Black Hole: On Sales Reps' Follow-up of Marketing Leads," *Journal of Marketing* 77 (January 2013), pp. 52–67.

24. Jeff Green, "The New Willy Loman Survives by Staying Home," *Bloomberg Businessweek*, January 14, 2013, pp. 16–17.

25. Willem Verbeke and Richard P. Bagozzi, "Sales-Call Anxiety: Exploring What It Means When Fear Rules a Sales Encounter," *Journal of Marketing* 64 (July 2000), pp. 88–101. See also Douglas E. Hughes and Michael Ahearne, "Energizing the Reseller's Sales Force: The Power of Brand Identification," *Journal of Marketing* 74 (July 2010), pp. 81–96; Jeffrey P. Boichuk, Willy

Bolander, Zachary R. Hall, Michael Ahearne, William J. Zahn, and Melissa Nieves, "Learned Helplessness among Newly Hired Salespeople and the Influence of Leadership," *Journal of Marketing* 78 (January 2014), pp. 95–111.

26. Gilbert A. Churchill Jr., Neil M. Ford, Orville C. Walker Jr., Mark W. Johnston, and Greg W. Marshall, *Sales-Force Management*, 9th ed. (New York: McGraw-Hill/Irwin, 2009). See also Eric G. Harris, John C. Mowen, and Tom J. Brown, "Reexamining Salesperson Goal Orientations," *Journal of the Academy of Marketing Science* 33 (Winter 2005), pp. 19–35.

27. Andrea L. Dixon, Rosann L. Spiro, and Magbul Jamil, "Successful and Unsuccessful Sales Calls: Measuring Salesperson Attributions and Behavioral Intentions," *Journal of Marketing* 65 (July 2001), pp. 64–78; Verbeke and Bagozzi, "Sales-Call Anxiety: Exploring What It Means When Fear Rules a Sales Encounter," pp. 88–101.

Chapter 18

Managing Marketing Responsibly in the Global Economy

In this chapter, we will address the following questions:

1. What factors should a company review before deciding to enter global markets? (Page 276)
2. What are the major ways of entering foreign markets? (Page 278)
3. To what extent must the company adapt its marketing to each foreign market? (Page 279)
4. What are the keys to effective internal marketing? (Page 282)
5. How can companies be socially responsible marketers? (Page 283)

Marketing Management at Patagonia

Patagonia, maker of high-end outdoor clothing and equipment, has always put environmental issues at the core of what it does. Company founder Yvon Chouinard actively promotes a post-consumerist economy in which goods are "high quality, recyclable, and repairable." Under Chouinard's leadership, Patagonia ran a full-page ad in the New York Times headlined "Don't Buy This Jacket." Below a photo of the retailer's R2 jacket was text explaining that despite its many positive features, the jacket still imposed many environmental costs (using 135 liters of water and 20 pounds of carbon dioxide to manufacture). The ad concluded by promoting the Common Threads Initiative asking consumers to engage in five behaviors: (1) reduce (what you buy); (2) repair (what you can); (3) reuse (what you have); (4) recycle (everything else); and (5) reimagine (a sustainable world). With $400 million in worldwide annual sales, Patagonia is always trying to find better environmental solutions for everything it does and makes.[1]

Healthy long-term growth for a brand requires holistic marketers to engage in a host of carefully planned, interconnected marketing activities and satisfy a broad set of constituents and objectives, especially if they seek growth outside domestic markets. In this chapter, we consider how firms expand into global markets, how they use internal marketing, and how they address social responsibility, sustainability, and ethics.

Competing On a Global Basis

Many companies have been global marketers for decades—firms like Shell and Toshiba. But global competition is intensifying in more product categories as new firms make their mark on the international stage. In a **global industry**, competitors' strategic positions in major geographic or national markets are affected by their overall global positions.[2] A **global firm** operates in more than one country and captures R&D, production, logistical, marketing, and financial advantages not available to purely domestic competitors.

To sell overseas, many successful global U.S. brands have tapped into universal consumer values and needs—such as Nike with athletic performance. Global marketing extends beyond products. Services represent the fastest-growing sector of the global economy and account for two-thirds of global output, one-third of global employment, and nearly 20 percent of global trade. For a company of any size or type to go global, it must make a series of decisions (see Figure 18.1).

FIGURE 18.1 Major Decisions in International Marketing

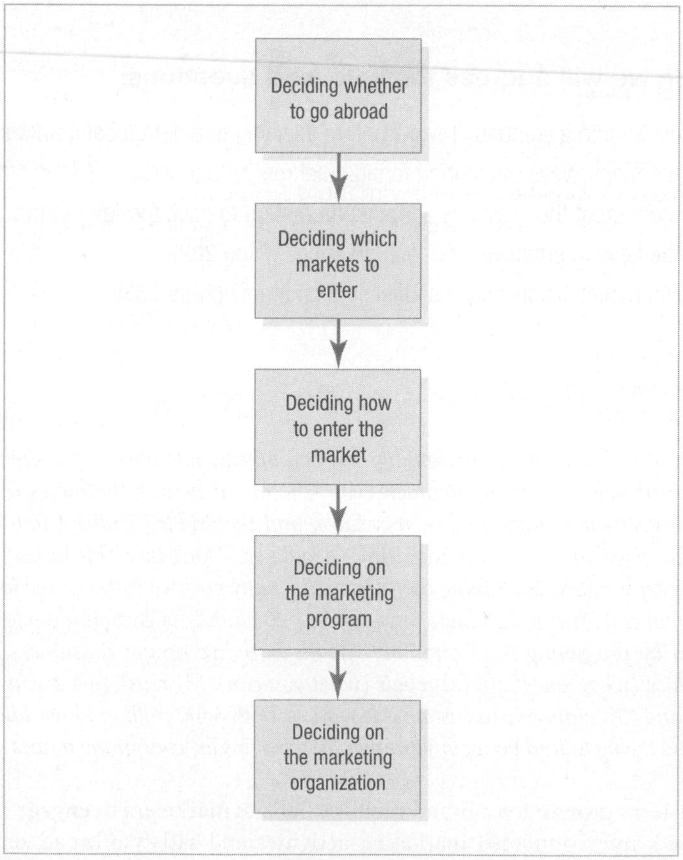

Deciding Whether to Go Abroad

Several factors can draw companies into the international arena. Some international markets present better profit opportunities than the domestic market. A firm may need a larger customer base to achieve economies of scale or want to reduce its dependence on any one market. Sometimes a firm decides to counterattack global competitors in their home markets, or it sees its customers going abroad and requiring international service.

Before making a decision to go abroad, the company must also weigh several risks. First, the company might not understand foreign preferences and could fail to offer a competitively attractive product. Second, it might not understand the foreign country's business culture or how to deal effectively with foreign regulations. Third, it might lack managers with international experience. Finally, the other country might change its commercial laws, devalue its currency, or undergo a political revolution and expropriate foreign property.

Deciding Which Markets to Enter

In deciding to go abroad, the company needs to define its marketing objectives and policies. What proportion of international to total sales will it seek? Most companies start small when they venture abroad. Some plan to stay small; others have bigger plans. Typical entry strategies are the *waterfall* approach, gradually entering countries in sequence, and the *sprinkler* approach, entering many countries simultaneously. Increasingly, firms—especially technology-intensive firms or online ventures—are *born global* and market to the entire world from the outset.

The company must also choose the countries to enter based on the product and on factors such as geography, income, population, and political climate. Competitive considerations come into play too. It may make sense to go into markets where competitors have already entered to force them to defend their market share as well as to learn from them how they are marketing in that environment. Getting a toehold in a fast-growing market can be a very attractive option even if that market is likely to soon be crowded with more competitors.[3]

Many companies prefer to sell to neighboring countries because they understand them better and can control their entry costs more effectively. Also, given more familiar language, laws, and culture, many U.S. firms prefer to sell in Canada, England, and Australia rather than in larger markets such as Germany and France. Companies should be careful, however, in choosing markets according to cultural distance. Besides overlooking potentially better markets, they may only superficially analyze real differences that put them at a disadvantage.[4]

In general, a company prefers to enter countries that have high market attractiveness and low market risk and in which it possesses a competitive advantage. Also, regional economic integration—the creation of trading agreements between blocs of countries—has intensified in recent years. This means companies are more likely to enter entire regions at the same time.

Deciding How to Enter the Market

The broad choices in entering a market are *indirect exporting, direct exporting, licensing, joint ventures,* and *direct investment,* shown in Figure 18.2. Each succeeding strategy entails more commitment, risk, control, and profit potential.

- **Indirect and direct export.** Companies typically start with indirect export, working through independent intermediaries, and may move into direct export later because this order of entry requires less investment and less risk. Many companies use direct or indirect exporting to "test the waters" before building a plant overseas. Successful companies adapt their Web

FIGURE 18.2 Five Modes of Entry into Foreign Markets

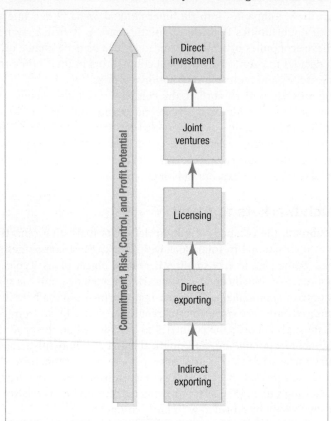

sites to provide country-specific content and services to their highest-potential international markets, ideally in the local language.

- **Licensing.** The licensor issues a license to a foreign company to use a manufacturing process, trademark, patent, trade secret, or other item of value for a fee or royalty. The licensor gains entry at little risk; the licensee gains production expertise or a well-known product or brand name. The licensor, however, has less control over the licensee than over its own production and sales facilities. If the licensee is very successful, the firm has given up profits, and if and when the contract ends, it might find it has created a competitor.

- **Joint ventures.** Foreign investors may join local investors in a **joint venture** company in which they share ownership and control, sometimes desirable for political or economic reasons. However, the partners might disagree over investment, marketing, or other policies. One might want to reinvest earnings for growth, the other to declare more dividends. Joint ownership can also prevent a multinational company from carrying out specific manufacturing and marketing policies on a worldwide basis.

- **Direct investment.** The ultimate form of foreign involvement is direct ownership: The foreign company can buy part or full interest in a local company or build its own manufacturing or service facilities. One advantage is that the firm secures cost economies through cheaper labor or raw materials, government incentives, and freight savings. Also, the firm strengthens its image in the host country because it creates jobs. In addition, it deepens its relationship with the government, customers, local suppliers, and distributors. Another advantage is retaining full control over its investment, with the ability to develop manufacturing and marketing policies that serve its long-term international objectives. Finally, the firm ensures its access to the market in case the host country insists that locally purchased goods must have domestic content. The main disadvantage is exposure to risks like blocked or devalued currencies, worsening markets, or expropriation. Note that, rather than bringing their brands into certain countries, many companies choose to acquire local brands for their brand portfolio.

Deciding on the Marketing Program

Companies must decide how much to adapt their marketing strategy to local conditions.[5] At one extreme is a *standardized marketing program* worldwide, which promises the lowest costs; Table 18.1 summarizes some pros and cons. At the other extreme is an *adapted marketing program* in which the company, consistent with the marketing concept, believes consumer needs vary and tailors marketing to each target group.

Most products require at least some adaptation because of global differences.[6] The best global brands are consistent in theme but reflect significant differences in consumer behavior, brand development, competitive forces, and the legal or political environment. Oft-heard—and sometime modified—advice to marketers of global brands is to "Think Global, Act Local" so brands will be relevant to consumers in every market. Warren Keegan has distinguished five product and communications adaptation strategies (see Figure 18.3).[7]

Product Strategies **Straight extension** introduces the product in the foreign market without any change, a successful strategy for consumer electronics, among other products. **Product adaptation** alters the product to meet local conditions or preferences, developing a *regional version* of its product, a *country version*, a *city version*, or different *retailer versions*. **Product**

TABLE 18.1	Globally Standardized Marketing Pros and Cons

Advantages

Economies of scale in production and distribution

Lower marketing costs

Power and scope

Consistency in brand image

Ability to leverage good ideas quickly and efficiently

Uniformity of marketing practices

Disadvantages

Ignores differences in consumer needs, wants, and usage patterns for products

Ignores differences in consumer response to marketing programs and activities

Ignores differences in brand and product development and the competitive environment

Ignores differences in the legal environment

Ignores differences in marketing institutions

Ignores differences in administrative procedures

FIGURE 18.3 Five International Product and Communication Strategies

	Product		
	Do Not Change Product	Adapt Product	Develop New Product
Do Not Change Communications	Straight extension	Product adaptation	Product invention
Adapt Communications	Communication adaptation	Dual adaptation	

invention creates something new. It can take two forms: *backward invention* (reintroducing earlier product forms well adapted to a foreign country's needs) or *forward invention* (creating a new product to meet a need in another country). When they launch products and services globally, marketers may need to change certain brand elements.[8] Even a brand name may require a choice between phonetic and semantic translations.[9]

Global Communication Strategies   Changing marketing communications for each local market is a process called **communication adaptation**. If it adapts both the product and the communications, the company engages in **dual adaptation**. Consider the message. The company can use one message everywhere, varying only the language and name. Or it can use the same message and creative theme globally but adapt the execution. Another approach, which Coca-Cola and Goodyear have used, consists of developing a global pool of ads from which each country selects the most appropriate. Finally, some companies allow their country managers to create country-specific ads, within guidelines. Personal selling tactics may need to change too.

Price   Multinationals selling abroad must contend with **price escalation**, raising the price to cover the added cost of transportation, tariffs, middleman margins, and the risk of currency fluctuations so it can earn the same profit. Pricing choices include setting a uniform price in all markets, a market-based price in each market, or a cost-based price in each market. Many multinationals are plagued by the **gray market**, which diverts branded products from authorized distribution channels either in-country or across international borders. Dealers in the low-price country buy and ship the goods to another country to take advantage of price differences. Multinationals try to prevent gray markets by policing distributors, raising their prices to lower-cost distributors, or altering product characteristics or service warranties for different countries.[10]

Counterfeit Products   As companies develop global supply chain networks and move production farther from home, the chance for corruption, fraud, and quality-control problems rises.[11] Sophisticated overseas factories seem able to reproduce almost anything. Fakes take a big bite of the profits of luxury brands such as Hermès, LVMH Moët Hennessy Louis Vuitton, and Tiffany, but faulty counterfeits can literally kill people. Cell phones with counterfeit batteries, fake brake pads made of compressed grass trimmings, and counterfeit airline parts pose safety risks to consumers. Toxic cough syrup in Panama, tainted baby formula in China, and fake teething powder in Nigeria have all led to the deaths of children in recent years.[12]

FIGURE 18.4 Whole-Channel Concept for International Marketing

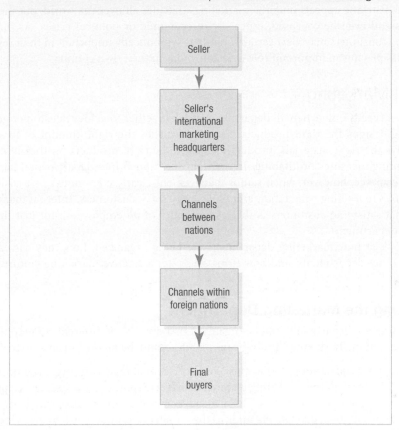

Distribution   Taking a whole-channel view of distribution, there are three links between the seller and the final buyer (see Figure 18.4). When multinationals first enter a country, they prefer to work with local distributors with good local knowledge, but friction often arises later.[13] Distribution channels across countries vary considerably, as do the size and character of retail units. Large-scale retail chains dominate the U.S. scene, but much foreign retailing is in the hands of small, independent retailers. Markups are high, but the real price comes down through haggling. Breaking bulk remains an important function of intermediaries and helps perpetuate long channels of distribution, a major obstacle to the expansion of large-scale retailing in developing countries. Although large retailers are increasingly moving into new global markets, some have had mixed success abroad.

Country-of-Origin Effects   *Country-of-origin perceptions* are the mental associations and beliefs triggered by a country. Government officials want to strengthen their country's image to help domestic marketers that export and to attract foreign firms and investors. Marketers want to use positive country-of-origin perceptions to sell their products and services. Global marketers know that buyers hold distinct attitudes and beliefs about brands or products from different countries.[14] The mere fact that a brand is perceived as successful on a global stage—whether it sends a quality signal, taps into cultural myths, or reinforces a sense of social responsibility—may lend credibility and respect.[15]

Marketers must look at country-of-origin perceptions from both a domestic and a foreign perspective. Patriotic appeals underlie marketing strategies all over the world, but they can lack uniqueness and even be overused, especially in economic or political crises. As international trade grows, consumers may view certain brands as symbolically important in their own cultural identity or as playing an important role in keeping jobs in their own country.

Internal Marketing

Marketing succeeds only when all departments work together to achieve customer goals: when engineering designs the right products, finance furnishes the right amount of funding, purchasing buys the right materials, production makes the right products on the right schedule, and accounting measures profitability in the right ways. Such interdepartmental harmony can only truly coalesce, however, when senior management clearly communicates a vision of how the company's marketing orientation and philosophy serve customers. Internal marketing emphasizes that satisfying customers is the responsibility of *all* employees, not just those in the marketing department.

Let's look at how marketing departments are being organized, how they can work effectively with other departments, and how firms can foster a creative marketing culture across the organization.[16]

Organizing the Marketing Department

Modern marketing departments can be organized in a number of different, sometimes overlapping ways: functionally, geographically, by product or brand, by market, or in a matrix.

- **Functional organization.** In the most common form of marketing organization, functional specialists (such as the marketing research manager) report to a marketing vice president who coordinates their activities. The main advantage is administrative simplicity. This form also can result in inadequate planning as the number of products and markets increases and each functional group vies for budget and status.

- **Geographic organization.** A company selling in a national market often organizes its sales force (and sometimes its marketing) along geographic lines.[17] Some companies are adding *area market specialists* (regional or local marketing managers) to support sales efforts in high-volume markets.

- **Product- or brand-management organization.** Companies producing a variety of products and brands often establish a product- (or brand-) management organization. This does not replace the functional organization but serves as another layer of management. A group product manager supervises product category managers, who in turn supervise specific product and brand managers. This makes sense if the company's products are quite different or there are more than a functional organization can handle. Other alternatives are *product teams*, assigning two or more minor products to one manager, and *category management* (focusing on product categories to build the firm's brands).

- **Market-management organization.** When customers fall into different user groups with distinct buying preferences and practices, a *market-management organization* is desirable. Market managers supervise several market-development managers, market specialists, or industry specialists and draw on functional services as needed. Market managers are staff, with duties like those of product managers. This organization shares many advantages and disadvantages of product-management systems. Many companies are reorganizing along market lines and becoming *market-centered organizations*. When customers have diverse and complex requirements, a *customer-management organization*, which deals with individual customers rather than the mass market or market segments, may be appropriate.[18]

- **Matrix-management organization.** Companies that produce many products for many markets may adopt a *matrix organization* employing both product and market managers. However, this is costly and can create conflicts about authority and responsibility. Some corporate marketing groups assist top management with overall opportunity evaluation, provide divisions with consulting assistance on request, help divisions that have little or no marketing, and promote the marketing concept throughout the company.

Relationships with Other Departments

Under the marketing concept, all departments need to "think customer" and work together to satisfy customer needs and expectations. Yet departments define company problems and goals from their own viewpoints, so conflicts of interest and communications problems are unavoidable. The marketing vice president or the CMO must usually work through persuasion rather than through authority to coordinate the company's internal marketing activities and coordinate marketing with finance, operations, and other company functions to serve the customer. Many companies now focus on key processes rather than on departments because departmental organization can be a barrier to smooth performance. They appoint process leaders, who manage cross-disciplinary teams that include marketing and salespeople.

Building a Creative Marketing Organization

Many companies realize they're not yet really market and customer driven—they are product and sales driven. Transforming into a true market-driven company requires, among other actions: (1) developing a company-wide passion for customers; (2) organizing around customer segments instead of products; and (3) understanding customers through qualitative and quantitative research. Although it's necessary to be customer oriented, it's not enough. The organization must also be creative. The answer is to build a capability in strategic innovation and imagination. This capability comes from assembling tools, processes, skills, and measures that let the firm generate more and better new ideas than its competitors.[19] See "Marketing Insight: The Marketing CEO" for concrete actions that will improve marketing capabilities.

Socially Responsible Marketing

Effective internal marketing must be matched by a strong sense of ethics, values, and social responsibility.[20] The most admired—and most successful—companies in the world abide by high standards of business and marketing conduct that serve people's interests, not only their own. Procter & Gamble has made "brand purpose" a key component of the company's marketing strategies, with award-winning cause programs such as Tide laundry detergent's "Loads of Hope."[21] This differentiation is only one rationale for investing in corporate social responsibility. Another is to build a bank of public goodwill to offset potential criticisms. In addition, companies need to understand the social pressures and opportunities facing their companies as they make decisions about investing in social responsibility.

Corporate Social Responsibility

Raising the level of socially responsible marketing calls for making a three-pronged attack that relies on proper legal, ethical, and social responsibility behavior.

marketing insight

The Marketing CEO

What steps can a CEO take to create a market- and customer-focused company?

1. *Convince senior management of the need to become customer focused.* The CEO personally exemplifies strong customer commitment and rewards those who do likewise.

2. *Appoint a senior marketing officer and marketing task force.* The marketing task force should include the CEO; C-level executives from sales, R&D, purchasing, manufacturing, finance, and human resources; and other key individuals.

3. *Get outside help and guidance.* Consulting firms have considerable experience helping companies adopt a marketing orientation.

4. *Change the company's reward measurement and system.* As long as purchasing and manufacturing are rewarded for keeping costs low, they will resist accepting some costs required to serve customers better. As long as finance focuses on short-term profit, it will oppose major investments designed to build satisfied, loyal customers.

5. *Hire strong marketing talent.* The company needs a chief marketing officer who not only manages the marketing department but also gains respect from and influence with other C-level executives.

6. *Develop strong in-house marketing training programs.* Design marketing training programs for corporate management, divisional managers, marketing and sales personnel, manufacturing personnel, and others.

7. *Install a modern marketing planning system.* The planning format will require managers to think about the marketing environment, opportunities, competitive trends, and other forces as they prepare strategies—and hold them accountable for performance.

8. *Establish an annual marketing excellence recognition program.* Business units that believe they've developed exemplary marketing plans should submit a description of their plans and results. Reward winning teams and share winning ideas across the company.

9. *Shift from a department focus to a process-outcome focus.* Appoint process leaders and cross-disciplinary teams to reengineer and implement key fundamental processes.

10. *Empower the employees.* Encourage and reward employees for new ideas and empower them to settle customer complaints.

Legal Behavior   Organizations must ensure every employee knows and observes relevant laws.[22] For example, it's illegal for salespeople to lie to consumers or mislead them about buying a product. They may not offer bribes to influence a B-to-B purchase. Their statements must match advertising claims, and they may not obtain or use competitors' technical or trade secrets through bribery or industrial espionage. They must not disparage competitors or competing products by suggesting things that are not true.

Ethical Behavior   It's not always easy to draw a clear line between normal marketing practice and unethical behavior. Some issues can generate controversy or sharply divide critics, such as acceptable marketing to children.[23] Of course, certain business practices are clearly unethical or illegal. These include bribery, theft of trade secrets, false and deceptive advertising, exclusive dealing and tying agreements, quality or safety defects, false warranties, inaccurate labeling, price-fixing or undue discrimination, and barriers to entry and predatory competition.

Companies must adopt and disseminate a written code of ethics, build a company tradition of ethical behavior, and hold their people fully responsible for observing ethical and legal guidelines. The general distrust of companies among U.S. consumers is evident in research showing the percentage of those who view corporations unfavorably is almost 40 percent.[24]

Social Responsibility Behavior   Increasingly, people want information about a company's record on social and environmental responsibility to help them decide which companies to buy from, invest in, and work for.[25] Corporate philanthropy also can pose dilemmas. Merck, DuPont, Walmart, and Bank of America have each donated $100 million or even more to charities in a year. Yet good deeds can be overlooked—even resented—if the company is seen as exploitive or fails to live up to a "good guys" image. Some critics worry that cause marketing or "consumption philanthropy" may replace virtuous actions with less thoughtful consumer buying, reduce emphasis on real solutions, or deflect attention from the fact that markets may create many social problems to begin with.[26]

Sustainability

Sustainability—the ability to meet humanity's needs without harming future generations—now tops many corporate agendas. Major corporations outline in great detail how they are trying to improve the long-term impact of their actions on communities and the environment. Coca-Cola, AT&T, and DuPont have even installed Chief Sustainability Officers.[27]

As one sustainability consultant put it, "There is a triple bottom line—people, planet, and profit—and the people part of the equation must come first. Sustainability means more than being eco-friendly, it also means you are in it for the long haul."[28] Some feel companies that score well on sustainability exhibit high-quality management in that "they tend to be more strategically nimble and better equipped to compete in the complex, high-velocity, global environment."[29] Consumer interest is also creating market opportunities, such as for organic products.

Heightened interest in sustainability has also unfortunately resulted in *greenwashing,* which gives products the appearance of being environmentally friendly without living up to that promise. One study revealed that half the labels on allegedly green products focus on an eco-friendly benefit (such as recycled content) while omitting information about significant environmental drawbacks (such as transportation costs).[30] Because insincere firms have jumped on the green bandwagon, consumers bring a healthy skepticism to environmental claims. They are also unwilling to sacrifice product performance and quality, nor are they necessarily willing to pay a price premium for green products.[31] Unfortunately, green products can be more expensive because ingredients are costly and transportation costs are higher for lower shipping volumes.

Cause-Related Marketing

Many firms blend corporate social responsibility initiatives with marketing activities.[32] **Cause-related marketing** links the firm's contributions toward a designated cause to customers' engaging directly or indirectly in revenue-producing transactions with the firm. Cause marketing is part of *corporate societal marketing (CSM),* which Minette Drumwright and Patrick Murphy define as marketing efforts "that have at least one noneconomic objective related to social welfare and use the resources of the company and/or of its partners."[33] Drumwright and Murphy also include traditional and strategic philanthropy and volunteerism in CSM.

A successful cause-marketing program can improve social welfare, create differentiated brand positioning, build strong consumer bonds, enhance the company's public image, create a reservoir of goodwill, boost internal morale and galvanize employees, drive sales, and increase the firm's market value.[34] Specifically, from a branding point of view, cause marketing can (1) build brand awareness, (2) enhance brand image, (3) establish brand credibility, (4) evoke brand feelings, (5) create a sense of brand community, and (6) elicit brand engagement.[35] It has a particularly interested audience in socially minded 18- to 34-year-old Millennial consumers who, not surprisingly, are more likely than the general population to use social media to learn about cause activities and engage with companies about them.[36]

TABLE 18.2	The Social Marketing Planning Process

Where Are We?

- Choose program focus.
- Identify campaign purpose.
- Conduct an analysis of strengths, weaknesses, opportunities, and threats (SWOT).
- Review past and similar efforts.

Where Do We Want to Go?

- Select target audiences.
- Set objectives and goals.
- Analyze target audiences and the competition.

How Will We Get There?

- Product: Design the market offering.
- Price: Manage costs of behavior change.
- Distribution: Make the product available.
- Communications: Create messages and choose media.

How Will We Stay on Course?

- Develop a plan for evaluation and monitoring.
- Establish budgets and find funding sources.
- Complete an implementation plan.

Cause-related marketing could backfire, however, if consumers question the link between the product and the cause or see the firm as self-serving and exploitive.[37] To avoid backlash, some firms take a soft-sell approach to their cause marketing. Most firms choose causes that fit their corporate or brand image and matter to their employees and shareholders.[38]

Social Marketing

Cause-related marketing supports a cause. **Social marketing** by nonprofit or government organizations *furthers* a cause, such as "say no to drugs" or "exercise more and eat better."[39] Different types of organizations conduct social marketing in the United States. Government agencies include the Centers for Disease Control and Prevention and the U.S. Environmental Protection Agency. Nonprofit organizations include the American Red Cross, the United Way, and the American Cancer Society.

While social marketing uses a number of different tactics to achieve its goals, the planning process follows many of the same steps as for traditional products and services (see Table 18.2). Social marketing programs are complex; they take time and may require phased programs or actions. Marketers should evaluate program success in terms of their objectives, measuring criteria like incidence of adoption, speed of adoption, continuance of adoption, low cost per unit of adoption, and absence of counterproductive consequences.

Executive Summary

When deciding whether to go abroad, a company needs to define its international marketing objectives and policies, weigh the risks, decide which and how many countries to enter, and determine the mode of entry (indirect exporting, direct exporting, licensing, joint ventures, or direct investment). Each succeeding strategy entails more commitment, risk, control, and profit potential. Firms going global have to decide how much to adapt their marketing strategy to local conditions. Country-of-origin effects can influence both consumers and businesses.

Internal marketing emphasizes that satisfying customers is the responsibility of *all* employees, not just those in the marketing department. Marketing departments can be organized in a number of ways: functionally, geographically, by product or brand, by market, or in a matrix. Companies must practice social responsibility through their legal, ethical, and social words and actions. Cause marketing can be a means for companies to productively link social responsibility to consumer marketing programs. Social marketing is done by a nonprofit or government organization to directly address a social problem or cause.

Notes

1. Mat McDermott, "Patagonia's New Wetsuits Will Be Made from Plants," *TreeHugger.com*, November 19, 2012; Brian Dumaine, "Patagonia Products: Built to Last," www.cnn.com, August 13, 2012; Tim Nudd, "Ad of the Day: Patagonia," *Adweek*, November 28, 2011; Diane Cardwell, "At Patagonia, the Bottom Line Includes the Earth," *New York Times,* July 30, 2014.

2. Michael E. Porter, *Competitive Strategy* (New York: Free Press, 1980), p. 275.

3. Michael J. Silverstein, Abheek Singhi, Carol Liao, and David Michael, *The $10 Trillion Prize: Captivating the Newly Affluent in China and India* (Boston: Harvard Business School Publishing, 2012).

4. Johny K. Johansson, "Global Marketing: Research on Foreign Entry, Local Marketing, Global Management," Bart Weitz and Robin Wensley, eds., *Handbook of Marketing* (London: Sage, 2002), pp. 457–83.

5. Johny K. Johansson, "Global Marketing: Research on Foreign Entry, Local Marketing, Global Management," Bart Weitz and Robin Wensley, eds., *Handbook of Marketing* (London: Sage, 2002), pp. 457–83.

6. For some organizational issues in adaptation, see Julien Cayla and Lisa Peñaloza, "Mapping the Play of Organizational Identity in Foreign Market Adaptation," *Journal of Marketing* 76 (November 2012), pp. 38–54.

7. Walter J. Keegan and Mark C. Green, *Global Marketing*, 4th ed. (Upper Saddle River, NJ: Prentice Hall, 2005); Warren J. Keegan, *Global Marketing Management,* 7th ed. (Upper Saddle River, NJ: Prentice Hall, 2002).

8. Ralf van der Lans, Joseph A. Cote, Catherine A. Cole, Siew Meng Leong, Ale Smidts, Pamela W. Henderson, Christian Bluemelhuber, Paul A. Bottomley, John R. Doyle, Alexander Fedorikhin, Janakiraman Moorthy, B. Ramaseshan, and Bernd H. Schmitt, "Cross-National Logo Evaluation Analysis: An Individual-Level Approach," *Marketing Science* 28 (September–October 2009), pp. 968–85.

9. F. C. (Frank) Hong, Anthony Pecotich, and Clifford J. Shultz II, "Language Constraints, Product Attributes, and Consumer Perceptions in East and Southeast Asia," *Journal of International Marketing* 10 (June 2002), pp. 29–45.

10. David Blanchard, "Just in Time—How to Fix a Leaky Supply Chain," *IndustryWeek,* May 1, 2007.

11. David Rocks and Nick Leiber, "Made in China? Not Worth the Trouble," *Bloomberg Businessweek*, June 25, 2012, pp. 49-50.

12. Steve Hargreaves, "Counterfeit Goods Becoming More Dangerous," www.money.cnn.com, September 27, 2012.

13. David Arnold, "Seven Rules of International Distribution," *Harvard Business Review,* November–December 2000, pp. 131–37; Rajdeep Grewal, Alok Kumar, Girish Mallapragada, and Amit Saini, "Marketing Channels in Foreign Markets: Control Mechanisms and the Moderating Role of Multinational Corporation Headquarters–Subsidiary Relationship," *Journal of Marketing Research* 50 (June 2013), pp. 378–98.

14. Zeynep Gurhan-Canli and Durairaj Maheswaran, "Cultural Variations in Country-of-Origin Effects," *Journal of Marketing Research* 37 (August 2000), pp. 309–17. For some different related issues, see also Lily Dong and Kelly Tian, "The Use of Western Brands in Asserting Chinese National Identity," *Journal of Consumer Research* 36 (October 2009), pp. 504–23; Yinlong Zhang and Adwait Khare, "The Impact of Accessible Identities on the Evaluation of Global versus Local Products," *Journal of Consumer Research* 36 (October 2009), pp. 524–37; Rohit Varman and Russell W. Belk, "Nationalism and Ideology in an Anticonsumption Movement," *Journal of Consumer Research* 36 (December 2009), pp. 686–700.

15. Douglas B. Holt, John A. Quelch, and Earl L. Taylor, "How Global Brands Compete," *Harvard Business Review* 82, September 2004, pp. 68–75; Jan-Benedict E.

M. Steenkamp, Rajeev Batra, and Dana L. Alden, "How Perceived Brand Globalness Creates Brand Value," *Journal of International Business Studies* 34 (January 2003), pp. 53–65.

16. Grant McKracken, *Chief Culture Officer* (New York: Basic Books, 2009).

17. Todd Guild, "Think Regionally, Act Locally: Four Steps to Reaching the Asian Consumer," *McKinsey Quarterly* 4 (September 2009), pp. 22–30.

18. Larry Selden and Geoffrey Colvin, *Angel Customers & Demon Customers* (New York: Portfolio [Penguin], 2003).

19. Gary Hamel, *Leading the Revolution* (Boston: Harvard Business School Press, 2000).

20. William L. Wilkie and Elizabeth S. Moore, "Marketing's Relationship to Society," Barton A. Weitz and Robin Wensley, eds., *Handbook of Marketing* (London: Sage, 2002), pp. 1–38.

21. David Hessekiel, "Cause Marketing Leaders of the Pack," www.forbes.com, January 31, 2012.

22. Elisabeth Sullivan, "Play by the New Rules," *Marketing News*, November 30, 2009, pp. 5–9; for further reading, see Dorothy Cohen, *Legal Issues in Marketing Decision Making* (Cincinnati, OH: South-Western College Publishing, 1995).

23. E. J. Schultz, "Senators Target Tax Deduction—This Time for the Children," *Advertising Age*, May 16, 2014; Lyndsey Layton, "In a First, Agriculture Dept. Plans to Regulate Food Marketing in Schools," *Washington Post*, February 25, 2014; Janet Adamy, "Tough New Rules Proposed on Food Advertising for Kids," *Wall Street Journal*, April 29, 2011. For relevant academic research, see Tirtha Dhar and Kathy Baylis, "Fast-Food Consumption and the Ban on Advertising Targeting Children: The Quebec Experience," *Journal of Marketing Research* 48 (October 2011), pp. 799–813.

24. Kent Hoover, "Favorability Ratings Up for Both Businesses and Labor Unions," *American Business Daily*, June 27, 2013.

25. Mary Jo Hatch and Majken Schultz, *Taking Brand Initiative: How Companies Can Align Strategy, Culture, and Identity through Corporate Branding* (San Francisco: Jossey-Bass, 2008); Majken Schultz, Yun Mi Antorini, and Fabian F. Csaba, *Corporate Branding: Purpose, People, and Process* (Køge, Denmark: Copenhagen Business School Press, 2005); Ronald J. Alsop, *The 18 Immutable Laws of Corporate Reputation* (New York: Free Press, 2004).

26. Angela M. Eikenberry, "The Hidden Cost of Cause Marketing," *Stanford Social Innovation Review* (Summer 2009); Aneel Karnani, "The Case against Corporate Social Responsibility," *Wall Street Journal*, August 23, 2010.

27. Dina Spector, "The Simple Way Stonyfield Farm Cut $18 Million in Expenses," *Business Insider*, February 23, 2012.

28. Sandra O'Loughlin, "The Wearin' o' the Green," *Brandweek*, April 23, 2007, pp. 26–27. For a critical response, see also John R. Ehrenfeld, "Feeding the Beast," *Fast Company*, December 2006–January 2007, pp. 42–43.

29. Pete Engardio, "Beyond the Green Corporation," *BusinessWeek*, January 29, 2007, pp. 50–64.

30. David Roberts, "Another Inconvenient Truth," *Fast Company*, March 2008, p. 70; Melanie Warner, "P&G's Chemistry Test," *Fast Company*, July/August 2008, pp. 71–74.

31. Ying-Ching Lin and Chiu-chi Angela Chang, "Double Standard: The Role of Environmental Consciousness in Green Product Usage," *Journal of Marketing* 76 (September 2012), pp. 125–34; Michael Hopkins, "What the 'Green' Consumer Wants," *MIT Sloan Management Review* (Summer 2009), pp. 87–89.

32. Larry Chiagouris and Ipshita Ray, "Saving the World with Cause-Related Marketing," *Marketing Management* 16 (July–August 2007), pp. 48–51; Hamish Pringle and Marjorie Thompson, *Brand Spirit: How Cause-Related Marketing Builds Brands* (New York: Wiley, 1999); Sue Adkins, *Cause-Related Marketing* (Oxford, UK: Butterworth-Heinemann, 1999); "Marketing, Corporate Social Initiatives, and the Bottom Line," Marketing Science Institute Conference Summary, *MSI Report No. 01-106,* 2001.

33. Minette Drumwright and Patrick E. Murphy, "Corporate Societal Marketing," Paul N. Bloom and Gregory T. Gundlach, eds., *Handbook of Marketing and Society* (Thousand Oaks, CA: Sage, 2001), pp. 162–83.

34. Christian Homburg, Marcel Stierl, and Torsten Bornemann, "Corporate Social Responsibility in Business-to-Business Markets: How Organizational Customers Account for Supplier Corporate Social Responsibility Engagement," *Journal of Marketing* 77 (November 2013), pp. 54–72; Sean Blair and Alexander Chernev, "Doing Well by Doing Good: The Benevolent Halo of Social Goodwill," *Marketing Science Institute Report 12-103, 2011*, www.msi.org; Xueming Luo and C. B. Bhattacharya, "Corporate Social Responsibility, Customer Satisfaction, and Market Value," *Journal of Marketing* 70 (October 2006), pp. 1–18; C. B. Bhattacharya and Sankar Sen, "Consumer-Company Identification: A Framework for Understanding Consumers' Relationships with Companies," *Journal of Marketing* 67 (April 2003), pp. 76–88; Sankar Sen and C. B. Bhattacharya, "Does Doing Good Always Lead to Doing Better," *Journal of Marketing Research* 38 (May 2001), pp. 225–44.

35. Paul N. Bloom, Steve Hoeffler, Kevin Lane Keller, and Carlos E. Basurto, "How Social-Cause Marketing Affects Consumer Perceptions," *MIT Sloan Management Review* (Winter 2006), pp. 49–55; Carolyn J. Simmons and Karen L. Becker-Olsen, "Achieving Marketing Objectives through Social Sponsorships," *Journal of Marketing* 70 (October 2006), pp. 154–69; Guido Berens, Cees B. M. van Riel, and Gerrit H. van Bruggen, "Corporate Associations and Consumer Product Responses: The Moderating Role of Corporate Brand Dominance," *Journal of Marketing* 69 (July 2005), pp. 35–48; Donald R. Lichtenstein, Minette E. Drumwright, and Bridgette M. Braig, "The Effect of Social Responsibility on Customer Donations to Corporate-Supported Nonprofits," *Journal of Marketing* 68 (October 2004), pp. 16–32; Stephen Hoeffler and Kevin Lane Keller, "Building Brand Equity through Corporate Societal Marketing," *Journal of Public Policy and Marketing* 21 (Spring 2002), pp. 78–89. See also Special Issue: Corporate Responsibility, *Journal of Brand Management* 10, nos. 4–5 (May 2003).

36. "2013 Cone Communications Social Impact Study: The Next Cause Evolution," www.conecomm.com; C. B. Bhattacharya, Sankar Sen, and Daniel Korschun, "Using Corporate Social Responsibility to Win the War for Talent," *MIT Sloan Management Review* 49 (January 2008), pp. 37–44.

37. Mark R. Forehand and Sonya Grier, "When Is Honesty the Best Policy? The Effect of Stated Company Intent on Consumer Skepticism," *Journal of Consumer Psychology* 13 (2003), pp. 349–56. See also Aradhna Krishna, "Can Supporting a Cause Decrease Donations and Happiness? The Cause Marketing Paradox," *Journal of Consumer Psychology* 21 (July 2011), pp. 338–45.

38. Stefanie Rosen Robinson, Caglar Irmak, and Satish Jayachandran, "Choice of Cause in Cause-Related Marketing," *Journal of Marketing* 76 (July 2012), pp. 126–39.

39. Philip Kotler, David Hessekiel, and Nancy Lee, *Good Works: Marketing and Corporate Initiatives That Build a Better World ... and the Bottom Line* (Hoboken, NJ: John Wiley & Sons, 2012); Philip Kotler and Nancy Lee, *Social Marketing: Influencing Behaviors for Good* (Thousand Oaks, CA: Sage, 2008); Alan Andreasen, *Social Marketing in the 21st Century* (Thousand Oaks, CA: Sage, 2006).

Glossary

A

adoption   an individual's decision to become a regular user of a product.

advertising   any paid form of nonpersonal presentation and promotion of a product by an identified sponsor.

advertising objective   a specific communications task and achievement level to be accomplished with a specific audience in a specific period of time.

aspirational groups   groups a person hopes to join.

associative network memory model   conceptual representation that views memory as consisting of nodes and interconnecting links, where nodes represent stored information or concepts and links represent strength of association between information or concepts.

attitudes   a person's enduring favorable or unfavorable evaluations, emotional feelings, and action tendencies toward some object or idea.

available market   the set of consumers who have interest, income, and access to a particular offer.

average cost   the cost per unit at a given level of production; it equals total costs divided by production.

B

banner ads   *see* display ads.

belief   a descriptive thought that a person holds about something.

brand   a name, term, sign, symbol, or design, or a combination of these, intended to identify the offering of one seller or seller group and differentiate it from competing offers.

brand associations   all brand-related thoughts, feelings, perceptions, images, experiences, beliefs, attitudes, and so on, that become linked to the brand node.

brand audit   a consumer-focused series of procedures to assess the health of the brand, uncover its sources of brand equity, and suggest ways to improve and leverage its equity.

brand community   a specialized community of consumers and employees whose identification and activities focus around the brand.

brand contact   any information-bearing experience that a customer or prospect has with the brand, its product category, or its market.

brand dilution   when consumers no longer associate a brand with a specific product or highly similar set of products and start thinking less of the brand.

brand elements   trademarkable devices that identify and differentiate the brand.

brand equity   the added value a brand endows on products and services.

brand extension   using an established brand to launch a new product.

brand knowledge   all the thoughts, feelings, images, experiences, and beliefs associated with the brand.

brand line   all the products (including line and category extensions) sold under a particular brand.

brand mix   the set of all brand lines that a particular seller offers.

brand personality   the specific mix of human traits attributed to a particular brand.

brand portfolio   the set of all brands and brand lines a particular firm offers in a particular category or market segment.

brand promise   the marketer's vision of what the brand must be and do for consumers.

brand valuation   estimating the brand's total financial value.

branded variants   specific brand lines supplied to specific retailers or distribution.

branding   endowing products and services with the power of a brand.

branding strategy   the number and nature of both common and distinctive brand elements applied to the firm's offerings.

brick-and-click   existing companies that have added an online site for information or e-commerce.

business market   all the organizations that acquire goods and services used in the production of other products or services that are sold, rented, or supplied to others.

C

capital items   long-lasting business goods that facilitate developing or managing the finished product.

category extension   using a parent brand to enter a different category from the one it currently serves.

category membership   the products or sets of products with which a brand competes and which function as close substitutes.

cause-related marketing   marketing that links a firm's contributions to a designated cause to customers' engaging directly or indirectly in revenue-producing transactions with the firm.

channel conflict   when one channel member's actions prevent another member from achieving its goal.

channel coordination   when channel members are brought together to advance the goals of the channel.

channel power   the ability to alter channel members' behavior so they take actions they would not have taken otherwise.

co-branding   also called dual branding or brand bundling, combining two or more well-known brands into a joint product or marketing them together in some fashion.

communication adaptation   changing marketing communications programs for each local market.

communication-effect research   determining whether an ad is communicating effectively.

company demand   company's estimated share of market demand at alternative levels of company marketing effort in a given period.

company sales forecast   expected level of company sales based on a chosen marketing plan and an assumed marketing environment.

competitive advantage   a company's ability to perform in one or more ways that competitors cannot or will not match.

competitive frame of reference   defining which other brands a brand competes with and which should be the focus of competitive analysis.

conformance quality   the degree to which all produced units are identical and meet promised specifications.

consumer behavior   the study of how individuals, groups, and organizations select, buy, use, and dispose of goods, services, ideas, or experiences to satisfy needs and wants.

containerization   putting goods in boxes or trailers that are easy to transfer between two transportation modes.

contractual sales force   manufacturers' reps, sales agents, and brokers who are paid a commission based on sales.

convenience goods   consumer goods that are purchased frequently, immediately, and with minimal effort.

core competency   attribute that is a source of competitive advantage by contributing to perceived customer benefits, has applications in a wide variety of markets, and is difficult for competitors to imitate.

core values   the belief systems that underlie attitudes and behaviors and determine people's long-term choices and desires.

corporate culture   the shared experiences, stories, beliefs, and norms that characterize an organization.

countertrade   when buyers offer items instead of cash as payment for a purchase.

crowdsourcing   obtaining expertise or a different perspective from paid or unpaid outsiders for a new-product project.

cues   minor stimuli that determine when, where, and how a person responds.

culture   the fundamental determinant of a person's wants and behavior.

customer churn   rate of customer defection.

customer database   an organized collection of comprehensive information about individual customers or prospects that is current, accessible, and actionable for lead generation, lead qualification, sales, or customer relationship management.

customer lifetime value (CLV)   the net present value of the stream of future profits expected over the customer's lifetime purchases.

customer-perceived value (CPV)   the difference between the prospective customer's value of all the benefits and all the costs of an offering and the perceived alternatives.

customer relationship management (CRM)   process of managing detailed information about individual customers and all customer touch points to maximize loyalty.

customer-value hierarchy   five product levels that must be addressed by marketers in planning an offering.

D

data mining   use of statistical and mathematical techniques to extract useful information about individuals, trends, and segments.

data warehouse   collection of data drawn from company contact with customers that marketers can analyze to draw inferences about an individual customer's needs and responses.

database marketing   the process of building, maintaining, and using databases to contact, transact with, and build relationships with customers.

demand chain planning   the process of designing the supply chain based on adopting a target market perspective and working backward.

design   the totality of features that affect how a product looks, feels, and functions to a consumer.

direct (company) sales force   full- or part-time paid employees who work exclusively for the company.

direct marketing   the use of consumer-direct (CD) channels to reach and deliver goods and services to the customer without using marketing middlemen.

direct marketing channel   channel arrangement in which the manufacturer sells directly to final customers; also known as a zero-level channel.

direct-order marketing   marketing in which direct marketers see a measureable response, typically a customer order.

direct product profitability (DPP)   a way of measuring a product's handling costs from the time it reaches the warehouse until a customer buys it in the store.

display ads (or banner ads)   small, rectangular boxes containing text and perhaps an image that firms pay to place on relevant Web sites.

dissociative groups   groups whose values or behavior an individual rejects.

drive   a strong internal stimulus impelling action.

dual adaptation   adapting both the product and the communications to the local market.

E

e-commerce   using a Web site to transact or facilitate the sale of goods and services online.

environmental threat   challenge posed by an unfavorable trend or development that, in the absence of defensive marketing action, would lead to lower sales or profit.

ethnographic research   uses concepts and tools from anthropology and other social science disciplines to provide deep cultural understanding of how people live and work.

everyday low pricing (EDLP)   charging a constant low price with little or no price promotion or special sales.

exclusive distribution   channel strategy in which a producer severely limits the number of intermediaries to maintain control over resellers' service level and outputs.

expectancy-value model   consumers evaluate products and services by combining their brand beliefs—the positives and negatives—according to importance.

experience curve   decline in the average cost that occurs with accumulated production experience; also known as the *learning curve*.

experimental research   the most scientifically valid research designed to capture cause-and-effect relationships by eliminating competing explanations of the findings.

F

fad   a craze that is unpredictable, of brief duration, and without long-term significance.

family brand   *see* master brand.

family of orientation   parents and siblings.

family of procreation   spouse and children.

features   characteristics that supplement a product's basic function.

fixed costs   also known as *overhead*, costs that do not vary with production level or sales revenue.

focus group   a gathering of 6 to 10 people selected for demographic, psychographic, or other considerations and convened to discuss various topics with a professional moderator.

forecasting   the art of anticipating what buyers are likely to do under a given set of conditions.

form   the product's size, shape, or physical structure.

frequency programs (FPs)   programs to reward customers who buy frequently and in substantial amounts.

G

generics   unbranded, plainly packaged, less expensive versions of common products.

global firm   a firm that operates in more than one country and captures R&D, production, logistical, marketing, and financial advantages in its costs and reputation that are not available to purely domestic competitors.

global industry   an industry in which the strategic positions of competitors in major geographic or national markets are fundamentally affected by their overall global positions.

going-rate pricing   prices based largely on competitors' prices.

gray market   branded products diverted from authorized distribution channels in the country of product origin or across international borders.

H

heuristics   rules of thumb in the decision process.

high-low pricing   in retailing, charging higher-than-EDLP prices on an everyday basis with frequent promotions that temporarily lower prices.

holistic marketing concept   based on the development, design, and implementation of marketing programs, processes, and activities that recognize their breadth and interdependencies.

horizontal marketing system   channel arrangement in which two or more unrelated firms put together resources or programs to exploit a marketing opportunity.

I

industry   group of firms offering a product or class of products that are close substitutes for one another.

informational appeal   elaborates on product or service attributes or benefits, assuming that consumers will process the communication very logically.

ingredient branding   a special case of co-branding that creates brand equity for materials, components, or parts contained in a branded product.

innovation   any good, service, or idea that someone *perceives* as new, no matter how long its history.

innovation diffusion process   the spread of a new idea from its source of invention or creation to its ultimate users or adopters.

integrated logistics systems (ILS)   materials management, material flow systems, and physical distribution, aided by information technology.

integrated marketing   mixing and matching marketing activities to maximize their individual and collective effects.

integrated marketing channel system   marketing channel in which the strategies and tactics of selling through one channel reflect the strategies and tactics of selling through one or more other channels.

integrated marketing communications (IMC)   a planning process designed to assure that all brand contacts received by a customer or prospect for a product, service, or organization are relevant to that person and consistent over time.

intensive distribution   channel strategy in which the producer places its offerings in as many outlets as possible.

internal marketing   element of holistic marketing that involves hiring, training, and motivating able employees who want to serve customers well.

interstitials   advertisements, often with video or animation, which pop up between changes on a Web site.

J

joint venture   a company in which multiple investors share ownership and control.

L

learning   changes in consumer behavior arising from experience.

licensed product   using the brand name licensed from one firm on a product made by another firm.

life-cycle cost   the product's purchase cost plus the discounted cost of maintenance and repair less the discounted salvage value.

life stage   a person's major concern, such as going through a divorce, taking care of an older parent, or deciding to buy a new home.

lifestyle   a person's pattern of living in the world as expressed in activities, interests, and opinions.

line extension   using a parent brand on a new product within a category it currently serves.

loyalty   a deeply held commitment to rebuy a market offering in the future despite situational influences and marketing efforts that might cause switching behavior.

M

market   groupings of customers.

market demand   the total volume that would be bought by a defined customer group in a defined geographical area in a defined time period in a defined marketing environment under a defined marketing program.

market forecast   the market demand corresponding to the level of industry marketing expenditure.

market logistics   planning the infrastructure to meet demand, then implementing and controlling the physical flows of materials and final goods from points of origin to points of use to meet customer requirements at a profit.

market-penetration pricing   pricing strategy where firms set the lowest price, assuming the market is price sensitive, to drive higher sales volume.

market potential   the limit approached by market demand as industry marketing expenditures approach infinity for a given marketing environment.

market share   level of selective demand for a company's product.

market-skimming pricing   pricing strategy where prices start high and slowly drop over time to maximize profits from less price-sensitive customers.

marketer   someone who seeks a response from another party (the prospect).

marketing   identifying and meeting human and social needs; the activity, set of institutions, and processes for creating, communicating, delivering, and exchanging offerings that have value for customers, clients, partners, and society at large.

marketing audit   a comprehensive, systematic, independent, and periodic examination of a company's or business unit's marketing environment, objectives, strategies, and activities.

marketing channel system   the particular set of marketing channels a firm employs.

marketing channels   sets of interdependent organizations participating in the process of making a product or service available for use or consumption; also called trade channels or distribution channels.

marketing communications   means by which firms attempt to inform, persuade, and remind consumers—directly or indirectly—about the products and brands they sell.

marketing communications mix   advertising, sales promotion, events and experiences, public relations and publicity, online and social media marketing, mobile marketing, direct and database marketing, and personal selling.

marketing concept   approach to marketing in which the job is to find the right products for your customers, not the right customers for your products.

marketing dashboard   concise set of interconnected performance drivers that marketers throughout the organization can view.

marketing funnel   tool used to identify the percentage of the potential target market at each stage in the decision process.

marketing implementation   the process that turns marketing plans into action assignments and ensures they accomplish the plan's stated objectives.

marketing information system (MIS)   the people, equipment, and procedures to gather, sort, analyze, evaluate, and distribute needed, timely, and accurate information to marketing decision makers.

marketing intelligence system   set of procedures and sources that managers use to obtain everyday information about developments in the marketing environment.

marketing management   the art and science of choosing target markets and getting, keeping, and growing customers through creating, delivering, and communicating superior customer value.

marketing metrics   the set of measures organizations use to quantify, compare, and interpret marketing performance.

marketing network   the company and its supporting stakeholders, with whom it has built mutually profitable business relationships.

marketing opportunity   area of buyer need and interest that a company can profitably satisfy.

marketing plan   the central instrument for directing and coordinating the marketing effort; a written document that summarizes what the firm knows about the marketplace, how it will reach its marketing objectives, and how it will direct and coordinate its marketing.

marketing public relations (MPR)   publicity and other activities that build corporate or product image to facilitate marketing goals.

marketing research   the systematic design, collection, analysis, and reporting of data and findings relevant to a specific marketing situation facing the company.

markup   pricing an item by adding a standard increase to the product's cost.

mass customization   how a company meets each customer's requirements, on a mass basis, by individually designing products, services, programs, and communications.

master (family) brand   a parent brand that is associated with multiple brand extensions.

media selection   finding the most cost-effective media to deliver the desired number and type of exposures to a target audience.

membership groups   groups having a direct influence on consumer behavior.

microsite   a limited area on the Web managed and paid for by an external advertiser/company.

mission statement   statement of what the organization exists to accomplish, which provides employees with a shared sense of purpose, direction, and opportunity.

mobile apps   bite-sized software programs that can be downloaded to smart phones.

motive   a need that is aroused to a sufficient level of intensity to drive someone to take action.

multichannel marketing   using two or more marketing channels to reach customer segments in one market area.

O

omnichannel marketing   multiple channels working seamlessly together, matching each target customer's preferred ways of doing business, delivering the right product information and customer service regardless of whether customers are online, in the store, or on the phone.

opinion leader   person who offers informal advice or information about a specific product or product category.

organizational buying   the decision-making process by which organizations establish the need for purchases and identify, evaluate, and choose among alternative brands and suppliers.

P

packaging   all the activities of designing and producing a product's container.

paid search   (or **pay-per-click ads**) marketers bid on search terms; when a consumer searches for those words using Google, Yahoo!, or Bing, the marketer's ad will appear on the results page, and advertisers pay only if people click on links.

parent brand   an existing brand that gives birth to a brand extension or sub-brand.

partner relationship management (PRM) forming and managing mutually satisfying, long-term relations with key partners such as suppliers and distributors.

penetrated market   the set of consumers who are buying the company's product.

perception   process by which people select, organize, and interpret information inputs to create a meaningful picture of the world.

performance marketing   part of holistic marketing that involves understanding the financial and nonfinancial returns to business and society from marketing activities and programs.

performance quality   the level at which the product's primary characteristics operate.

personal communications channel   two or more persons communicating face to face or person to audience through a phone, surface mail, or e-mail.

personal influence   the effect one person has on another's attitude or purchase probability.

personality   distinguishing human psychological traits that lead to relatively consistent and enduring responses to environmental stimuli.

place advertising   (also known as **out-of-home** advertising) a broad category including many creative and unexpected forms to grab consumers' attention.

point of purchase (P-O-P)   the location where a purchase is made, typically thought of in terms of a retail setting.

points-of-difference (PODs)   attributes or benefits that consumers associate with a brand, positively evaluate, and believe they could not find with a competitive brand.

points-of-parity (POPs)   attribute or benefit associations that are not necessarily unique to the brand but may be shared with other brands.

positioning   designing a company's offering and image to occupy a distinctive place in the minds of the target market.

potential market   the set of consumers with a sufficient level of interest in a market offer.

price discrimination   pricing approach in which a firm sells an offering at two or more prices that do not reflect a proportional difference in costs.

price escalation   when a multinational firm raises the price to cover the added cost of transportation, tariffs, middleman margins, and the risk of currency fluctuations so it can earn the same profit.

principle of congruity   communicators can use their good image to reduce some negative feeling toward a brand but in the process might lose some esteem with the audience.

private-label brand   a brand that retailers and wholesalers develop; also called a reseller, store, house, or distributor brand.

product   anything that can be offered to a market to satisfy a want or need.

product adaptation   altering the product to meet local conditions or preferences.

product assortment   *see* product mix.

product concept   proposes that consumers favor products offering the most quality, performance, or innovative features.

product invention   creating something new.

product line   products within a product class that are closely related because they perform similar functions, are sold to the same customer groups, are marketed through the same channels, or fall within given price ranges.

product mix   also called a *product assortment,* the set of all products and items a particular seller offers for sale.

product mix pricing   the firm plans a set of prices that maximizes profits on the total product mix.

product system   a group of diverse but related items that function in a compatible manner.

production concept   holds that consumers prefer products that are widely available and inexpensive.

profitable customer   a person, household, or company that over time yields a revenue stream exceeding by an acceptable amount the company's costs for attracting, selling, and serving that customer.

prospect an individual or group from whom a marketer seeks a response such as a purchase, a vote, or a donation.

psychographics the science of using psychology and demographics to better understand consumers.

public any group that has an actual or potential interest in or impact on a company's ability to achieve its objectives.

public relations (PR) a variety of programs designed to promote or protect a company's image or its individual products.

publicity the task of securing editorial space—as opposed to paid space—in print and broadcast media to promote something.

pull strategy channel strategy in which the producer uses communications to persuade consumers to demand the product from intermediaries, inducing the intermediaries to order it.

pure-click companies that have launched a Web site without any previous existence as a firm.

push strategy channel strategy in which a producer uses its sales force or other means to induce intermediaries to carry, promote, and sell the product to end users.

Q

quality the totality of features and characteristics of a product or service that bear on its ability to satisfy stated or implied needs.

R

reference groups all the groups that have a direct or indirect influence on a customer's attitudes or behavior.

reference price internal or external price against which a customer compares an observed price.

relationship marketing building mutually satisfying long-term relationships with key parties to earn and retain their business.

retailer any business enterprise whose sales volume comes primarily from retailing.

retailing all the activities in selling goods or services directly to final consumers for personal, nonbusiness use.

role the activities a person is expected to perform.

S

sales promotion a collection of incentive tools, mostly short term, designed to stimulate quicker or greater purchases of particular products or services by consumers or the trade.

sales quota sales goal set for a product line, company division, or sales representative.

satisfaction a person's feelings of pleasure or disappointment that result from comparing a product's perceived performance to expectations.

scenario analysis developing plausible representations of a firm's possible future using assumptions about forces driving the market and different uncertainties.

selective attention mental process of screening out some stimuli while noticing others.

selective distribution channel strategy in which a manufacturer relies on only some of the intermediaries willing to carry a particular product.

selling concept holds that consumers and businesses, if left alone, will not buy enough of the organization's products.

service any act or performance one party can offer to another that is essentially intangible and does not result in the ownership of anything.

sharing economy how consumers extract more value from what they already own by sharing bikes, cars, clothes, couches, and other items.

shopper marketing how manufacturers and retailers use stocking, displays, and promotions to influence consumers actively shopping for a product.

shopping goods goods that consumers compare on the basis of suitability, quality, price, and style.

showrooming letting buyers physically examine a product and collect information in a store, although buyers will make their actual purchase later, from the retailer online or from a different retailer, typically to secure a lower price.

social classes homogeneous and enduring divisions in a society, hierarchically ordered and with members who share similar values, interests, and behavior.

social marketing   marketing by nonprofit or government organizations to further a cause.

social media   a means for consumers to share text, images, audio, and video information with each other and with companies, and vice versa.

specialty goods   consumer goods with unique characteristics or brand identification for which enough buyers are willing to make a special purchasing effort.

status   one's position within a group or society.

straight extension   introducing a product in a foreign market without any change in the product.

strategic business unit (SBU)   a business that can be planned separately from the rest of the company, with its own set of competitors and a manager responsible for strategic planning and profit performance.

strategic marketing plan   plan that lays out the firm's target markets and value proposition, based on an analysis of the best market opportunities.

strategy   firm's game plan for achieving its goals.

sub-brand   combining a new brand with an existing brand.

subcultures   groups with shared values, beliefs, preferences, and behaviors emerging from their special life experiences or circumstances.

supersegment   a set of market segments sharing some exploitable similarity.

supply chain   the partnerships a firm forges with suppliers and distributors to deliver value to customers; also known as a value delivery network.

supply chain management (SCM)   managing the supply chain from procurement of inputs through efficient conversion into finished products and then the movement of products to final destinations.

T

tactical marketing plan   plan that specifies the firm's marketing tactics, including product features, promotion, merchandising, pricing, sales channels, and service.

target costing   determining the cost that must be achieved to sell a new product at the price consumers are willing to pay, given its appeal and competitors' prices.

target market   the part of the qualified available market the company decides to pursue.

target-return pricing   determining the price that will yield the firm's target rate of return on investment.

telemarketing   the use of telephone and call centers to attract prospects, sell to existing customers, and provide service by taking orders and answering questions.

total costs   the sum of the fixed and variable costs for a given level of production.

total customer benefit   the perceived monetary value of the bundle of economic, functional, and psychological benefits customers expect from a market offering.

total customer cost   the perceived monetary value of the bundle of costs customers expect to incur in evaluating, obtaining, using, and disposing of the market offering.

transformational appeal   elaborates on a nonproduct-related benefit or image.

trend   a direction or sequence of events with momentum and durability.

U

unsought goods   goods that the consumer does not know about or normally think of buying.

V

value chain   a tool for identifying ways to create more customer value; nine strategically relevant activities that create value and cost in a specific business.

value delivery network   *see* supply chain.

value delivery system   all the experiences the customer will have in obtaining and using the offering.

value network   a system of partnerships and alliances that a firm creates to source, augment, and deliver its offerings.

value pricing pricing method in which the firm wins loyal customers by charging a fairly low price for a high-quality offering.

value proposition set of benefits that a marketer proposes to deliver to satisfy customers' needs.

variable costs costs that vary directly with the level of production.

vertical marketing system (VMS) a channel arrangement in which the producer, wholesaler(s), and retailer(s) act as a unified system.

viral marketing a form of online word of mouth, or "word of mouse," that encourages consumers to pass along company-developed products and services or audio, video, or written information to others online.

W

warranties formal statements of expected product performance by the manufacturer, legally enforceable.

wholesaling all the activities in selling goods or services to those who buy for resale or business use.

Z

zero-level channel *see* direct marketing channel.

Brand, Company, and Name Index

Subject Index